BEARING FALSE WITNESS?

An Introduction to the Christian Countercult

Douglas E. Cowan

Foreword by Jeffrey K. Hadden

Westport, Connecticut
London

Library of Congress Cataloging-in-Publication Data

Cowan, Douglas E.
  Bearing false witness? : an introduction to the Christian countercult / Douglas E.
Cowan ; foreword by Jeffrey K. Hadden.
      p. cm.
  Includes bibliographical references and index.
  ISBN 0–275–97459–6 (alk. paper)
      1. Anti-cult movements—United States.   2. Evangelicalism—United States.
  I. Title.
BP604.2.U6C68   2003
239'.9—dc21   2002029867

British Library Cataloguing in Publication Data is available.

Library of Congress Catalog Card Number: 2002029867
ISBN: 0–275–97459–6

First published in 2003

Praeger Publishers, 88 Post Road West, Westport, CT 06881
An imprint of Greenwood Publishing Group, Inc.
www.praeger.com

Printed in the United States of America

The paper used in this book complies with the
Permanent Paper Standard issued by the National
Information Standards Organization (Z39.48–1984).

10 9 8 7 6 5 4 3 2 1

Copyright Acknowledgments

The author and publisher gratefully acknowledge permission for use of the following
material:

Part of chapter 2 appeared previously in the *Journal of Contemporary Religion* as
"Exits and Migrations: Foregrounding the Christian Counter-cult" 17(3) (2002): 339–
54 and is reproduced here by the kind permission of Carfax Publishing and editors
Peter B. Clarke and Elisabeth Arweck.

Part of chapter 9 appeared previously in *Religious Studies and Theology* as "No
Harmony: Some Notes on Evangelical Christian Response to Buddhism" 19(2)
(2000): 17–52 and is reproduced here with the kind permission of the journal.

Scattered quotations appeared previously in EMNR's *Manual of Ethical and
Doctrinal Standards,* and are reproduced here with the kind permission of John W.
Morehead, president of EMNR.

For Irving R. Hexham

Contents

Foreword *by Jeffrey K. Hadden*   ix

Acknowledgments   xv

I. Perspectives on the Christian Countercult   1

1. Confronting Cults   3

2. From Extraction to Migration: The Christian Countercult in Sociological Perspective   15

3. "For the Bible Tells Me So": Constructing the Countercult Cosmology   29

4. Definition and Counterdefinition: The Countercult as Reality-Maintenance   43

II. Typologizing the Countercult   61

5. A Territory under Siege: The Early Countercult in the Twentieth Century   63

6. Demon Siege: The Countercult on the Fringe   79

7. The Siege Continues: Modern Countercult Continua   95

8. The Siege in Cyberspace and the Democratization of the Countercult   115

III. Countercult Apologetics   131

9. From False Worlds to True, Part 1: Other Religions According to the Countercult   133

10. From False Worlds to True, Part 2: Cults, the Occult, and the New
    Age Rage   155

11. The Countercult against Christianity: The Case of Rome   171

12. "Gittin' Thar Fustest with the Mostest": Antipathy, Authority, and
    Apologetics   191

    Notes   213

    References   223

    Index   247

Foreword

The last quarter of the twentieth century saw the production of a large body of literature about cults, sects, and new religious movements. This literature has taken two distinct forms. On the one hand, oppositional voices contend that leaders of cults possess something approaching supernatural powers, which makes it possible for them to "brainwash" persons with whom they come in contact. Leaders of these groups hold followers as virtual slaves, always ready to do their unscrupulous bidding. The second body of literature, which is largely the product of social scientists, has been highly skeptical of this mind control model. Scholars do not reject the notion that religious groups are capable of exercising considerable influence on those who come in contact with them; however, the preponderance of research points to the conclusion that individuals seem to act largely of their own volition in making decisions to join, stay, or leave religious groups.

In retrospect, it is clear that much of the scholarly literature can be understood as a response to the negative writings about cults. The reasons are understandable. From very early on, new religious groups were part of the youth counterculture phenomenon. Their public visibility caught the attention of both the press and young sociologists, for whom the allegations of brainwashing had a highly mysterious and intriguing quality. Not surprisingly, those who made such allegations (and sought to reverse them through unscrupulous practices such as deprogramming) were soon before the courts, and the findings of scholars became part of the permanent legal record.

Applying social movement theory to the problem, scholars framed the conflict as a struggle between anticult movements and the new religious movements. While most social scientists saw themselves as objective observers of the conflict, some, believing religious liberties were being abridged, were openly sympathetic to the new religions. And the large proportion concluded that their research findings did not support the negative assessments made by the adversaries of these new religious movements.

It is not unusual in movement/countermovement struggles for the argument to be framed in terms of "those who are not with us are against us." This occurred fairly early in the conflict as the anticult movement labeled scholars as *cult apologists*. Thus, whether they liked it or not, scholars came to be perceived as part of the conflict they were studying. Scholars of new religions continue to live with this labeling.

Much new scholarship now promises to move the study of new religious movements beyond the narrow focus that characterized the conflict literature that commenced with the youth counterculture. Today, comparative and historical studies are broadening our understanding of how new religions emerge, interact with their host culture, and eventually accommodate themselves or perish.

Another important dimension of cult conflict, however, has largely been neglected by scholars over the past quarter-century. Here, the central focus is conflict regarding *correct beliefs* or *doctrine*. This battleground is substantially centered in evangelical Protestant groups, especially independent and nondenominational traditions.

That scholars should have neglected this conflict is of particular interest since it has existed more-or-less unabated since the early nineteenth century. Indeed, its roots are found even further back, in the venerable tradition of Christian apologetics, the systematic argumentation on behalf of the truth of Christian doctrine as it is found and interpreted in the scriptures. In the eighteenth century, for example, much of the focus of apologetics centered on arguments against deism.

In the nineteenth century, Roman Catholics from southern Europe came by the millions to the United States, bringing with them teachings that many Protestants rejected as false and heretical. Catholic immigration was followed by the appearance of several rapidly growing sectarian movements that were also seen as heretical. Mormons and Jehovah's Witnesses were the most visible, but literally dozens of movements appeared with doctrines that these Protestants believed false. In this regard, Christian apologetics takes two forms: (1) to *warn* the faithful of the false doctrines that have appeared on the scene; and (2) to *rescue* those who have fallen for the false doctrines. At stake, in both instances, is the *salvation* and *soul* of those who have been lured away from the true faith.

Douglas Cowan's *Bearing False Witness?* tells the story of evangelical zeal that has been largely overlooked by other scholars of the cult phenomenon in America during the past quarter-century. His analysis traces the historical roots of this theologically grounded movement, showing how it has both continued and changed over the decades.

The deeper we get into Cowan's analysis, the clearer it becomes that we are looking at two dimensions of the same story. The anticult movement, which has attracted the attention of social scientists for more than thirty years now, is primarily a secular movement. While cults are acknowledged to be religious in character and religious symbolism figures prominently in them, the cult tales of the late twentieth century are essentially secular tales. Charismatic leaders develop highly manipulative skills that are virtually impossible for the novice to resist. The heroes of this drama are parents who take great risks to rescue their (often adult) children from organizations that have created highly developed forms of mind control. In this endeavor, they are assisted by an emerging class of quasi-professionals who initially called themselves *deprogrammers,* but later adopted more legitimate sounding titles such as *exit counselors.* The fundamental conception of the anticult paradigm is secular in nature. The cult has inhibited the individual's capacity to control fully his or her mental resources. The goal of removing the individual from the cult is the restoration of an alert and properly functioning mind.

From the beginning to the present day, on the other hand, the evangelical precursor to the anticult movement has sought to rescue the *soul* from a variety of evils that constitute a threat to individual *salvation.* In this telling of the tale, the world is a dangerous place inhabited with false gods, demons, evil spirits—all of which are responsible for the rise of new and controversial religious movements. The modern world differs from the nineteenth and early twentieth century in that we are experiencing this proliferation of threats to individual salvation. The goal of the evangelical Christian countercult is twofold: to protect those who are saved, and to rescue those who have fallen under the influence of these evils.

A few contemporary scholars, most particularly J. Gordon Melton, have taken note of the distinction Cowan makes between the evangelical movement that focuses on spiritual salvation and the restored control of one's mental or psychological resources that characterizes the secular anticult movement. In fact, Cowan follows Melton's terminology in using *countercult* to characterize the evangelical movement.

Two primary reasons may be offered to account for the considerable attention devoted to the secular anticult movement as compared to the evangelical countercult. First, the novelty of the new religions that attracted many youth also attracted the attention of mass media. Those parents who initiated the anticult movement also developed skills in attracting the media to tell their stories. By contrast, the countercult movement focused its resources on more-established new religions. These groups were neither particularly attractive to middle-class college youth, nor did their beliefs appear to be substantially at variance with traditional groups, and thus, they lacked appeal to the media.

A second factor leading to neglect of the countercult movement is that social scientists had generally ignored anything at all about evangelicals. With the exception of Bryan Wilson's notable work, there was essentially no literature on evangelical groups. Others, however, had picked up on the task of studying evangelical groups by the time Cowan began pursuing his research.

As is often the case, Douglas Cowan's interest in studying the countercult movement emerged out of biographical experience. Born and raised on Vancouver Island, in the western Canadian province of British Columbia, Cowan studied for the ministry at St. Andrew's Theological College. In 1989 he was ordained in the United Church of Canada, the largest Protestant denomination in the country. And, as is typical in many denominations, new ordinands have little say about their first pastoral charge.

When interviewed regarding his first assignment, Cowan was asked how he felt about "interfaith dialogue," to which he replied, "Fine. Why?"

"We're thinking of Cardston and Magrath for you," replied the church official, naming two small towns in the southwest corner of Alberta. "And, well, there are some Mormons there. . . ."

Cardston and Magrath represent the northern line of early Mormon advance when many Latter-day Saints were leaving Utah in the mid-1880s as a result of the Edmunds and Edmunds-Tucker Acts. Charles Card, the founder of Cardston, was one of Brigham Young's sons-in-law. Until 1992 Cardston was the only Mormon temple city in Canada, and of the five thousand residents there, just over four thousand are Latter-day Saints.

The young Rev. Cowan was assigned to the United Church.

When he learned of his charge, Cowan went to his local Christian bookstore and asked for some good reference material. Without hesitation, the clerk replied, "Oh, we have the best book on the market," and handed him a copy of *The God Makers* by Ed Decker and Dave Hunt. Knowing nothing about Mormons, and unaware of the slant of the book, he took it home and read it that afternoon. Of the literally hundreds of anti-Mormon books on the market, *The God Makers* ranks among the most pernicious.

Understandably, Cowan was apprehensive and unprepared for the interfaith dialogue he was about to encounter. What he discovered, not surprisingly, was that the people in Cardston were like people everywhere. Further, the line that separated those who were wonderful and caring from those who weren't did not run between the Mormon and United Church communities.

The cognitive dissonance that set in between Cowan's expectations based on reading *The God Makers* and his experience of living among Mormons soon led him to begin collecting Christian countercult materials. He presented the first results of his research at a regional meeting of the American Academy of Religion in 1990.

Cowan learned that a systematic study of the evangelical countercult movement was no easy task. The movement has many leaders, a large proportion of whom are prolific writers, and basically, they choose to be unavailable to scholars who are interested in understanding them. Cowan's resources consisted of hundreds of books, newsletters, and transcripts of radio and television programs. While the writings of individual authors tend to be duplicative, sufficient changes in their perspectives exist to make sampling difficult. So Cowan read hundreds of manuscripts and took copious notes.

Over the past few years, I have had the pleasure of reading several manuscript versions of this book, all the previous much longer than this version. It is clear that Cowan has distilled the essential history, themes, and content of countercult literature and that he has offered an analysis that draws upon the application of a brilliant theoretical interpretation.

As the title suggests, *Bearing False Witness?* is nuanced with multiple levels of meaning. In it, Cowan focuses on what is perceived by evangelicals to be the essential truth about particular Christian doctrines. The content might just as well have focused on the doctrinal messages of a particular Islamic faith tradition, or Judaic, or Hindu, for that matter.

The core of Cowan's analysis is to understand the dynamics of how people communicate in order to make persuasive arguments to a particular audience. While he is personally troubled by what many of us would see as prejudice, even hatred, that many countercult apologists express toward those who do not believe as they do, his goal is to understand how the structure of certain beliefs leads necessarily to logical conclusions. With rare lapses, he has maintained a dispassionate cool-headedness throughout the book.

Persuasive arguments rest at the core of all communication. Insofar as our arguments are not persuasive to a particular target audience, we have not succeeded in communicating our message. Cowan has probed the content of various types of evangelical communication, sorting out styles and techniques that result in effective communication. The sum of his effort is that he demonstrates why certain styles of communication are more effective to some kinds of audiences than to others.

For the most part, this volume will appeal to readers who will not be persuaded by the arguments of the evangelical countercult movement, but if they read with care they will better understand how and why so many can be attracted to the witness of the countercult preachers. And, perhaps also, they will see the utility of Cowan's analysis for understanding why other belief systems that proliferate around the world are able to attract large followings.

Jeffrey K. Hadden
University of Virginia

Acknowledgments

A great number of people deserve recognition for their varied contributions to this work. At the University of Calgary, to a teacher, colleague, and friend, I would like to offer my deepest appreciation first to Irving R. Hexham. From its initial conception as a doctoral dissertation to the current incarnation as an introduction to the Christian countercult, Irving has exemplified the finest tradition of an academic mentor. At Calgary also, I would like to express my thanks to A. W. Barber, Hugo Meynell, and David Taras. I would like to acknowledge my gratitude to the Social Sciences and Humanities Research Council of Canada for a doctoral fellowship that aided tremendously in gathering together the initial research materials.

At the University of Missouri-Kansas City, for their many helpful comments and suggestions, I would like to thank my colleague, Gary L. Ebersole, as well as graduate students who read and critiqued parts of the book: Kevin O'Brien, Paul Thomas, and Glenn Young.

Finally, at the University of Virginia, for his friendship, encouragement, wisdom, and the contribution of a foreword, many thanks are due Jeffrey K. Hadden.

The loving and consistent support of my parents, who quietly knew decades ago that this was the path my life would take and I just needed to wake up to that fact, has been so important over the past few years that mere words seem superfluous. So I will simply say, "Thank you, Mom and Dad."

Finally, what to say about my wife, Joie? Her pride and her courage, her support and her encouragement, her challenge and her love—all make this her work as much as mine. There is nothing more to say. *Res ipsa loquitur.*

Part I
Perspectives on the Christian Countercult

1

Confronting Cults

> The only reason for becoming familiar with other religions and other religious writings would be in order to show those who follow these false systems wherein the error lies and thereby to rescue them.
>
> —Dave Hunt, countercult apologist

INTRODUCING THE CHRISTIAN COUNTERCULT

One can experience the Christian countercult in a variety of ways. Walk into almost any evangelical bookstore, for example, and you will undoubtedly find a section labeled "Other Religions," "Cults and Sects," "False Religions," or something similar. Although these sections range from a few shelves to entire display cases, most contain titles such as *Cult Watch* (Ankerberg and Weldon 1991a), *Cult-Proofing Your Kids* (Martin 1993), *The Kingdom of the Cults* (Martin 1997), and *Occult Invasion* (Hunt 1998). Some of these books are organized along encyclopedic lines and describe an assortment of alternative religious groups and traditions; others focus on just one group and often include specific suggestions for evangelizing group members. Some, such as Martin's *Kingdom of the Cults,* are designed as a permanent desk reference; others, such as Alan Gomes's *Truth and Error: Comparative Charts of Cults and Christianity* (1998), are meant to be carried in one's briefcase, overcoat, or pocketbook. At some point, though, all compare and contrast the various religious leaders, groups, and movements the authors consider with evangelical or fundamentalist Protestantism.

On the other hand, perhaps you live near a Latter-day Saints temple, one of more than sixty in the United States alone. Walking past the temple one day you may encounter evangelical Christians from countercult ministries such as Saints Alive in Jesus (Ed Decker), Utah Lighthouse Ministry (Jerald and Sandra Tanner), or Mormonism Research Ministry (Bill McKeever) passing out leaflets on the street. An especially popular activity at new temple openings, when the Church of Jesus Christ of Latter-day Saints invites the non-Mormon public to view a temple prior to its consecration, countercult apologists often give out tracts explaining why they believe Mormonism is not Christian. They engage visitors in conversation to that same end and very occasionally picket the streets and avenues leading to the temple grounds.

Finally, imagine that a family member or friend has just announced her decision to start auditing with the Church of Scientology, to put herself under the shepherding movement of the International Church of Christ, or to take dharma vows as a Zen Buddhist. Upset by this unexpected religious choice, you turn to the Internet—the most active source of quick-and-easy information in human history—to learn more about the group. Depending on your search terms, however, rather than official Web sites for the group in question, any one of hundreds of countercult Web sites could appear. "Answers in Action," the "Bible Truth Mormonism Page," "Ex-Masons for Jesus," and "Jehovah's Christian Witness" are just a few of the sites dedicated to various aspects of evangelical countercult apologetics.

These are just some of the venues in which the Christian countercult movement operates. With roots that stretch back to the theological shifts of the nineteenth century, including the emergence of such sects as the Mormons, Jehovah's Witnesses, and Christian Science, the Christian countercult is that branch of evangelical Protestantism most concerned about the growth of religious pluralism and with the advent of new and often controversial religious movements. Because these movements expand the range of available religious choice in society, they invariably threaten the sense of ontological uniqueness that has marked Christianity since its rise to dominance in the West. Long before the secular anticult appeared in the late 1960s and gained public attention in the 1970s with often lurid stories of brainwashing and deprogramming (see chapter 2), evangelical Protestants had been cataloguing and comparing emergent religious movements in North America. From Eber Howe's *Mormonism Unvailed* (1834) to George Hamilton Combs's *Some Latter-day Religions* (1899), from William Irvine's *Heresies Exposed* (1935, originally published in 1917 as *Timely Warnings*) to Walter Martin's *Kingdom of the Cults* (in fourth edition, 1997), and from occasional sermons in evangelical pulpits to the advent of professional apologetics organizations such as the Christian Research Institute, Spiritual Counterfeits Project, and Personal Freedom Outreach, the Christian countercult has been enormously influential in constructing and maintaining the popular image of new and controversial religious movements in North America.

As a social movement, in many ways the countercult is multifaceted and indistinct, with exponents that range from the academic to the popular, and the erudite to the absurd. It encompasses large corporations as well as individual ministries; its membership includes both full-time apologists who have devoted their professional lives to researching and writing about new religious movements, and ordinary Christians who only want to know how to respond to the evangelistic advances of Mormon missionaries or Jehovah's Witness pioneers. The resources the countercult brings to bear on what it regards as the growing problem of cults, sects, and so-called false religions vary also— print publication of books, magazines, and newsletters; radio broadcasting; audio- and videocassette production; direct mail appeals; proactive evangelistic encounters; professional and avocational Internet Web sites; as well as lecture series, training workshops, and countercult conferences. The polymorphous character of the movement means, among other things, that there are no reliable membership statistics available. Since religious pluralism characterizes the social environment in which the countercult resides, movement intellectuals (a concept discussed more fully below) regard all committed Christians as potential participants in the countercult movement. Thus, while fewer than 100 apologists publish commercially and consistently in North America, the actual number of Christians engaged in countercult apologetics at all levels is impossible to determine.

Bearing False Witness? is an introduction to this Christian countercult movement. Even though some of the countercult exponents I discuss range from the extremes represented by writers such as Constance Cumbey, Dave Hunt, and Texe Marrs to the more erudite portrayals of evangelical Christianity one finds from apologists such as Robert Bowman, Walter Martin, and Carl Mosser, I contend that the organizing principles of countercult apologetics remain the same throughout. That is, the cognitive praxis of the countercult movement revolves around two poles: the apologetic, the ongoing construction and maintenance of the evangelical Christian worldview; and the evangelistic, the continuing effort to convert to evangelical Christianity those who follow other religious traditions.

THE COUNTERCULT AS REALITY PERCEIVED AND MAINTAINED

Whether one accepts the concerns of the Christian countercult as valid, or agrees with their interpretation and evaluation of various social, cultural, and religious phenomena, is less important than the fact that *they* believe. They *believe* in the validity of these analyses, and this belief contributes to their behavior in the world. One of the fundamental premises of a sociology of knowledge, however, is that *perceived* reality is not inevitably congruent with *actual* reality. It may well be, but it is not necessarily so. However, because individuals and groups operate within the constraints of perceived reality, it is this dynamic that governs behavior. Social action is predicated on the perception of reality, but not necessarily the accuracy of that perception. Thus, my task here is to describe the *subjective* construction of reality that governs countercult action, to understand as far as one is able the various units of knowledge, clusters of belief, information filters, and logical processes around which countercult groups constitute themselves, the lenses through which they interpret the world around them, and according to the precepts of which they make choices to act in that world.

In their classic study *The Social Construction of Reality*, Peter Berger and Thomas Luckmann argue that "the sociology of knowledge must concern itself with whatever passes for 'knowledge' in a society, regardless of the ultimate validity or invalidity (by whatever criteria) of such 'knowledge' " (1966: 15). Because belief in the validity of something has the power to motivate social action related to that thing, *"the sociology of knowledge is concerned with the social construction of reality"* (1966: 15, emphasis in the original). Thus, I am interested in (1) reality as it is socially constructed by the Christian countercult; (2) the ways in which information is managed and presented in order to maintain and reinforce that reality in the face of threats to its validity, essentiality, and inevitability; and (3) the struggle to sustain the evangelical Christian construction of reality as the only legitimate expression of religious life.

Take, for example, evangelical scholar John Newport's description of the need for a serviceable Christian apologetic in the face of the potential disconfirmations represented by the so-called New Age movement. "Evangelical Christianity cannot embrace the New Age worldview," he writes. "But it can and must establish contact with those who have turned to the New Age movement in their search for spiritual meaning. Their needs can be satisfied only by biblical religion" (Newport 1998: 607). While there is some ambiguity in his terminology, given that Newport writes of the New Age as opposed to specific new or controversial religious movements that may regularly be considered parts of it, his comments illustrate a number of the basic principles at work in Christian countercult apologetics.

- First is a *conflict of worldviews.* The worldview (or construction of reality) represented by the New Age (or the particular cult, sect, or new religious movement under discussion) is regarded as fundamentally incompatible with, and therefore a problem of practical life for, those who subscribe to a Christian worldview.

- Second, the *Christian worldview is held to be unique, exclusive, and insuperable.* Predicated on an interpretation of divine revelation that insists Christianity be set apart from all other religious traditions, the Christian countercult presents its subjective construction of reality as the only one that is entirely congruent with objective reality.

- Third is a *mandate to convert* those who inhabit competing worldviews. Communication must be established with adherents of these worldviews, and information managed in such a way as to effect their conversion—their migration, as it were— from the false world to the true.

Thus, the Christian countercult operates in two separate but related domains: apologetics and missiology.

Let me offer an initial postulate informing this study: When a social structure evolves in which relatively open choice is available with respect to the particular construction of reality residents may inhabit without significant social sanction, specific conceptual mechanisms are required to maintain a reasoned inhabitance in one reality over another. Put differently, there needs to be ongoing reinforcement that the choice to live as a Christian, for example, is superior to all other possible choices. However, the option for one's own subjective reality also locates the individual *outside* of other subjective realities. Clarifying which universe one *does* inhabit also declares which universe (or universes) one *does not* and, by implication, *ought not* inhabit. Thus, paraphrasing Foucault (1980), as an ongoing struggle for authentic existence, the Christian countercult apologetic represents "relations of power," not simply "relations of meaning."

If every person understood and participated in reality in precisely the same way, then the need for reality-maintenance would hardly arise. Everyone, no matter what his or her age, sex, or social position, would inhabit the world according to the same set of subjective givens; indeed, those givens—what Berger and Luckmann call "recipe knowledge"—would assume an ontological monolithicity simply because no significant differences of opinion or interpretation were offered to challenge the essential nature of the perception. But, such is not the case. No such uniformity exists, and arguably never has. "Incipient counter-definitions of reality and identity," write Berger and Luckmann, "are present as soon as any such individuals congregate in socially durable groups" (Berger and Luckmann 1966: 185).

What is really shaken by potential disconfirmation of one's subjective reality is faith in the reliability of one's *perception* as an accurate reflection of the *actual*. Expectation is shaken by experience, and cognitive dissonance sets in with the realization that the way we *believe* things to be may not be the way they *actually* are. Countercult apologists do not defend their particular worldview simply because they believe that it keeps them or anyone else within the domain of evangelical or fundamentalist Christianity; rather they believe theirs is the only subjective reality that is completely congruent with reality as it is.

Of course, this is not to say that no correspondence exists between countercult perception and social reality. Indeed, many of the phenomena about which the Christian countercult writes and against which it contends are quite obvious in the postmodern world. For decades in North America there has been heightened interest in Eastern religious traditions, spirituality, and meditative techniques. The rediscovery and/or reinvention of Neopagan beliefs and practices is also increasing—absent now the social opprobrium and often lethal consequences that accompanied their presence in the past. More and more material is available each year on a variety of phenomena from psychic techniques and UFO contact experiences to the use of remote viewing to augment these experiences, from the attempted integration of science and mysticism to a growing abundance of so-called divination devices ranging from the ancient (the *I Ching*) to the New Age *(Inner Child Cards)*. New religious expression—whether formed around the "space brothers" and their message of universal peace, J. Z. Knight's channeled messages from the Atlantean warrior Ramtha, or apocalyptic interpretations of Christian Scripture—is constantly erupting. Thus, the question is not whether these phenomena exist, but what they mean in the context of social evolution. How are they regarded by those with whom they are in competition? Let me cite one example.

"I believe there is an evil intelligence behind cults (including UFO cults), the New Age Movement, and much of what we call modern spirituality" writes countercult apologist William Alnor, who is also a fundamentalist pastor, director of Eastern Christian Outreach, and a visiting journalism professor at Texas A&M University–Kingsville.

However, I have found that many people are not willing to accept that there is a definite demonic agenda behind many contemporary religious strands. I believe that one of the biggest deceptions of all is the inability to discern the intelligence behind evil. I have shown that there is an intelligent evil behind the UFO cults that permeates New Age occultism. It is most concerned with blocking what God has said in his Word and voiding what the true Christ did on the cross two thousand years ago. . . . UFO cults and the current obsession with the unseen and the realm of space are not of God. They are evil and demonic in every language and in every culture. (Alnor 1998: 152)

Again, whether Alnor's perception of reality accords with objective reality is not the issue. It is upon that perception that Alnor, the target audience for his countercult ministry, and arguably the members of his church congregation will base their behavior. Indeed, it was this perceived reality that Alnor offered to the media as so-called expert testimony in the wake of the 1997 Rancho Santa Fe suicides. "Because I wrote about the group that became the Heaven's Gate cult in my 1992 book *UFOs in the New Age*," he writes, "I have made a number of media appearances to try to explain the event. The answers to why it happened are part of the fundamental human condition—the conflict between good and evil itself. I believe it is important for people to be inoculated against religious deception, which began in the Garden of Eden and since then has destroyed many" (Alnor 1998: 15–16).

The claim that all religious traditions other than Christianity develop from a common, deceptive rootstock is prevalent among countercult apologists. Social scientific research, on the other hand, contends that all cults are not the same, regardless of superficial similarities (cf. Dawson 1998; Melton 1992; Zablocki and Robbins 2001). Death by suicide is one of the very few things that the Heaven's Gate "Away Team" had in common with those who died in Jonestown, Guyana, and even that apparent similarity is tenuous at best. Finally, when lumped together as religious phenomena, as some countercult apologists are wont to do, both Latter-day Saints and Scientologists object vigorously. The issue, then, becomes one of achieving an authoritative voice.

In the context of an open religious economy, several different voices compete for authoritative positions in the discourse on cults, sects, and new religious movements, and each brings to that discourse a distinct interpretation of events. First are the new religious movements themselves. Whether they are new because of religious novelty and innovation (e.g., Scientology, Heaven's Gate, various emergent neopaganisms), because they have reinterpreted dominant religious traditions to supposedly uncover heretofore hidden meanings (e.g., Latter-day Saints, Jehovah's Witnesses, Christian Science), or because they have only recently emerged in the particular religious economy under consideration (e.g., Buddhism or Hinduism in North America), each has its own emic perspective, its own self-understanding of religious history, beliefs, and practice. Next, there is the dominant religious tradition in the economy; in the North American context, this has meant the various Christianities. Whether they welcome the pluralism that defines the expansion of that economy, as the ecumenical and interfaith movements of mainline liberal Protestantism have, or regard it as problematic, as have evangelical and fundamentalist Protestantisms, their voices contribute to the shape and tenor of the discourse. For those who regard new religious movements as problematic, opposition voices can emerge from within a religious tradition (e.g., the evangelical Christian countercult) or outside of any particular tradition (e.g., the secular anticult). Often, academic voices try to mediate understanding and interpretation across these competing voices. Finally, arguably the most influential voice in the discourse, but one that potentially engages all the others, is that of the mass media. In situations of social conflict, new religious movements cannot avoid the media spotlight, and media power to contribute to the common stock of cultural knowledge cannot be overstated. The degree to which media attribute the so-called authoritative voice in any story, for example, is the degree to which that particular narrative is privileged in the ensuing cultural conversation. In North America, mainstream media treatment of new religious movements has been almost entirely prejudicial, rarely privileging the voices of the movement members, and more often than not relying on oppositional voices for the information they pass on to news consumers (cf. Beckford 1994; Richardson 1995; Richardson and van Driel 1997; Shupe and Hadden 1995; Silk 1997; van Driel and Richardson 1988; Wright 1997).

In this discourse, Christian countercult writers and speakers identify themselves most often as apologists, and take as their biblical mandate the apostle Jude's admonition to "earnestly contend for the faith which was once delivered unto the saints" (Jude 3 KJV). Since the Second World War, the countercult has become a specialized branch of neo-evangelical apologetics and seeks to offer reasoned arguments for the superiority of Christianity in the face of pluralistic challenges to the faith. In the context of this ongoing reality-maintenance, and unlike those in the secular anticult movement discussed in chapter 2, countercult apologists are clear that migration *from* the worldview inhabited by the adherent *to* that of evangelical/fundamentalist Christianity is the ideal outcome of their mission.

THE COGNITIVE APPROACH AND THE UNAVOIDABLE LACUNAE

A social movement such as the Christian countercult can be investigated in a number of ways. Demographic analysis of the countercult constituency, participant-observation at evangelistic venues such as a Latter-day Saints temple opening, archival research at the Spiritual Counterfeits Project or the Christian Research Institute, or in-depth interviews with prominent countercult apologists—all are possibilities, and each would disclose certain aspects of the movement. For this book, however, I have chosen to combine elements from two analytic approaches: a sociology of knowledge, particularly as it has been mediated through the work of Peter Berger and Thomas Luckmann (1966; Berger 1967), and the cognitive approach to social movements articulated by Ron Eyerman and Andrew Jamison (1991). Inasmuch as Berger and Luckmann's work has been discussed extensively since its publication, and Eyerman and Jamison's approach is relatively new, I concentrate for the moment on the latter's two principle concepts: cognitive praxis and movement intellectuals.

"By studying social movements as cognitive praxis," write Eyerman and Jamison, "we mean that they are producers of knowledge and that knowledge creation itself should be seen as a collective process. . . . We want to argue that social movements are actually constituted by the cognitive praxis that is entailed in the articulation of their historical projects" (1991: 43). For them, there are three dimensions to a social movement's cognitive praxis: cosmology, technology, and organization. Cosmology we recognize readily as the worldview by which a social movement is bounded, the "basic assumptions or beliefs" that all participants take "more or less for granted" (Eyerman and Jamison 1991: 66)—what I term below the "cognitive boundary markers" of the Christian countercult. The concept of a technological dimension derives from their original work on European environmental movements. By this, though, they mean the specific problems to which the movement is responding—what Karl Mannheim called the problems of practical life—and the various critiques organized around those problems. Finally, the organizational dimension refers to the ways in which movements develop, evolve, professionalize, and democratize.

The central concept of the cognitive praxis approach is that social movements are producers of knowledge, and that the new knowledge a movement produces (or the new ways in which extant knowledge is framed or articulated) actually constitutes "the core identity of a social movement" (Eyerman and Jamison 1991: 44). This approach to the problem avoids the need to locate a movement's identity solely (or even principally) in the individuals, groups, or coalitions that populate it at a certain point in time. No different from any other social actor, countercult apologists function in a number of different social spheres. William Alnor is a countercult apologist, journalism professor, and fundamentalist pastor. In addition to their countercult activities, many of Alnor's colleagues are also evangelical academics and pastors, while others participate in the countercult only occasionally and avocationally. How, then, does a researcher tease out the strands of social action that reflect countercult apologetics as opposed to some other facet of a participant's life? The answer is to consider the countercult movement on the basis of the cognitive content around which it is formed and the social praxis that both embeds and transmits that content.

This approach allows for a larger picture of the movement's historical development and social project to emerge. "We conceive of social movements as processes through which meaning is constituted," contend Eyerman and Jamison (1991: 44), an approach that seems to me particularly useful for the study of a movement as polymorphous as the Christian countercult.

If cognitive praxis is "the concepts, ideas and intellectual activities that give [social movements] their cognitive identity" (Eyerman and Jamison 1991: 3), then "movement intellectuals" are those actors who make that cognitive praxis historically visible. While they offer a more theoretically complete explanation of the concept than I have time for here, for Eyerman and Jamison, movement intellectuals are "those individuals who through their activities articulate the knowledge interests and cognitive identity of social movements" (1991: 98). In terms of the countercult, this means those apologists who create or in some other way contribute to the intellectual product on which the countercult movement depends for its social praxis. As Eyerman and Jamison note, in studying social movements, "the cognitive dimension can be found in specific texts, in movement documents, programs, books, articles, etc. In short, it can be 'read,' that is, reconstructed from really existing materials" (1991: 68).

Whether these contributions come from movement participants with recognized academic or clerical credentials, or those whose participation is linked to personal experiences with new religious movements, all are movement intellectuals to some degree. As Eyerman and Jamison point out, however, it is important to remember that "all activists do not participate equally in the cognitive praxis" of a social movement (1991: 94). That is, not everyone who wants to contribute to the ongoing development of the countercult has similar access to the principle mechanisms of countercult production—print media, broadcasting, and audio-video production. While the advent of the Internet is changing this situation to some degree, and allowing for a democratization of countercult apologetics hitherto unavailable (see chapter 8), evangelical trade publishing, for example, is still restricted to those authors whom publishing houses regard as commercially viable, or who have the personal resources to publish their own material.

This brings me to the particular materials that interest me in this study— the public face of the Christian countercult, the *social* construction of countercult apologetics, which means, by and large, that which is readily available on the shelves of the Christian bookstores noted above. Because the range of countercult consumers extends from the impulse buyer to the apologetic aficionado, I take it as an axiom that far more Christians purchase and read countercult materials through evangelical bookstores (or now access countercult resources online) than have either the time or the inclination to attend seminars or conferences, participate actively in countercult organizations, or pursue countercult apologetics beyond those bookstore purchases, Internet searches, and perhaps an occasional encounter with Mormon missionaries or Witness pioneers. While a smaller number will subscribe to countercult journals and newsletters, relatively few will have the opportunity to enter into extended dialogue with principal movement intellectuals, those who produce the materials countercult consumers purchase. Why not, then, conduct personal interviews, archival research, or participant-observation? I regard this as less useful because the average countercult consumer would not have access to these kinds of intellectual product; rather, their perception of cults, sects, and new religious movements is informed and shaped by that which is publicly and readily available.

This approach to the problem is not inconsistent with the understanding of some countercult apologists themselves. During the initial phases of research and writing, for example, I made several attempts to interview Dave Hunt, not as a movement intellectual who was representative of the countercult as a whole, but as a significant contributor to certain aspects of its cognitive praxis. While an opportunity to learn more of Hunt's background, to clarify issues of interpretation, and to inquire whether his views had changed over the years might have been valuable, it is not necessary to an investigation of the Christian countercult as cognitive praxis. Indeed, Hunt himself believes that the need to speak with a writer directly is obviated by the writer's primary responsibility to clarity and precision upon publication. While hardly unequivocal as a methodological dictum, he makes a compelling argument for the very approach I have employed in this book. In the first issue of his *Berean Call* newsletter (February 1986), in answer to the manner in which he and co-author T. A. McMahon took evangelical Christianity to task in their book *The Seduction of Christianity* (Hunt and McMahon 1985; see chapter 12), Hunt (1986: 2) writes:

It is not necessary to talk with a writer or speaker in order to be accurate and fair. It is a rather weak excuse to say that some writer/leader really didn't mean what he said. Then he should have said what he meant. Unfortunately, there are thousands and, in the case of some, millions who have read and/or heard and taken it at face value, as any reasonable person would. Words have meaning and it is assumed that the normal meaning applies. Even if one of these teachers has changed his beliefs, we must still deal with what has been published for the sake of those who have been affected by it.

Again, this is not to say that personal interaction with writers or speakers might not prove valuable; undoubtedly, it would. It is to say that in the analysis of social movements according to the cognitive praxis by which those movements are constituted and informed, it is not essential.

No study of social movements is ever complete. While a particular project may be finished, there are always other stories that could have been told, other groups or movement intellectuals who could have been included, other modes of analysis that could have been used to shed light on a particular movement's cognitive praxis. In any project, these constitute the unavoidable lacunae that emerge as the different phases of research appear, progress, and ultimately draw to a close. In this book, I have made no attempt to include every countercult ministry, identify every movement intellectual, or account for every shift and nuance of countercult apologetics as it has developed in the late twentieth century. As a result, I suspect that some countercult apologists will be upset because they are included here, others because they are not or because they feel that their efforts have been insufficiently explored. To reiterate Eyerman and Jamison, however, the approach I am taking moves away from explicitly identifying social movements solely on the basis of the individuals, groups, and coalitions that participate in them.

I have chosen not simply to catalogue the Christian countercult. Rather, through a close analysis of hundreds of books, pamphlets, newsletters, journals, audio- and videocassettes, and Web sites, I have tried to accomplish three major tasks. In part I, I outline the cognitive praxis by which the countercult as a social movement is defined. Part II describes some of the major trends in countercult development and the various organizational continua along which different countercult groups and apologists operate. Finally, part III surveys the manner in which the members of the Christian countercult depict various religious groups in our society. That is, what is the countercult's core identity? How is it organized to manifest that identity? And, how does it constitute the adversarial Other in the face of whom that identity finds meaning?

From Extraction to Migration: The Christian Countercult in Sociological Perspective

In the past three decades, numerous books and articles, both popular and academic, have dealt with various aspects of the secular *anticult* movement.[1] Only recently, though, have scholars specifically begun to considers it Christian correlate: the evangelical *countercult* movement (cf. Cowan 1990; Introvigne 1993, 1995a, 1995b; Langone 1995; Melton 1992, 2000; Saliba 1999). More often than not, the countercult has been subsumed as a mere variant of what has been perceived as a larger anticult movement (e.g., Barker 1982; Bromley and Shupe 1987; Shupe and Bromley 1980).

In 1993, a brief but significant flurry of interest in the difference between the two movements surfaced following Italian scholar Massimo Introvigne's presentation to the Center for Study on New Religions conference. Introvigne proposed a rationalist/postrationalist model to draw the distinction between the secular anticult and the religious countercult (he acknowledged but did not limit his analysis to evangelical Christians) and predicted that the differences between the two movements would result in ongoing enmity between them. Various discussions ensued between Introvigne and those who recognized the validity of the distinction he and fellow scholar J. Gordon Melton had made, and others who felt it might in some way detract from or dilute the vigor of their own anticult argument (cf. Introvigne 1993, 1995a, 1995b; Langone 1995). In response, for example, the executive director of the American Family Foundation, Michael Langone, criticized Introvigne for proposing a typological distinction between the two groups that was "an oversimplification and subtly derogatory" (1995: 171). Langone argued that Introvigne's typology "leads to a construction or exaggeration of differences, as well as an underestimation of similarities" (Langone 1995: 172–73). That the two movements ought to be working together against a common enemy was the not so subtle message in Langone's reply.

Apparent similarities aside, though, the distinction Introvigne and Melton recognized is important. Significant enough differences exist between the anticult and the countercult, for example, in their respective cult conceptualizations, epistemologies, threat perceptions, and organizational motivation and methods, that further discrimination between the two movements is in order and that more intentional research on the latter should be undertaken.

THE CHRISTIAN COUNTERCULT IN SOCIOLOGICAL PERSPECTIVE

Very broadly put, the secular anticult proceeds according to different versions of the brainwashing or thought control hypothesis and takes as its point of departure allegations of physical and mental abuse, attacking a number of nontraditional religious groups on the basis of alleged civil liberties violations (cf. Bromley 1998, 2001; Bromley and Richardson 1983; Conway and Siegelman 1979; Hassan 1990, 2000; Hein 2000; Singer and Lalich 1995; Tobias and Lalich 1994; Zablocki 1997, 1998; Zablocki and Robbins 2001). The working hypothesis is that at some point in the recruitment and conversion process, the cognitive ability of the potential recruit is compromised by the religious group, and the capacity to make rational, informed decisions is impaired. Once recruits are active within the group, this process continues and intensifies.

The Christian countercult, on the other hand, operates from an almost entirely different perspective. For the countercult, alternative religious expressions—cults and sects—present a problem of practical life (Mannheim 1952) not primarily because of their alleged recruiting and retention methods, but because of their ontology; they are a threat to society not by virtue of their reputedly antisocial behavior, but simply by virtue of their existence. Because they expand the range of choices available in the religious marketplace, choices that are deemed unacceptable by the countercult, the very presence of nontraditional religious groups threatens the worldview inhabited by conservative Christians and challenges that worldview's various claims to an ultimate authority and a unique veracity. In the face of this, whether professional or avocational, countercult apologists function as "significant others" (Berger and Luckmann 1966) in the ongoing maintenance of the evangelical/fundamentalist worldview, and the reinforcement of its claim to a matchless authenticity (cf. Clark and Geisler 1990; Groothuis 1986, 1988; Hunt 1996; Melton 2000; Sire 1997).

That the Christian countercult has been subsumed under the rubric of its often more sensational cousin should not surprise. While exorcisms may occur with varying regularity in some evangelical and fundamentalist domains (cf. Cuneo 2001; Larson 1989b, 1996, 1999; Modica 1996), the lurid descriptions of deprogramming that attracted high levels of media attention in the 1970s and early 1980s exist almost entirely within the world of the anticult. Unless they were evangelical or fundamentalist Christians themselves, if outraged or anxious family members or friends of new religious movement recruits sought to do anything about their loved ones' involvement in these groups, they usually worked through elements of the anticult, not the countercult. As well, until the late 1980s and mid-1990s, the Christian countercult was restricted either to religious publishing houses and/or the often prohibitively expensive path of print self-publishing. Even though groups such as the Christian Research Institute (CRI) and the Spiritual Counterfeits Project (SCP) have been around for decades (Hexham 1981; Martin 1965), relatively little attention has been focused on them in either the secular media or the scholarly literature.

Two processes have led to the recent expansion and democratization of the countercult, though, that warrant a more intentional and disciplined investigation. First, following the organizational shake-up of the Christian Research Institute after the death in 1989 of its founder and guiding light, Walter R. Martin, a number of new countercult groups and ministries have come into existence. Many people who had worked either for Martin or briefly for his successor, Hank Hanegraaff, left the organization under a variety of circumstances and began countercult ministries of their own. Robert M. Bowman, for example, was a special projects editor with CRI until a conflict with Hanegraaff resulted in his leaving the organization in 1992. Since then he has been involved with a number of countercult ministries, including Apologia Report (an Internet venture run by another ex-CRI employee, Rich Poll) and the Atlanta Christian Apologetics Project; he has worked as publications editor for the Watchman Fellowship and now operates his own Institute for the Development of Evangelical Apologetics. Similarly, Ron Rhodes, a former senior researcher at CRI, left in the wake of these same troubles and both aligned himself with Poll's Apologia Report and started his own apologetics organization, Reasoning From Scriptures Ministries.

Second, for most of its postwar history, few avenues or opportunities have existed for nonprofessional countercult apologists to enter the field. Publication—either commercial or self-funded—was limited to those with the necessary resources for print publication, audio- and videocassette production, and, for the evangelically well-heeled, radio broadcasting. The advent of the Internet, however, as well as the increasing availability of Web authoring tools, domain and Web site hosting, and server support, has resulted in an explosion of interrelated countercult Web sites. This aspect of the phenomenon is more fully explored in chapter 8.

With these parallel expansions, and because the Christian countercult represents the first sustained categorization and systematization of new and emergent religions in North America, preceding the earliest efforts of the secular anticult by more than half a century, it is important to distinguish between them.

EXTRACTION AND MIGRATION: THE ANTICULT AND THE COUNTERCULT

At least five separate areas differentiate the countercult from the anticult. Although these areas are not categorically discrete and do interpenetrate one

another, isolating and comparing them does help illustrate the differences between the two movements. They are (1) the definition of "cult" employed by
both movements; (2) each movement's explanation for the prevalence of cultic
behavior; (3) the personal and organizational motivation behind the anticult
and the countercult, and the perceived danger to which each is responding;
(4) the objective or goal of the different movements; and (5) the methods
employed to achieve those goals. Through these distinctions, what becomes
clear is that although they are concerned with very similar social problems, for
the most part, the anticult and countercult conceptualize, explain, and respond
to these problems in very different ways.

Definition of "Cult"

Because it lays bare the conceptual grounding of the movements themselves—the foundation of their cognitive praxes—how each defines the word
"cult" is the obvious point of departure for differentiating between them. In
many ways, whether for the anticult or the countercult, everything that follows
derives from these respective definitions.

Margaret Singer, a prominent figure in the secular anticult movement and
the author (with exit counselor Janja Lalich) of *Cults in Our Midst* (1995),
provides a good example of the definition employed by the anticult. While she
prefers the phrase "cultic relationships," Singer defines a cult according to three
interrelated sets of criteria: "1. The origin of the group and the role of the
leader. 2. The power structure, or relationship between the leader (or leaders)
and the followers. 3. The use of a coordinated program of persuasion (which
is called thought reform or, more commonly, brainwashing)" (1995: 7). She
then expands on each of these broader categories, further refining (but in no
way really clarifying) her definition (Singer and Lalich 1995: 7–28).

Michael Langone, who edits the American Family Foundation's *Cultic Studies Journal*, lists twelve "statements" that "often characterize manipulative
groups." Among these, Langone states that "the group is focused on a living
leader to whom members seem to display excessively zealous, unquestioning
commitment"; "the group is preoccupied with bringing in new members"; "the
group is preoccupied with making money"; "the group has a polarized us-
versus-them mentality, which causes conflict with the wider society"; and "the
group is elitist, claiming a special, exalted status for itself, its leader(s), and
members" (Langone 1999b).

Following Stark and Bainbridge's compelling argument in *The Future of
Religion* (1985: 19–20), the major problem with both these sets of characteristics is that they are subjective correlates rather than empirically measurable
attributes. What, for example, constitutes "excessive" as opposed to "appropriate" zeal? Indeed, what may appear inappropriate or even manipulative to
one person hardly registers on another's perceptual radar. What is the evan-

gelical Christian church growth movement—or, indeed, the Christian countercult—but an organized and systematic attempt to bring new members into
that stream of Christianity? As well, a number of well-established religious
traditions employ what Langone calls "mind-numbing techniques," in which
he includes "meditation, chanting, [and] speaking in tongues"; yet, these would
hardly qualify as cults in the context of the Western religious economy. Finally,
many groups that are often popularly characterized as cults no longer have a
living leader and have relied instead on a Weberian routinization of charisma
to survive and evolve.

Concerns such as these exemplify the problem of how many of these characteristics must be present, and to what degree, before a group qualifies as a
cult. On the other hand, how does one determine the times when these same
statements do *not* characterize manipulative groups? Because the anticult consistently confuses correlates with attributes in this way, there is no stability of
definition; they present instead what Stark and Bainbridge have called the "un-
ideal type" (1985: 19–20), a labeling process more suited to the political evaluation and stigmatization of unpopular groups than an analysis of their social
and cultural location.

In fact, the dubious nature of the correlates used by Langone and his colleagues at the American Family Foundation is unwittingly recognized and
highlighted in an article that he has felt forced to include in the "Cults 101"
section of the foundation's Web site (www.csj.org). "I have had to point out
why the United States Marine Corps is not a cult so many times," Langone
writes, "that I carry a list to lectures and court appearances" (1999a). The fact
that he has had to point out the differences that many times indicates the
fundamentally ambiguous nature—and corresponding futility—of the American Family Foundation definition.

While there is some variation in the specifics of the definition used by members of the Christian countercult, there is considerably less inherent ambiguity.
Although it may, on occasion, deploy aspects of the anticult definition as supportive correlates, for the countercult the definitions of both "cults" and "false
religions" are always made with reference to normative claims of Christian
uniqueness, exclusivity, and insuperability. Usually rendered in terms of evangelical and/or fundamentalist theology, these claims establish the standards by
which all other religious groups, beliefs, and practices are evaluated.

Of all the postwar countercult apologists, Walter Ralston Martin (1928–89)
is arguably the most influential (see chapter 5). Despite continuing allegations
that Martin misrepresented his educational credentials, his matrilineal descent
from Brigham Young, and the authenticity of his ordination, he remains, perhaps, *the* major figure on the twentieth-century countercult horizon. In *The
Rise of the Cults* (1980), Martin defined the phenomenon of new religious
movements thus: "*By cultism we mean the adherence to doctrines which are
pointedly contradictory to orthodox Christianity and which yet claim the dis-*

tinction of either tracing their origin to orthodox sources or of being in essential harmony with those sources. Cultism, in short, is any major deviation from orthodox Christianity relative to the cardinal doctrines of the Christian faith" (Martin 1980: 12, emphasis in the original).

Even this theologically oriented definition is not as clear as it would become as the countercult developed during and after the 1970s. Was Martin referring, for example, to *deviance by Christians* from what he considered orthodox Christianity, as his first sentence seems to indicate, or a *theological variance from Christianity by anyone*, no matter what the variant's position, as his second sentence suggests? The list of groups with which he dealt in his magnum opus, *The Kingdom of the Cults* (Martin 1965, 1977, 1985, 1997), and that have been considered cults by the Christian Research Institute and other countercult apologists who have followed in its wake suggests very strongly the latter.[2] In an attempt to reconcile the ambiguity, however, a number of countercult apologists do make the distinction between what they refer to as "sociological" definitions of cults (i.e., using a definition closely related to that deployed by the anticult), and the more theological definition employed by Martin and others. Where neither of these apply, a third category—false religions—is often introduced.

"Cult," then, becomes a function of deviance from Christian orthodoxy by putative Christian groups; "false religions," world faiths such as Islam, Hinduism, and Buddhism, are considered anathema by virtue of their de facto rejection of Christian doctrines. Whether a cult or a false religion, operationally the distinction is made according to doctrinal predicates; any religious movement, group, or tradition that differs from Christianity is to be rejected and repudiated, and its adherents considered potential targets for missionizing and conversion.

Many countercult writers are highly critical of the anticult's reliance on brainwashing and thought control and reject them as either useful definitions of or explanatory mechanisms for cultic involvement (see, for example, Gomes 1998; Groothuis 1986, 1988; Passantino and Passantino 1997). Writing in the fourth edition of *The Kingdom of the Cults*, for example, CRI California cofounder Gretchen Passantino critiques the anticult's use of the mind-control model for similar reasons as put forth above. It is simply too subjective, too prone to its own abuse. "*Doctrinal* aberration should distinguish the cults from Christianity," the Passantinos declare, "not mere social aberration" (1997: 55, emphasis in the original). In their own countercult ministry, Answers in Action (http://answers.org), the Passantinos define a cult as "a religious group that identifies itself with Christianity, or at least claims compatibility with Christianity, and yet which denies one or more of [Christianity's] cardinal biblical doctrines" (Passantino and Passantino 1990a). Once again, however, a review of the groups considered cults by the Passantinos reveals that *any* group that deviates from "these cardinal biblical doctrines" so qualifies.

Bob Larson, a fundamentalist Christian radio talk-show host, writer, and traveling lecturer uses a similar definition. "The term *cult*," he writes in *Larson's New Book of Cults*, "as used in this book is generally understood to have a negative connotation that indicates morally reprehensible practices or beliefs that depart from historic Christianity" (1989a: 19). "Morally reprehensible practices" that are part and parcel of historic Christianity notwithstanding, at first glance it seems that a cult can be identified either by moral reprehensibility or by deviance from "historic Christianity." However, it becomes clear that the latter defines a cult more clearly for Larson than does the former. For him, two attributes constitute a cult: "(1) if it ignores or purposely omits central apostolic doctrines; or (2) if it holds beliefs that are distinctly opposed to orthodox Christianity" (Larson 1989a: 19–20).

While some ambiguity may still linger in the above definitions, among the clearest examples of the countercult definition *in practice* are those deployed by evangelical sociologist Ron Enroth and countercult apologist Jay Howard. In *The Lure of the Cults*, Enroth states: "Any group, movement, or teaching may be considered cultic to the degree it deviates from biblical, orthodox Christianity" (1979: 20). Howard concurs. For him, a cult is "any group promoting a person or set of teachings that rejects the historic, central teachings of the Christian church" (Howard, Fink, and Unseth 1990: 23; for definitions similar to this, see Ankerberg and Weldon 1991a, 1999; Enroth 1977; Marrs 1990; McDowell and Stewart 1983; Scott 1993; van Baalen 1960; Williams 1997). While the anticult relies on putative sociological and psychological definitions of "cult" to support its conceptualization, and suffers thereby, the countercult grounds its opposition to new and alternative religious groups, as well as established world religions, in a theological understanding of the exclusive, unique, and all-sufficient nature of conservative Christianity. These different definitions also fix how each movement explains so-called cultic behavior.

Explanation of Cultic Behavior

Deriving tautologically from its definition of a cult, the anticult also explains cultic behavior in terms of brainwashing and/or thought control models. Men and women join and remain within new and controversial religious movements because their normal cognitive faculties have been interrupted by the thought control processes deployed by the new religious movement. Chanting and indoctrinational lectures, a low-protein diet, excessive service in the face of inadequate periods of rest together constitute a program by which the ability of individuals to make rational choices is impaired (see Bromley and Richardson 1983; Conway and Siegelman 1979; Freed 1980; Hassan 1990, 2000; Melton 1999; Singer and Lalich 1995; Tobias and Lalich 1994; for a contrary view, however, see Bainbridge 1978; Barker 1984). The explanatory calculus in this is simple: since no one in their right mind, operating with full cognitive information and consent, would make the kind of life choices made by those who join new and controversial religious movements, those who do join must, therefore, have had their ability to make such choices impeded or eliminated (Hill 1980).

While the modes of cultic behavior according to the anticult may inform the countercult at certain junctures, the Christian countercult locates the phenomenon within the much larger domain of cosmological conflict. That is, cults, sects, and, in many cases, any religion other than evangelical or fundamentalist Christianity simply constitute one more skirmish line in the ongoing battle between God and Satan. Consider the following three examples.

Widely regarded as an academic wunderkind of the countercult, Douglas Groothuis, now an associate professor at the theologically conservative Denver Seminary, regards Christians who engage cults and new religious movements as entering into the arena of spiritual warfare. Writing of the New Age movement in particular, Groothuis declares that "despite whatever good intentions New Agers may have, it is Satan, the spiritual counterfeiter himself, who ultimately inspires all false religion" (1988: 38). He continues that all true Christians "are in combat conditions, with no demilitarized zones available this side of heaven" (Groothuis 1988: 39).

Dave Hunt, one of the most prolific countercult apologists, is similarly unambiguous about the origin of cultic groups, and regards any religious expression other than evangelical Christianity as satanically derived. In the nearly twenty years that separate his first major countercult effort, *The Cult Explosion* (1980), from its enlarged restatement as *Occult Invasion* (1998), Hunt's position has not varied. "Strange as it may seem," he writes, "most cults are basically the same" (Hunt 1980: 19). At the end of that book, he concludes that "in spite of apparently wide differences among the many cults, beneath the surface they all rest on a common foundation: the four lies Satan used to trick Eve. . . . Satan is the author of every cult and false religion, and his imprint is clearly seen on them all" (Hunt 1980: 239; for similar statements, see Hunt 1983, 1996, 1998; Hunt and McMahon 1988). Indeed, Hunt suggests that one of the reasons Satan exists is to provide these alternative spiritual choices; those whom God has created must make a conscious decision to worship God.

Motivation and Perceived Danger

Because it is grounded in the conceptual framework of brainwashing and thought control, the precipitating motivation for the secular anticult is the alleged abuses of civil liberties and human rights that such processes entail. As Langone writes, the anticult concentrates "on deed rather than creed" (1995: 169). Language opposing "captivity" and "freedom" abounds in the cognitive praxis of the anticult. Hassan (1990), for example, writes of *Combatting Cult Mind Control*, while his second book, *Releasing the Bonds* (2000), was self-published through Freedom of Mind Press. Clay (1987) titled his account of the so-called cult phenomenon in Canada, *No Freedom for the Mind*. Together, Tobias and Lalich (1994) promote "Freedom and Recovery from Cults and Abusive Relationships."

The countercult, on the other hand, is grounded in the perception of heresy and false religious consciousness, as well as the cosmological imperative to challenge the evil that both represent. While the anticult makes its appeal on humanitarian grounds, the countercult locates its struggle both theologically and soteriologically. "The only reason for becoming familiar with other religions and other religious writings," writes Dave Hunt, "would be in order to show those who follow these false systems wherein the error lies and thereby to rescue them" (1996: 68).

Both groups seek to provide a countervailing pressure to what they regard as a clear and present social danger. The countercult, however, serves another, more fundamental function—the ongoing legitimation and maintenance of the worldview of its target audience (see chapter 4). In an open religious economy the presence of alternative worldviews presents a multiplicity of potential disconfirmations of the evangelical or fundamentalist construction of reality. In the face of this latent instability, countercult apologists serve as significant others in the ongoing maintenance of those aspects of the evangelical worldview threatened by the existence of other, competing religious groups. In this, they function both as movement intellectuals and as principal negotiators of the "conceptual machinery of universe-maintenance" (see Berger and Luckmann 1966).

Unlike the anticult, few countercult ministries proactively seek encounters with adherents of new or controversial religious groups. While there are certainly those on the front lines, so to speak, most countercult efforts are apologetic rather than missiologic; most countercult material is produced for and marketed to evangelical Christians. The majority of countercult books, tracts, and tapes, for example, are found only in evangelical Christian bookstores—although more and more are finding their way into the secular marketplace. In this regard, many countercult apologists see themselves as "equipping the saints" for a spiritual battle to which they believe all Christians are called. Although some countercult materials are designed for use in either proactive or reactive evangelism (e.g., Bjornstad 1979; Bowman 1989a, 1989b; Concordia's How to Respond to series of booklets; Gomes 1998, and the Zondervan Guide to Cults and Religious Movements series that he edits; Howard, Fink, and Unseth 1990; Morey 1980; Watters 1987), the majority is produced to demonstrate and reinforce the conservative Christian worldview against all challengers.

The danger to which both the anticult and countercult respond is also a function of their respective explanations of cultic behavior. For the anticult, predicated on brainwashing and thought control, the danger is the abrogation of one's civil liberties by controversial religious groups. Motivated by a particular psychopathology or a desire for power and money, cult leaders strip their followers of these civil liberties in order to further their own ends. For the countercult, however, non-Christian religious expression—whether character- ized as cults or false religions—is a problem of soteriology and represents a major component of the Satanic program to take over the world. If the leaders of these groups do abrogate the civil liberties of their followers, that abrogation is at the behest of the true power behind the throne—Satan (e.g., Cumbey 1983, 1985; Groothuis 1986, 1988; Hunt 1980, 1998; Hunt and McMahon 1988; Larson 1989b, 1996, 1999; Matrisciana 1985; Rhodes 1994). This perception locates the countercult within an explicitly *dualistic* and *duelistic* cosmology that is explored more fully in chapter 3.

Objective

Deliverance is the axis around which many of the other differences between the two movements revolve. While both the anticult and countercult under- stand their ultimate objective in terms of rescue, each conceptualizes very dif- ferently what it means to be rescued. The anticult, for example, seeks the successful *exit from* the group in question and reintegration of the former cult member into family and society. Although the well-publicized kidnappings and forced deprogrammings in the 1970s have given way to the less overtly offen- sive and somewhat more sophisticated "exit counseling" provided by current incarnations of the anticult (cf. Giambalvo 1995; Hassan 1990, 2000; Shupe and Darnell 2000, 2001; Singer and Lalich 1995; Tobias and Lalich 1994),[3] extraction and reintegration into the dominant society remain the anticult's primary goals.

The countercult's objective, on the other hand, is not merely to effect the exit of the individual from the group in question. This accomplishes only half the mission. Salvation—both literal and metaphorical—is not achieved until the individual converts to evangelical Christianity. Where the anticult seeks to effect *exit,* the countercult seeks *migration.* Thus, the journey between "plau- sibility structures" (Berger 1967; Berger and Luckmann 1966) is made from the many false worlds to the one true world. Consider countercult apologists Ron Rhodes and Douglas Groothuis.

In *The Culting of America,* Rhodes states that "through the use of apolo- getics we can provide well-reasoned evidences to the non-believer as to why he ought to choose Christianity rather than any other religion. Apologetics can be used to show the unbeliever that all the other options in the smorgasbord of world religions *are not really options at all,* since they are false" (1994: 230, emphasis in the original). Notice how if one reverses the clausal order of the last sentence, placing "since they are false" in an appropriate periodicity, it becomes clear that apologetics serves to reinforce or confirm a falsity in world religions (and new religious movements) to which Rhodes has already given assent. According to Rhodes, all other worldviews than Christianity will ultimately fail by virtue of the flaws inherent in them (see also Clark and Geisler 1990; Geisler 1976; Sire 1997). Therefore, it is incumbent upon inhabitants of the so-called true worldview (i.e., conservative Christianity) to mediate the migration between worlds.

Similarly, Groothuis writes of what he calls "negative apologetics" (1988: 67). In this he assumes that unless one's worldview is built on a particular Christian foundation, it is ipso facto false, and the demonstration of that falsity is simply a pro forma operation. For example, in *Confronting the New Age* (1988), the book that remains by far his most popular work, he argues that any construction of reality not grounded in an evangelical interpretation of the Bible will ultimately demonstrate itself inadequate. The starting point from which his vision of negative apologetics proceeds, this is also the point at which its particular epistemic difficulties emerge. This seems at least implicitly recognized by Groothuis's senior colleague at Denver Seminary, Gordon Lewis. "Many Christians seem satisfied with a refutation of cultic doctrine and condemnation of the movements," he writes, a sentiment with which Groothuis would presumably not disagree. "But Christians are responsible to evangelize deceived people in the cults" (Lewis 1966: 10).

As I noted briefly above, a prominent subgenre within the broader counter-cult is material aimed specifically at the nihilation of competing religious worldviews when adherents of those worldviews interact with Christians. For many years, Concordia Publishing House has marketed a series of small booklets in what is known as The Response Series; included, for example, are pamphlets on "how to respond to" the Masonic Lodge, the Jehovah's Witnesses, the Mormons, the Occult, and Eastern religions. In the last few years, Zondervan has brought out a comparable series, the Zondervan Guide to Cults and Religious Movements. Both follow a similar format. Each booklet provides the Christian with a brief historical and theological overview of the particular group, and then key doctrines or beliefs are contrasted with those of conservative Christianity. These are followed (1) by "typical" arguments Christians can expect from the group, and (2) by counterarguments (often in Socratic format, with appropriate biblical references) and group-specific advice that may be used to effect evangelism and conversion.

Modi Operandi

By virtue of the kind of explanations to which it appeals, the anticult consists largely of psychologists, lawyers, and deprogrammers/exit counselors, as well as the family and friends of cult members. From small ad hoc support groups in the 1970s to its ongoing professionalization, this still accounts for the majority of the anticult constituency. The anticult specializes in information exchange and referral, deprogramming and exit counseling, and family group support (Giambalvo 1995; Hassan 1990, 2000; Singer and Lalich 1995; Tobias and Lalich 1994). As it is used by Hassan and the American Family Foundation, exit counseling is intended not only for the adherent, but also for the adherent's family and friends, who are most often the impetus for exit counseling. In this, a service provider/client relationship is established. Thus, at the microscopic level, the anticult is reactive; it responds to individual needs with which it is presented. At the macroscopic level, though, in many countries it is proactive, seeking to influence various levels of government about the appropriate response those bodies should take toward groups the anticult considers dangerous. In some countries, notably France, Germany, and Russia, the anticult lobby has met with not insignificant success (see, for example, Hexham and Poewe 1999; Introvigne 1998).

The countercult, on the other hand, and again because of the explanations it posits for cultic behavior, is populated by conservative Christian theologians and apologists—both lay and professional. While there is some occasional proactive witnessing, the countercult specializes in information exchange, support ministries for ex-members, and apologetic tools to equip Christians for their confrontations with cult groups and members. Two purposes are served by this: (1) the *apologetic-evangelistic*, which intends to operationalize the migration of the adherent to the Christianity of the countercult apologist; and (2) the *apologetic-reinforcement*, which serves to maintain, repair, and fortify the Christian worldview in the face of the de facto threat represented by the presence of the adversarial Other, that is, the cultic group or false religion in question.

Although both groups may share the reality of "apostates" as an organizational category, the use to which these apostates are put also varies according to the explanatory agenda of the group and its programmatic objective. For example, apostate testimony from the anticult concentrates on the freedom from mind control once the cultic group has been left (e.g., Appel 1983; Singer and Lalich 1995; Tobias and Lalich 1994). Apostate testimony deployed by the countercult, on the other hand, concentrates ultimately on the salvation the apostate now finds in Christ (e.g., Decker 1990; Decker and Hunt 1984; Geer 1986; Hunt 1980; Schnell 1956; Scott 1990, 1993, 1994; see also almost any fundraising letter from any of the major countercult organizations for ample anecdotal evidence).

In *Strange Gods* (1981), David Bromley and Anson Shupe begin their examination of "the great American cult scare" with five specific refutations of (then) common thinking around new religious movements. Among other things, they conclude that there was "no avalanche of rapidly growing cults," "no mysterious brainwashing process," and "no compelling reason to believe that all modern gurus and spiritual leaders are complete charlatans" (Bromley and Shupe 1981: 2, 3). While these conclusions may lay to rest certain aspects of the anticult movement's case (if not their perceptions), because of the very different grounding of the countercult movement, they do nothing to mitigate the problem of practical life to which these evangelical and fundamentalist Christians are responding. The anticult is concerned with abuses on the ground, as it were; the countercult, on the other hand, locates the cult controversies in the midst of a vast cosmology bounded by God on one side and Satan on the other, and centered in the conflict between the two. Recognizing, of course, that the two movements are not entirely discrete entities, by continuing to subsume one under the rubric of the other important distinctions in social process and influence will almost certainly go unnoticed. There are a number of research questions addressed throughout this book, however, that differentiation can usefully serve.

First, how ought scholars treat the distinctions between anticult (psychological) and countercult (theological) assessments of controversial religious movements methodologically and analytically? While Barker's (1984) empirical research into the Unification Church can demonstrate the fallacy of the brainwashing hypothesis as an explanatory mechanism for cultic involvement, theological explanations—whether framed in terms of cosmological conflict, spiritual deception, or demonic interference—are essentially nonfalsifiable. They require different analytic modes—sociologies of knowledge, of reality-construction and control, of cognitive praxis.

Second, whereas significant legal battles have been fought in the anticult domain over charges of kidnapping and deprogramming, as well as what Shupe and Darnell (2000, 2001) refer to as anticult "street crime," juridical analyses of the countercult could focus on issues of libel, slander, and the promotion of religious hatred and discrimination. Besides simply describing some of the more questionable statements made by countercult writers—for example, Dave Hunt's claim that the U.S. Armed Forces has for many years employed "official satanic chaplains"—and seeking to locate them within a particular cognitive praxis, I would argue that scholars have an obligation to develop ethical and rhetorical analyses as well as sociological and anthropological ones. On the other hand, how does a researcher weigh the right to a free exercise of one's own religion—for example, fundamentalist Christianity—when that exercise demands the denunciation and not infrequently the denigration of all other religions?

Third, how wide is the cognitive spectrum within which the countercult functions? I suggest that subsuming the countercult under the anticult hinders the ability of academics to explore the various operational levels the countercult inhabits. And, it is important to note that, while a similar religious construction of reality obtains across the countercult spectrum, there is, nevertheless, a spectrum. Fair-minded apologists such as John Morehead, Jon Trott, and Carl Mosser vie for shelf space and audience share with countercult extremists such as Constance Cumbey, Dave Hunt, and Texe Marrs; those regarded as academics in the countercult community are often outsold considerably by those with no academic credentials whatsoever. As well, the advent of the Internet has allowed a virtual explosion of amateur, mom-and-pop ministries to compete with professional countercult organizations such as the Christian Research Institute and the Spiritual Counterfeits Project (Cowan 2001, and chapter 8).

Finally, since a major function of the countercult is cognitive boundary support and worldview-maintenance for evangelical and fundamentalist Christians, investigating the countercult as a separate entity allows for more sophisticated analyses of discourse strategy, deployment of religious propaganda, and the construction and repair of religious plausibility structures in the face of potential disconfirmation.

"For the Bible Tells Me So": Constructing the Countercult Cosmology

In the academic study of religion, the concept of a "religious economy" has become an increasingly popular way of describing the current situation of religious pluralism in the West (Finke and Iannaccone 1993; Iannaccone 1990, 1994, 1995; Stark and Finke 2000; Young 1997). Various religious groups and traditions assume the role of competitors in an open or unregulated marketplace, tailoring their different wares to meet the shifting demands of an increasingly hard-to-please pool of consumers. The opening of this religious economy, the expansion of the range of religious choices individuals might make without fear of reprisal, is one dynamic to which the Christian countercult is responding. For a number of reasons, religious pluralism has thrown Christianity into crisis. And, as Berger so trenchantly points out, since "all socially constructed worlds are inherently precarious" (1967: 29), all require mechanisms by which they can be reinforced in the face of challenge. Building on the elegant, though not uncontroversial, theoretical models developed by Stark and Bainbridge (1987) and Stark and Finke (2000), I suggest four modest propositions as an entry into the more general discussion of countercult cosmology—the first component of the movement's cognitive praxis—and the way in which that cosmology is maintained.

The first proposition is axiomatic: as a religious economy opens, the range and variety of religious possibilities that may be entered into without censure or reprisal expands. The repeal of the Witchcraft Act in Great Britain (1951), for example, removed the level of official sanction against Neopaganism and allowed individuals such as Gerald Gardner to bring the popularization of witchcraft "out of the broom closet," as it were (see Hutton 1999; York 1995). In the United States, while there are without question unofficial levels at which social censure occurs, Constitutional freedom of religion guarantees empower people to participate in any faith they choose—or in no faith at all. Indeed, from a Constitutional vantage point the Church of Satan is as legitimate a religion as Christianity; individuals can choose to join the Hare Krishnas as freely as they might the Episcopalians. This circumstance leads to the second proposition.

Recognizing Stark and Finke's observation that "the overall level of religiousness will be higher where pluralism is greater or where regulation is lower" (2000: 219), as a religious economy opens, admitting greater numbers of religious possibilities and expanding the range of religious choices that may be entered into without social sanction, the *relative value* attached to any heretofore dominant religious meaning structure decreases. That is, it is no longer taken for granted that certain religious principles necessarily guide the development of society and culture. Whereas, at the colloquial level, it is not infrequently assumed that the framers of the Constitution were good evangelical Protestants and that the country was founded on explicitly Judeo-Christian principles (see, for example, interviews in Wolfe 1999; also Wuthnow 1995), that this is manifestly not the case now is of considerable concern to many evangelicals. The alleged introduction into the educational, commercial, and governmental life of the country of so-called anti-Christian philosophies such as secular humanism, the removal from public education of religious accoutrements such as school prayer, and the overall decline in "religious" (read: "Christian") values in society are all regarded by evangelicals as incontrovertible evidence that the relative value of Christianity has declined (see, for example, Bates 1993; Duncan n.d., 1981).

Third, as a religious economy opens, and the relative value of any heretofore dominant religious meaning structure decreases, the need for maintenance and reinforcement of that meaning structure increases. This is the basic principle of reality-maintenance about which Berger and Luckmann have written (1966), and that is discussed more fully in chapter 4. Essentially, when faced with a challenge to the plausibility, inevitability, and ultimate reliability of a particular meaning structure, adherents will seek ways to reinforce their ability to believe. In the case of evangelical Christianity, for example, while bumper stickers may proclaim pre-theoretically, and popular practice may bear out the maxim, "God said it. I believe it. That settles it," the reality is that considerably more sophisticated mechanisms of maintaining belief in the Bible as the only Word of God are regularly deployed. At a very basic level, all of these mechanisms have a common purpose: to demonstrate the objective (i.e., unconstructed) nature of divine revelation and thereby support the unique reasonableness of conservative Christian belief. This, then, yields the fourth of these modest propositions.

ANCHORING THE COUNTERCULT: THE BIBLE AS UNIVERSAL CANON

As a religious economy opens, and the need for maintenance and reinforcement of particular religious meaning structures increases, to the extent possible religious actors will seek to locate the validity of those structures within an external (i.e., objective) authority. This proposition anchors the most common attribute of Christian countercult apologetics: that the Bible is the unique and external authority by which all other religious traditions, beliefs, and behavior must be measured and ultimately judged, an authority that is inerrant, infallible, and insuperable. While most, if not all, major doctrines and practices of the Christian faith, whether through explicit location (e.g., the establishment of the Eucharist) or implicit derivation (e.g., the doctrine of the Trinity), find their primary source in the Bible, not all streams of Christianity accord the Bible the same authority, nor locate their lived faith within the same hermeneutic framework. Indeed, Christian thought from the early church fathers and mothers to modern exponents of movements as disparate as Southern Baptist fundamentalism (cf., for example, Ammerman 1990; Lindsell 1976; Toumey 1994), postdenominational Creation Spirituality (see, for example, Fox 1983, 1991, 1996), and Latin American theologies of liberation (see, for example, Boff 1978; Gutierrez 1973; Sobrino 1993; Tamez 1982) have relied on the Bible as the wellspring from which theology, liturgy, and doctrine flow. The same body of texts has generated widely divergent, often mutually incompatible, even mutually hostile interpretations.

Within the domain of the Christian countercult, it is the Bible understood as the Word of God "inerrant," "the standard by which all human teachings . . . are to be tested" (Bowman 1991b: 19) that anchors the movement's cognitive praxis. It delineates the boundaries of reality and provides the cipher by which the mysteries of creation and redemption are understood, the cosmic struggle between good and evil interpreted, and humanity's role within those determined. In this domain, the Bible both defines and imposes a cosmology that brooks no competition. Interpreted thus, it totalizes the problem of practical life presented by new and emergent religions and renders the countercult worldview monolithic. The "essential Christian belief [is] that *the Bible is the inspired, infallible, inerrant, and literal Word of God,"* writes countercult apologist and conspiracy theorist, Texe Marrs,[1] "given to man through God and undefiled by nature of its divine authorship" (1990: 56, emphasis in the original). This, then, is the "general axiom" (Mannheim 1952: 148) from which all others in the countercult cosmology derive. That this axiom has the potential to influence social action is clear from Marrs's working definition of a "cult": "A cult is a body or organized group of activists or believers who have involved themselves in a spiritual or social movement in opposition to the clear and direct Word of God" (1990: 55; similarly, see Ankerberg and Weldon 1991a, 1999; Howard, Fink, and Unseth 1990; Hunt 1996; Martin 1985).

Across the various continua of the countercult, though, adherents of the totalizing objectivity claimed for the principle of scriptural inerrancy refuse to accept the possibility of that principle's essentially subjective and, therefore, constructed nature. An epistemic circularity, the operative hermeneutic is, as Ken Wilber has noted, not unlike a conversation that proceeds " 'What is the most sacred and authoritative book ever written in the world?' 'The Bible.'

'How do you know?' 'It says so in the Bible.' " To which Wilber adds somewhat sarcastically, "This may sound odd, but that is not my fault" (1993: 21).[2] While countercult apologists often go to great lengths to demonstrate that their claim for biblical authority and exclusivity is, in fact, not circular (cf., for example, Bowman 1991b; Geisler 1976; Groothuis 1990; Hanegraaff n.d.; Hawkins 1996; Hunt 1996; McDowell 1979, 1981; Morey 1980), few address the socially constructed and reinforced nature of their position. Rather, most concentrate on convergent external factors that do not really address the issue of inerrancy (e.g., that there are a tremendous number of New Testament manuscripts that vary only slightly from version to version) or inductive arguments that depend for their vigor on the a priori acceptance of biblical inerrancy (e.g., an internal consistency in the Bible or prophecies from the Old Testament that have allegedly been fulfilled in Jesus, thus proving the reliability of the Bible). In fact, writes Dave Hunt of the latter, the "simple yet profound evidence" the Bible provides of its authenticity and reliability "is prophecy fulfilled, an irrefutable verification reserved to the Judeo-Christian Scriptures alone. No honest person can remain an unbeliever after even a brief study of prophecy" (1993a: 24).

Insofar as it adverts to biblical inerrancy, infallibility, and insuperability, countercult apologetics, almost by definition passes into solipsism precisely because there is neither verification nor falsification that could either confirm or disconfirm the countercult claim. There is no validating facticity; any possible validation remains subjective, a function of the apologist's personal adherence to this general axiom of biblical inerrancy. While it may be contextualized and reinforced through social interaction, and while it may be given communal, even sacramental form, authentication and adherence remain essentially internal processes. Following Karl Mannheim, though, once totalized in this manner, countercult apologists often "take flight into a supratemporal logic and assert that truth as such is unsullied and has neither a plurality of forms nor any connection with unconscious motivations" (Mannheim 1936: 42). That is, the Bible as the Word of God exists apart from social construction and evolution, and beyond cultural interpretation and contextualization (although, cf. Ehrman 1993).

Motivations and interpretations, however, both conscious and unconscious, abound. Implicit in the claim to the Bible's inerrancy are a number of derivative claims: (1) that the interpretation of the Bible offered by the countercult is the correct interpretation; (2) that interpretations offered by religious groups under consideration, in so far as these occur, are incorrect; and often, (3) that proof of the latter necessarily demonstrates the truth of the former. Walter Martin, for example, writes that while "cults continually emphasize the Bible," "without exception they place themselves in the roles of infallible interpreters of the Word of God, their dogmatism rivaled only by Jesuit scholars" (1985: 404).[3] Martin, on the other hand, contends that Christians "must be prepared to defend the claims of Scripture interpreted by the Holy Spirit" (1985: 407). Like many countercult apologists, Martin was either unaware of or ignored the fact that the hermeneutic infallibility he criticized in others was precisely the infallibility countercult apologists claim in practice, if not in principle.

In *Deceived by the Light*, for example, a critical evaluation of New Age bestseller *Embraced by the Light* (Eadie 1992), in which author Betty Eadie claims to have been granted metaphysical revelation by virtue of a series of near-death experiences, Douglas Groothuis declares that "because the Bible does not describe any NDEs, we can conclude that it does not view them as crucial for our understanding of life, death, and the beyond" (1995: 133). In this case, for Groothuis the problem of practical life—the veracity of NDEs examined against the backdrop of his adherence to biblical inerrancy—is simply obviated. Since the Bible does not speak of them, they are of no importance. That there are, however, many things that are not discussed in the Bible, but that exist nonetheless, is not a question Groothuis addresses. Rather, he simply critiques Eadie's story, using as his touchstone the most common question in countercult apologetics: "Are her views genuinely biblical?" (1995: 20). Put differently, does it measure up to the countercult apologist's particular interpretation of the biblical message? Even though Groothuis acknowledges that the reader must "keep in mind that Eadie is not offering her opinions or commentary on the Bible or on any other religious book" (1995: 22), he still insists that "we test Eadie's testimony against Scripture," and that we "hold her accountable to her own words" (1995: 22). His method here illustrates the supratemporal and supracontextual authority granted the Bible by the countercult. To be fair, Groothuis (and other countercult apologists who challenge new and emergent religions on the grounds of biblical compatibility) may very well be able to raze a story like Eadie's; he may very well be able to demonstrate her either a crackpot or a fraud. But, it must be born in mind that a demonstration that Eadie's subjective construction of reality is wrong (according to whatever criteria are applied) is not thereby a demonstration that the countercult construction is correct.[4]

This understanding, however, informs one of the most common countercult deployments of scriptural inerrancy: its use as an all-sufficient witnessing tool. For example, in *Counterfeits at Your Door*, written for those interacting with Mormons and Jehovah's Witnesses, James Bjornstad (1979) offers prepared missiologues supported by an abundance of scriptural references. In *Goddess Worship, Witchcraft and Neo-Paganism*, his contribution to the Zondervan Guide to Cults and New Religions, Craig Hawkins recommends the "Biblical Teaching Approach" as the first "approach for witnessing to neo-pagans" (1998: 76). Like Bjornstad, Hawkins advises those who encounter Neopagans to "pepper" their conversation with Scripture. And, despite the fact that Neopagans might be resistant to the Bible, "or only interpret it according to preconceived views," "it will accomplish what God desires. The Holy Spirit will work through the Bible to accomplish his will" (Hawkins 1998: 76). Like a talisman, the Bible operates magically to reinforce the witnessing (and the worldview) of the evangelist.

In another volume in the same series, entitled *Truth and Error: Comparative Charts of Cults and Christianity,* series editor Alan Gomes (1998) contrasts a number of new, emergent, and world religions with Christianity. Following a very brief introduction to the group under consideration, each chapter contains a "Parallel Comparison Chart" that contrasts various teachings of the group with passages from the Bible. The abbreviated nature of the format, however, presents what are often widely divergent religions and religious textual traditions as though they were essentially homogenous. "Buddhism, Taoism, and Other Far Eastern Religions" (including Bon, the pre-Buddhist indigenous religion of Tibet) are gathered together in one chapter, as are "Hinduism, TM, and Hare Krishna." Gomes, however, does not consider the differences between schools, streams of tradition, or historical and sociological development; rather, he compares textual excerpts from a variety of sources with selected biblical texts. Thus, the first of Buddhism's Four Noble Truths (which Gomes takes from the Pali Canon's *Samyutta-Nikaya*) is contrasted with John 16:20, 22, in which Jesus assures his disciples that "no one will take away your joy." From the Mahāyāna *Sikshasamuccaya* Gomes draws the description of a Bodhisattva, a being who vows to take on the suffering of all beings; this he compares with Isaiah 53:4–6 in which the "suffering servant" "took up our iniquities and carried our sorrows." Where the prophet Isaiah speaks of the "suffering servant of Israel," however, Gomes's own hermeneutic hand appears when he inserts the gloss "[Jesus Christ]" into the Isaianic text, replacing the original wording and retrojecting his own evangelical interpretation (1998: 85).

His socially constructed handling of Scripture aside, Gomes's presentation of these religious traditions produces what literary scholar Roland Barthes called the process of "mythicization." That is, "myth has an imperative, buttonholing character" (Barthes 1982: 110); myth becomes not so much a symbolic description of a particular phenomenon, but a value signified by that which is described. In this case, regardless of the particular tradition or text under consideration, the value signified is "not-Biblical." Mythologized in this way, the reader is not allowed to see the various traditions as an adherent might see them, only those decontextualized representations Gomes extracts to serve his apologetic. As Barthes writes, "Myth acts economically: it abolishes the complexity of human acts, it gives them the simplicity of essences" (1982: 132). As becomes clear throughout the discussion in this book, because the cognitive praxis of the Christian countercult often generates a world arranged with little regard for complexity or nuance, a world reduced to the uncomplicated comparison of carefully selected texts, the "simplicity of essences" is itself essential to its organizing cosmology.

According to that cosmology, the cults are everywhere. Modern Western society is in the midst a "cult explosion" (Hunt 1980), and an "occult invasion" (Hunt 1998); we are witnessing "the culting of America" (Rhodes 1994), and are urged to cult-proof our children (Martin 1993). According to Robert Morey, pastors must constantly face the problem of "the many cultists who are continuously knocking at the front doors of their parishioners," parishioners who are also "besieged by cultists at the airport and the local shopping malls" (1980: 10). As a result, Christians must be prepared to answer the challenge presented by adherents of these so-called false religions. Indeed, Morey claims that most parishioners are "tired of simply shutting the door on [Jehovah's] Witnesses" and instead want "special training" to deal with the problem. Accordingly, in *How to Answer a Jehovah's Witness* (subtitled *How to Successfully Take the Initiative When They Come to Your Door*), Morey points out the basic principles of worldview nihilation in countercult apologetics: "The first step is to undermine the reliability of the New World Translation in the mind of the Witness" (1980: 19), he writes, and then demonstrate to the Witness that the Watchtower Society itself is a "false prophet" (1980: 15). Once this has been accomplished, Morey suggests that the Witness be guided through an inductive "workbook" prepared by Morey on the deity of Christ. Consisting of leading questions supported by the appropriate biblical references in which the answers may be found, Morey's inductive approach is, in fact, very similar to that found in Watchtower literature itself.

Here as well, Morey illustrates an almost mathematical reliance on the Bible. For example, to demonstrate that the Yahweh of the Old Testament is, ontologically, the Jesus of the New Testament, Morey directs the participants in his study to parallel passages that purport to demonstrate that equivalence. Isaiah 9:6, a familiar Christian reinterpretation of the prophet's message of a coming messiah, is paired with Luke 1:31–33, the announcement to Mary of the Virgin Birth and a well-known textual lens through which Christians interpret the Isaianic passage. Though the Mighty God of Isaiah does not actually appear in Luke's narrative, but must be inferred, in a passage worth quoting at length Morey attempts to prove syllogistically the direct equivalence of one to the other. He writes:

There is also an irrefutable scriptural logic behind the proposition that Jesus is YHWH. In logic, the following syllogism is *always valid:*

$$A > B \quad a = b$$
$$\underline{B > C \text{ or } b = c}$$
$$A > C \quad a = c$$

In the same way, the teaching of Scripture can be arranged in conformity to the above syllogism.

Jesus is 'Mighty God' (Isa. 9:6)
$$\underline{\text{'Mighty God' is YHWH (Isa. 10:20–21)}}$$
Jesus is YHWH

The logical sequence cannot be shown to be invalid. The conclusion is automatic and irrefutable. (Morey 1980: 96–97; for a similar equation, see Rhodes 1997: 115–17)

COUNTERCULT DOGMATICS: THE DERIVATIVE KERYGMA

By itself, of course, biblical inerrancy means little. It is, in fact, useless without some religious content to which it might inerrantly point or some religious doctrine in the service of which it might be inerrantly deployed. What Morey's countercult calculus indicates is precisely the use to which that inerrancy is put in the establishment, maintenance, and reinforcement of a particular cosmology. Like biblical interpretation, Christian doctrine varies widely across the church. The Roman Catholic Church recognizes seven sacraments, Protestant denominations only two—baptism and the Eucharist. Even within the Eucharist, differences in understanding abound. In terms of the real presence of Christ, for example, Roman Catholics still hold to the doctrine of transubstantiation, Lutherans and Episcopalians that of consubstantiation. Among more liberal Protestants, the Lord's Supper is entirely symbolic, with no real presence in either of the other two senses. While the story of the Virgin Birth is integral to the annual reiteration of the Nativity throughout the Christian church, interpretation of that story varies from literal belief in a historic event, to symbolic reverence for a myth that still speaks to the hearts of believers, to utter disregard for the birth narratives as obsolete barriers to more sophisticated belief. Similar ranges of opinion obtain with respect to many aspects of Christian thought and belief: the nature and attributes of God, the character and purpose of revelation, the person and work of Christ, and the definition of and necessity for atonement. For some Christians, only the most tenuous belief in any of these is sufficient to be included in the Christian church; for others, such as the countercult apologists, the cognitive boundaries of acceptable belief are much more firmly established, much less accepting of alternative interpretations, and much more tenaciously maintained in the face of such alternatives.

Explicit in the inerrancy, infallibility, and insuperability of Scripture is its ontological uniqueness among the holy texts of humankind (see, for example, Ankerberg and Weldon 1999; Bowman 1991b; Groothuis 1990; Hunt 1996; Marrs 1990; Morey 1980, 1992). Each of the cognitive boundary markers by which the countercult worldview may be defined both derives from and reflexively supports that uniqueness. Following very closely upon what became known as the five points of fundamentalism, these markers are considered kerygmatic by the countercult, indispensable in determining the true nature of Christian belief. In addition to scriptural inerrancy, they include (1) the virgin birth of Jesus, his crucifixion and bodily resurrection; (2) his ontological divinity as the Second Person of the Holy Trinity; (3) a substitutionary theory of atonement; and (4) Jesus's literal and visible second coming. In the fundamentalist worldview (and that of the countercult), the first three are logically processual: the Virgin Birth ensures the ontological divinity of Jesus, which divinity provides the soteriological platform for the atonement. Although here I consider these primarily as they are articulated in the work of Dave Hunt, none in the evangelical or fundamentalist Christian countercult community would dispute their centrality. Indeed, as Ankerberg and Weldon note (1999: 678), these are the "crucial doctrines" that secure the singular nature of the incarnation on which the exclusivity of the countercult cosmology, missiology, and teleology depend.

"In Christianity alone," writes Hunt, in a passage drawing together this processual dogmatic, "the penalty for breaking God's laws is paid by God, who became a man through the virgin birth." Hunt continues: "He never ceased to be God and will never cease to be man. Jesus Christ is the one and only God-man, who as perfect and sinless could represent the human race, taking the penalty it deserved, and could fully pay that penalty. Only on that basis can pardon be offered to all who repent and receive Christ as savior" (1998: 230). Within this kerygmatic configuration, the Virgin Birth is essential for three reasons. First, it allegedly fulfills the Isaianic prophecy that "a virgin shall conceive" and bring forth the Messiah, thereby sustaining the inerrancy of Scripture. Second, it obviates the need for purification on the part of that Messiah, since sexual intercourse was not a factor in the conception and it is this biological/generational transmission that is regarded as problematic. Since God cannot dwell with sin, absent a human father the case can be made that Jesus was without sin. Third, thus sinless, the Messiah can fulfill his role as the ontologically divine savior in the universal drama of salvation (Ankerberg and Weldon 1999; Bowman 1992; Groothuis 1990; Hawkins 1996; Martin 1985; Rhodes 1997). The countercult cosmology is located squarely within these boundaries.

While few if any religious doctrines are demonstrable according to a strictly scientific method, countercult apologists argue strongly for the facticity of their beliefs, as well as the cosmological functions of the Virgin Birth and the ontological divinity of Christ. Although these are statements of faith, countercult apologists such as Hunt deploy them as though they are statements of indisputable fact. "There can be no doubt," he writes, "that Jesus Christ, who is God, came to this earth as a man through a virgin birth, lived a perfect, sinless life, died for our sins, and rose from the dead the third day. Historically, these events are firmly established" and "a matter of history" (Hunt 1993a: 111). Since Hunt freely mingles statements that might be construed as historically valid (i.e., that someone named Jesus was born, lived, and died) with those that are clearly faith based and require the acceptance of a particular construction of reality in order for them to have validity (i.e., the special circumstances surrounding Jesus's birth, life, and death), these assertions are not nearly so firmly established as Hunt believes. Beyond possible questions about the facticity of Jesus's existence (fairly well established, but still questioned from time to time; see Wells 1999), significant discussion can and does ensue even within the wider Christian communion about each aspect of the countercult's kerygmatic proclamation. Is Jesus of Nazareth really God? Can one legitimately equate the two in the unequivocal, ontological manner claimed? Is the Virgin

Birth really virgin, and is it, in fact, a fulfillment of prophecy? All these questions are resolved (if not answered) in the context of belief in an inerrant, infallible, insuperable Scripture.

These questions notwithstanding, the fact of the Virgin Birth is crucial to the countercult's subjective construction of reality. Because of the processual soteriology, challenging the validity of the Virgin Birth calls into question the validity of the entire construction. Just as Jesus's ontological divinity depends on it, the necessity for the Christ to be ontologically divine is related integrally to the doctrine of substitutionary atonement and derivatively to the *métier* of the Christian countercult. "Salvation is the one most important core belief in Christianity," writes Hunt (1994: 347; cf. Ankerberg and Weldon 1999; Decker and Hunt 1984; Groothuis 1986, 1988, 1990; Hawkins 1998; Howard, Fink, and Unseth 1990; Larson 1989a; Marrs 1990; Rhodes 1997; Winkler 1994). "The Bible says that there are two classes of people," he continues, in *A Woman Rides the Beast*, his contribution to modern anti-Catholic apologetics (see chapter 11), "those who are saved and those who are unsaved or lost" (1994: 347). While it is unclear precisely where the Bible says this, and Hunt offers no specific references, for the countercult the issue is not whether these two primary groups exist, but to which group each person belongs. In their cosmology, this division constitutes the principal fault line dividing humankind from God, and from each other. And, migration across the chasm separating the saved from the unsaved is the component of countercult apologetics toward which all others tend. "The primary goal of evangelicals," writes Hunt, "is to preach the gospel to the lost so they might be saved" (1994: 350).

COUNTERCULT CONSPIRACISM: COSMIC DUALISM AND THE COSMIC DUEL

Whether they are trapped in other world religions or have been lured away from the true path into some new and dangerous spiritual byway (cf. Enroth 1979), salvation of the lost is integrally linked to the cosmic battle between the forces of good and evil. This struggle constitutes the third attribute of the countercult cosmology. *Dualistic*, in that it posits opposing forces for good and evil in the universe—that is, God and Satan—countercult cosmology is also *duelistic*, in that this opposition is seen as an ongoing battle not only for the souls of humankind, but one in which humankind has the power to choose sides. "If this disease continues unchecked," writes Ron Rhodes, referring to the apathy of Christians in the face of "the cancer of cultism [that] has been free to spread at an incredible, unprecedented rate in America" (1994: 218), "you can count on the continued deterioration of America as well as the continued *culting* of America. If Christians do not act, *the cults will*. The war is on—and you as a Christian will be either a soldier in the midst of the conflict or a casualty on the sidelines. Which will it be?" (1994: 219, emphasis in the original). Nearly twenty years earlier, in *Youth, Brainwashing, and the Ex-*

tremist Cults, Enroth echoed this same sentiment. "From the Christian perspective, the so-called new-age cults represent the most recent manifestation of an age-old struggle—the battle between God and God's adversary, Satan. The phenomena described in this book are neither random nor accidental: they are profoundly patterned. As simplistic as it may sound to some, they indicate a demonic conspiracy to subvert the true gospel of Jesus Christ through human agents whose eyes have been blinded by the evil one" (Enroth 1977: 202).

The proliferation of new religions, and the increasing popularity of non-Christian world religions in what is often considered a Judeo-Christian culture, is regarded by many countercult apologists as compelling evidence that the cosmic battle is heating up. While perhaps more implicit in apologists such as Enroth than in others, this dualistic/duelistic cosmology is often expressed in conspiracist terms about the nature of the duality and the conduct of the duel. As opposed to "conspiracy theory," "conspiracism" is a more useful concept for explaining this aspect of countercult ideology. As Daniel Pipes notes, "Conspiracism resembles other 'isms' in defining an outlook that can become an all-encompassing concern" (1997: 22). Conspiracism recognizes that there are certain things happening in the world and, as Pipes puts it, "has many facts right but goes wrong by locating causal relationships where none exist" (1997: 30; cf. Coughlin 1999). It is the case, for example, that recent years have seen a significant increase in the number of new religious movements, the prominence with which these movements sometimes act in society, and a growing interest in spiritual paths that are decidedly different than those espoused by the countercult apologists. Superficially, it is the case that, doctrinally and practically, many—though by no means all—of these new religious movements appear quite similar. Countercult conspiracism obtains when these facts are located in an interpretive framework bounded by dualism and duelism, and conclusions are then drawn that make sense *only* within that framework.

If the inerrancy of Scripture and the kerygmatic beliefs that derive from it provide the *what* of the countercult worldview, in the maintenance and reinforcement of that worldview this conspiracism offers the *why*, the causal relationships that explain the reason things are they way they are. "The fact," writes Hunt, for example, "that the same revelation is consistently preached by supposed 'Space Brothers' from UFOs and spirit guides at seances and is experienced on LSD trip and during Eastern meditation (TM, yoga, Zen, etc.) indicates a common source of deception" (1980: 63).

Three components define the framework of this conspiracism. First, the overall understanding that a sinister conspiracy does exist governs the interpretation of all that occurs within its purview. Apparent or perceived congruencies between the beliefs and/or practices of problem religious groups point obviously to a common source of demonic inspiration for these groups. Like Hunt, Bob Larson writes: "The cults, no matter how diverse their origins, display a remarkable conformity of ideology. Considering that the source of cultic knowledge is the *gnosis* of Eden's serpent, the Bible-believing Christian is not surprised to observe such harmony" (1989a: 39).

The second component considers those who challenge the reality of the perceived conspiracy. If someone faults the exegesis, logic, interpretation, or conclusions of these apologists, then that person either (1) is an active participant in the conspiracy or (2) has been deceived by those who are active participants. While the countercult encompasses different modes of antipathetic discourse, this rhetoric of conspiratorial deception is common, both supported by and supplementing the principle understanding of Satan as the "father of lies" and the "great deceiver."

Countercult journalist Richard Abanes, for example, in *Cults, New Religious Movements, and Your Family*, writes of "ten non-Christian groups out to convert your loved ones"—among others, the Church of Scientology, the Church of Satan, and the Church of Jesus Christ of Latter-day Saints (1998b). Jay Howard, a "cult expert" and founder of the Association for Theological Studies (the Web site for which is called "Focus on the Faulty"), warns readers that groups fitting his "definition of a cult are not comprised of a few poor, misdirected souls. They are everywhere," he writes, and include the "Eastern cults," such as Hinduism and Buddhism, as well as Jehovah's Witnesses and Unitarian Universalists (Howard, Fink, and Unseth 1990: 23). For Howard, "False Teaching in Truth's Clothing" (1990: 7) constitutes the "classic cult scenario." Lutheran pastor Eldon Winkler concurs, titling his book *The New Age Is Lying to You* (1994). Ron Rhodes warns his readers both of the "deluge of cultic and occultic groups vying for the American mainstream" and of the "cultic and occultic penetration of America's businesses, health facilities, and public schools" (1994: 218). Finally, "there is an unparalleled mystical conspiracy threatening today's world," declares the front cover of Caryl Matrisciana's *Gods of the New Age* (1985), a conspiracy Matrisciana believes will usher in the Great Tribulation—a period of suffering unparalleled in human history.

Similarly, describing the biblical Eve as "Satan's Mistress," Texe Marrs's wife, Wanda, writes particularly of *New Age Lies to Women* (1989). Certain that "there is no longer any doubt that Satan has inspired his earth-bound, flesh and blood servants to go all out to entrap and snare women," Wanda Marrs even names those she believes are among the so-called New Age elite (W. Marrs 1989: 39).[5] "Satan has for many years wormed his way into the farthest reaches of our world," she concludes, "planting seeds in the form of demonic-led New Age teachers and leaders—seeds that are even now bearing cruel and evil fruit. Women, beware!" (W. Marrs 1989: 50).

Third, for the many countercult apologists who subscribe also to one of the various theories of fundamentalist dispensationalism, the so-called cult explosion is more evidence that the end-times are rapidly approaching. In this matter, Constance Cumbey, a Detroit-area lawyer and countercult apologist, is not one for equivocation. "There is absolutely no way," she writes in *A Planned Deception* (1985), "one can competently research the New Age Movement and not discover that its major purpose is bringing in a New World Order headed by the Antichrist" (1985: 2). In terms of Cumbey's conspiracism, the need for worldview-maintenance is grounded in the fact that there are scholars, both lay and professional, who study the same religious phenomena as the countercult, but who arrive at very different conclusions.[6] For Cumbey, however, those who have studied the New Age movement and have *not* come to her conclusions have either not carried out their research "competently," or are themselves in collusion with the architects of the New Age. In this regard, one might expect to find me included in this list as well. In terms of reality-maintenance, though, the reason for her implied conclusion is clear. Research on similar movements that produces dissimilar results challenges the validity of Cumbey's own work and thereby threatens the integrity of the subjective reality that work helps maintain. Put differently, it calls into question the essential correctness of her worldview.

. If Occam's Razor (also known as the principle of parsimony) suggests that all other things being equal the simplest solution to a particular problem is probably the correct one, then, in terms of the subjective construction of reality maintained by many countercult apologists, conspiracism as it relates to the ongoing battle between good and evil is the Razor's cognitive opposite. Since, in countercult cosmology, "all paths except Christ lead to destruction" (Hunt 1980: 78), an elaborate web of schemes within schemes must exist to attempt the destruction of Christianity and create the conditions for the rise of the Antichrist. Self-fulfilling prophecies, fashioned from the careful management of concept definition and the specific bounding of debate, are necessary to strengthen the sense of conspiracism and the validity of perceived persecution—both important components in the dualism/duelism of countercult cosmology. Writing of "A Calculated Destruction of Morals," for example, Hunt declares that "tragically the public education system in the United States is devoted to destroying Christian beliefs and replacing them with evolution, witchcraft, Hinduism, Buddhism, or Native American religion. In most schools in the Western world, *teaching* provides an excuse for *indoctrination*" (1998: 321, emphasis in the original). While the U.S. educational system might be somewhat less than perfect, Hunt offers no evidence that it is "devoted to destroying Christian beliefs." Rather, this is an inference based on his subjective construction of reality, but one with which not a few of his peers agree. Since the public educational system is not explicitly and exclusively pro-Christian, it must, therefore, be explicitly anti-Christian; since it is not dedicated to promoting Christianity, it must be dedicated to its destruction.

Definition and Counterdefinition: The Countercult as Reality-Maintenance

In *The Social Construction of Reality,* Berger and Luckmann note that "subjective reality is . . . always dependent upon specific plausibility structures" (1966: 174). That is, for any group, specialized social and cognitive mechanisms are required to establish and reinforce the essential correctness of the subjective reality the group inhabits. Of these plausibility structures, they identify *conversation* as the most prevalent and most important. "All who employ the same language are reality-maintaining others," they continue (1966: 173), and all contribute to the emerging cognitive praxis of the group or movement. In using similar language to describe the problem and its potential resolutions, participants both confirm the validity of their own reality and disconfirm that of competing realities. When the problem of practical life is the encroachment of alternative religious belief or practice, countercult apologists (1) *confirm* the Christian subjective reality as it is believed by adherents, (2) *negate* competing realities by which it is challenged, and (3) *propagate* the need for ongoing confirmation and negation by raising into popular consciousness issues and problems of which Christians may not have been aware.

This is part of the ongoing process of knowledge production to which movement intellectuals particularly contribute and illustrates another key feature in the evolving cognitive praxis of the Christian countercult: the continual identification of deviants as the Other against which the movement is organized. Without the constant incursion of the cults, without the progressive detection of potential disconfirmations to the evangelical worldview, there is less obvious need for countercult apologetics. As Eyerman and Jamison note, drawing on elements of primary group theory, "In mobilizing a sense of collective will, as well as in articulating felt needs, the classical movement intellectual thematizes in speeches, tracts, articles, and books the rudiments of a new collective identity. Central to this process of self-formation is the constitution of an Other against which the budding movement will interact" (1991: 101).

MOVEMENT INTELLECTUALS AND REALITY-MAINTENANCE

In a 1998 newsletter, for example, Texe Marrs warns "Continued Vigilance Necessary" as the U.S. government debates a bill that would establish "the dictatorial *Office of Religious Persecution Monitoring (ORPM)*" (1998b: 1, emphasis in the original). According to Marrs, "ORPM's mandate ostensibly is to identify and punish groups and nations that discriminate against their citizens based on religious convictions" (1998b: 1). While Marrs presents a not unreasonable précis of the proposed organization, he maintains that "the real intent of ORPM's framers was never to protect Christians. ORPM is to be a globally-connected law enforcement agency, headed by a Religious Czar, that will brand and punish as criminals those Christians who preach that Jesus Christ and the Holy Bible are exclusively the Truth. ORPM is designed to be an *oppressor* of true Christianity" (1998b: 1–2). With this notice, whether the ORPM comes into being or not, Marrs's readership is now aware of it as a potential problem.

Similarly, in *Confronting the New Age*, Douglas Groothuis points out that the "presence of the New Age Movement in so many areas of life should deeply challenge Christians to develop a thoroughly Christian mind able to discern the differences between counterfeit and reality" (1988: 173). Since his audience may not be aware of what specific phenomena constitute counterfeits opposed to Christianity, Groothuis identifies such issues as "Self-Esteem and the Christian"; "Visualization and Imagination"; "Imagination and Fantasy"; "Biofeedback Therapy"; and "Music for a New Age." Once again, until these were labeled by Groothuis, they may not have been seen by his readers as problems of practical life.

Once raised, though, these problems require some form of resolution. While it is unlikely that every member of a particular constituency needs the same level of resolution, reality-maintenance of some kind is necessary to obviate, integrate, or nihilate the problem. Ideally, the Christian countercult (and similar groups since the dawn of competing religious consciousness) wants the elimination of disconfirming influences. In some social situations—for example, Spain under the Roman Catholic Church in the fifteenth century, Iran under the rule of the Imams since 1979, Afghanistan under the Taliban from the early 1990s until the U.S. retaliatory strikes following the September 11 attacks on the World Trade Center and the Pentagon—the elimination of disconfirming influences can be accomplished through measures such as the Holy Office of the Inquisition, the Revolutionary Courts, or simply using field artillery to destroy the religious infrastructure of competing faiths.

Such measures, of course, are unavailable to the Christian countercult in the West. Given the theoretically grounded and often elaborately articulated nature of its belief structure, however, the apologetic method employed by the countercult seeks a similar elimination through constant engagement of the twin vectors of reality-confirmation and reality-disconfirmation. Put differently, on-going confirmation of the validity of the countercult's worldview (and, by extension, the worldviews of those for whom movement intellectuals act as authoritative voices) is effected *through* the ongoing, proactive disconfirmation of competing worldviews. At its most basic level, the conflict exemplified by the countercult's ongoing crusade against so-called cults and false religions is the battle between *a* world and *the* world. The very presence of alternative worldviews, which, at the empirical level, represent the potential for alternative world choices, forces those who inhabit what they believe to be *the* world (i.e., the *only legitimate* world) to confront the fact that theirs is simply one world choice among many.

In *The Sacred Canopy*, Berger states that, absent more stringent methods of reality-maintenance and enforcement, the most effective mode of religious legitimation is one in which the constructed nature of the worldview has been concealed from those who participate in it. It appears self-evident, axiomatic. As such, while it may in fact be cognitively apprehended and subjectively constructed, the specific symbolic universe countercult apologists are defending is for them ontological in nature. They are not apologists for a world that is *perceived* and *constructed* from the dialectic of human cognition and social imperative, but one *created* and *revealed* as a result of divine *fiat*, and to which they have been privileged through divine revelation. "Since God is the Lord and Owner of the entire created universe," writes Groothuis, "Christianity covers the whole of life" (1986: 169). Similarly, Rhodes declares that "certainly the suggestion that humanity is derived from a nonhuman ancestor cannot be reconciled with the explicit statement of man's creation in Genesis 2:7. Man did not evolve but rather was created from the dust of the ground" (1997: 155).

Both these quotes exemplify Berger's point that "religion legitimates social institutions by bestowing upon them an ultimately ontological status, that is, by *locating* them within a sacred and cosmic frame of reference" (1967: 33). The human articulation of particular religious experiences, recorded in both oral and written form, socially constructed and transmitted across generations, and interpreted according to the particular hermeneutic processes operant and available in each of those generations is elevated above the level of construction and subjectivity to that of revelation and ontology. One possible consequence of challenges to this ontology, then, and one that is deployed frequently in conservative Christian arguments for the veracity of the Bible, is the invitation to nihility. This invitation suggests that if one cannot trust everything about a particular construction of reality, then one can trust nothing. As apologists John Ankerberg and John Weldon declare in one of the "Doctrinal Appendices" to their *Encyclopedia of Cults and New Religions*, "Biblical claims leave us few options. Either the Bible is what it claims—the literal inerrant Word of God—or it is not possible to know if God has revealed Himself to us truthfully" (1999: 666). Threatening the established nomos of the subjective reality encourages its dissolution into anomy. As well, "when the socially defined reality has come to be identified with the ultimate reality of the universe, then its denial takes on the quality of evil as well as madness" (Berger 1967: 39). Thus, Groothuis, Rhodes, indeed many of those who have garrisoned Christian territory against a varied host of invaders are not simply defenders of a particular view of the world; they perceive themselves in almost Manichaean terms, as warriors in a dualistic battle of light against darkness.

A 1998 fundraising letter from Bob Larson, for example, is headlined "Do You Want Me In The Devil's Face?" Further on, in a passage worth quoting at length for its use of the rhetoric of cosmological warfare, Larson recalls a conversation with "*a pastor* who is all too typical of some in the pulpit."

'Yes, I've heard of you,' he said as he started the conversation. 'You're the guy who's out there on the edge of spiritual warfare. *You're always in someone's face!* I prefer a gentler, more pastoral approach. *I pick up the pieces* after people like you.' I was hurt. I wanted to respond forcefully in defense, but out of respect for his position as a pastor, I didn't. He's partially right. I am on the edge where few people want to be! I am in people's faces, warning them about sin and Satan. But *that pastor is dead wrong* about who picks up the pieces! *I'm the one, with God's help, who picks up the pieces of shattered lives that so many in the ministry won't touch!* I pick up the pieces of people who have been battered and bruised by demons and bring them to Jesus for deliverance! I won't apologize for that. On the contrary, I am committed to reaching those whom many Christians have ignored. But being on the edge isn't a place that many people want to be, and I must often stand alone. There aren't many friends like you who are willing to be there with me. (Emphasis in the original.)

Similarly, Groothuis points out the "need to remember that the Christian witness to the New Ager is a spiritual offensive into enemy territory" (1988: 68). "Christians are involved in literal, spiritual warfare" he writes elsewhere; they "are in combat conditions, with no demilitarized zones available this side of heaven" (Groothuis 1988: 39).

Statements such as this help answer a question that arises occasionally in the analysis of the Christian countercult and its emphasis on reality-maintenance: Why go on? Why sustain the constant flow of books, tracts, audio- and videocassettes, newsletters, and, now, electronic information—all of which are elements of the conversation Berger and Luckmann posit as essential to the process of reality-maintenance? Why? Because "men forget," writes Berger simply (1967: 40), and repetition, as the old maxim goes, is the mother of learning.

Inherently precarious, any number of experiences, events, and ideas appear daily on one's cognitive horizon to threaten the subjective plausibility, the perceived inevitability, and ultimate legitimacy of one's worldview. For some, it may be the discovery of a particular fossil series that threatens the worldview of those who hold to any number of variant Creation scenarios (see Numbers 1992; Toumey 1994). For others, the discovery of scrolls nearly two millennia old—for example, the Nag Hammadi library—jeopardizes a subjective reality predicated on a particular understanding of the uniqueness of a particular revelation—that is, the New Testament. These are but two examples of cognitive threats, dissonant occurrences that contribute to a general consciousness that the world one inhabits is, in fact, neither definitely plausible, nor necessarily inevitable, nor uniquely legitimate. And, as threats, they require some measure of response. How, then, ought these threats be met?

Berger and Luckmann call the mechanisms by which threats to one's subjective reality are met "conceptual machineries of universe-maintenance," those particular apologetic and conservative processes that work to ensure the healthy maintenance and ongoing preservation of a specific symbolic universe. As a mechanism of knowledge production, this conceptual machinery operates in the dialectical space between threat and response. As Eyerman and Jamison point out, "knowledge is . . . the product of a series of social encounters," and emerges "between movements and their established opponents" (1991: 57). Thus, this kind of conceptual machinery is charged not only with the ongoing legitimation of a particular worldview, but also with the demonstration of its inherent superiority over any other realities that might rise to challenge it. Indeed, the predication of superiority is necessary because the "appearance of an alternative symbolic universe poses a threat because its very existence demonstrates empirically that one's own universe is less than inevitable" (Berger and Luckmann 1966: 126). For countercult apologists such as John Ankerberg, Constance Cumbey, Douglas Groothuis, Dave Hunt, Bob Larson, Texe Marrs, Walter Martin, Caryl Matrisciana, Ron Rhodes, and John Weldon, the mere thought that there are religious realities that people inhabit quite happily, and in which they do not accept the legitimacy of the exclusive religious claims on which the very existence of evangelical/fundamentalist reality is predicated, is enough to provoke the countercult response. This dissonance becomes even more pronounced when they inhabit a counterdefinition that is perceived to be in diametric opposition to that of the countercult.

"Thou shalt not suffer a witch to live," declares the author of Exodus (22:18 KJV). By the Middle Ages the Christian church had determined that the crucial reason for this censure was that a witch had made a pact with the devil (Guazzo [1608] 1988; Kramer and Sprenger [1484] 1971; Levack 1995; Midelfort 1972). But, what happens when one lives in a culture where—pacts with the devil notwithstanding—witches are not only suffered to live, but are also free to open bookshops, publish newsletters, magazines, and Web sites, gather together for rituals, and apply for state recognition as a legitimate religion? It is precisely this kind of unresolved tension that generates the need for a therapeutic maintenance of one's own reality. "The question 'Who am I?' " write Berger and Luckmann, "becomes possible simply because two conflicting answers are socially available" (1966: 186). Put differently, an answer to the question "Who am I?" is *required* precisely because more than one answer *is* possible. Further, when the socially available answers multiply from a duality (e.g., Christian versus non-Christian) to a plurality (i.e., Christian as merely one possibility among many), the need for reality- and identity-maintenance in the face of manifold potential disconfirmations becomes even more pronounced.

Of the possible conceptual machineries of universe-maintenance they discuss, Berger and Luckmann concentrate on two: therapy and nihilation. In their formulation, these function as opposites. "Therapy uses a conceptual machinery to keep everyone within the universe in question. Nihilation, in its turn, uses a similar machinery to liquidate conceptually everything *outside* the same universe" (Berger and Luckmann 1966: 132). As far as it goes, this appears correct. However, I suggest that therapy and nihilation do not function as opposites, but rather as dependent aspects of a larger cognitive process and praxis. Therapy is one component in the process of reality-maintenance; nihilation is one means by which a therapeutic model of reality-maintenance realizes its objective.

In fact, rather than simply the two they describe, I suggest at least three aspects to this therapeutic machinery: (1) an at least internally coherent theoretical framework into which those events that require maintenance may be integrated, (2) a methodology by which the events may be properly identified and accurately interpreted in the context of the orthodoxy determined by item (1), and (3) some procedure by which the event can be satisfactorily integrated into the adherent's subjective reality. With each successive integration, each successful repudiation of a challenge to its integrity, the subjective reality is strengthened and reified. Following the medical terminology implied by a therapeutic model these three elements may be called a *hygienics*—a basic perception of systemic health, which implies but does not define the variable indicators of nonhealth; a *pathology*—including the diagnostic tools necessary to identify events of nonhealth (i.e., deviance) correctly, and, since nihilation may not be the most effective therapeutic instrument in all cases, to indicate which therapy is appropriate to resolve the identified deviance; and a *therapy*—or, rather, a range of therapies the choice of which depends on the nature and severity of the diagnosed deviance. Together, these constitute a cognitive process and praxis by which the deviant event is rendered either healthy or inert, either of which would maintain the vigor of the system itself. While delineated in this way for heuristic purposes, it should be noted that these elements function interdependently and dialectically; no hard and fast division exists between them.

HYGIENICS: THE NOMIC VISION

The hygienics of any subjective reality is the nomic vision that determines "the world as it should be." In "the best of all possible worlds," there is an exact correspondence between the subjective interpretation of reality and an objective observation of reality as it is. The traffic light one perceives as green actually is green and is not simply remembered as such in the face of a potential moving violation. The belief that God created the universe *ex nihilo* in six literal, terrestrial days is actually what occurred at the beginning of cosmic time. Of course, the first example is readily falsifiable; a variety of evidence ranging from eyewitness testimony to computer monitoring of the traffic signal pattern can demonstrate what color the light was at any given moment. Thus, the exact correspondence between perception and reality can be disputed and determined. The second example, on the other hand, is not falsifiable; while some may dispute it, may argue for or against it on the basis of a wide variety of epistemologies, it cannot be either verified or falsified. Once again, it requires that a statement of faith be offered as a statement of fact. Similarly, because reality as it is does not always accord exactly (or often even closely) with reality as it is perceived to be, the nomic vision's function is more often ethical than actual. That is, it specifically details the world *as it should be*, rather than as it is now. The nomic vision is determined by the present, but oriented toward the future. It is an ideal type from which all situations and phenomena deviate in some regard. In the context of reality-maintenance, this ideal-type hygienics provides the template against which incidents of deviance are measured.

In the Christian countercult—though hardly limited to it—this *hygienics* is provided by the particular set of cognitive boundary markers that define evangelical cosmology—that is, the five fundamentals discussed earlier that find their principal orientation and predication in "The Bible is the only Word of God." In terms of a therapeutic model, these markers function in two ways. First, they identify and define the cognitive topography according to which the group is constituted; and second, while subjective in essence, they provide what comes to be regarded as objective, external standards according to which conformity and deviance can be evaluated.

As noted above, "biblical claims leave us few options. Either the Bible is what it claims—the literal inerrant Word of God—or it is not possible to know if God has revealed Himself to us truthfully" (Ankerberg and Weldon 1999: 666). Despite the logical fallacy of an irrelevant conclusion, Ankerberg and Weldon offer a number of similar statements, all designed to demonstrate the uniqueness of the Bible (and, by implication, its divine origin), as well as the place of the Bible as a divine blueprint for humanity. Among these, they contend that the Bible alone "offers objective evidence to be the Word of God," and "contains the greatest moral standards of any book" (Ankerberg and Weldon 1999: 670). It is "the most translated, purchased, memorized and persecuted book in history," they continue, though what, precisely, this proves remains unclear (Ankerberg and Weldon 1999: 671). Finally, "only the Bible provides historic proof that the one true God loves mankind" (Ankerberg and Weldon 1999: 671). In this, they demonstrate very well what Kenneth Boa and Robert Bowman call the classical apologetic approach, in which an a priori biblical authority is "the conclusion toward which an apologetic is directed" (2001: 110). "In other words," they write, despite their discussion of the normative rules of biblical interpretation (Ankerberg and Weldon 1999: 671–72), "the church does not sit in judgment upon the content or legitimacy of the Bible; the Bible sits in judgment upon the content or legitimacy of religious bodies claiming to be Christian" (Ankerberg and Weldon 1999: 662).

Working *from* a list of divine attributes *to* the inerrancy and authority of Scripture, Ankerberg and Weldon continue this line of argument. For example, because "a sovereign God is able to preserve the process of inspiration from error" and "a righteous God is unable to inspire error," therefore the Bible is the inerrant word of God. Because "an omniscient God knows every contingency that might arise to inhibit inerrancy," and "an immutable God could never contradict His word," therefore the Bible is the inerrant word of God (Ankerberg and Weldon 1999: 670). None of which necessarily follows. In the countercult construction of countercult reality, however, they don't have to. By and large, the audience for whom Ankerberg and Weldon are writing, and to whom their books are marketed, is already predisposed to believe this so-called evidence, whether it conforms to the principles of logic or not, whether it actually warrants the authors' conclusions or not. Because this target audience is already willing to see in these correspondences confirmation of the world as they believe it to be, a biblical mandate—often selectively interpreted—determines the shape and content of the hygienic, the nomic vision.

Groothuis (1986, 1990) presents broadly similar arguments, all of which tend toward a single conclusion: the objective nature of Christianity (properly defined) versus the subjective (and, therefore, problematic) nature of every worldview that differs from it. In language distinctly reminiscent of Harold Hill, a popular charismatic writer from the 1970s, who regularly described the Bible as the "Manufacturer's Handbook," Groothuis declares that "Christianity is also objective, providing a standard beyond and above the created world by which to evaluate all of life. Truth is not based on subjective experience but on God's revelation of himself in the Bible and through Christ" (1986: 170). "The God of the Bible has given us an objective operating manual for the planet," he continues, "that we may be equipped to obey him in every area of life and thought" (Groothuis 1986: 170).

Despite the countercult's own trek through subjective space, their hygienic is this blueprint laid out for humanity in God's "objective operating manual for the planet." Key, of course, as all countercult apologists are at considerable pains to point out, is the correct interpretation of this manual. Since conflicting interpretations of Scripture have been a part of the church's life almost from the beginning, establishing that one is working with the correct interpretation is central to any argument for the inherent superiority of a worldview that appeals to the Bible as a source of external authority. Emphasizing "the crucial need for intellectual honesty in looking at the Bible," Groothuis, for example, (1988: 87) often appends the phrase "properly interpreted" to general statements about the nature of the Bible. Ron Rhodes, a former CRI researcher, now publishes a Reasoning from the Scriptures series (which, to this point, includes Jehovah's Witnesses, Mormons, Roman Catholics, and Masons; Rhodes 1993, 1995, 2000, 2001b). For decades, Rhodes's mentor at CRI, Walter

Martin, was on the radio as *The Bible Answer Man;* since Martin's death, Hank Hanegraaff has assumed this position. Indeed, in the conclusion to *Reasoning From the Scriptures with the Jehovah's Witnesses,* Rhodes quotes Martin: "'Remember how dense you and I were—until the Lord managed to break through. Because cultists are bound in the chains of slavery to sin, you need to be patient'" (Martin, quoted in Rhodes 1993: 407). The derogatory language is less important here than the operant hermeneutic—the belief that scriptural interpretation on the part of the countercult apologist does not enter into the picture; rather, it is the "Lord" who "breaks through." Since few countercult apologists do not appeal to the nomic value of their own interpretation of the Bible in evaluating and ultimately condemning religious groups different from their own, in practice "properly interpreted" means an interpretation that agrees with theirs.

PATHOLOGY: DIAGNOSIS FOR THE DISCONFIRMED WORLDVIEW

When someone or something challenges the hygienics of a particular worldview, the *pathologic* and *diagnostic* functions of the conceptual machineries of universe-maintenance begin to operate. *Pathology* is the process by which specific deviances from the particular hygienic are identified and according to which appropriate therapy is established. If the hygienics of universe-maintenance provide the template against which the determination is made *whether* something is wrong, the pathologic function diagnoses precisely *what* is wrong and to what degree.

In the Christian countercult, incidents of deviance vary from the doctrinally suspect to the categorically heretical, and the extent of the deviance informs the kind and degree of reality-maintenance required. Some need only a minor readjustment, a therapeutic realignment to restore the transgressor to healthy participation in doctrinal orthodoxy. Word Faith teacher Benny Hinn, for example, who has made some rather unorthodox statements about the nature of God, is regarded as a doctrinal annoyance by some evangelical Christians; to others, however, he is a full-blown heretic. Of Hinn, former Mormon and now evangelical pastor James Spencer wonders, "How many dumb statements make someone a heretic? If an otherwise orthodox preacher makes a doctrinal mistake, is he a heretic?" (1993: 42). In a case such as this, presumably all that would be required is a bit of doctrinal clarity, perhaps some televised repentance and humility, and an implicit promise not to make such problematic statements again.

Other deviances, however, are not so easily resolved; they require more stringent measures—worldview nihilation, what Groothuis calls "negative apologetics." Any appeal to extra-biblical revelation, for example—whether *The Book of Mormon,* or a new version of the Bible such as the *New World Translation* (Jehovah's Witnesses)—presents a significant problem for countercult apologists. Likewise, doctrinal and ritual differences—from the place of the Temple in the Church of Jesus Christ of the Latter-day Saints to the denial of the Trinity by Jehovah's Witnesses—are enough to render a group permanently suspect in the eyes of the countercult. While opinions vary on *how* to confront groups such as the Latter-day Saints or Jehovah's Witnesses, the evangelical countercult is all but united in its condemnation of them as heretical.

THERAPY: RECONFIRMING THE WORLD AS IT OUGHT TO BE

What remains, then, is for the therapeutic model to treat the deviant event in such a way that the incumbent worldview is legitimated and maintained. Some incidences of deviance will require nihilation as an instrument of therapy if the plausibility of the evangelical countercult worldview is to be maintained, others will not. The latter, for example, may assume a shared subjective reality from which specific, minor deviances have been noted; these conform more closely to Berger's and Luckmann's formulation of the problem. The former move beyond Berger's and Luckmann's conception and begin to account for larger subjective realities, those inhabited by alternative religious collectivities as opposed to deviant individuals. At this level, whatever machinery of universe-maintenance is employed, it is faced with the task of engaging and integrating not deviance from a shared subjective reality, but the often greater problem of divergent, competing, and potentially disconfirming worldviews. In this section, two examples—one in which nihilation is required, and one in which it is not—will serve to illustrate the manner in which pathology and therapy operate in the context of universe-maintenance.

Therapeutic Integration

As noted, integration is not a point in cognitive space, but a spectrum of therapeutic intervention determined by the relative seriousness of the transgression. As one point on the spectrum, for example, consider the "holy war" (Numbers 1992: 289) waged in the Southern Baptist Convention during the past few decades over the issue of biblical inerrancy (cf. Ammerman 1990; Lindsell 1976: 91–104; Toumey 1994: 60–62). All participants in the SBC conflict operate from commonly understood frames of reference; a similar subjective reality obtains for both major parties, the cognitive boundaries of which are not seriously questioned by either side. Both factions in the dispute—who, in their struggle for the convention presidency, came to be known as "fundamentalists" and "moderates"—locate themselves explicitly within the same symbolic universe: conservative Baptist Protestantism. Yet, both sides accused the other of illegitimately appropriating the symbolism of that universe for their own ends (Ammerman 1990: 72–126). Paul Pressler, a leader in the inerrantist faction, "insisted that the fight was about one thing and one thing only—beliefs about the Bible" (Ammerman 1990: 80).

Two camps, both of which define their identity as Baptists according to particular beliefs about the Bible, dispute the nomic force that belief should wield in the community and the manner in which that *nomos* should regulate behavior. Insofar as the holy war within the Southern Baptist Convention is about the Bible, though, the important point from the perspective of therapeutic integration is that neither side in the dispute requires a complete worldview shift on the part of the other for resolution to be reached. Neither requires the complete dissolution of the other's subjective reality in order for their own reality to be maintained and validated. While it has split the denomination, and generated significant heartache and conflict with the Southern Baptist community, at its core this is a family fight, sheep from the same fold who are perceived to have gone astray. Which sheep have strayed, of course, depends entirely on who one asks. While they disagree strongly over the exact nature of Scripture and the precise nomic value it has in society, neither group would question the essential Christianity of the other. Therapy, then, is a matter of one side convincing the other that their own position on Scripture is the correct one.

Therapeutic Nihilation

Conversely, an example of the requirement for nihilation in the service of reality-maintenance is the fundamentalist Christian response to the perceived incursion of competing religious systems—for example, Buddhism, Hinduism, Islam, and Neopaganism—in an increasingly pluralistic context. Because there is often no shared fold to which deviant sheep might be returned, such an incursion requires the nihilation of the competing worldview—a wolf threatening the sheepfold that must be destroyed cognitively if not actually.

Rhodes's discussions of other religious groups, for example, are almost uniformly couched in the language of legitimized suffering of Christians and a Christian society at the hands of religious interlopers; that is, in his view, when the founding fathers of the United States framed the Constitution, they never intended for freedom of religion to be extended beyond the parameters of puritan Christianity (1994: 7–9). According to Rhodes, that extension—what he labels "the 'culting' of America"—is largely responsible for the current degradation of society. Rhodes's target audience is reflected in his rhetorical call to action. That is, are they "concerned Christians," as the cover of his book says they should be if they pay attention to the "shocking implications" that he will reveal? Will the reader "be a soldier in the midst of the conflict or a casualty on the sidelines" (Rhodes 1994: 219)?

A continual denigration of the enemy is clear from the language used by many countercult apologists; disease, infestation, and invasion metaphors all both articulate and aggravate the antipathy with which the enemy is regarded.

This emotional, often violent language, which is so value-laden that it becomes difficult for the reader to separate the flow of the argument from the tenor of the rhetoric, contributes therapeutically to the nihilation of competing world-views. Words such as "infiltrated" (i.e., Hinduism; Rhodes 1994: 21), "pene-trate" (*passim;* one of Rhodes's favorites), and "invasion" (i.e., Islam; Rhodes 1994: 22–23) abound. As well, antipathetic disease metaphors are very common in his writing, further distancing the unhealthy or dangerous "them" from the wholesome and virtuous "us." "Of course," he concludes, "there are no skull-and-crossbones POISON warning labels stamped on the cults, labels like those found on bottles containing deadly elements. Tragically, though, innumerable people in the United States are drinking down spiritual cyanide by the mega-dose and are completely oblivious to the fact that they are bringing about their own doom" (Rhodes 1994: 26).

In a passage very like Rhodes's, Spencer points out that "hard cases are not easily won to Christ" (1991: 21). According to Spencer, a "hard case" is anyone over eighteen who is not by that time a Christian. To convert these hard cases, Spencer advocates confrontational evangelism, which is similar to Groothuis's negative apologetics and for which Christians must be specially equipped. "Equipping," he insists, "is both spiritual and intellectual. It is necessary to understand how the devil has poisoned those he has marked for destruction, to know the antidote for the poison and how to administer the antidote" (Spen-cer 1991: 21–22). An excellent illustration of the therapeutic model.

In many cases, the antidote is therapeutic nihilation of the worldview in question. In *Christian Apologetics,* Norman Geisler, one of the most respected evangelical names in the field, writes that "we have argued two things thus far, one explicitly and the other implicitly. First, we have argued that every major nontheistic world view may be internally non-contradictory, but that they are, nonetheless, somehow self-defeating and false. Second, by implica-tion, this would mean that theism, the only remaining non-contradictory view, would be true by the process of elimination" (1976: 237). The a priori ani-mosity Geisler brings to these other worldviews and the fallacy of limited alternatives explicit in his conclusion notwithstanding, these are also good ex-amples of the basic framework of worldview nihilation deployed by the countercult.

THE APOLOGETIC HUBRIS OF ORTHODOXY

Over against "false religions"—those whose constructions of reality are ob-viously and demonstrably different from Christianity—there is the somewhat thornier problem of *heresy.* If false religions represent the danger from with-out, heresies are the dangers that lurk within the church, the theological or doctrinal viruses that disguise themselves as natural components of the body of Christ. Those Christians who are even moderately familiar with Buddhism, Hinduism, or Scientology readily recognize that they present radically different constructions of reality than the Christians' own. Few are taken in. As many countercult apologists would contend, it is much easier to avoid the devil when you can see him coming, pitchfork waving, flames shooting from his ears, pointed tail cracking like a bullwhip in the sulfurous breeze. When he appears as an angel of light, however, speaking the language of faith as though he knows what he's talking about, claiming to expand and illumine truths in which one already believes, he is infinitely more dangerous. On this, eminent evangelical scholar Harold O. J. Brown notes, "Honorable enemies are regarded with less hostility than the traitor in one's own camp. The Christian life is often presented as spiritual warfare; if the pagans are the enemies, the heretics are the traitors" (1988: 3).

While initial attempts to develop an explicit sociology of orthodoxy and heresy all lament the scholarly inattention paid to this important domain of religious interaction (Berlinerblau 2001; Henderson 1998; Kurtz 1983; Weber 1951; Zito 1983), progress to date has been somewhat limited. In any sociology of orthodoxy and heresy, though, one of the most fundamental issues is that of historical and theological precedence. Put simply, does orthodoxy precede heresy, and heresy then merely deviate from the established orthodoxy, or does what becomes orthodoxy develop out of the contested interaction between what are later declared competing heresies? The well known Bauer thesis (Bauer 1971), lately expanded by Gerd Lüdemann (1995; cf. Ehrman 1993; Kraft 1975; Lüdemann and Janssen 1997; Robinson 1988), contends the latter: early Christianity did not comprise an established orthodoxy that later spawned rival heresies. Rather, in the first centuries of the church, numerous understandings of the Jesus event competed for dominance, and orthodoxy depended in large measure upon where one lived, in whose apostolic lineage the church in that region was founded, and to which texts that lineage had access and considered authoritative.

However they may take account of the Bauer thesis, evangelical scholars such as Brown argue the opposite. "Heresy as a formulation of doctrine," writes Wayne House, a constitutional scholar and editor of the short-lived *Journal of Christian Apologetics,* "appears on the scene earlier and more completely than does orthodoxy" (1997: 33). "Am I suggesting that it is truly prior to orthodoxy?" he continues. "No!" Following Harold Brown, on whom House relies considerably for the substance of his discussion, the evangelical argument for the priority of orthodoxy is that heresy "presupposes orthodoxy" (Brown 1988: 4); that is, in order for heresy to exist, there must have been a preexisting orthodoxy—in the therapeutic model, a hygienics—from which beliefs could then deviate. Because it illustrates so clearly aspects of both therapeutic reality-maintenance and the epistemic circularity inherent in what I am calling "the apologetic hubris of orthodoxy," Brown is worth quoting at some length.

There is one very good argument that the story of heresy provides to persuade us that it itself is secondary, a reaction to orthodoxy, and not the other way around. It is impossible to document what we now call orthodoxy in the first two centuries of Christianity; heresy often appears more prominently, so much so that orthodoxy looks like a reaction to it. But we can document orthodoxy for all the centuries since then—in other words, for close to seventeen centuries of the church's existence. And we discover that orthodoxy, which has become and been an identifiable constant for so long, continues to evoke the same reaction. Century after century, man's religious imagination leads him to re-create ancient heresies in reaction to the same orthodoxy, which has now been constant for so long. Were the very first heresies, which we glimpse *before* we glimpse orthodoxy, also reactions? If they were, then it can reasonably be argued that the story of Christian theology is the story of truth. If not, then it would be necessary to concede that the history of orthodoxy is the history of a usurpation—as indeed many eminent scholars have argued and still argue. It is not necessary to make this concession, and the history of orthodoxy is the history of truth. (Brown 1988: 5)

In his introduction to an edition of *The Communist Manifesto*, distinguished Oxford historian A. J. P. Taylor noted a propensity for self-serving definition in that "Marx wanted socialism to win and rigged the dialectic to ensure that it should. . . . He decided beforehand what he wanted to discover and sure enough discovered it" (1985: 10). A similar exegetical dynamic obtains in Brown's understanding of the development of orthodoxy and (then) heresy. While a number of logical fallacies tumble together in the lengthy passage quoted above—including arguments from longevity (i.e., the length of orthodoxy's tenure in the church argues for its veracity as an expression of ontological reality) and the fallacy of an irrelevant thesis (i.e., if the heresies faced by the early church were reactions to orthodoxy, then the ontological veracity of orthodoxy is supported)—the key sentence is Brown's last: "It is not necessary to make this concession [i.e., that orthodoxy is a history of political and theological usurpation], and the history of orthodoxy is the history of truth." Put differently, if anything like the Bauer thesis were conceded, then any evangelical claim to an ontological, ahistorical orthodoxy is placed in considerable jeopardy; the worldview hygienic is threatened. Since the exclusive religious claims made for Christianity by evangelicals cannot tolerate such an admission of social construction, the concession cannot be made, and other explanations for the phenomena must be found. In the inaugural issue of the *Journal of Christian Apologetics*, House (1997) suggests some of these other explanations. And, in what he calls the "six reasons heresy might arise," he offers a good example of the pathological function in worldview-maintenance.

First, House declares, the most obvious mark of heresy is that it fails "to hold to the historic teachings of the church (1997: 35). As an argument for a precedent hygienic, this, of course, requires that the "historic teachings of the church" be in some way readily available; that they do, indeed, predate any competing heresy; and that their objective and ahistorical (i.e., unconstructed) nature renders them easily distinguishable from competing deviances. Even House acknowledges, however, that these deviances rarely if ever concern "explicit doctrine." "Rather," he writes, heresy is identified by its "lack of adherence to implicit teachings extracted from the Bible" (House 1997: 35). House continues that "the sacred text sets forth the proper and necessary information from which one develops a theology but the text itself is not a theology" (1997: 35).

Here we see the first emergence of the hubris of apologetic orthodoxy. As do virtually all of the countercult apologists, House avoids discussing the socially constructed nature of theology—orthodox or not—*that is explicit in his own formulation of the problem.* He admits that what are commonly called "the historic teachings of the church" are not themselves explicit, but rather implicit (at best); they do not reveal themselves in any overt fashion from the pages of Holy Writ, but must be "extracted" from it. That is, he acknowledges, at least implicitly, that a particular hermeneutic must be at work; a process of selection and interpretation determines which aspects of the biblical witness will be extracted, how these aspects will be integrated into a theological framework, and what particular ecclesiastical interests the construction of that framework will serve. Countercult apologetic orthodoxy, on the other hand, requires an overarching interpretation—a determinate extraction, if you will—that is ontologically correct quite apart from any interpretative process by which it was generated. While he acknowledges that "one develops a theology" from the biblical text, House does not consider the necessarily interpretative, constructed, and, ultimately, subjective nature of that development. Put differently, a central question obtains: what determines the correctness (or orthodoxy) of one theological development over another—apart from the investment each party has in being correct?

Rather, House suggests that "Arius and his followers were not ignorant of Holy Scripture but erred by drawing wrong inferences from the teachings about the generation of the Son" (1997: 35). Indeed, Arius was not ignorant of Scripture, but how was it determined that the inferences he drew were wrong? Only by holding his teachings up against those promulgated by others—teachings that were as developmental, one might even say experimental, as those of Arius (cf. Gregg and Groh 1981; Williams 1987). This unwillingness to acknowledge the socially determined process of theological construction seriously weakens the claims made by countercult apologists for the ontological validity of their particular construction of theological reality.

The second aspect of House's pathology derives from his first. Heretics, it appears, were unwilling "to live with tension in Christian theology" (House 1997: 35), by which House means that those aspects of what became orthodox theology, but which could not be explained rationally (e.g., the Trinity and the *homoousios* of Christ), were no less true for being mysterious and simply had to be accepted as such. This particular symptom of heresy even more directly embeds the apologetic process in subjective interpretation and the political manipulation of meaning. "In understanding divine mysteries of the nature of God," House continues, "often one must pronounce the understanding of God's unity and plurality as not contrary to logic but nonetheless inscrutable. This

Arius, and the heretics before and after him, have chosen not to do. The truth about the Trinity of God, the dual natures of Christ, as well as other doctrines requires one not to err on the left or the right" (1997: 35).

As noted above, countercult apologists define their mission according to both negative and positive aspects: reasons why a person should *not* believe in a particular religious worldview versus reasons why one *should* accept the evangelical Christian worldview as the only one that accords with objective reality. Yet, as apologists have since the time of Arius, when these rationally grounded arguments run afoul of paradox, inconsistency, or contradiction, retreat is often made to the inscrutability of God. Essentially an argument from mystery, House and other apologists contend that orthodox theology—especially trinitarianism and the *homoousios* of Christ—are not illogical, they are merely enigmatic. They are implicit from Scripture, not explicit; they must be extracted and derived; they cannot be comprehended rationally—yet, these are the only correct interpretations possible and must be accepted as such, all other arguments and interpretations notwithstanding. "Because it is a mystery," however, is an argument only marginally more elegant than "because we say so"; it is no more compelling in and of itself.

Highlighting the ahistorical and decontextualized nature of any claim to an ontological orthodoxy, a "lack of proper ecclesiastical structure for the confrontation of heretics" is House's third reason for the rise and "staying power" of heresy (1997: 36). House argues that the apologists of the early church "successfully attacked" a variety of heresies regardless of government support for or interference with their efforts; in this, he locates the success of what became orthodoxy in the ineluctable will of God. Later, heresy was "brought under control" because, as it evolved, the church looked to the Patristic authors and the decisions of the ecumenical councils as the touchstones of articulated faith. Recalling Brown's argument above, House once again assumes that the orthodoxy that prevailed did so because it was objectively correct—however implicit and derivative its origination. That is, it is orthodox because it is correct, not correct because it was declared orthodox.

Finally, lighting on the heretical yardstick of Christian fundamentalism, heresy is a result of the "rejection of the authority of the canonical Scripture, and the acceptance of the teaching of the apostles" (House 1997: 38). The heretics were so because they did not correctly interpret Scripture. An assertion common in countercult apologetics, few books, pamphlets, or video- and audiotapes miss the opportunity to emphasize how nontraditional religious groups have supposedly twisted Scripture (see Geisler and Rhodes 1997; Sire 1980). That there may be competing interpretations of contested passages rarely enters into the discussion. However, once again retrojecting an ahistorical doctrinal consensus that almost certainly did not exist, House offers what is, arguably, his most troubling statement: "We in the English speaking world enjoy many advantages over the theologians who developed the creeds of the church. Generally, we do not have the confusion brought about by differences of meanings between languages, such as Latin and Greek" (1997: 38). This implies—indeed, almost proclaims—for the English speaker or reader a transparency of meaning, as well as a purity of translation and transmission between the documents and records of the early church—such as they are—and modern evangelical apologists. Assuming that not only the translations, but the entire sociological structures of knowledge and interpretation, the different "cultures of inquiry" (Hall 1999; McCarthy 1996) that existed from the early church through the Ecumenical Councils are, of course, correct, House avoids the central concern in that deceptively simple phrase, "the authority of the canonical Scripture." That is to say, "the authority of Scripture" is a vacant concept without some ethic, some mandate, some *interpretation* of the relevant material over which it can exercise authority.

Many apologists treat the Bible as though it were a completely open book, the meaning of which is utterly clear, limpid, and available to the diligent and pious reader (e.g., Ankerberg and Weldon 1999: 661–72). Recall, for example, Dave Hunt on prophecy as the so-called irrefutable verification of the biblical witness: "No honest person can remain an unbeliever after even a brief study of prophecy" (1993a: 24). Or countercult journalist William Alnor on alleged doctrinal changes resulting from differing interpretations of the Bible: "Historical documents prove that there were never any rewrites, revisions, second editions, or cutting out of *any doctrines* of Christianity" (1998: 106, emphasis in the original; while in an endnote to this [1998: 188 n.25], Alnor adds, "What one sees in today's Bible, simply put, is what has always been there," see Ehrman 1993). Or Ron Rhodes, who concedes that the Bible's lucidity is not always all that it could be: "Scripture is clear that one of the ministries of the Holy Spirit is to illumine the minds of Christians so they can understand Scripture" (1997: 33). He continues: "The Holy Spirit's 'signal' (that is, His illumination) is always perfect. But because of varying circumstances (perhaps sin, or not fully walking in the Spirit, or being overly concerned about the affairs of the world, or being blinded by Satan), Christians have varying degrees of success in receiving the Spirit's illumination" (1997: 33).

Though he dismisses the caveat that "heresy is the position held by the group that loses" (House 1997: 29)—arguing instead that such a claim does not properly consider "a biblical and credal view of the nature of truth"—House nevertheless insists that there was an objective orthodoxy from which it was possible to deviate and in the face of which it was possible to compromise. Despite his acknowledgment that the beliefs of the church evolved over time, having been extracted from Scripture, as it were, mined from the implicit and rendered explicit only in their interpretation, he affirms an ontological orthodoxy set in place by God, and there for the righteous to find.

All of these reasons intend toward a discussion of therapy—that is, what the church should do about heresy and about heretics. How should suspect doctrines be judged? What sanctions should be applied to those found in violation? Who should have the authority to make those decisions? Pointing out that

"Athanasius was in a small minority at the beginning of the Nicean Council" (1997: 39), House suggests that, sometimes, heresy is uncovered by a lone voice, around which an ecclesial consensus eventually forms through force of argument and exegesis. This assumes, of course, that a level playing field exists for all participants in the dispute. Conversely, he wonders, "What about several countercult organizations issuing a joint proclamation? Would this be equivalent to the actions of a synod?" (House 1997: 39). If House means for this latter suggestion to be taken seriously, it is another example of the arrogance with which the countercult often conducts itself.

Finally, in a romantic if somewhat chimeric view not uncommon to fundamentalists, House once again implies that there was in the early church a clearly defined standard of belief and practice upon which all (or most) were agreed. "Today's church," he writes, "does not have the cohesion the church had at its beginning. There is no one ecclesiastical *court* to which one can appeal. If an individual is teaching heresy and is forced out of one organization that individual can join another, or start an independent branch of the Church with little censure" (House 1997: 40, emphasis in the original). House's argument does not consider the possibility that, if such idealistic conditions ever really existed in the church (and even the biblical witness is clear that they did not), they were very likely imposed and enforced by those with the power to do so, lasting only until the next theological challenge to their dominance.

The reality is that challenges to theological dominance have arisen throughout the history of the church—from the so-called Judaizers against whom Paul argued to the Gnostic opponents of Irenaeus, from the Cathars in the Languedoc to the Latter-day Saints in the American Midwest, and from the Church of Scientology in downtown Los Angeles to the Hindu temple just down the street. While each of these has generated some measure of response from the established church, it is the particular answer of the Christian countercult in the twentieth century to which we now turn.

Part II
Typologizing the Countercult

A Territory under Siege: The Early Countercult in the Twentieth Century

In *Apologetics in a New Age,* David Clark and Norman Geisler lament that "Christian apologists have been caught unaware. Christians have become successful at defending their faith against Epicurean atheism, but they are relatively defenseless in the face of Stoic pantheism. For this reason, Christian apologists must turn their attention in a new direction by developing new arguments for a new age" (1990: 12). For all countercult intents and purposes, that new age began in the nineteenth century with the appearance of upstart groups such as the Latter-day Saints, Jehovah's Witnesses, Christian Science, and the New Thought churches, as well as a resurgence of spiritualism. This emerging religious pluralism, which many of the nation's founders saw as inseparable from civil liberty, resulted not in the ghettoization of what was regarded as the strange and the intrusive, but often in conversion to these new sects by members of more established traditions. Protestant missionaries writing from the field may have opined that "the four marks of Paganism were Tauism, Boodism, ancestor worship, and opium addiction" (Fields 1992: 72), but church leaders on the ground at home were more concerned about people leaving one set of pews and choosing another, more "patently ridiculous" set.

"For climacteric comicality," writes George Hamilton Combs (1864–1951), a Disciples of Christ minister from Kansas City, Missouri, "Mormonism should be awarded the palm. Its romancing is refreshing in its very audaciousness. Jules Verne dreaming is here eclipsed. Baron Munchausen marvels seem commonplace. . . . Untruth was never more picturesque" (1899: 205). Mary Baker Eddy's *Science and Health with Key to the Scriptures* he dismisses as "such a hodge-podge of crudities [as] was never found before between the covers of one book" (Combs 1899: 235). "Pass can this delusion none too swiftly to that oblivion which is its doom" Combs concludes (1899: 243).

But, pass these upstarts did not, and we can only wonder with what dismay Combs watched, in the more than half-century of life that remained to him, the growth of the Latter-day Saints, the Watchtower Bible and Tract Society,

and myriad other groups that threatened the security of his Protestant evangelicalism. Others, however, took up his banner, and laid the foundation for
the modern Christian countercult movement.

"ISMS": EMERGENT RELIGIONS AND *THE FUNDAMENTALS*

At the beginning of the twentieth century, "two prominent Christian lay-
men"—anonymous for a time, but now known to have been southern California oil barons Lyman and Milton Stewart—financed the assembly,
publication, and free distribution of *The Fundamentals: A Testimony to the
Truth* to "ministers of the gospel, missionaries, Sunday School superintendents,
and others engaged in aggressive Christian work throughout the English speaking world" (Torrey [1917] 1996: 5). Originally published between 1910 and
1915 as a reaction to the advent of theological liberalism, higher criticism of
the Bible, and the theory of evolution at the end of the nineteenth century,
The Fundamentals articulated what its contributors held to be the kerygmatic
elements of an authentic Christian faith: (1) the inerrancy, infallibility, and
insuperability of Scripture; (2) the virgin birth of Jesus and his crucifixion and
bodily resurrection; (3) Jesus's ontological divinity as the Second Person of the
Holy Trinity; (4) Jesus's literal and visible second coming; and (5) a substitutionary theory of atonement.[1] While these are easily recognizable as the cognitive boundary markers by which the modern evangelical countercult is
defined, when considering them it is important to recognize that few of the
contributors to *The Fundamentals* would have considered themselves anything
other than solidly mainstream at the time the essays were produced. So-called
fundamentalism had not yet acquired the pejorative connotation by which it
is often characterized today. By and large, these authors were simply and vigorously defending what they perceived as traditional Christianity against implicit threats from within and explicit threats from without.

Rather than the unlettered and unsophisticated devotees so beloved of modern North American cinema and presented to the world as fundamentalists,
the authors collected in *The Fundamentals* represented some of the most respected voices in the Christian academy at the time. Among them, William
Caven (former principal of Knox College in Toronto), George Robinson (Mc-
Cormick Theological Seminary), George Frederick Wright (Oberlin College),
and James Orr (United Free Church College in Glasgow) each contributed essays refuting higher criticism of Scripture and arguing for the Bible's uniqueness and divine inspiration. Wright and Orr also wrote pieces criticizing
scientific challenges to biblical creationism. Benjamin B. Warfield (Princeton
Theological Seminary), R. A. Torrey (dean of the Bible Institute of Los Angeles,
now Biola University), Orr, and others answered concerns raised by the "new
theology" and the social gospel.

Specifically religious challenges to the so-called true church included "Romanism," an old favorite of Protestant apologists (see chapter 11). Besides the plethora of post-Reformation propaganda, contributors to *The Fundamentals* could hardly have been unfamiliar with such nineteenth- and early twentieth-century anti-Catholic material as the *Awful Disclosures of Maria Monk* (Monk 1876), *The Priest, the Woman and the Confessional* (Chiniquy 1880), or Blakeney's *Protestant Catechism* (Blakeney 1911). Aware, though, that "if I undertake to prove that *Romanism is not Christianity*, I must expect to be called 'bigoted, harsh, uncharitable' " (Medhurst [1917] 1996: 288, emphasis in the original), T. W. Medhurst set out to prove "that the teaching of Rome is at least as different from that of the Sacred Writings as that which Paul calls 'another gospel' " ([1917] 1996: 290)—that is, "a *Satanic delusion*" ([1917] 1996: 289, emphasis in the original). For his part, J. M. Foster was even less equivocal than Medhurst, urging his readers to consider two "undeniable facts": "*ROME IS THE NATION'S ANTAGONIST BECAUSE IT IS A CORRUPT AND CORRUPTING SYSTEM OF FALSEHOOD AND IDOLATRY THAT POLLUTES OUR LAND*" (Foster [1917] 1996: 301) and "*ROME IS THE NATION'S ANTAGONIST BECAUSE IT IS A POLITICAL SYSTEM OF FOREIGN DESPOTISM*" ([1917] 1996: 309, emphasis in the original).

For his contribution to *The Fundamentals,* William Moorehead, a professor at the United Presbyterian Theological Seminary (Xenia, Ohio), chose to consider the Millennial Dawn of Charles Taze Russell (1852–1916), which became, of course, Jehovah's Witnesses. Moorehead discussed "Dawnism"—its adherents he called "Dawnists"—from the perspective of what he regarded as their categorical deviances from orthodox Christianity. Particularly alarmed at the prodigious output of Russell's publishing house,[2] Moorehead writes: "That the teaching of Dawnism has done immense harm is certain; that it is calculated to subvert the faith of Christians by substituting for the truth of Jesus Christ the calamitous doctrines of Mr. Russell cannot be denied; for the whole system is anti-Scriptural, anti-Christian, and a deplorable perversion of the Gospel of the Son of God" ([1917] 1996: 110). Russell's understanding of the atonement he called "a wretched caricature," "an inadequate and puerile conception" (Moorehead [1917] 1996: 116). The resurrection fared little better: "Wicked and disastrous as are the teachings of Millennial Dawn noted above, this is immeasurably worse, if that be possible. Here the climax in audacity and falsehood is reached" (Moorehead [1917] 1996: 117). Noting an analogy with the emergence of Mormonism, Moorehead concludes that the "Millennial Dawn is essentially polytheistic; and as it has always happened with polytheism, this system, should it endure, will ultimately sink into idolatry" ([1917] 1996: 128).

When the original volumes of *The Fundamentals* were published, the main competing religious groups with which the writers were concerned were the Mormons, Jehovah's Witnesses, Christian Scientists, and Roman Catholics. Overt influence by more radically different religious traditions was considerably less prevalent than it is today. The first World Parliament of Religions took place in 1893; there had been some Eastern (i.e., Hindu and Buddhist) influence on the American Transcendentalists, especially Ralph Waldo Emerson and Henry David Thoreau, significant influence on the early Theosophists, especially Helena Petrovna Blavatsky and Henry Steel Olcott, as well as some minor missionary activity in the United States. But, outside of an essay on spiritualism—in which "the millions of China, Japan and India" are portrayed as "the demonized races of the heathen world" (Pollock [1917] 1996: 166)— the major defense of traditional Christianity in *The Fundamentals* is made against deviant Christian sects that had emerged and established themselves in the nineteenth century.

That which *The Fundamentals* defended against indicated the direction (or directions) from which the underwriters, editors, and contributors believed the threat to come. Rather than battle the incursion of "demonized races of the heathen world" (apparently not much of an issue), they chose to defend Christianity on the basis of biblical veracity and reliability, credal fidelity, and theological orthodoxy. Since the essayists still regarded Christianity as a self-evidently true ontology, anger and frustration at the so-called upstarts come through clearly in much of their work. For them, Christianity was, quite simply, an accurate representation of "the way the world is" (implying as well, of course, "the way the world ought to be"), and required only the nihilation of its challengers to reassert its legitimate authority. This is little different from the approach taken by many of the modern countercult apologists.

Internecine differences aside, the beliefs reflected in both *The Fundamentals* and modern countercult apologetics are similar with respect to *what* they seek to defend (i.e., biblical Christianity), and what they seek to protect that reality *from* (i.e., challenges to biblical Christianity's plausibility, inevitability, and unique legitimacy). Indeed, modern apologists—fundamentalist or otherwise—owe a tremendous, if often unacknowledged, intellectual debt to their conservative Christian predecessors. Together, they stand in the stream defined first by the author of the letter of Jude (vv. 3b–4a NRSV), enjoining those who claim to be Christian to "contend for the faith that was once for all entrusted to the saints. For certain intruders have stolen in among you."

"UNPAID BILLS": JAN KAREL VAN BAALEN AND *THE CHAOS OF CULTS*

A common feature of many small and medium-sized towns in North America is a church signboard placed prominently at the main entrances to the municipality. Listed there, sometimes according to their relative popularity, other times alphabetically, are the different places of worship to which visitors and townsfolk might be drawn. Grace Lutheran Church, St. Mary's Roman Catholic Parish, Knox Presbyterian, and St. Cyprian's Episcopal Church—all offer their varied services to the worshipping public. While there was a time when those listings contained only religious groups accepted by the culture at

large, lately St. Andrew's has vied for signboard space with the Kingdom Hall
of Jehovah's Witnesses, and the telephone number for St. Mary's parish now
falls just below those of the five different wards of The Church of Jesus Christ
of Latter-day Saints.

What alarms those who contend that such signboards should be limited to
accepted Christian denominations only (with, perhaps, an occasional grudging
nod toward the local synagogue) is the simple fact that in North America's
expanding religious economy, they have not been so limited. "For example,"
writes Christian Reformed minister and early countercult apologist Jan Karel
van Baalen in the introduction to the 1960 edition of his classic work *The Chaos
of Cults,* "Mormonism, Christian Science, Unity, and similar non-Christian
cults are allowed to list their services and hours of worship on the same bulletin
boards at the entrance of cities and towns, and in hotel lobbies, with evangelical
churches whose every tenet these cults not merely deny but combat" (1960:
6). That this presented a problem of practical life for van Baalen is clear. "The
writer believes," he concludes, "that it would be well to stop this practice" (van
Baalen 1960: 6).

Outside of Christian Reformed circles, Jan Karel van Baalen (1890–1968) is
best known for the four editions of *The Chaos of Cults,* subtitled *A Study in
Present-Day Isms,* and one of the first modern encyclopedic treatments of
emergent religions that discussed the phenomenon in any systematic fashion.[3]
He did, however, have a brief career as a pamphleteer on the side of positive
Calvinism during the "common grace" controversy that rocked the Christian
Reformed Church between 1921 and 1928 (Bratt 1984; Engelsma 1996). Indeed,
it was precisely this understanding of common grace—that the grace of God
is at least implicit in all humanity—that contributed to the more temperate
character of his writings, a quality often lacking in those who have followed
him in the field of countercult apologetics. While not always the case in practice,
Irving Hexham and Karla Poewe note, for example, that "although van Baalen
was devastating in his theological criticism of various groups, he made an effort
to be scrupulously fair. His objections were doctrinal, not personal or vindic-
tive" (1997: 3).

When confronting adherents of a different religious tradition, for example,
van Baalen advised that one should "never show that you suspect the cultist
of dishonesty or mercenary motives" (1960: 392). That is, they should be approached as though the *motives* behind their religious choice are as authentic
and honorable as anyone else's. This is in direct contrast to much of the rhetoric
of seduction, deceit, and aggression that has followed van Baalen in the Christian countercult. For van Baalen, though, a reasonable demeanor was not
merely a tactical consideration, but one that emerged from the heart of his
contribution to the common grace dispute. Even in groups he considered thoroughly heterodox, he believed that "there is a sufficient amount of common
grace working in most men for them to resent being suspected of evil" (van
Baalen 1960: 393).[4]

However much it may have tempered the tone of his writing, this under-standing did not prevent van Baalen from making clear the distinction between the different and impermeable boundaries of religious adherence. Christian orthodoxy, as defined by the historic creeds, was still the canon against which all other belief systems were to be measured. "What have Mormonism or Russellism to say in the face of such confessions?" he asks, referring to the Formula of Concord (1576) and the Belgic Confession of Faith (1561). "What has Mother Mary Baker Eddy to lay alongside them?" (van Baalen 1960: 384–85; cf. van Baalen 1948). In a remark often attributed to him, but which he makes clear originated elsewhere, van Baalen writes that "there is an old saying that 'the cults are the unpaid bills of the church' " (1960: 420). That is, alter-native religions flourish where the institutional church has failed, an insight not inconsistent with social scientific research into the rise of new religious movements (see, e.g., Bainbridge 1997; Braden 1949; Stark and Bainbridge 1985, 1987; Stark and Finke 2000).

While he appeared more willing than many to give credit where credit is due, whatever other good may be attributed to heterodox groups, they still stand well beyond the pale of so-called legitimate Christianity. Establishing his own articulation of *extra ecclesiam nulla salus*, van Baalen writes that "there are but two religions in the world. The one is autosoterism, that salvation is from man" (1960: 15). Consigning all other religious traditions to a generic "paganism," van Baalen asks in the introduction to the first edition of *Chaos*, "What, then, is the great difference between Christianity and paganism? There can be no doubt but that Christianity stands apart from all other 'great reli-gions' in that it teaches a God-made salvation while the others are all auto-soteric" (1938: 18). Even despite his penchant for fair treatment of heterodox traditions, for van Baalen the boundaries between religions were drawn with simple efficiency; there were only two possible religious primary groups to which humankind could belong: Christians, and everybody else.

Having identified these groups, and the problem of practical life to which he responded, two aspects of van Baalen's contribution to Christian countercult apologetics should be noted. The first is his clear articulation of the funda-mental boundary marker for authentic Christianity—the Bible, inerrant, in-fallible, and insuperable. "What is Christianity?" van Baalen asks, answering, "To this query the reply of all the evangelical groups has ever been that the inspired Scriptures are the only source of saving knowledge and the determin-ing factor of what is to be believed" (1960: 378). For example, advising those who confronted the adherents of other religions, van Baalen writes simply "that God has spoken in His Son, the infallible record of which we have in the Bible" (1960: 395). A bit further, van Baalen deployed a common evangelical argument and instructed the apologist, "You may point to the sinlessness of Jesus as an evidence of Christianity, or you may refer to His miracles and His resurrection as indisputable evidence of His divinity" (1960: 398).

Further, given the fact that many of the groups with which van Baalen dealt also quote Scripture, in good Reformed tradition he asks, "Where is the true doctrine?" (van Baalen 1960: 382). "To this second paramount question the answer is, *In the great historic creeds of the Church universal*" (van Baalen 1960: 383, emphasis in the original). The appeal to subordinate formularies such as the historic creeds is common in both the Christian countercult, as well as conservative reform and renewal movements within mainline Protestant denominations that are experiencing decline in numbers and division over denominational policies and direction (cf. Cowan forthcoming [b]). Because many of the doctrinal positions claimed by Christians are only implicit in Scripture and must be extrapolated from the convergence of a particular interpretation of the biblical witness, the desire to establish the *veritas* of one's own interpretation, and the distillation of apologetic argument in the face of challenges to that interpretation, subordinate formularies such as the creeds offer explicit (although not always unambiguous) statements of orthodox belief that function as charters for the reinforcement and maintenance of the dominant worldview. Indeed, continues van Baalen, "it is base ingratitude, not to say detestable conceit, and ingratitude not only toward men but toward God, to ignore the results of the sincere and arduous labors of godly and Spirit-filled men of past generations" (1960: 383). Over time, these charters reify belief and are, in turn, themselves reified. In Bergerian terms (Berger and Luckmann 1966), they externalize, objectivate, and internalize, exerting a control over adherents that completely submerges their constructed nature. The creeds come to control the religious lives of adherents, rather than help them articulate the beliefs that inform those religious lives. Credal subscription becomes the sine qua non of group affiliation and membership.

Having established what he understood to be the nature and content of authentic Christianity, how, then, did van Baalen define a cult? Broad-reaching, vague, and of little practicality beyond the cognitive boundaries of his evangelical Christianity, van Baalen's working definition designated as a cult " 'any religion regarded as unorthodox or even spurious' (Webster)" (1960: 389); following on this, he noted in passing that "the word 'sect' is here taken in the sense of a somewhat odd denomination" (1960: 390). In the context of knowledge production and the control of that knowledge, the questions are begged, regarded as orthodox by whom, and according to what standards odd?

Second, from the perspective of a sociology of knowledge, van Baalen's reason for his own participation in the countercult is worthy of note. An avocation for him—he remained an active clergyman in the Christian Reformed Church—why did he choose this particular response to the problem of practical life represented by what he regarded as the cults? Faced with an expanding religious economy and the continuing emergence of alternative religious possibilities, van Baalen and many who have followed him in countercult apologetics believe themselves to be in a territory under siege, a people whose very freedom to worship is at risk. As noted, there are two main directions from which this threat may come: from *within*—that is, an aberrant Christianity that challenges in some way the received claims of traditional orthodoxy; or from *without*—that is, the introduction into North America of religious traditions that lay no claim to Christian belief of any sort. Because they challenge the inevitability of the Christian worldview, both induce an ongoing state of cognitive dissonance, and both press the machinery of universe-maintenance and dissonance management into service.

For the countercult, these challenges are not simply differences of theological opinion. They are spiritual warfare, and the countercult apologist is often the lone defender on the field of battle. "Not only has the cultist repudiated the orthodox religion you represent," van Baalen writes to those "approaching adherents of the cults," "he is actually hostile to it" (1960: 389). "The cultist you are about to visit is your *opponent*" (van Baalen 1960: 391, emphasis in the original). Occasionally, van Baalen was not immune to the kind of antipathetic rhetoric seen in some of his countercult successors. While he considered Mormonism, however heterodox, "a marvelously composite faith," the accomplishments of which "cannot fail to arouse admiration" (van Baalen 1960: 197), and Swedenborgianism the product of a "genius and a scholar of the first dimension," a man with "a deep religious sense" (van Baalen 1960: 186, 187), he reserved some of his harshest criticism for "Russellites." For van Baalen, Jehovah's Witnesses are "a notable exception" to the more "conciliatory" demeanor of emergent religions in the postwar period. "They are the deadliest and fiercest enemies of the Christian religion extant today," he writes. "Their zeal is in keeping with their hatred of all the evangelical doctrines, such as the Trinity, the Deity of Christ, and the true Biblical teaching concerning atonement; and they do not hesitate to denounce all others as enemies of Jehovah's kingdom on earth, grouping and labeling them the organization of 'Satan the Devil' " (van Baalen 1960: 266).

When confronting adherents of any of these groups, van Baalen advocated a worldview nihilation similar to the negative apologetics advanced by Douglas Groothuis. "In an argument with an adherent of a different faith," he instructed readers, "you should be able to attack and refute his stand. Refute his principle, the foundation of his system" (van Baalen 1960: 395). In the case of Jehovah's Witnesses, Mormons, or Seventh-Day Adventists, for example, this meant negating the adherent's claim that their view has any a priori biblical grounding whatsoever. "Destroy the foundation, and the excrescences will disappear," van Baalen counseled (1960: 396).

For van Baalen, the problem of practical life when he began his countercult work was clear: "For some decades now," he wrote in the first edition of *The Chaos of Cults*, "Christianity has been in the unenviable position of a religion going through a major crisis and battling for its very right of existence" (van Baalen 1938: 15). Though this passage was deleted from later editions, the text he added presaged much of what others would write in years to follow. In later editions, van Baalen warned the faithful: "The true Christian will be hated of all men for their aloofness, their refusal to recognize others as equally good; they will be accused of holding back unity and progress, world-peace, and similar desirable goods. Probably it will all end in renewed persecution" (1960: 14).[5]

Whether van Baalen's prediction of a renewed persecution based on evangelical Christianity's unwillingness to accept an expanding religious economy comes true or not remains to be seen. What is not in doubt is the surfeit of Christian countercult material that has followed in van Baalen's wake, and the belief among modern countercult apologists that the rise of new religious movements, the continued introduction of established world religions into the North American context, and the conversion of former Christians to these faiths constitute something on the order of a clear and present danger.

"KINGDOM COME": WALTER RALSTON MARTIN AND *THE KINGDOM OF THE CULTS*

According to the brief biographical note in the 1997 edition of Walter Ralston Martin's magnum opus, *The Kingdom of the Cults* (Martin 1965, 1977, 1985, 1997; hereafter *Kingdom*), Martin (1928–89) "was fondly and respectfully known as the 'father of Christian cult apologetics' " (1997: 7). Indeed, of all the postwar countercult apologists, Martin was arguably the most influential and, in many regards, the most controversial. "More than anyone else," write Hexham and Poewe, "Walter R. Martin shaped modern attitudes to contemporary religions" (1997: 3). At Martin's memorial service, some of the most prominent evangelicals in North America either gathered or sent messages of tribute, including Ted Engstrom, President Emeritus of World Vision, James Dobson, President of Focus on the Family, and Bill Bright, founder of Campus Crusade for Christ. Norman Geisler, apologist and former professor of systematic theology at Dallas Theological Seminary, says that Martin's "insightful mind, his forceful logic, and his dedication to orthodox Christianity were seldom, if ever, equaled in the field of contemporary cults." Gordon Lewis, founder of the Evangelical Ministries to New Religions and senior professor of Christian philosophy and theology at Denver Seminary, declares that "Walter Martin awakened the sleeping giant of the church to the deadly dangers of deceptive doctrines. He understood the cultic mentality, highlighted reasons for the cults' magnetic appeals, and challenged the church to consider neglected doctrine." Fellow apologist Ronald Enroth remembered the encouragement Martin offered others in countercult ministries, concluding, "He represented for all of us an exemplary model of scholarship, fairness, and biblically-based analysis."[6]

Martin's approach to cults and emergent religions, however, differed markedly from that of van Baalen, as did his preparation for the task at hand. Whereas van Baalen received his ordination in the Christian Reformed Church and his advanced theological education at Princeton Theological Seminary, Martin's ordination and education are matters of ongoing debate. His critics claim that his credentials are ambiguous at best, fraudulent at worst; his defenders, family members who continue his work and former colleagues from the Christian Research Institute, continue to contend for their authenticity.

The dust jacket of the fourth edition of *Kingdom*, which was listed by *Newsweek* in 1985 as one of the ten best-selling spiritual books in America (Lyons 1985), claims that "Dr. Walter Martin held four earned degrees, having received his doctorate from California Coast University in the field of Comparative Religions." The dust jacket of the 1985 edition adds that Martin "received his education at Stonybrook School, Adelphi University, Biblical Seminary, New York University, and California Western University."[7] However, Robert and Rosemary Brown, two Arizona Latter-day Saints who have dedicated significant effort to exposing various levels of fraud associated with anti-Mormon polemics,[8] devote a substantial portion of the third volume of *They Lie in Wait to Deceive: A Study in Anti-Mormon Deception* to the veracity of Martin's academic and professional claims (Brown and Brown 1986: 2–65).

"Investigating Walter Martin has been fun," they write. "Most investigations, I would assume, require a lot of work before substantial evidence is accumulated. What makes investigating Walter Martin so interesting is that everywhere you turn you hit pay dirt!" (Brown and Brown 1986: 64). For example, Martin declares on the flyleaf of *The Maze of Mormonism* that he was a direct descendant on his mother's side from Brigham Young (Martin 1978: 3), and that this fact had been confirmed for him by a Mormon genealogist. Robert Brown confronted Martin on a radio talk show with evidence that indicated such descent was an "impossibility" (Brown and Brown 1984: 82). When challenged by Martin to make a statement to that effect that might be tested legally, Brown declined to do so on the air. In their book, however, the Browns remain unequivocal: "We will make a definite statement here that WALTER RALSTON MARTIN IS NOT A DESCENDANT OF BRIGHAM YOUNG. Any attempt to use his name in connection with Brigham Young is an attempt to deceive you—an attempt to impress you with credentials he does **not** have" (Brown and Brown 1984: 84; emphases in the original).

Working from original sources—official broadcast transcripts, communications with denominational and institutional officials, and court records, most of which are reproduced in their books—the Browns have amassed an array of documentation to support their assertions that Martin "falsely claimed degrees from schools he attended only briefly" (Brown and Brown 1986: 64), and that he "received a questionable Ph.D. degree in 1976," although he had been referring to himself as "Doctor" for at least ten years prior to that (Brown and Brown 1986: 65).

Arguments surrounding the legitimacy of Martin's credentials have long figured in the lore of the Christian Research Institute (CRI), the countercult think tank he founded on October 1, 1960, and which has gone on to become arguably the largest organization of its kind in the world. In 1993, four years after Martin's death and in response to ongoing challenges that threatened the essential credibility of the organization, CRI published "Does Dr. Walter Martin Have a Genuine Earned Doctor's Degree?" (Christian Research Institute 1993). The CRI reply rehearses the Browns' claims and disputes neither where Martin got his degrees, nor the fact that California Coast University is a distance-education institution offering no resident programming. It does dispute, however, the significance of these facts. While many, like the Browns, have claimed that Martin received his Ph.D. through a mail-order degree mill, for the CRI this is not important. "Yes, Walter Martin's doctoral degree is legitimate," reads the reply, "and, no, it really does not matter. Down through the centuries God has used both the great and the simple to bring the gospel message" (Christian Research Institute 1993). The Browns, on the other hand, contend that through Martin's continual reference to himself as "Doctor," and the implicit cachet attached to a doctoral degree, it really *does* matter. In their view, a " 'mail order degree' " from a "correspondence school" that "advertises that 'No Classroom Attendance Is Required' " (Brown and Brown 1986: 41) ought not be either confused or equated with a degree from a more traditional institution (see chapter 12).[9]

Questions of academic, personal, and professional integrity aside, Walter Martin remains a major figure, perhaps *the* major movement intellectual on the modern Christian countercult horizon. As historian and former Jehovah's Witness, M. James Penton, writes:

Although Martin was a person of monumental ego who gave a highly misleading picture of himself, that fact in itself says very little about the nature of his scholarship. Nor does it indicate anything about the claim that he made to speak for "orthodoxy" within the Reformed or Calvinist tradition. Yet it is important to examine these matters, for Martin has influenced great numbers of persons who have come out of cultic and sectarian movements. (Penton n.d.: 1)[10]

In *The Rise of the Cults* (1955), Martin defined the problem of new and emergent religions thus: *"By cultism we mean the adherence to doctrines which are pointedly contradictory to orthodox Christianity and* which yet claim the distinction of either tracing their origin to orthodox sources or of being in essential harmony with those sources. Cultism, in short, is any major deviation from orthodox Christianity relative to the cardinal doctrines of the Christian faith" (1955: 12, emphasis in the original). In the 1980 edition of this book, to "cardinal doctrines on the Christian faith" Martin appended, "particularly the fact that God became man in Jesus Christ" (1980: 12). As noted in chapter 2, this theologically oriented definition is not entirely clear. Was Martin referring to *deviance by Christians* from what he considered orthodox Christianity, as his first sentence appears to indicate, or a *theological variance from Christianity by anyone*, no matter what the variant's position, as his second sentence at least implied? His list of groups considered in the various editions of *Kingdom* suggests the latter, for among these are Spiritism ("the Cult of Antiquity"); Zen Buddhism ("the second oldest of all the cult systems considered in this book"); Baha'i ("A non-Christian cult of distinctly foreign

origin"); "The Black Muslim Cult" (in which "one can see emerging the outlines of what is most certainly a black Ku Klux Klan"); Scientology; "Eastern
Religions" (including Rajneeshism, the International Society for Krishna Consciousness (ISKCON), and Transcendental Meditation); and Islam, which Martin admits "is not a cult, but a major world religion," but which he included
in later editions of the book because "the West has experienced an unanticipated
invasion—Islam" (1985: 364).

These ambiguities notwithstanding, Martin began *Kingdom* with a definition
of "cult" that is essentially sociological in nature. Starting from a definition
used by Northwestern scholar Charles Braden in *These Also Believe: A Study
of Modern American Cults and Minority Religious Movements* (1949), Martin
writes: " 'By the term 'cult' I mean nothing derogatory to any group so classified. A cult, as I define it, is any religious group which differs significantly
in some one or more respects as to belief or practice from those religious groups
which are regarded as the normative expressions of religion in our total culture'" (Braden, quoted in Martin 1965: 11; cf. Braden 1949: xii). Braden, "a
lifelong Methodist," "an ordained clergyman," "a university teacher in the
History of Religions for many years," and "an unrepentant liberal" (1949: xi),
sought to give his understanding of cults the greatest latitude available in the
analysis of those religious systems that differ from the dominant.[11]

Martin, however, failed to include Braden's complete definition. That is, Braden did not leave off where Martin finished. "If any reader who belongs to a
group discussed here," Braden actually continues, "prefers to think of himself
as a member of a minority religious group rather than a cult, there can be no
objection" (1949: xii). Indeed, no matter what their affiliation—and Braden
included in his encomium Unity, Christian Science, Theosophy, Jehovah's Witnesses, British Israelism, and Mormonism, all of which Martin condemned with
varying degrees of opprobrium—Braden (like Atkins [1923] and, to a lesser
degree, Clark [1949] before him) believed that "in general the cults represent
the earnest attempt of millions of people to find the fulfillment of deep and
legitimate needs of the human spirit, which most of them seem not to have
found in the established churches" (1949: xi). They are, in fact, some of the
very "unpaid bills of the church" to which van Baalen referred.

Despite his albeit truncated use of Braden's definition, Martin operated from
a very different understanding of popular religious phenomena than did the
Northwestern religious scholar. "I may add to this," Martin wrote in 1965,
"that a cult might also be defined as a group of people gathered about a specific
person or person's interpretation of the Bible" (1965: 11). Two of *Kingdom's*
subsequent editions (1985, 1997) emend this to read "misinterpretations of the
Bible." Indeed, it was this conceptualization that set the tone for his entire
body of work, and the bulk of Christian countercult apologetics. For Martin,
anything that differed from his interpretation of Scripture was, ipso facto, suspect—at the very least heterodox and at most heretical. As with van Baalen,
Martin's preeminent boundary marker was the primacy of Christian Scripture

as inerrant, infallible, and insuperable. Even though his ordination in the General Association of Regular Baptists was revoked in 1953, and his claims to ordination in both the American Baptist Convention and the Southern Baptist Convention are, at the very least, suspect (Brown and Brown 1986: 9–27), he continues to declare in each edition of *Kingdom* that "I am a Baptist minister, an evangelical holding to the inerrancy of Scripture" (e.g., Martin 1997: 18).

Until his death in 1989, Martin worked tirelessly to further the cause of countercult apologetics, continuing to manage affairs at the Christian Research Institute and to act as host of its flagship radio program, *The Bible Answer Man*. In addition to numerous articles in the *Christian Research Journal* and *Christian Research Newsletter*, Martin published popular works on Jehovah's Witnesses (Martin and Klann 1974), the Latter-day Saints (Martin 1978), and new religious movements in North America (Martin and Passantino 1980). *Kingdom* remains his most enduring work, however. Not infrequently referred to as a textbook by those in the field, it has been issued in revised edition on an average once every decade since its initial publication in 1965. A fifth edition, unaffiliated with the Christian Research Institute, is scheduled for publication in 2004.

Beginning his analysis in *Kingdom* with "the psychological structure of cultism," Martin described the cognitive factors that he believed were common among cults. Indeed, presaging the reductivism that often characterizes aspects of the modern countercult apologetic, Martin declares that "the cultic psychological patterns evidenced in manic proportions at Jonestown are present to some degree in each and every cult" (1985: 27). Of these patterns, he identified three as primary. First, "belief systems of the cults are characterized by closedmindedness" (Martin 1985: 26). Second, since they confuse their "dislike of the Christian message with the messenger," cultic adherents are personally antagonistic toward Christians. And, third, "all cultic belief systems manifest a type of institutional dogmatism and a pronounced intolerance for any position but their own" (Martin 1985: 27). Martin offered no evidence for any of these sweeping generalizations.

However, since each manifests a particular aspect of intolerance, Martin offered a cogent sociological insight into the nature of intractable belief. "The problem of intolerance," he writes (1985: 28), "is closely linked to institutional dogmatism or authoritarianism, and those systems which embody this line of reasoning are resistant to change and penetration since the cults thrive on conformity, ambiguity and extremeness of belief." While a plausible description of many new and emergent religious movements, Martin (and virtually all countercult apologists since) ignored the application of his own analysis to the evangelical countercult itself. Consider the third of his three so-called common factors, that is, "almost without exception, all cultic belief systems manifest a type of institutional dogmatism and a pronounced intolerance for any position but their own." While the Christian countercult operates across a variety of continua (many of which are discussed in the following chapters), their adherence to the fundamental principles of countercult cosmology demonstrates Martin's third factor quite well. In fact, his statement could easily be rewritten, "almost without exception, Christian countercult apologists manifest a type of institutional dogmatism and a pronounced intolerance for any position but their own."

Dave Hunt, for example, responding to a question about the uniqueness and exclusivity of the Bible in the context of other scriptures, and in a statement worth repeating for the manner in which it epitomizes much of the Christian countercult agenda, writes: "The only reason for becoming familiar with other religions and other religious writings would be in order to show those who follow these false systems wherein the error lies and thereby to rescue them" (1996: 68; cf. Barker 1998a, 1998b, 1998c). Douglas Groothuis uses similar language in his consideration of the New Age, arguing that "despite whatever good intentions New Agers may have, it is Satan, the spiritual counterfeiter himself, who ultimately inspires all false religion" (1988: 38). In the introduction to *Cult Watch* (a book dedicated to "our good friend, Walter R. Martin"), television evangelist John Ankerberg and his co-author, former CRI researcher John Weldon, identify the need for "an absolute standard by which to judge other beliefs, practices, and actions" (1991a: ix). They continue:

That standard is God Himself, and it may be known through His revealed word, the Bible. The Bible alone provides the infallible standard by which ideas and practices can be judged. Because Christianity alone is based on God's Word [which excludes, of course, any other scripture from that domain], it stands unique among all the world's religions and philosophies. And if Christianity is true to Scripture, it can speak authoritatively to any situation because it offers God's mind on the subject. Indeed, the only reason the Bible has absolute authority is because the Bible really *is* God's revelation to man. (Ankerberg and Weldon 1991a: ix)

Similar examples are easily multiplied across the continua of the countercult.

KEEPING UP WITH THE "CULTS"

Though his prose is of a considerably different tenor than either Martin's or van Baalen's, and though he referred in this passage only to Latter-day Saints, George Hamilton Combs also epitomized the countercult agenda: "If this power shall pit itself further against our institutions," he writes, "let it be crushed into powder. Let Christian sentinels be ever alert, and, at slightest hint of Mormon encroachment sound the tocsin of war" (Combs 1899: 222).

In the century since Combs lamented the rise of Mormonism, the religious economy of North America has only expanded. Christian Science may have posted a steady decline since the 1950s, but the Latter-day Saints and Jehovah's Witnesses continue to grow. So-called aberrant Christianities—the apocalyptic beliefs and the apocalyptic end of the Branch Davidians at Waco, sexual scandals within the Children of God (now The Family), the transformation of the Holy

Order of MANS from a "Rosicrucian-style monastic community" to "a traditionalist Eastern Orthodox sect" (Lucas 1995: 141), and the rise of the Boston
Church of Christ amid renewed cries of "brainwashing"—continue to appear,
each bringing its own particular challenge to the dominance of the "established" Christian worldview. Eastern traditions, once considered the province
of the beat and the offbeat (see Cowan 1996), have entered the mainstream of
religious life. From George Harrison chanting the Hare Krishna mantra to
Richard Gere shepherding the fourteenth Dalai Lama around New York City,
Hinduism and Buddhism have advanced in the religious marketplace through
both conversion and immigration.

And then there are the New Age and Neopaganism. With interest increasing
in everything from Ásatru to est, from Faerie Wicca to the Church of Scientology, and from the Tarot to the Qabalah, the Christian worldview represented
by such individuals as Van Baalen, Martin, and contributors to *The Fundamentals* required more and more reinforcement. It became painfully clear that
"the chaos of the cults" was not going to disappear anytime soon; in fact, it
promised to get even more chaotic. Before proceeding to the parallel processes
of professionalization and democratization that have marked the countercult
in recent years, I would like to consider the end of the countercult spectrum
opposite that occupied by van Baalen and Martin—the fringe for whom the
"tocsin of war" is a daily call to battle.

6

Demon Siege: The Countercult on the Fringe

Before being "gloriously saved in 1984," and beginning a countercult ministry to those in the occult, Bill Schnoebelen claims to have been a Wiccan High Priest, a Satanist High Priest, a Master Mason, an Old Order Catholic priest, a Temple Mormon, and teacher of witchcraft, Qabalah, and ceremonial magick with over sixteen years experience (www.withoneaccord.org). In *The Beautiful Side of Evil*, Johanna Michaelson, a popular evangelical writer and speaker, declares that "we are raising a generation of children to be psychics, shamans, mediums, and occultists. . . . These children, soon to be adults, will at the right time 'intuitively' grasp the importance of taking the final Luciferic Initiation in order to enter the 'New Age' " (1989: 15). In *Alien Encounters*, Chuck Missler, an end-times conspiracist, radio host, and publisher from Couer d'Alene, Idaho, concludes that "Satan and his cohorts" have been "creating alien ships and masquerading as extraterrestrials" in order to bring into being the "global ecumenical religious belief system" required by the Antichrist (Missler and Eastman 1997: 302). Countercult journalist William Alnor concurs. Though he admits he is "no fan of reckless speculations and guessing games over specific end-times events and personalities" (1992: 55), Alnor wonders whether the entertainment industry—from movies such as *Close Encounters of the Third Kind, ET,* and *Starman* to science fiction novels such as Arthur C. Clarke's acclaimed *Childhood's End*—has been intentionally preparing society for an alien landing.

Examples such as these inform the domain of countercult conspiracism that seems the most remote from reality, and in which the ability to integrate apparently unrelated events into a grand cosmological narrative the most pronounced. At this end of the spectrum, little or no concern exists for the refinements of interreligious dialogue; the subtleties of whether or not one ought to be in dialogue with nonfundamentalist Christians simply do not exist. Here the battle lines between the divine and the demonic are drawn with no ambiguity, and the fantastic, often hyperbolic claims of apologists compete for the attention of their respective audiences.

TALKING BACK WITH BOB LARSON

For people who receive them throughout the year, fundraising appeals from Bob Larson (b. 1944), a fundamentalist Christian radio talk-show host, traveling lecturer, and freelance exorcist, arrive on an average about every three weeks. Each letter is theme oriented and contains a number of common elements—an emotional opening, a careful recitation of Larson's efforts to free those held in bondage to whatever current crisis looms on the spiritual horizon, and an appeal for funds. Lest a too-quick browse of the letter miss them, all the key points Larson wants to make are carefully underlined, highlighted, or italicized—occasionally all three. Warnings about the Satanic plot to take over the world crowd together with brief anecdotes detailing real-life exorcisms (often with testimonial snippets about how difficult the exorcism was on Larson both personally and professionally); instructions on books that *must* be read, videos that *must* be seen, audio tapes that must be *heard* to be believed are followed closely by ordering instructions and the appropriate gift of money that would enable Larson to send them.

"For a gift of $50 to back and bless our ministry," begins one typical appeal (all emphases in the original), "I'll send you THE SATANIC TAKEOVER video, plus my latest Spiritual Warfare Training Tape entitled, 'Evolution and the Dinosaurs.' This cassette reveals that dinosaurs didn't die off—they're still alive today! Furthermore, dinosaurs were on the ark with Noah! No one can hear this cassette and believe in evolution." In another offering, Larson invites his listeners to commit $20.00 per month and join his "S.W.A.T. (Spiritual Warfare Action Training) team. S.W.A.T. members receive a monthly tape from me talking about important spiritual warfare issues." While closing salutations vary for these appeals, each is similar in tone. "Yours for the hurting," says one; "Yours in the fight against evil," reads another; "Yours in the victory over Satan," closes a third.

Raised in Nebraska and converted to evangelical Christianity at the age of nineteen, within a few years of his conversion Bob Larson was busy writing books on the "Hindu heresy" of the hippie subculture (Larson 1969), allegedly lecturing across North America on the evils of rock-and-roll music, and leading evangelistic crusades. According to the publishers of his third book, *Hippies, Hindus and Rock and Roll*, at that time Larson was "one of the most promising young writers of religious literature" (1969: 4). Beyond a reference to "McCook, Nebraska," though, no actual publisher is listed in the book itself. There is, however, an identical address for Bob Larson himself in the small town of McCook (1999 population: 7,800), from which readers could order a variety of materials ranging from long-play records *(The Humorous Gospel*

Songs of Bob Larson) to five-inch reel-to-reel tapes *(Bob Larson Speaks Out on Rock Music)* (Larson 1969: 92).

From the beginning of his ministry, the boundaries of acceptable Christianity have been as clearly defined for Larson as for any countercult apologist. His evaluations of new religious movements are just as unequivocal. However, as noted earlier, whereas other apologists often attempt to temper their working definitions of the term "cult," Larson is unambiguous. Each entry in *Larson's New Book of Cults*, for example, considers religious groups from a number of different perspectives: the founder(s), major symbology, the organization's purpose (as Larson perceives it), and the errors, inevitably, to which it succumbs. "In brief," he writes of Buddhism, "the goal is maximum well-being with a minimum of active effort" (1989a: 82). In another perhaps unconscious reflection of the countercult cosmology to which he himself adheres, Larson declares that in the view of Islam, "all other religions are seen as satanic expressions of polytheism" (1989a: 96). And, "from Satan's standpoint," he concludes, "UFOs may be preparing the modern mind to accept a casual familiarity with supernatural phenomena" (Larson 1989a: 436).

Under "Errors" Larson lists the main reasons particular religious groups, movements, or phenomena ought to be regarded as heretical or blasphemous. Considering Hinduism, for example, Larson writes: "The polytheistic and idolatrous practices are pagan forms of worship that constitute collusion with demonic forces" (1989a: 70). Buddhism fares little better; it is made up of "idolatrous sects that advocate demonic ceremonialism and the propitiation of spirits constitutes a form of witchcraft that is scripturally forbidden (Deut. 18)" (Larson 1989a: 82). Similar to Alnor, Hunt, Missler, Rhodes, Wimbish, and other countercult writers, his main critique of postwar interest in UFOs is that the "Bible does not give the slightest hint that extraterrestrials exist. . . . Secular UFO interest fails to consider the possibility that such phenomena may be supernatural (demonic) in nature" (Larson 1989a: 436; cf. Alnor 1992, 1998; Larson 1997; Missler and Eastman 1997; Rhodes 1998; Wimbish 1990).[1] On the other hand, the Bible also says very little about laptop computers, CD-ROMs, electric guitars, and radio broadcasting, but that has not prevented Larson and his colleagues from both using and profiting from them. As well, the possibility that these phenomena *are* of extraterrestrial origin is simply precluded.

Covering groups, movements, and phenomena ranging from the Ku Klux Klan to martial arts, and from Appalachian snake handlers to Scientology, *Larson's New Book of Cults*, one of twenty-five books he claims to have written, is an encyclopedic if uneven attempt to categorize and, more importantly, homogenize the problem of alternative religious worldviews. His main interest in the last several years, however—Satanism and the phenomenon of demon possession—has produced three books: *Satanism: The Seduction of America's Youth* (1989b), *In the Name of Satan*, which is subtitled *How the Forces of Evil Work and What You Can Do to Defeat Them* (1996), and *Larson's Book*

of Spiritual Warfare (1999). If the information in his fundraising letters is at
all credible, then Larson spends a vast amount of his time in this form of
deliverance ministry. And it is for this interest that I find him most intriguing
as an apologist and as a movement intellectual who contributes to the cognitive
praxis—and the public persona—of the Christian countercult.

In the past decade, demonic encounters have become Larson's professional
stock-in-trade. He claims that his first encounter with a demon, though, occurred in 1967 during "a Hindu ceremony of Thaipusam" in Singapore—a
story that he has recounted in at least three places, and one that has been
modified slightly in the telling (cf. Larson 1969: 71–79, 1996: 3–9, 1999: 11–
16). In the 1969 version, because "it was so horrible that a verbal description
would not suffice to describe it," Larson arranged to stay in Singapore to witness the festival and drove to the temple grounds with "several missionaries"
(1969: 71). In the later version, an exaggerated air of mystery surrounds Larson's search for the Thaipusam festival. This is heightened by his assertion
that "this ritual of self-mutilation" (Larson 1996: 3) can be found in only two
places: Kuala Lumpur and Singapore. "Even in Hindu-dominated India," he
continues, "this rigorous ceremony of piercing and lacerating one's body is
outlawed" (Larson 1996: 3). In the decades between the two versions, the missionaries with whom Larson rode have disappeared. By 1996, no one seemed
willing to talk to Larson about the mysterious ritual. "After going through the
normal tourist channels and finding no one who would talk about Thaipusam—
much less tell me in which temple it would take place—I met a missionary
who had witnessed this ceremony several years before. With his directions in
hand, and the help of a curious taxi driver, I finally found the temple" (Larson
1996: 4). Given that Thaipusam is a national holiday in Malaysia, and attended
by hundreds of thousands of Singapore's Hindu population, Larson's somewhat
cloak-and-dagger description seems just a bit disingenuous.

In the original version, before leaving Nebraska Larson had apparently
"scheduled a city-wide crusade in the beautiful Conference Hall in Singapore"
(1969: 71) and then delayed leaving the city until he had seen Thaipusam. In
neither of the later versions of the story, however, is this crusade mentioned.
Among North American evangelicals in the late 1960s the word "crusade"
stirred up images of Billy Graham filling the University of Tennessee's Neyland
Stadium, Little Rock's War Memorial Stadium, and New York's Madison
Square Garden. While talk of a citywide crusade would almost certainly evoke
similar images in Larson's readers, why does the reference disappear so completely in later revisions of the story?

One possibility the Singapore crusade is not mentioned in revised versions
is that Larson simply invented it for inclusion in *Hippies, Hindus, and Rock
and Roll* in order to increase the profile of his nascent ministry. Or, it could be
that he did indeed *schedule* such a citywide crusade, though one to which few
if any participants actually came. Finally, if while in Singapore he did witness
to people as he traveled around the city—talking to them on street corners,

passing out tracts, maybe singing a humorous gospel song or two—this could have become in his construction of reality a citywide crusade. Indeed, if the crusade was not simply invented for the book, this last seems the most plausible explanation.

Tracing Larson's different redactions of this event illustrates an important aspect of the countercult's cognitive praxis. In an effort to accord their ministries more importance than might otherwise be the case, many countercult apologists regularly exaggerate both anecdotal atrocities and anecdotal miracles associated with their efforts. In Ed Decker's case, for example, a poorly cooked meal in another country was represented to Saints Alive in Jesus supporters as a conspiracy on the part the Masonic Lodge to rid the world of its greatest challenger by poisoning his food; that Decker did not actually succumb is evidence of the divine blessing his mission and ministry enjoys. Larson's funding appeals often contain similar examples. "The task I face looks daunting," he wrote in September 1998. "Every time I get behind the radio microphone or stand in front of the television camera, I confront the forces of Hell."

A few months earlier, in a fundraising letter headlined "Let Me Help You Demon-Proof Your Life!" Larson told his supporters that "I feel your pain. Whatever you are going through right now I understand" (1998: 1). In support of this, he listed a veritable catalogue of tragedy: his mother, aunt, grandmother-in-law, and "closest spiritual advisor" all died within a few weeks of each other; during that same period his second child was born, his three-year-old nephew and three-month-old niece "were murdered," and he suffered "a severe accident that could have taken my life!" (Larson 1998b: 1, emphasis in the original).

I impaled my right thigh on an 18-inch iron spike. The spike entered just above my knee, hit the femur bone, and traveled eight inches up my leg. I spent four hours in the emergency ward getting stitches and X-rays. The doctor was amazed I didn't break my leg, or put the spike through my stomach and kill myself. He warned me that I'd be on crutches for three weeks and might not ever walk normally. In spite of these dire predictions, God miraculously healed my leg. I walked on crutches only two days. Three days after the accident I swam. Two weeks after the injury I was jogging again. Within three weeks I was running six miles a day! When my regular family doctor first saw my leg 10 days after the injury, he exclaimed, "This is a miracle. Your leg isn't even bruised. I've never seen an injury like this heal so quickly!"

That Larson suffered some kind of accident is not the issue. He very likely did. What is of interest here is the hyperbolic, somewhat inconsistent description of the injury and the anecdotal miracle Larson attaches to it. From all this trauma—including, if true, his callous use of the tragic deaths of the two young children—Larson concludes that "my entire life has been a training exercise in understanding the supernatural dimension of things that happen in our lives" 1998b: 2, emphasis in the original). If, on the other hand, his account of the deaths of these children is not accurate, or he has embellished them to serve his own ends, that highlights the often egregious nature of his funding appeals. His solution to "the adverse circumstances we all face," though, is worth quoting at length.

To help you get through your personal pain, I've put together what I call a DEMON-PROOFING PROTECTION PACKAGE! It includes the following:

- SONGS OF SPIRITUAL WARFARE: A 10-tune cassette featuring the praise and worship songs I have found most effective to defeat demons.

- DEVIL-PROOFING PRAYERS: A video that teaches you specific prayers to pray to keep you and your family free from Satan's attacks.

- S.W.A.T. TAPES: Six tapes with six hours of the most intense teaching on demons and deliverance you'll ever find anywhere.

- EXORCISM IN ACTION: My latest, never-before-released video, of the most incredible moments of spiritual warfare during recent rallies. You'll see what thousands have seen live, in-person as I've traveled from city to city across America, doing public exorcisms!

If you were to order this DEMON-PROOFING PROTECTION PACKAGE from our resource list the total price would be $150.00!

It is spiritually critical for you to have this information before Satan attacks your life. So, I'm making it available one-time only for a tax-deductible gift of just $100 or more! (Larson 1998b: 3)

In subsequent funding appeals, neither the deaths of these people (including the children) nor Larson's injury and miraculous healing appear again.

Following his trip to Asia in 1967, Larson encountered his first demon "on American soil" in 1971 in St. Louis (1996: 11–22, 1999: 17–29). "Since then," he points out, "I have been involved with hundreds of exorcisms. Some have lasted no more than a few minutes, while others have gone on for hours, weeks, months, and even years" (Larson 1996: 21). In terms of his construction of reality, Larson inhabits the world of spiritual warfare about which fellow evangelical Frank Peretti writes in his popular novels (Peretti 1986, 1989, 1995; cf. Lewis 1996b). A Manichaean world in which the literal presence and malevolent influence of demons are far more common in human affairs than not, participation in the ongoing spiritual battle between the realms of light and dark is the paramount task, and one in which Larson often casts himself as the lone warrior standing in the breach between good and evil. "I've seen more demonic supernaturalism than any living human I've known," he writes in *In the Name of Satan* (Larson 1996: 150).

Similarly, at a 1998 seminar, Larson told the audience that he is "probably the worldwide expert on the occult. No one knows more about spiritualism and demon possession than I do" (Larson 1998a). "World's Most Recognized Authority on the Supernatural and Spiritual Success," read part of the newspaper advertisement for the seminar. Headlined "FIRST EVER LIVE PUBLIC EXORCISM IN CANADA," the ad promised that seminar attendees would learn how to "Determine if you or someone else has a demon; Remove ancestral curses from your family; Confront someone who has a demon; Free yourself from tormenting evil spirits; Overcome thoughts of depression and suicide; Release your children from demons of rebellion; Turn your fear of the unknown into personal power" (Larson 1998a). Despite Larson's efforts, however, no exorcism took place. In response to his exhortations, a small number of people repented of various sins and turned their lives over to Jesus. However, when faced by a young woman who came to the seminar dressed in goth attire, he confessed that he could not cast out of her the "demon of teen rebellion." After confronting her in a most belligerent manner,[2] Larson announced after just a few minutes, "I'm prevented from doing anything about the demon inside her. She has bipolar disorder, and that would have to be dealt with first" (1998a). Presumably, suspicious diagnoses such as this are the reason Larson's publisher, Baker Books, has felt the need to include a disclaimer at the beginning of each of his books on spiritual warfare, pointing out that they are "not intended to replace proper medical consultation or appropriate psychological therapy. Readers are encouraged to consult physicians and professional counselors prior to drawing any conclusions about the demonic diagnosis or physical, mental, or emotional ills" (Larson 1996: ii; 1999: iv).

Like Walter Martin before him, and Hank Hanegraaff now, Larson is not without his detractors both within the countercult and without, and his ministry has come under scrutiny in recent years for allegations ranging from taped shows broadcast as though they were live (in order to keep donations flowing), financial misrepresentation and nondisclosure, and the claims of a former Bob Larson Ministries vice president that it was she, not Larson, who wrote the majority of the novel *Dead Air* (1991), a work for which Larson claims sole authorship (Trott 1993; cf. Parks 2002).

While Lori Boespflug joined Bob Larson Ministries first as a secretary, according to an investigative report in *Cornerstone Magazine*, she rose to the position of vice president in less than a year (Trott 1993).[3] In addition to writing many of the fundraising advertisements that Bob Larson Ministries mails out regularly, Boespflug maintains that it was she, not Larson, who authored most of *Dead Air*. A year after it was published, she was also contracted by Larson to write *Dead Air*'s sequel, *Abaddon* (Larson 1993). In support of her claims, Boespflug provided *Cornerstone* a copy of her agreement with Larson, dated 7 April 1992:

You hereby agree to provide me on or before May 1, 1992 an outline of the first two hundred (200) pages of the sequel; and on or before July 1, 1992, an outline of the remaining two hundred (200) pages of the sequel. If so requested by me, said outlines shall contain or be accompanied by character sketches, narratives, fact research and sample dialogue, all collectively referred to herein as ("the creative material"). Also, if so requested, you shall assist me in any and all editing of the sequel that may be necessary before its final acceptance by the publisher. (Larson, quoted in Trott 1993)

Boespflug told *Cornerstone* that she had completed the first hundred pages of *Abaddon* when she was fired by Larson in June 1992 (Trott 1993).

A comparative reading of both *Dead Air* and *Abaddon* suggests that Boespflug's claims are not without foundation. Both novels deal with a radio talk show host and his investigation of Satanic ritual abuse. And, while there are obvious similarities between them, there are also significant differences in characterization, plot development, dialogue and scene construction, as well as the overall flow of the prose. In fact, they read less as novels by the same author, than as two novels in the shared world format of popular science fiction (e.g., *Dr. Who, Star Wars, Star Trek*), a subgenre in which different authors utilize established characters, milieu, and thematic vectors to continue a shared general narrative.

At the end of *Dead Air*, Larson includes what appears to be a standard disclaimer, but is not. "The incidents in this story are based on actual experiences," he writes. "Names of people and places have been changed and details of the accounts of their experiences have been altered in order to protect the privacy of the people involved" (Larson 1991: 350). Boespflug denies this as well, alleging that "Larson allowed her to make up the story but inserted chunks of his radio callers' stories into the mix. She notes that no evidence existed to back up the stories Larson inserted into the text" (Trott 1993).

While the purchase of ghost writing on Larson's part is arguable in Boespflug's case, plagiarism is certain in his discussion of a UFO group headquartered in Québec, Canada. In *UFOs and the Alien Agenda*, several passages on the Raëlian UFO movement have been taken all but verbatim from Canadian scholar Susan Jean Palmer's 1995 essay, "Women in the Raëlian Movement: New Religious Experiments in Gender and Authority." While Larson cites other essays from the collection in which Palmer's essay appears—indicating that he is familiar with the volume—none of the references are to Palmer, and her material accounts for roughly one-third of Larson's chapter.

Potential problems notwithstanding, and despite the criticism of some of his countercult peers, for twenty years Larson's radio program, *Talk Back with Bob Larson*, has continued daily in hundreds of markets across North America[4]; his books continue to be published by such established evangelical houses as Baker Books and Thomas Nelson and stocked in most Christian bookstores (occasionally even showing up in mainstream booksellers such as Barnes and Noble, and Borders); thousands of people continue to attend his "Spiritual Freedom" rallies; and he continues as a significant movement intellectual. Spiritual warfare is a hot topic on the evangelical landscape, and Larson remains in the thick of the fray. How seriously Larson is taken by his audience is a research topic for another time, but the fact that commercial media continue to publish and promote his work indicates without question a profitable market for his particular brand of pop demonism and deliverance. The same cannot be said for one of his conspiracist confrères, Texe Marrs.

THE BIBLE AND BLACK HELICOPTERS: TEXE AND WANDA MARRS

Hecate's Loom describes itself as "Canada's International Pagan Magazine." An eclectic collection of poetry, articles, personal journey narratives, artwork, and book reviews for the Neopagan community, it is published quarterly according to the major seasons of the Neopagan year. In 1995, one of its contributors, a Wiccan solitary living on Vancouver Island, reviewed *New Age Cults and Religions*, by countercult apologist and conspiracist Texe Marrs (cf. also Abanes 1996: 205–207). "I picked up the book out of curiosity," writes Linda Doerksen, "to perhaps find out about other religious systems, and in doing so received the shock of my life" (1995: 37). Following a brief and not inaccurate description of Marrs's book, Doerksen reacted. "I felt as if all my panic buttons had been punched. I no longer want to be out of the broom closet, with the risk of meeting someone like the author of this book. Fear, anger, and anger at being afraid have invaded my life in a way I have never experienced" (Doerksen 1995: 38).

For, if apologists such as Frank Beckwith, John Morehead, Carl Mosser, and Paul Owen represent the rational and academic countercult treatment of new religious phenomena (see chapters 7 and 12), Marrs and his wife, Wanda, occupy a very different point on the spectrum. Together, the Marrs are cofounders of Living Truth Ministries, a countercult newsletter and self-publishing business based in Austin, Texas.[5] A former U.S. Air Force officer, Marrs relies on ultra-right-wing conspiracy theories and unqualified scriptural interpretations to support his vision that we are living in the end-times feared (and implicitly welcomed) by many fundamentalist Christians. In this vision, every challenge to his fundamentalist construction of reality he regards as part of the Satanic plot to subdue the Earth and eliminate its only true guardians—Christians such as Texe and Wanda Marrs.

"Pity and have mercy on the children, and pray for their protection," he writes in *Ravaged by the New Age: Satan's Plan to Destroy Our Kids*, "because Satan—the Father of Lies and the grotesque inventor of all wickedness—has targeted the innocents for bondage, pain and destruction" (T. Marrs 1989b: 13). Sounding very much like Larson, Marrs concludes that "abundant evidence exists that the startling hidden agenda of the Evil One calls for total world domination by the year 2000" (T. Marrs 1989b: 13). Wanda Marrs concurs, writing in *New Age Lies to Women*, "I feel it imperative to emphasize once again that to become an incarnation of the Goddess—to be molded in her image—is to become *demon-possessed*. It is Satan's ultimate goal to possess every woman and every human being. It is a goal he has already achieved with millions of people, and many more are to come in these last days. Satan considers women merely as lambs for the slaughter" (W. Marrs 1989: 177, emphasis in the original).

For Marrs, the evidence of satanic conspiracy is ubiquitous. In an article representative of his newsletter (1997c: 1–2), for example, he asks, "Does the

Walt Disney corporate logo conceal three cleverly disguised '6s'—thus, 666?"
Mindful of the litigious nature often fundamental to large corporations,
though, Marrs is careful to avoid writing anything that could be construed as
libel. That is, he virtually always either frames potentially libelous allegations
as open-ended questions and possibility statements, or else places potentially
damning "evidence" in the mouths of unnamed others—"friends of the ministry" who call, write, or e-mail Marrs with their information. In the article
above, entitled "Devil Companies, Devil Products, Devil Logos," in addition to
Walt Disney he names Lucent Technologies ("formerly AT&T's Bell Labs"—
"Some say it stands for Lucifer's Enterprises"); Reebok International, which
"recently gave one of its lines of women's running shoes the telling name,
Incubus"; Honeywell, which "is reportedly pushing a pro-homosexual philosophy" and "has, for years, had a subsidiary company based in Europe named—
believe it or not—*Lucifer Manufacturing!*"; Microsoft, which is apparently
under the corporate covers with "Soviet Communist Mikhail Gorbachev"; and
Apple Computers, with its famous bite-out-of-the-apple logo. "But," asks
Marrs, "have Bill Gates and Microsoft linked up with a devilish company in
Apple?" According to Marrs (1997c: 2, emphasis in the original), when Apple
cofounders Stephen Jobs ("a weird, New Age guru-type") and Steven Wozniak
("also an advocate of Aquarian Age culture") "first marketed their earliest,
crude personal computer, they put a price tag of $666 on the product. 666!
Coincidental—or on purpose? *You* decide." (Even worse, the actual price was
supposedly $666.66.) No supporting documentation is offered for any of these
claims. Further, Marrs names, but does not directly accuse of similar New Age
conspiracy: Proctor & Gamble; America On-Line and CBS, both of which have
"a pyramid with an all-seeing eye inside it" as their logo; Intel, Saturn, Shell
Oil (whose "logo appears to be the golden shell of Aphrodite, the goddess who,
pagan legend says, rose from the sea"), and Texaco Oil (whose logo "displays
the Egyptian Tau cross in a black and red coloration") (1997c: 2).

This conspiracism is reinforced by what he considers personal attacks on his
ministry by these same forces of darkness. In January 1999, citing "an unfair,
politically-directed attack by the Internal Revenue Service" (1999: 1), which
made him feel as though he were "in Soviet Russia, in Castro's Cuba, or in
Hitler's Nazi Germany," Marrs and his wife closed down one ministry, Flashpoint, and launched a new one, Power of Prophecy. This new venture he claims
is "totally free of IRS and Big Brother government control, a ministry not tied
to the IRS's controlled 501(c)3 status" (Marrs 1999: 2; Marrs 1998a). In this
new ministry, Marrs assures his supporters that "not one word will ever be
edited out or censored by the IRS or the feds. I guarantee it" (1999: 2). For
Marrs, as for Larson, Cumbey, Hunt, and other countercult apologists at this
end of the conspiracism continuum, the problem of practical life could not be
clearer.

The New Age appears to be the instrument that Satan will use to catapult his Antichrist
to power. Once he is firmly entrenched, he will unite all cults and religions into one:

the New Age World Religion. When Christians refuse to be initiated into this Satanic religious system, they will be dealt with very harshly. Many will be put to death. The New Age is working hard today to set up an environment of hatred toward Christians and what they stand for, so the public mood will be ready when the Antichrist begins his brutal anti-Christian programs. (Marrs 1987: 262)

In his pursuit of this conspiracist agenda, including a dedicated Web site called Conspiracyworld.com that went online in 2001, First Amendment protections seem tailor-made for Marrs. Well-known evangelicals such as Jack van Impe, Hank Hanegraaff, and Chuck Colson he characterizes as "papal underlings." And, with the exception of Pope John Paul II, he regards Billy Graham, arguably the most recognizable evangelical in the world, as "the chief deceiver in the world today." Marrs's barely concealed antisemitism comes through in a tape offered by his ministry, entitled *The Esther Option*. "Is there an ongoing plot by religious Jews," he asked in a 1998 advertisement for the tape, "to use Monica Lewinsky to unseat President Bill Clinton and replace him with Vice President Al Gore?" More to the point, Marrs continues: "Do Zionist Jews hold Monica Lewinsky up and acclaim her as their new 'Queen Esther'? In fact, Orthodox Rabbis and other right-wing Jews in Israel and the U.S. are privately acclaiming Monica Lewinsky to be the 'Salvation of Israel'."

Not surprisingly, Rome is also a target. "Blatant Satan worship is now rampant within the Catholic Church," he wrote in 1997. "High-ranking churchmen are guilty of this heinous crime against God" (Marrs 1997d: 1). And not only the Catholic Church. "This wickedness is found in some of today's Methodist and Charismatic churches," Marrs continues, "and especially in Episcopal and Anglican churches" (1997d: 3). Allegedly citing Catholic critic Malachi Martin, Marrs deploys a well-known (if potentially apocryphal) remark attributed to Paul VI: "The smoke of Satan has entered the very sanctuary of St. Peter's Cathedral" (1997d: 1). While there is still some dispute in the Catholic Church about the veracity of the attribution—some link it to the traditionalist, Marian Bayside movement and their claim that a purported papal imposter had physically replaced Paul VI to disrupt the church (Cuneo 1997: 152–77)—if accurate the Pope's remark most probably refers in a generally metaphorical way to the discord that characterized the church after Vatican II and, particularly, Paul VI's 1968 promulgation of *Humanae Vitae*. According to Marrs, however, following the "smoke of Satan" remark, "the Pontiff went on to explain that he had knowledge of a midnight hour, Black Satanic Mass having been conducted at the altar of St. Peter's, on the exact spot where the Pope himself regularly says mass" (Marrs 1997d: 1). Should supporters wish to learn more about these revelations, Marrs offers an audiotape for sale, allegedly proving, among other things, "Pope John Paul II's public endorsement of voodoo, black magic, Hinduism, Talmudic Judaism, and other false religions."

In addition to numerous books linking various aspects of national and international government with a New Age conspiracy to rule the world and usher in the era of the Antichrist (cf. Marrs 1987, 1989a, 1989b, 1992), Marrs has reserved significant criticism for former First Lady Hilary Rodham Clinton in *Big Sister Is Watching You: Hilary Clinton and the White House Feminists Who Now Control America—And Tell the President What to Do* (Marrs 1993). Calling Rodham Clinton and a number of female Clinton appointees variously "femiNazis" and "Hillary's hellcats," Marrs claims that they "control a heartless police establishment more efficient than Stalin's dreaded *Cheka* and more feared than Himmler's bloody *SS Corps*" (1993: 15), one that is responsible for a compendium of atrocities, not least the tragic death of more than seventy Branch Davidians at Waco. Unabashedly attributing a "neo-Nazi theology" to Rodham Clinton (1993: 27), Marrs declares that she is, "for the femiNazis, the fleshly embodiment of their heavenly Goddess. She is the Madonna of the New Age, the High Priestess of WomanChurch" (1993: 28). As well, each of the women Clinton appointed to various positions within his administrations has earned particular "monikers" from Marrs. Oscar-nominated actress Jane Alexander, whom Clinton appointed Chairperson of the National Endowment for the Arts, Marrs declared the "Czarina of Homoerotic Art"; Surgeon General Jocelyn Elders became "The Condom Queen"; Attorney General Janet Reno, about whom Marrs has the most to say, is the "Duchess of Doom," so named because Marrs declares she gave a direct order "to murder and burn alive" the Branch Davidians (1993: 159–68).

In similar fashion to the use Larson made of the (alleged) deaths of his niece and nephew, perhaps the most problematic examples of Marrs's conspiracism concern Chandra Levy, a Washington congressional intern who disappeared in late April 2001, and whose disappearance generated a firestorm of media coverage because of her alleged sexual involvement with congressman Gary Condit (D-Calif.).[6] Five months after Levy's disappearance, Marrs published two articles that linked the young intern to the "darkly vicious satanic forces" that he believes control Washington. "Was Chandra Levy Sacrificed to Satan?" asks one article, in which Marrs suggests that Condit is a "practicing satanist" (Marrs 2001b). Once again carefully couching his allegations in the form of leading questions rather than direct accusations, Marrs writes: "The last time anyone (other than Condit and associates?) heard from Chandra was *April 30th*. It just so happens that April 30th is *walpurgisnacht* on the witchcraft calendar, the night of the Grand Climax, when a chosen innocent victim—invariably a young woman—is sacrificed to Pan, the horned god (a.k.a. 'Devil')" (2001b). Marrs considers Condit suspicious because he "is known to have secret ties to the satanic Hell's Angels motorcycle cult. He owned and anonymously rode on back roads a *Harley Davidson*" (2001b). Regarding the Washington, D.C., police search of Condit's condominium and the oft-repeated media anecdote that Levy had helped rearrange it, Marrs asks: "*What* was in Condit's closet? Could it be that evidence of satanic and/or barbaric, sadistic conduct—chains, whips, symbols, masks, etc.—were discovered and inventoried by police investigators?" (2001b, emphasis in the original).

Like any successful worldview, the primary element of a serviceable conspiracy theory is the ability to integrate new data into its construction of reality. In "The Mysterious Riddle of Chandra Levy" (Marrs 2001a), a chapter in Marrs's interpretation of events that demonstrates most clearly his own unassailable conspiracism, Marrs provides the answer to Levy's disappearance. Having initially conjectured that she might have been the victim of a satanic conspiracy of which Condit is a part, following the September 11, 2001, attacks on the World Trade Centers and the Pentagon, Marrs concludes that her disappearance and the attacks are "intimately connected." As it turns out, Levy was not just another congressional intern in the D.C. area, but a "youthful recruit of the Israeli Mossad," and it was in this capacity that she worked in Washington. As a spy for Mossad, in addition to Condit Levy "was introduced to the perverted inner sex lives of numbers of other congressmen, all of whom are part of D.C.'s exclusive satanic brotherhood" (Marrs 2001a: 1). Not surprisingly, this group is an integral part of the mysterious Illuminati, a staple of religiopolitical conspiracy theories since the eighteenth century. Because it demonstrates so clearly the ability of a conspiracy theory to integrate even the most disparate events, Marrs's conclusion in the matter is worth quoting at length.

I believe that at that point Chandra Levy had somehow stumbled onto the most shocking intelligence secret of the last few decades—the horrific Illuminati plot to manipulate the so-called Arab Islamic terrorists to smash airliners into the World Trade Center Towers and the Pentagon. This unauthorized disclosure sealed Chandra Levy's doom. On May 1st, a date numerologically and occultly significant in the Illuminati's witchcraft and satanic calender, she was disposed of during a ritual at D.C.'s mysteriously gothic Rock Creek Park, a large, forested area which is shaped like a goat's head—the hideous head of Baphomet, the Masonic goat-god, representative of the coming antichrist. (Marrs 2001a: 1–2)

Little escapes Marrs's conspiracist biblicism: unmarked black helicopters that patrol the East River past the so-called Tower of Babble (the United Nations building), crop failures and an impending shortage of drinking water, the Masonic plot to take over America, and the Illuminati plot to take over the world. All have a role to play in the unfolding eschaton, and all will ultimately serve the pleasure of the Beast 666—the so-called Universal Human Control System. According to the jacket notes on Marrs's *Project L.U.C.I.D.*, his best known contribution to the growing eschatological bookshelf, "All data on you is linked, networked, and processed by a Central Gestapo, where faceless bureaucrats give orders to police, military, and intelligence agencies. This is the new, global police state, made up of the FBI, KGB, CIA, DEA, DIA, NSA, IRS, EPA,

NCIC, USDA, FDA, NRO, BATF, FINCEN, INS, DOJ, WTO, Europol, Interpol, Mossad, and the MAB" (1996; Marrs 1997b).

THE CONSPIRACY FACTOR IN COUNTERCULT DISCOURSE

Beyond the sensationalism often required by an increasingly competitive countercult market, and the appetite twentieth-century fin de siècle culture appears to have for the bizarre and the preposterous (witness the popularity of Jerry Springer, for example), what purpose do the claims of apologists such as Larson and Marrs serve? The subtle brilliance of this kind of conspiracism is that there is no event or circumstance that cannot be integrated into the larger cosmological schema. It bears repeating that the most important component of a successful conspiracy theory is precisely this ability to incorporate all aspects of new data into its construction of reality. In the conspiracist worldview—whether religious, political, economic, military, or some combination of these—nothing is insignificant. In what is almost a rationalist parody of chaos theory, the very nature of the conspiracy requires that events that on the surface bear no relation to one another be intimately and causally connected. If it cannot integrate events—*especially* events that appear unrelated—then it will ultimately founder as an explanation. The inability to integrate events suggests at least the possibility that history occurs not as the result of some grand and sinister scheme, but instead as a multicausal confluence of experiences, agendas, individual actions, social coalitions, and random events, all of which are later interpreted into a coherent framework known to observers as "history." Because this possibility gainsays the monocausality on which conspiracism depends, it fatally disables the conspiracy theory itself. Unable to abide ambiguity, conspiracism allows for no loose ends. Thus, in Christian dispensationalist discourse, if peace breaks out in the Middle East it must be able to be interpreted as a sign that the antichrist is coming (see, e.g., Hunt 1983, 1990); on the other hand, if war erupts in the same region, that too must be a sign of the end-times (cf., for example, Marrs 1989a, 1992; Walvoord 1990).

Despite Christian fundamentalism's well-documented beginnings as a reaction against the modernist project, because it assumes that, while the knowledge gained might not always be pleasant, complete knowledge about the world *can* be achieved, countercult conspiracism is actually a function of modernity; the world as it is experienced and perceived can be understood in rational, propositional terms. There *is* a clear, indisputable, and correct interpretation of the Bible that exists entirely apart from anyone's attempts to understand it. There *is* a standard of meaning available that is not subject to the whims and fancies of interpretation. This is seen most obviously in the fundamentalist obverse of countercult conspiracism—biblical prophecy. As with all other aspects of countercult apologetics, the interpretation of prophecy is bounded by one specific caveat: the Bible is never and can never be wrong. If something appears contradictory or inaccurate, it is not the text that is in error; there must simply be another way of looking at it. Indeed, Dave Hunt declares that unless one is predisposed toward the kind of prophetic determinism by which countercult conspiracism is framed, there is little value in approaching the text at all. If it appears that biblical prophecy has fallen short in some respect, the fault cannot lay with the Bible. "No Christian can accept that for a moment," he writes, "not because our faith in the Bible is blind, but because we have carefully examined it and know it to be the infallible Word of God. There can be no mistakes or failed prophecies. We must, therefore, seek another interpretation" (Hunt 1993a: 150).

In this context prophetic determinism plays two important roles in the countercult movement's cognitive praxis: (1) it offers a reflexive framework by which the countercult apologist or reader can identify current events within the context of an inerrant Scripture, and at the same time reinforce belief in that same inerrancy; and (2) it furnishes explanations for those events that are rendered plausible only in the context of that framework.

First, insofar as it is derived from the interpretation of an inerrant and infallible Scripture, this prophetic determinism provides an eschatological framework in which countercult apologists such as Hunt, Marrs, and Cumbey can locate current events. Anything that happens anywhere in the world must have a place in the divine plan simply by virtue of there being a divine plan. Additionally, the ability to locate events successfully within this eschatological framework, to establish to one's own satisfaction the validity of the connections between circumstances in the world and the unfolding of the end-times, reflexively reinforces the plausibility of that framework.

Second, and in this the countercult fringe differs only in degree from the more mainstream, countercult conspiracism not only describes *what* is happening in the world, but explains *why* it is happening. In the wake of any social crisis—from the September 11 attacks to a small child killed or injured crossing the road, from the failure of one's business to the diagnosis of cancer in one who has avoided carcinogens all her life—"Why?" becomes the question of moment. As has been well known since the patristic era, the problem of evil and suffering is one of the most durable and robust challenges to the existence of an omnipotent, omnibenevolent God. While orthodox Christianity has never officially supported the thoroughgoing duotheism of, say, Zoroastrianism, in which negative experiences can be attributed to the actions of an evil God equal in power to a benevolent God (i.e., Ahriman versus Ahura Mazda), at times in Christian history the power of the Devil has appeared at least to rival if not equal the power of God. For the countercult, then, the rise of new religious movements, however steep or gradual that increase has been, is not the product of an expanding religious economy supported by a constitutional guarantee of religious freedom and a cultural ethos in which religious preference and practice is often jealously guarded as a private experience; rather, it is clear evidence that the first enemy of God is hard at work in the war for humanity's soul.

7

The Siege Continues: Modern Countercult Continua

While it is a considerably more coherent social entity than, for example, the New Age movement (see chapter 10), and while it remains anchored in a shared evangelical/fundamentalist cosmology, the Christian countercult as it has evolved since Walter Martin first published *The Kingdom of the Cults* still encompasses a wide variety of ministries, approaches, and beliefs about the problems of practical life represented by new and controversial religious movements. At the turn of the twentieth century, the precursors to the postwar countercult (e.g., Combs 1899; the various contributors to *The Fundamentals*; and van Baalen 1938) were concerned, by and large, with sectarian challenges originating within the broader framework of Christianity (e.g., Christian Science, the Church of Jesus Christ of Latter-day Saints, the Watchtower Bible and Tract Society). Since World War II, however, that concern has expanded to meet the challenge of new and emergent religions—the advent into mainstream North America of Eastern religious traditions, a growing variety of Neopaganisms, and the aforementioned New Age movement.

This expansion has resulted in (1) the development of a systematic cognitive praxis, a countercult apologetic focused on the reinforcement of an authoritative Christian meaning structure and mechanisms for maintaining the plausibility of that structure in the face of the growing diversity of challenges to it; and (2) in terms of countercult organization and the production of resources, parallel processes of professionalization and democratization. Unlike the secular anticult, which tended over time to become increasingly concentrated in professional and semiprofessional associations, the countercult has both professionalized and democratized. Professionalization has occurred in such organizations as the Christian Research Institute, the Spiritual Counterfeits Project, Watchman Fellowship, the Utah Lighthouse Ministry, the Berean Call, Answers in Action, and Saints Alive in Jesus. This process is continuing to evolve organizationally through coalitioning movements such as the Evangelical Ministries to New Religions.

The increased availability of countercult material, though, and particularly the development and expansion of Internet self-publishing (see chapter 8), has also led to the democratization of countercult resources, a circumstance that has expanded the pool of movement intellectuals, including now a wide variety of avocational and crossover participants. That is, while the initial resources may have been produced by a professional or semiprofessional class of apologists—Eyerman and Jamison's "established intellectuals" (1991: 108–13)—these resources have been explicitly intended for use by all Christians. Democratization, then, has appeared at the level of so-called mom-and-pop or street-level organizations, ministries that operate at various levels of apologetic sophistication ranging from Matt Slick's "Christian Apologetic and Research Ministry" (a one-man show run on the Internet out of a spare back bedroom) to more organizationally complex entities such as Anton Hein's "Apologetics Index," a very elaborate Web site that is now intimately connected with the "Apologia Report," an Internet countercult ministry operated by former employees of the Christian Research Institute. What I am calling "crossover ministries" are those that began as avocational ventures and developed over time into more professional (or at least commercial) enterprises.

Democratization both gives rise to and accounts for two other developments in the countercult domain. First, the countercult varies across a number of particular, discriminate continua. Even though all evangelical/fundamentalist countercult apologists hold to specific doctrinal and cognitive boundary markers, their individual interpretations of these markers, the place they think the countercult has or should have in the unfolding of Christian salvation-history, and their own beliefs about the manner in which countercult activities are or ought to be conducted can be conceptualized in a number of ways. However, while each of these conceptualizations may help elucidate countercult belief and activity, none describes that activity fully. Second, the wide variation in these models is a predictable result of the democratization process. Once a resource has been produced and released into the public domain—whether commercially or pro bono—the producer has given up any effective control he or she might have had over the use to which that product is put. Occasionally, when various aspects of countercult conceptualization and mission focus come into conflict, it is over these precise conceptualizations, and considerable interpersonal and interagency tension may develop (see chapter 12).

TYPOLOGIZING THE COUNTERCULT

Typologically, the Christian countercult can be organized a number of ways. Is its organizational structure professional, semiprofessional, crossover, or avocational? Does it concern itself with one religious group or group cluster, or with all religious traditions other than Christianity? Is it operated by former members of new or controversial religious movements, people who have never been members of these groups, or some combination of the two? Derivatively, is its intended audience current or former members of target religious groups? Or evangelical Christians alone? Since each countercult ministry occupies some place in answer to each of these questions, but no group occupies precisely the same place, I have chosen to present them in a rather different form—as aspects of the intersections between various discriminate continua. While other configurations of these continua are possible, and bearing in mind that these coordinate representations are offered merely as heuristic devices rather than definitive typological locations, consider the following three possible matrices.

In the first matrix, shown in Figure 7.1, the horizontal axis depicts the organizational character of the ministry. "Avocational" represents those countercult ministries that are operated neither by professional apologists nor as primarily commercial enterprises. Both on the Internet, and in real life, these are the mom-and-pop, street-level ministries, and they often have the flavor of a hobby (recognizing how seriously some people take their hobbies), a side interest that is adjunct to one's professional life. Software consultant Timothy Campbell, for example, is an ex-Witness who started his countercult Web site (members.aol.com/beyondjw) in 1995 "to let other ex-Witnesses know that they are not alone, and that they are not bad people." "Darkness to Light" (www.dtl.org) is Gary Zeolla's site for "explaining and defending the Christian faith." Roy Howdyshell is a retired Washington, D.C., firefighter and newly ordained Baptist minister who operates the Refuge Outreach Ministry (www.refuge-outreach.org) as an "outreach to churches on Cults and Counterfeit teachings of the Christian faith, and teachings on Mind Control, J.W., Mormon and Counterfeit Religions/Denominations, etc."

At the other end of the continuum are fully orbed, professional countercult organizations such as the Christian Research Institute, the Watchman Fellowship, the Spiritual Counterfeits Project, and Personal Freedom Outreach. These are characterized by (1) a primary organizational commitment to countercult apologetics, and (2) the regular employment of staff as movement intellectuals,

Figure 7.1
The Countercult from Avocation to Profession

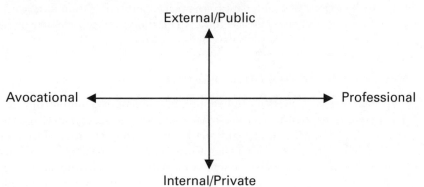

whose principal responsibility is the production and dissemination of apologetic resource material, the intentional instruction of Christians in the implementation of countercult apologetics, and/or the proactive evangelization of non-Christian religionists.

The vertical axis represents the cardinal domain in which the ministry's activities are conducted. Whether through publications, workshops, lectures, or "cult awareness impact crusades," is ministry activity limited to the evangelical community, and not intended for an audience beyond that community? Morey's *How to Answer a Jehovah's Witness* (1980), Bjornstad's *Counterfeits at Your Door* (1979), Rhodes's Reasoning from the Scriptures With series(e.g., 1993, 1995, 2000, 2001b), as well as the Zondervan Guide to Cults and Religious Movements and Concordia's How to Respond To series, for example, are all designed specifically for use by evangelical Christians. On the other hand, ministry activity also takes place beyond the specific boundaries of the evangelical church—on the steps of a new Latter-day Saints temple, or when the annual conference of Jehovah's Witnesses happens to meet at a local convention center.

Figure 7.2 maintains the internal-external axis, but intersects it instead with the provision of information versus proactive evangelism. This is the array illustrating the tension between evangelical boundary maintenance and evangelistic missionizing. A countercult group that is both information oriented and internally located would be most concerned with reality-maintaining aspects of the countercult apologetic. They are defending the faith. "Contend for the Faith," for example (www.geocities.com/Athens/Delphi/8449), is an Internet apologetics ministry operated by Justin Taylor and Matt Perman, whose "goal is to present to the world the reasonableness and excellence of Christian truth for the glory of God and the good of His church." Conversely, a ministry that is oriented both evangelistically and externally functions in the principal domain of mission—members of Saints Alive in Jesus leafleting in Temple

Figure 7.2
The Countercult from Boundary-maintenance to Evangelism

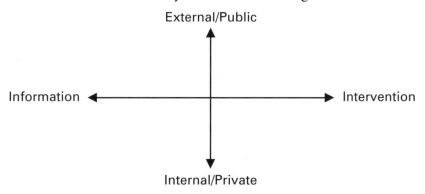

Square, Salt Lake City, or Bob Larson on the radio five days a week, battling Satan, Satanists, and those suspected of being Satanists.

Finally, Figure 7.3 returns the avocational-professional axis but distinguishes ministries according to their staffing. Given that the normative religious position for countercult apologists as I have been discussing them here is evangelical/fundamentalist Christianity, the question is whether staff members are converts to Christianity from target religious groups, or Christians who have never been part of suspect groups. Saints Alive in Jesus, for example, is the colloquial name for the Ex-Mormons for Jesus Evangelistic Association. Watchman Fellowship includes among its staff former Latter-day Saints, RLDSs (Reorganized Church of Jesus Christ of Latter-day Saints [now the Community of Christ]), Jehovah's Witnesses, and occultists, as well as those who have been members only of evangelical Christian churches.

THE COUNTERCULT PROFESSIONALS

Since many of the modern professional countercult organizations have been in existence for some time, in-depth histories could be written about each one. In this section, I consider them briefly in light of their stated organizational imperatives, especially as those imperatives impact U.S. constitutional guarantees of religious freedom. Although it is not uncommon for countercult apologists to profess a robust commitment to this constitutional security, the manner in which it is interpreted says much about the nature of the organization.

Excursus: The Countercult and the First Amendment

Recognizing that they, too, benefit from religious freedom, few if any countercult apologists would suggest that the First Amendment ought to be re-

Figure 7.3
Staffing the Countercult

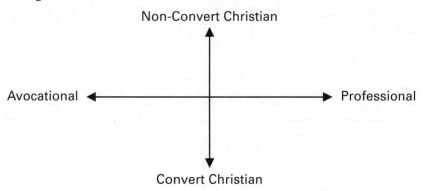

pealed. Rather, they often question what the constitutional framers meant or intended by the amendment. Since they acknowledge that simple differences in belief will not obviate the constitutional guarantee, it is at this point that many apologists often introduce distinctions between belief and practice, alleging, for example, that Satanists can believe what they want as long as they don't sacrifice animals or humans. While accurate, when stated thus, with no evidence offered that Satanists actually engage in these practices (a charge they vigorously deny), the repetition of this particular countercult convention serves to keep popular stereotypes about Satanism firmly in view (see, e.g., Branch 1990).

Two principle vectors inform countercult interpretation of the First Amendment. On the one hand, in keeping with either an implicit or explicit conspiracism, some apologists maintain that religious freedom will be used as a pretext to persecute conservative Christians. Texe Marrs, for example, believes that in the so-called New World Order, fundamentalist Christianity will be the only religion actively prohibited under the First Amendment (see chapter 6). On the other hand, countercult apologists often claim that their own polemical and evangelistic imperative is explicitly protected under that same amendment.

Based in Chattanooga, Tennessee, John Ankerberg hosts the *John Ankerberg Show*, a debate-style, current events television program, and operates the Ankerberg Theological Research Institute, an Internet clearinghouse for short countercult articles that are available on a subscription basis. Together with John Weldon, formerly with the Christian Research Institute and now senior researcher for the Ankerberg Institute, he has written a number of books dealing with various aspects of new religious movements. In their *Encyclopedia of Cults and New Religions*, Ankerberg and Weldon address the issue of "responsible religious freedom," and suggest that "Christian leaders should call for and institute a national discussion over how we protect legitimate religious freedoms and simultaneously protect ourselves from 'freedom of religion' " (1999: xxviii). The issue of what constitutes a legitimate religious freedom and who is permitted to make that decision is central to this discussion. Because it so concisely illustrates both of the vectors noted above, and neatly locates them within the context of American manifest destiny, Ankerberg and Weldon's concerns are worth quoting at length.

In America, the problems raised by the dominance of relativism and secularism vis à vis first amendment religious issues is forbidding at best. A generation ago we had very few cults and no problem with intolerance or persecution of Christians because the cultural consensus was Christian. This seems to have been the divine plan. In establishing a nation solidly based in clear Christian beliefs and principles . . . God may have ordained a built-in penalty that could not be avoided should we forsake our Christian foundations and responsibilities. In other words, the First Amendment only works as long as we accept Christian principles. If it does not, then it gets what it gets—all kinds of religious evils protected by the very amendment which God intended to bless the nation. (Ankerberg and Weldon 1999: xxix)

Notwithstanding the debatable historical accuracy of claims to "a nation solidly based in clear Christian beliefs and principles,"[1] Ankerberg and Weldon's words here call to mind Napoleon the pig's famous dictum from Orwell's *Animal Farm:* "All pigs are equal, but some pigs are more equal than others." "The First Amendment only works as long as we accept Christian principles," they write. Put differently, we ought to have just enough freedom of religion to allow us to choose to be Christian. Within the context of countercult cognitive praxis, the logic of this argument is unassailable: since evangelical Christianity is the only true religion, religious freedom is only possible and legitimate when that freedom is used to embrace evangelical Christianity. Because countercult apologists regard theirs as the only authentic religious path, and regard all others as false religions, true religious freedom can logically be found only in Christianity. Therefore, in discharging the Great Commission (Matt. 28:19–20), apologists believe that they have not only a right but a duty to fulfill the countercult imperative to evangelize and convert. When that right is questioned, when target religious groups object to the kind of distortion and misrepresentation that often marks countercult characterizations of them, apologists often contend that *their* free exercise of religion under the First Amendment is being infringed. In a curious reinterpretation of the concept of tolerance, some apologists argue that it is actually intolerant to suggest they cannot criticize other religions on the basis of their own religious worldview.

Anton Hein, for example, a freelance Internet apologist and former moderator of Apologia Report's Web-based apologetics discussion list, AR-forum (see chapter 8), contends that the right to freedom of religion includes "the right and freedom to present relevant information about religions, movements, leaders, doctrines, and practices in order to help people make informed decisions about various belief systems" (Hein n.d.). Presenting what he considers relevant information from the perspective of an evangelical/fundamentalist Christian, Hein concludes, however, that "those who deny others the right to hold and express religious views that challenge the validity of competing and/or contradictory religious views, in so doing promote religious intolerance."

In terms of First Amendment freedom of religion, countercult apologetics exist in the liminal state Canadian human rights authority Alan Borovoy calls "the collision of freedoms" (Borovoy 1988). How does the exercise of one freedom limit or impinge the exercise of another? In the case of a conflict, which freedom is held to override the other? In the context of the Christian countercult, which freedom has priority—an individual's freedom to choose his or her own religious path, or the countercult's freedom to exercise its evangelistic imperative? While a number of different organizations could have been considered in this section, I have chosen two of the more well known groups—

the Christian Research Institute and the Watchman Fellowship—to illustrate
aspects of this tension.

"A Systematic Defense": Christian Research Institute

Begun in 1960 by Walter Martin, whom the current online historical brief
erroneously asserts was "the first evangelical Christian clergy to recognize the
threat and opportunity presented to the Christian church by cults and alternative religious systems" (www.equip.org), the Christian Research Institute
(CRI) is arguably the most recognizable professional countercult organization
around. Indeed, four decades after its inception that same snippet contends that
the CRI is "the largest, most effective apologetics ministry in the world." Since
Martin's death, the organization has been governed by Hendrik (Hank) Hanegraaff, who, in the face of often bitter criticism both from Martin's family
and from former CRI staff members, has maintained that he was Martin's
designated successor. Since some of the issues related to recent controversies
in the CRI are dealt with in chapter 12, in this section I discuss the broader
goals of the CRI in the context of the evolving professionalization of the
countercult.

In *The Kingdom of the Cults* (1965, 1977, 1985, 1997), Martin outlined a
program that he believed necessary to pursue the "primary task of the Christian church"—evangelizing the cults. Recognizing that the central problem in
this pursuit was a lack of information on the part of rank-and-file evangelicals,
whether clergy or lay, he also correctly interpreted several important cultural
drifts: the Latter-day Saints and the Watchtower Society were both quite obviously growing at considerable rates; there was an increasing awareness of
alternative religious traditions in the postwar United States (though perhaps
not, strictly speaking, the so-called explosion of cults apologists often claim;
cf. Finke and Stark 1992; Hunt 1980); the expanding religious economy did
appear to be diluting the more apparent influence enjoyed by the Christian
church to that point; and, finally, the youth counterculture of the 1960s was
challenging many of the social and cultural foundations on which that influence
had been built and that it had served to reinforce (Tipton 1982; though also
Cowan 1998). Writing on Zen in the first edition of *Kingdom*, for example,
Martin declares that increased interest in Eastern religion had to be taken seriously by evangelicals. Rarely one for equivocation where new religious movements were concerned, Martin writes that, "while it is true that Zen has become
associated in the minds of some people with bearded beatniks sipping Espresso
in Greenwich Village–type Bohemian clubs and garrets, theirs is but a superficial mastery of Zen terminology, and an almost pathetic attempt to identify
their lack of moral and social responsibility with a religio-philosophic system
of thought which impresses the Western mind with its virtually irrational and
pantheistic approach to religion and, for that matter, reality" (1965: 234).

Rather than bemoan the growing problem, however, Martin saw the opportunity for a research and education facility designed specifically for this emerging mission field. Outlined in *Kingdom* as "The Road to Recovery," Martin's vision comprised four interrelated components. Each of these contributed to the emergent professionalization of the countercult, and together they formed Martin's blueprint for a systematic countercult apologetic and an organized defense of the faith—an established cognitive praxis for the countercult movement.

First and foremost, adequate research had to be carried out in order to determine the scope and extent of the so-called cult problem faced by evangelicals. This research had several aspects. Martin knew, for example, that there was an abundance of countercult material available—some of it useful, some of it less so. Much of this information he had already used in writing *The Kingdom of the Cults*. He was the first to suggest, however, that it needed to be "validated, codified, and carefully weighed by mission agencies and field representatives of the major denominations and independent Christian groups" (1977: 353). Martin was clear that the professionalization of the countercult was not to serve as an end in itself but was to be one resource brought to a spiritual battle in which he passionately believed every Christian was or ought to be involved. In this battle, Martin also realized that theological resources alone would be insufficient. He wanted sociological and demographic data compiled, information that would tell the countercult where target groups were growing, where they were not, and what might be the contributing social factors for each. Further, rather than simply decide unilaterally how countercult apologetics and evangelism ought to be performed, Martin wanted to access the considerable human resources already available to the church. "Questionnaires must be sent out to key personnel in all Christian movements," he writes, "seeking their reaction to the challenge of the cults in those areas under their jurisdiction. In this way, a broad perspective of cult methodology will be obtained" (Martin 1977: 353).

The Christian Research Institute was Martin's attempt to meet these challenges. Rather than a frontline ministry, handing out evangelical tracts to participants at a local pagan festival, for example, Martin envisioned the CRI as "a bureau of information on comparative religions," readily available to Christian pastors, missionaries, and lay people. In Martin's view, easy access to this information was essential. Like ammunition on the battlefield, it did little good sitting in a warehouse well behind the front lines. Effective resource mobilization was crucial to the fight.

In 1977, when the second edition of *Kingdom* was released, computers were just making their way over the cultural horizon. While personal computers were still a few years away, both institutional and public libraries were beginning to acquire crude electronic data retrieval systems. As the host of *The Bible Answer Man*, Martin was already on the radio daily and was familiar with the technology required for that endeavor. He also saw the value in computer systems and proposed a "Christian Research Lending Library" to take advantage of the evolving technology (Martin 1977: 354). Somewhat idealistically (perhaps influenced by cinematic portrayals of computers at the time), he envisioned a system not unlike the World Wide Web and the Internet. "Through our projected computer network," he writes, "individuals would be able to tap our resources via computer terminals. This person would be able to type his question on a console and receive an almost instantaneous reply complete with documentation" (Martin 1977: 354). Martin's techno-idealism notwithstanding, as an intentional clearinghouse for countercult information the CRI began both to centralize and to standardize countercult material—to crystallize the cosmological and technological aspects of its cognitive praxis. Collecting and evaluating material, making available both in print and through the *Bible Answer Man* that which Martin's countercult protocols deemed acceptable, the CRI began to establish for the first time a coherent body of countercult apologetic literature. As a movement intellectual, Martin was instrumental in establishing this early cognitive praxis of the Christian countercult, often playing, as Eyerman and Jamison point out, "the role of gatekeeper, deciding what was relevant for discussion and who was competent to participate" (1991: 113).

Whether provided in hard copy or electronically, *what* information these individuals and groups would need was the second major component of the CRI vision. In the years during which Martin was compiling *Kingdom*, other Christian groups were not sitting idle. Evangelist William Biederwolf (1867–1936) wrote a series of "booklets on the Isms" that were later collected and republished by Eerdmans in the early 1950s. A decade later, the Church of England brought out its Modern Heresies booklet series; 1963 saw the publication of an adult Sunday School curriculum entitled *Christianity and the Cults*, introduced by Harold Lindsell, who would go on just a few years later to edit *Christianity Today*. What was available in the early 1960s, though, was uneven and scattered, ranging from these early adult-education attempts to reinforce the worldview of evangelicals in the face of the challenge represented by new religious movements to extended anecdotal atrocity tales such W. J. Schnell's *Thirty Years a Watchtower Slave* (1956). From the masses of data available—and drawing on both the nascent countercult and the targeted religious groups themselves—Martin sought to distill and condense the most useful information for active countercult evangelism. Simple and efficient were the watchwords of his apologetic. In contrast to what has happened with other organizations, though, including the CRI, Martin originally intended these materials to be made available as inexpensively as possible.

Martin also understood clearly that this was not solely an evangelical enterprise. In addition to working through such established distribution networks as the American Tract Society, the New York Bible Society, and the International Missionary Council, he believed that cults did not concern only evangelicals, but that this might be an issue over which liberals and conservatives could set aside their theological differences in pursuit of a common solution to a common problem. Unless there was a coherent front presented, he reasoned, unless liberals and conservatives worked together in an effort to "erect a systematic defense against the proselyting of the cults" (Martin 1977: 355), the problem would soon escalate out of control. That liberal churches did not join with Martin in his crusade must surely have been a disappointment to him, not least because he recognized how that fractured both the reality and the perception of Christian response to new religious movements (on this, see Saliba 1999).

Third, deriving from his desire to see vast quantities of information disseminated as quickly and easily as possible, Martin declares unequivocally that an "educational reevaluation" had to occur within the Christian church, particularly its evangelical branches. "It is a fact," he writes, reflecting on the curricula then available in seminaries and Bible colleges, "that at present less than five percent of all such institutions in the United States require as a prerequisite of graduation that a student take a course on comparative religions, or non-Christian American cults, a fact which staggers the imagination, when one can see the obvious inroads the cults have made both at home and abroad" (Martin 1977: 356). It was at this point that Martin asserted the CRI's founding position on religious freedom. "We are not to suggest that the activities of these movements be curtailed by law, or that they should become the target of an evangelical barrage of abuse. Full freedom of worship and the right to promulgate one's convictions are historic planks in the platform of Protestant evangelicalism" (Martin 1977: 356).

Martin's answer, however well or poorly the countercult movement overall has followed his ethical dicta with regard to "an evangelical barrage of abuse," was a comprehensive educational program aimed not at members of new or controversial religious movements, but at Christians and Christian educational institutions. He maintained that it was futile to provide arguments and refutations for use in evangelization—which, revealingly, is something Christians do, as opposed to the so-called proselytization or recruitment of cults—if there was no solid doctrinal foundation underpinning that witness. Both went hand-in-glove: information that nihilated or refuted the worldview of the new religious movement adherent had to be reinforced by material that assured the evangelist of the inevitable superiority of the Christian worldview.[2] For Martin, this pedagogical sea change had to begin with the educational institutions in which church leaders were trained. If pastors could not speak authoritatively to their congregations about new religious movements, the Christian church had little right to expect those congregation members to speak out. Today, more and more evangelical institutions offer degree programs in Christian apologetics, some in which students can choose to concentrate on new religious movements. And, in many of these programs, *The Kingdom of the Cults* is still used as either a primary or secondary textbook.

The last plank in Martin's plan for a professionalized countercult was scholarly and semischolarly outreach within the evangelical community. In addition to education, it made little sense to him to assemble and refine countercult material and then make no attempt to disseminate it. To address this, Martin suggested specialized countercult conferences that could occur at various organizational levels of the church—congregational, denominational, interdenominational, or academic. If these conferences could "both explain the divergent doctrines of the cults and, at the same time, strengthen the faith of Christians in the great fundamental teachings of Christianity" (Martin 1977: 359), apologetic missiology and apologetic boundary-maintenance would come together.

In the years since his proposal, Martin's archetypal apologetic has been realized more in the ideal than the actual. Indeed, some of the most questionable countercult scholarship in recent years has come from individuals most closely associated with Martin and CRI. Since Martin's death, CRI has undergone significant changes in personnel and apologetic orientation. As I discuss more fully in chapter 12, not a few former CRI employees believe that it has gone far afield of Martin's original vision. In the early professionalization of the countercult, however, especially in terms of the many strands of research Martin sought to weave together in service of his apologetic agenda, the contribution and impact of the Christian Research Institute cannot be overestimated.

"A Conspiracy to Commit Evangelism": Watchman Fellowship

Like the Christian Research Institute, Watchman Fellowship (WF) is well known in the countercult community. An interdenominational organization founded in 1979 and headquartered in Arlington, Texas, it maintains a number of satellite offices and, according to its statement of purpose, serves as "a resource for cult education, counselling, and non-coercive intervention." While "non-coercive intervention" is not defined, the array of countercult material produced and marketed by Watchman Fellowship suggests that their intention is actually more evangelistic than strictly interventionist. In addition to publishing *The Watchman Expositor*, a monthly magazine similar to the *Christian Research Journal*, as well as a series of individual *Watchman Fellowship Profiles*, the group maintains a speaker's bureau on which interested parties may call for lectures, workshops, and "Cult Awareness Impact Crusades." Crusades conducted by these speakers occur regularly across the country and cover such familiar topics as the Latter-day Saints, Jehovah's Witnesses, and the New Age. Of more interest, though, is the claim that in its twenty-year-plus history, WF has resourced not only church groups, but also law enforcement agencies, educational institutions, and civic organizations. If this is accurate, and not merely rhetorical overstatement on the part of the group, then the manner in which

Watchman Fellowship interprets and responds to the issue of religious freedom seems relatively important.

In a "Public Information" section included in each issue of *The Watchman Expositor*, WF sets out its religious position very clearly. "Watchman Fellowship endorses a biblically based, conservative, evangelical position, proclaiming that all must turn from sin to trust the death, burial, and resurrection of the second person of the Trinity, Jesus Christ, as the only remedy for sin and the sole foundation for true religion." Biographical sketches of the WF staff support this understanding—many are former members of target groups, and a number carry clerical credentials from fundamentalist denominations. "Watchman Fellowship endorses freedom of religion in both thought and expression," the disclaimer continues. "While endorsing the rights of everyone to hold and practice divergent beliefs, Watchman Fellowship is compelled to exercise its freedoms (religious, speech and press) to expose questionable doctrines and abusive or manipulative practices, and to offer spiritual alternatives in the form of traditional Christian faith."

On at least one occasion that compulsion has led to controversy. In January 2000, the AP wire picked up a story about a WF Cult Awareness Impact Crusade to be held at the two largest Southern Baptist churches in the Winston-Salem area of North Carolina. According to James Walker, the leader of these particular crusades, the wire story, which was abbreviated from local news sources, "created a firestorm of controversy in the community" (Walker 2000). As a result, a WF editorial (likely also written by Walker) concludes: "It will not take long before such groups work together, as representatives of world religions such as Islam and Judaism have, to label such educational and evangelistic outreaches as intolerant acts that could lead to hate crimes against members of minority religions" (Watchman Fellowship 2000).

The tone of these and similar articles suggests that some evangelicals are puzzled that anyone could object to the countercult activities of organizations such as the Watchman Fellowship. "We believe in freedom of religion," protests Walker, in another brief article, this one entitled "Conspiracy to Commit Evangelism" (Walker 2000). In fact, he continues, evangelicals go considerably further than simple open-mindedness. "We do more than just tolerate the existence of other faiths—we celebrate religious diversity. I believe Mormons have every right to believe in Mormonism, but I also believe that I have a right and a responsibility to try to evangelize them." In the same issue of *The Watchman Expositor*, R. Philip Roberts argues that, far from being intolerant of other religions, evangelicals are actually in the forefront of demanding freedom of religion for all faiths (Roberts 2000). Roberts continues:

Intolerance used to refer to bigotry or prejudice against those who were different from someone simply because of who they were by virtue of differing characteristics such as race or ethnicity. Now intolerance is defined as simply questioning the legitimacy or truthfulness of another's religious views. Those who do so have allegedly made the mistake of assuming that subjective religious "truth" should be objectively true for everyone else. Those who hold that truth is objective and universal, and that some religious views are not true, are labeled as fundamentalists. (Roberts 2000)

Yes, exactly—the Christian countercult has raised a subjective construction of religious reality to the level of objective ontology, the kind of ontology very often espoused is fundamentalist, and adherence to this ontology is offered as grounds for questioning the legitimacy of competing religious views. If, however, all the countercult brought to the expanding religious economy were "simple questions" about the truth or legitimacy of another tradition (two very different concepts that seem to function synonymously at least for Roberts), then there would be little to question about the countercult. As this book seeks to document, however, the reality of the countercult cognitive praxis is often something considerably different.

While it does not come up as an explicit discussion of First Amendment issues, the concept and process of interreligious dialogue implies—indeed requires—the kind of freedoms guaranteed by the Constitution. How a group understands interreligious dialogue, then, is one window into the way in which that group interprets the freedom of religion. In 1998, WF devoted most of an issue of *The Watchman Expositor* to the problem of interreligious dialogue and its implications for evangelism and countercult ministry. Most of the articles in the issue were written by Jason Barker, a former Jehovah's Witness and now director of the Southwest Institute for Orthodox Studies, a countercult organization intended for the members of the Orthodox Church in America (Barker 1998a, 1998b, 1998c, 1999). Contending that while interreligious dialogue is not evangelism, "neither does it preclude evangelism," Barker's central thesis is that "interreligious dialogue is related to evangelism in two ways: 'Christians must practice dialogue with non-Christians (1) to understand the situation of non-Christians and how the Gospel answers their needs; (2) answer questions raised by people . . . to involve them in a personal encounter with the claims of God' " (Barker 1998a: 7, ellipses in the original).

Trying to put the best face on interreligious dialogue that he can, while still maintaining a commitment to the exclusivistic claims of evangelical Christianity and the missiological imperative of countercult cognitive praxis, Barker demonstrates the tensions inherent in the collision between a dualistic worldview and a pluralistic world. Misunderstanding Leonard Swidler's well-known "Dialogue Decalogue" (Swidler 1983), which provides the framework for his discussion on the practicalities of interreligious dialogue from an evangelical/countercult perspective, Barker suggests that "one area in which the participants should have an equal education is in regards to the religion(s) with whom they are dialoging. Each participant should be knowledgeable about the beliefs and practices of the other religious community" (1998b: 9). Barker means this to conform to Swidler's seventh commandment (i.e., "Dialogue can only occur between equals"), and he suggests that "the dialogue will be unequal if only one participant is knowledgeable about the other's religion" (1998b: 9). While this may be the case, he avoids entirely both the intention of Swidler's exercise, which is to encourage conversations in which few participants may know anything about the others, but have gathered in dialogue to *learn;* and the conflict between his interpretation of this and Swidler's immediately preceding dictum: "There should be no preconceptions as to areas of disagreement." Rather, Barker suggests that one way a suitable balance might be achieved is if "each participant [holds] a doctorate in religious studies," believing somewhat naively that "the ability to review the scholarship of participants will also ensure that all motives for dialogue are honest and sincere" (1998b: 9). It seems similarly naive to suggest that someone with a doctorate in apologetics from Biola University is not going to bring a preconception or two to the dialogue table when she meets with a professor of theology from the Unification Church's seminary in Barrytown, New York—or vice versa.

For Barker, dialogue is little more than a Trojan horse for mission. The purpose is to learn about target groups in order to make one's witnessing more effective—hardly the agenda Swidler had in mind. Indeed, he acknowledges that few "current participants in interreligious dialogue" will approve of the manner he suggests Swidler's dicta be used (Barker 1998b: 11). His response to this objection places WF's position on the dialogue afforded by constitutional guarantees of religious freedom in clear perspective. Recognizing that there are those who "will refuse to dialogue with a Christian who is committed to the essentials of historic Christianity," he concludes that there will be occasions when "the missiological differences between evangelicalism and the religion in question make dialogue impossible" (Barker 1998b: 12). Even in these cases, Barker concludes, again somewhat ingenuously: "Evangelicals must attempt to engage in dialogue not only because the clarified understanding of other religious communities will increase the efficacy of evangelism and apologetics, but also because that understanding will improve the ability of Christians and non-Christians to peaceably co-exist in a pluralistic society" (1998b: 12). As a whole, Barker's approach to interreligious dialogue seems less an honest attempt to engage those who believe differently than a somewhat artificial effort to put a positive spin on countercult apologetics through an appeal to the rhetoric of dialogue.

In addition to the light they shed on the Watchman Fellowship's understanding of the uses to which religious freedom ought be put, Barker's articles also illustrate that the professionalization of the countercult does not mean necessarily any increase in its intellectual sophistication. As noted briefly, Barker's articles are filled with problematic interpretations of theology, church history, as well as the process and philosophic underpinnings of interreligious dialogue. The Spanish Inquisition, for example, he refers to as a case of "sectarian strife" (Barker 1998b: 10). Misrepresenting his source (Cobb 1985: 379), he confuses Hindu theology with the Buddhist concept of Nirvana (Barker 1998a). He describes the gospel pericope in which Jesus is found in the temple conversing with the teachers there as an example of "sustained interreligious conversation" (though, implying that Jesus was not a Jew, he does suggest this is more appropriately referred to as "interfaith dialogue"; Barker 1998a: 7); and he opines that interreligious dialogue will increase the self-understanding of Christians, helping them to differentiate between the pure gospel and the cultural lenses through which people too frequently interpret the gospel. As do other countercult apologists, Barker ignores the reality that there is no pure gospel apart from the cultural lenses through which it is interpreted.

"The Urge to Merge": Evangelical Ministries to New Religions

Duplication of effort, internecine conflict over nonessential doctrinal items, and different assessments of controversial religious groups—all of these have been recognized by apologists as detrimental to the countercult enterprise. Lack of accountability and standards of intellectual and spiritual preparation for evangelism further hamper the ability of the countercult to fulfill what many believe ought to be its primary mission. Indeed, dissension has even arisen within the countercult about what that primary mission ought to be: boundary-maintenance for Christians, or proactive evangelism of non-Christian religionists (cf. Morehead 2000, 2002).

In an effort to address these preceived deficiencies and increase effectiveness, participants at a 1982 conference on cults and new religious movements voted to establish a permanent countercult coalition—Evangelical Ministries to Cultists—to be coordinated by Gordon Lewis, a senior professor at Denver Seminary and widely respected figure in the countercult movement (Pement 1999). Designed to follow the dictates of the 1974 Lausanne Covenant (ratified at the first International Congress on World Evangelization), especially Lausanne's "Affirmation 7" on cooperation in evangelism, the original founders included such countercult luminaries as Walter Martin, James Bjornstad, and Ronald Enroth. As former Evangelical Ministries to New Religions Executive Director Eric Pement notes, however, it was not long before the founding members of the organization realized that the name they had chosen was more likely to offend the very people they hoped to reach. Thus, in late 1984, the name was officially changed to Evangelical Ministries to New Religions (EMNR). In addition to organizing annual conferences on countercult evangelism and apologetics, offering various countercult publications, and providing referral services for speakers and workshop leaders, one of the most significant steps taken by the EMNR in recent years has been the creation of the *Manual of Ethical and Doctrinal Standards* (*MEDS*; Evangelical Ministries to New Religions 1997), to the principles of which each member or member organization is expected to adhere.

In many ways, the *MEDS* is a remarkable document and could very well constitute a model for the way in which countercult ministries conduct their affairs. While coalitioning movements such as the EMNR, which has grown in the past two decades to include numerous countercult organizations and individual apologists, can serve any number of specific functions, in the *MEDS* these marshal under three broad categories: (1) the clarification of organizational doctrines and objectives, (2) the establishment of professional standards of ethical and missiological conduct, and (3) the collection and administration of acceptable countercult apologetic material.

While acceptable doctrinal positions are not spelled out explicitly in the *MEDS*, the 1974 Lausanne Covenant and the 1989 Manila Manifesto (which came out of the Second International Congress on World Evangelization) provide the standards of faith and belief to which EMNR members are expected to conform. The infallibility and authority of the Bible, the uniqueness and universality of Christ, and world evangelization as the central mission of the Christian church are the cornerstones on which the Lausanne Covenant and all that has proceeded from it are built. Based on this, the first two EMNR principles call its membership to "clarify essential principles of doctrine, ethics, and ministry by which movements may be distinguished as sub-Christian, cultic, or non-Christian," and to "evaluate the doctrine, ethics, and ministerial practice of controversial groups" (Evangelical Ministries to New Religions 1997). The third principle highlights the tension implicit in any attempt at a coalitioning movement: "Recognize the qualified and credentialed ministries reaching the unreached in the new religions and cults" (Evangelical Ministries to New Religions 1997).

The issue here is obvious: who decides what constitutes "qualified and credentialed ministries"? While the *MEDS* is clear that the EMNR was formed as an umbrella group, and the intention was not for the organization "to assume a magisterial role," implicit in any evaluation of potential members is a power relationship determined precisely by the conceptual framework of "qualified and credentialed." Given the breadth of the countercult and the extreme variance in terms of ministry preparation, academic or professional training, and overall countercult vision, "Qualified in what way" and "Credentialed by whom" are just two of the questions raised by the *MEDS* document. The *MEDS* concedes that "many devoted and Spirit-led Christian ministries and missionaries will never affiliate with EMNR." According to their list of member organizations, this includes well-known countercult groups such as the Christian Research Institute, the Spiritual Counterfeits Project, the Berean Call, Answers in Action, Saints Alive in Jesus, and Utah Lighthouse Ministry. That this variance exists within the countercult community has not gone unnoticed by the EMNR. "As in any coalition" the document continues, "we expect to find believers with varying levels of competence, maturity, and ministerial experience. Some Christians possess the skills and knowledge necessary to present a balanced approach to this difficult field. Some of us have engaged in unjust or superficial judgments against others. On occasion some have judged presumptuously, making nonessential matters a test for Christian fellowship" (Evangelical Ministries to New Religions 1997).

Much of the document betrays a reaction to various tensions and scandals within the larger evangelical community, and the ethical standards articulated are clearly intended to address those issues. "There are occasions," the document states, "when Christians sin against one another by attitude, tone, timing, or delivery in their attempt to correct. As a result, some have earned the label 'witch hunter' or 'heresy hunter' " (Evangelical Ministries to New Religions 1997). In this regard, both Spencer (1993) and the Passantinos (1990b) produced work criticizing such countercult writers as Dave Hunt and Constance Cumbey, as well as organizations such as the Spiritual Counterfeits Project and the Christian Research Institute. These conflicts are considered in more detail in chapter 12. Important here is the EMNR's attempt to address in some organizational fashion the disunity generated by these circumstances.

The majority of the *MEDS* document is designed to ensure harmonious relations among evangelical Christians. Protections against slander and libel, standards of ethical, financial, and moral conduct, and the potential for a variety of sanctions are all intended to safeguard the integrity of the countercult witness. Very little, however, is devoted to similar protections for the objects of countercult activity. Put differently, while there is an elaborate ethic of missiologic conduct incumbent upon countercult apologists in their interaction with other apologists, very little governs evangelistic encounters with target religious groups or individuals. All discussion of this is relegated to three short paragraphs, under the heading, "Public critique of non-Christians."

The *MEDS* acknowledges that countercult interaction with non-Christians ought to be conducted in the same spirit of gentleness and humility that informs interaction within the countercult. EMNR members are enjoined to "avoid the use of harsh language where possible," to "beware of presuming to discern the motives, intents or inner thoughts of non-Christians," and to "bear in mind that our goal is to win them, not to alienate them" (Evangelical Ministries to New Religions 1997). "In our printed and oral presentations against error," the document continues, "EMNR members must recall that a 'bad witness' can sometimes undo months or years of 'seed-planting' on the part of others. We must avoid the use of 'loaded language' or emotional terminology which will breed contempt in the audience rather than compassion" (Evangelical Ministries to New Religions 1997).

The *MEDS* itself, however, falls into precisely the trap it charges EMNR participants to avoid. For, in this same section, not five sentences earlier, in fact, we read: "Though unbelievers are slaves to sin and possessed of a darkened, rebellious nature toward God, we have no warrant for impugning their motives in all cases" (Evangelical Ministries to New Religions 1997). Which suggests, first, that there are situations in which such censure would be warranted, and that countercult apologists possess the wisdom to know the difference. And, second, one wonders just how a devout Neopagan, for example, a person at least as committed to her spiritual path as the countercult apologist is to his, would hear the phrase "slaves to sin and possessed of a darkened, rebellious nature toward God"? While this may be what countercult apologists believe, I would suggest that this is precisely the kind of loaded language groups such as the EMNR are striving to eschew.

In terms of the ongoing professionalization of the countercult, one of the most important sections of the *MEDS* deals with self-representation, in which five critical areas outline standards for professional credentialing, authorship, testimony, employment, and accomplishments. In this, the EMNR recognizes that embellishment, hyperbole, the solipsistic interpretation of events as either anecdotal atrocities or anecdotal miracles, and the outright invention of one's past are all detrimental to the countercult agenda. Regarding "Educational Degrees and Ordination," for example, the *MEDS* reads: "EMNR members shall not advertise themselves as having degrees of higher education unless the degree has been legitimately earned at an institution requiring in-class instruction or through an accredited 'distance education' facility" (Evangelical Ministries to New Religions 1997). For some in the EMNR, for example, Gordon Lewis or Douglas Groothuis, this does not present any difficulty. For another of the coalition's founders, however, the venerable Walter Martin, the issue of whether he claimed for his degrees more academic freight than they could legitimately carry remains open. Similar issues have been raised about countercult apologists such as John Ankerberg, Hank Hanegraaff, John Weldon, and James White (see chapter 12).

Since, in the domain of the countercult, nouns such as "expert," "authority," and "specialist" are used regularly, often coupled with adjectives such as "international," "renowned," and "leading," the potential for and temptation to misrepresent one's credentials is high. Further, since there is no real accrediting body, no official *magisterium*, indeed no formal requirement for special education of any kind, the problem becomes that much more complex. Anyone who wants to can hang out a shingle (or launch the Internet equivalent thereof) that reads: "Countercult Apologist: Slaves to Sin Saved Here."

Like most taboos, it makes little sense to enact an ethical standard like this if the need for such a standard had not been made evident. With the democratization of the countercult, however, it is easy to see how the symbolic power of name and title is employed to an often exaggerated, apologetic purpose. Consider these few examples. The "Christian Research and Apologetics Ministry" (see chapter 8) is operated by "a guy, whose last name is Slick, who has a full time job fixing computers, and who writes and researches 'anti cult' material from a spare bedroom" (Slick 2001). The "Resource Center for Theological Research" is the project of Jeff Downs, an undergraduate student at Lancaster Bible College, and two student friends. "Christian Research and Evangelism" is operated by a lay Sunday School teacher from Sioux City, Iowa. "Christian Answers for the New Age" is the apologetics ministry of Marcia

Montenegro, a former astrologer and all-around New Age devotee. Few of these names reveal anything about the credentials of the operators.

In conclusion, through its doctrinal and ethical standards, EMNR seeks to hold the countercult community accountable for its claims—a commendable goal, but one that has not elicited the kind of support its organizers envisioned. As noted above, many countercult organizations, both large and small, are not represented in the EMNR. There are a number of possible explanations for this. First, interagency tensions between various countercult groups and individual apologists often prevent the kind of coalitioning anticipated by the EMNR's founders. Interpersonal conflicts, the collision of egos, differences in biblical interpretation and doctrinal adherence, division over which groups ought to be labeled "cults" and which not—all contribute to the often bitter feuds within the countercult domain that are exemplified in books such as *Heresy Hunters* (Spencer 1993) and *Witch Hunt* (Passantino and Passantino 1990b). Second, in many cases, if the EMNR model of peer accountability were responsibly implemented, the apologetics deployed by many countercult ministries would be badly shaken. Hyperbole and embellishment, deception and misrepresentation, questionable scholarship and outright lies can all be found within the countercult domain. In fact, for a number of ministries some combination of these constitutes the apologetic stock-in-trade. Ministries such as the two considered in the preceding chapter, for example, might not want to subject themselves to the kind of accountability suggested by the EMNR. Third, there is no unanimous agreement within the countercult community on what the Christian response ought to be to the problem of practical life presented by new and controversial religious movements. Some see proactive evangelism as the most faithful response, while others favor solid Christian boundary-maintenance. However successful it has been, though, the EMNR represents that end of the countercult spectrum that most strives for respectability and recognition both within the wider Christian community and beyond.

The Siege in Cyberspace and the Democratization of the Countercult

In the first centuries of the Christian church, apologists wrote with sharpened styli and lampblack ink, carefully tracing Latin characters onto parchment scrolls, folios, and codices. Their works bore names such as *Adversus haireses* (Irenaeus), *Contra Celsum* (Origen), and the *Praescriptionibus adversus haereticos*, Tertullian's *Prescription against Heretics*. In our modern—and some say postmodern—world the styli have become keyboards, the ink minute bundles of energy, and the dry leaves of parchment glowing computer screens. And, in the countercult, the *Prescription against Heretics* is now the "Cult Awareness Research Ministries," the "Ex-Masons for Jesus," and "Dave's Cult Page."

When Irenaeus and Origen wrote, if their books traveled at all they took weeks or months to reach their destinations. Now, anyone with access to the Internet can find and view countercult Web sites in a matter of seconds; downloading material and printing it consumes mere minutes. With the advent of handheld computers and PDAs, many of which are equipped to connect to the Internet wirelessly, this material is available to the apologist wherever there is cellular service or an infrared data port. More important for our purposes here, though, is the fact that anyone with basic equipment, software, and server access can now contribute to a movement that began in Christianity with the early apologists and continues unabated to this day. It is this access, perhaps more than any other single factor, that has contributed to the democratization of the countercult in recent years.

Until the late 1980s and early 1990s, countercult apologists were restricted, by and large, either to religious publishing houses or to the often prohibitively expensive path of self-publishing. The advent of the Internet, however, as well as the ready availability of Web authoring tools, domain hosting, and server support, has resulted in an explosion of interrelated countercult sites. Now, those who have felt called to this ministry but in the past have been unable to participate can, for the price of Microsoft Frontpage and a local Internet service provider, actively participate in the countercult. As emergent movement intellectuals, they can help shape the cognitive praxis of modern countercult apologetics, rather than simply make use of it in their daily lives. Indeed, in terms of Web site numbers, the Christian countercult presence on the Internet far exceeds that of the secular anticult. I suggest some reasons for this below.

THE COUNTERCULT ON THE INTERNET: LIBRARY, PLATFORM, AND COMMUNITY

Currently, the countercult in cyberspace contains hundreds of separate Web sites, which can be typologized according to a number of the continua discussed above. Some, notably those managed by professional countercult ministries, are not designed to *provide* significant countercult resources over the Internet at all, the dreams of Walter Martin notwithstanding. Instead, they function as cyber-storefronts, offering minimal online material but advertising the ministry's commercial print, video, and audio products. They participate in an information supermall, rather than an information superhighway—which is, I think, a better metaphor for the Internet anyway. On the other hand, a number of often very elaborate Web sites are operated by avocational countercult apologists. As another discriminate continuum by which countercult ministries may be distinguished, some of these sites include extensive discussion of new religious movements (NRMs), the apologetic agenda of the church, and the need to confront and counteract alleged cultic influence in society; others contain little more than a front page, perhaps an e-mail address (but not always), and a few hyperlinks to more detailed pages contained on other sites. While some avocational operators produce their own material, others borrow material freely from more established sources. Finally, while some sites are generalist, in that they treat any and all groups considered heterodox by the operators, others are group specific, functioning more on the order of electronic exit resource and postexit Christian e-communities.

With the growing availability of home page software and server support, it is these avocational countercult sites that have sprung up like fairy rings in the cyber-forest. They range from "Amazing Grace," which is run by a retired Imperial County sheriff and fingerprint expert, to the "Cult Awareness and Information Center," operated by an Australian ex-Jehovah's Witness; from "Dave's Cult Page," the Internet project of an undergraduate journalism student at California State University, Northridge, to "Doc Bob's JW Page," which is operated by another former Witness, who admits he is neither a doctor nor does he play one on TV.

Besides the obvious commercial applications for the professional countercult, the Internet provides, for the first time in Christian history, an intervailing, mutually supportive network that extends both in time and space beyond the physical boundaries of community and congregation. On the Web, the "consistent and continual conversation" that Berger and Luckmann (1966: 172–79) stress is so important to the ongoing maintenance of plausibility structures

exists on a scale unimagined even a scant decade ago. In the ongoing democratization of the countercult, it creates a space for the emergence of these new
movement intellectuals. And, in the evolution of countercult cognitive praxis,
the Internet is used in three major ways: as a library, as a platform, and as a
community.

LIBRARY: "EVERYTHING I NEED TO KNOW IS AT MY FINGERTIPS"

In his contribution to *Religion on the Internet*, Ken Bedell notes that the
"hunger for information [is] almost universal. At all levels of church organization people expect that they can find answers to questions on the Internet"
(2000: 191). A columnist in a leading British Internet magazine urges readers
to "Use the Net like Polyfilla and fill the gaps in your knowledge with ready-
made, instant info bites" (Wright 2000: 51). Providing these "ready-made,
instant info bites" is the most obvious use to which the Web is put by the
countercult. Rather than have to seek out and purchase resources from Christian bookstores, persons looking for information on Wicca, Buddhism, the Hare
Krishnas, Jehovah's Witnesses, or whatever group is of interest to them, can
simply click onto Web sites for the Apologetics Index, Baptist World Cult Evangelism, Cultwatch, or the Midwest Christian Outreach, and "fill the gaps" in
their knowledge. Since most countercult sites are collections of either brief
essays or hyperlinks to other brief essays, access to information is quick and
easy. But, like so much of what is available in the information supermall, a
good deal of the information is superficial and of questionable reliability.

Like the countercult in print, the countercult on the Net is an electronic
library designed less to *inform* the Christian visitor about the group in question, than to *confirm* for the visitor why that group is heterodox (read: cultic),
why it should be avoided, and why conservative Christianity is the only viable
option in place of it. As well, again like the countercult in print, the countercult
on the Net is intended as an equipping force to supply Christians with apologetic resources for their own encounters with NRM members. When Jehovah's
Witnesses or Mormons knock at one's door on a Saturday morning, when Sally
and Bobby return from college and announce they have found their spiritual
path in Scientology, when one's own pastor attends a conference on religious
freedom sponsored by the Holy Spirit Association for the World Unification
of Christianity (i.e., the Moonies), the countercult on the Internet places at the
fingers of distraught Christian parents and congregants resources to dispute
the religious claims of these other worldviews. Rather than a *public* library,
though, it is like those few shelves in an evangelical Christian bookstore or
seminary library that are devoted to "Cults and Sects" or "False Religions."

Consider as an example of a professional site, the "Ankerberg Theological
Research Institute" (www.johnankerberg.org), the Web presence of the *John
Ankerberg Show*. A fairly standard framed Web site, the "Articles" link in-

cludes collections of short essays on Roman Catholicism, Islam, and various aspects of the New Age. Each essay, which is usually no more than two printed pages, concludes with an offer to purchase a book or tape on that topic, as well as a .pdf copy of the article. Far from providing any in-depth analysis or discussion, the Ankerberg Theological Research Institute site is really an advertising forum for the published books, tracts, and video- and audiotapes produced by Ankerberg and his associates. In this it mirrors many of its secular Internet compeers. And this should in no way surprise. They are in the ministry business, and a cyber-storefront in the information supermall is becoming an indispensable aspect of that business. Because of this, like other professional countercult Web sites (e.g., that of the Spiritual Counterfeits Project), there is often less actual information available online than on many avocational sites. Because they illustrate different aspects of the countercult in cyberspace, I want to consider very briefly three of these avocational sites: the "Christian Apologetics and Research Ministry," the "Apologetics Index," and "Resource."

Christian Apologetics and Research Ministry (www.carm.org)

Begun originally as little more than the Internet project of an interested layperson, "Christian Apologetics and Research Ministry" (CARM) is now a 501(c)3 Internet countercult ministry. A fairly elaborate, well-designed site, it includes pages on Christian Doctrine, Apologetics, Major and Minor Cults, Religions, Philosophy, and Evolution. In his biographical statement, though, the owner (who is now an ordained evangelical minister) writes: "CARM is simply one man, me, Matt Slick. I write all the articles on the site—except for the testimonies and archived debates on the evolution board." Though it does appear that Slick has occasional help from volunteers in managing the site, he is clear that the site's content is entirely his responsibility.

Slick's choice of cultic and sectarian movements is interesting. Rarely, for example, does one see Christadelphianism listed as a "major cult." No edition of Walter Martin's *The Kingdom of the Cults* references it, and the Christian Research Institute has only one virtually insignificant reference in the scores of articles available online. Similarly curious is Slick's juxtaposition of Eckankar and Christian Identity; that is, one of the most benign NRMs is listed adjacent to what is arguably one of the most hateful. However, when one considers his own account of CARM's history, and the fact that he is solely responsible for content, the site's eclectic nature gains some context. In various ways over the past two decades, Slick has engaged in random countercult evangelism—including a volunteer beach ministry, and an ad in a local newspaper that read simply: "Learn the truth about Mormonism, Jehovah's Witness, Christian Science, and Unity. Call . . ." In his definition of "cult," though, while cleaving fairly close to the spirit of the countercult, Slick writes somewhat idiosyncratically: "Generally, a cult is a group that is unorthodox, esoteric, and has a devotion to a person, object, or a set of new ideas."

From this activity, Slick stored all his notes, sermons, talks, bible studies, and journals on computer disk. In 1995 he simply converted them to .html files and loaded them onto a site he called the "Christian Apologetics and Research Ministry." Five years later, he claims 14,000 front page hits per week and is endeavoring to make his Internet ministry a full-time operation—a crossover ministry. Moving from the avocational countercult to the Internet professional, for example, he offers his "Christian Apologetics Notebook" in three-ring binder format. Essentially the CARM Web site content in hard copy, Slick claims to have sold more than 3,000 of these notebooks on the Web. He has also self-published the same notebook as *Right Answers for Wrong Beliefs* (Slick 2002). Finally, for those who might think either a notebook or a paperback too cumbersome, Slick produces the entire Web site for sale on CD-ROM.

CARM maintains numerous discussion forums, as well as an online dictionary of theology—again written by Slick. A request form for those wishing to link from CARM to their own Web sites requires subscription to an electronic confessional statement. Numerous other countercult sites link to CARM, though, many with laudatory comments on the "objectivity" of the information Slick presents. As other Web authors and countercult apologists find his site, the various links between them both increase the size of the chorus, boosting the perceived authority of the individual voices, and further democratize the countercult community. "Contend for the Faith," for example, an apologetics Web site operated by Justin Taylor and Matt Perman, lists Slick as one of "the top defenders of Christianity, philosophers, and ethicists on the Web"— virtual approbation for Slick's emerging profile as one of the next generation's movement intellectuals. However, unless one looks specifically for Slick's personal information—that is, "I produce the entire site in my office at home in my spare time"—CARM's Web presentation could easily suggest to a visitor that it is a multistaffed, professionally credentialed, research organization.

Apologetics Index (www.gospelcom.net/apologeticsindex)

Many academics involved in the study of new religious movements are familiar with the work of Dutch countercultist Anton Hein and his "Apologetics Index" (AI) Web site. Indeed, a number of distinguished researchers—including Eileen Barker, David Bromley, Jeffrey Hadden, Irving Hexham, Massimo Introvigne, Gordon Melton, and Anson Shupe—are listed on Hein's site as dedicated "cult apologists" of varying degrees of prominence.[1] Hein claims to have been involved in online countercult activities "since the days of 300 baud modems and 50MB hard drives."[2] Whatever the past, he has built an enormous site that is updated daily and contains over 4,000 separate pages, as well as several thousand links to an amazing array of apologetic material. In many ways, it seems as though "Apologetics Index" is what Matt Slick might one day want his site to become.

Organized in the style of an online encyclopedia, Hein's material extends from *A Course in Miracles* to Zen Buddhism, with thousands of stops along the way. Linked articles quote passages from other sources—ranging from media reports to other countercult apologetic material to scholarly journals and monographs—most of which are then interwoven with Hein's own commentary. He regularly criticizes the above-mentioned cult apologists, for whom he shows particular contempt, and Scientology, to which he regularly refers as a "hate group." And, while he purports to support freedom of religion, like many countercult apologists Hein interprets that to include, most importantly, the "freedom to present research information that helps people make informed decisions about various movements, belief systems and world views."[3] In addition to the various articles, essays, broadsides, and hyperlinks, for years Hein also published the *Religion News Report,* an online clippings service of items related to evangelical countercult apologetics. Recently, he has taken advantage of Weblog programming and changed the *Religion News Report* to *Religion News Blog,* which allows for more sophisticated feeback from his readers. *Religion News Blog* is not generally the writings of Anton Hein, however. Rather, he reprints a wide variety of news articles and inserts his own commentary into the Weblog text.

His consideration of the March 1997 deaths of the Movement for the Restoration of the Ten Commandments of God sect in Uganda is a useful example of the manner in which information is often framed and presented on AI. Headlined "Uganda Doomsday Cult," its subheadings include "Other Ugandan Cults," "Controlling Cults," and "Cult Apologists Rush In." While the first two are simply reprinted media reports that ignore the fact that the Movement for the Restoration of the Ten Commandments of God was made up of fundamentalist Roman Catholics and was led by a renegade Catholic priest, "Cult Apologists Rush In" is Hein's own criticism of such scholars as Massimo Introvigne, James Lewis, Gordon Melton, and Catherine Wessinger. Following his critique of each of these, Hein concludes: "Let's hope that in the aftermath of the Uganda cult tragedy, authorities and individuals will learn to recognize cult danger signs, pay attention to ex-member testimonies, and reject the misguided propaganda of cult apologists."[4]

In addition to reality-maintenance, Hein has also used the Internet in more proactive countercult apologetics. In the years that Canadian scholar Irving Hexham's Nurel-l was an active Internet discussion group dedicated to the academic consideration of new religious movements (cf. Cowan 2000b), Hein was a vocal countercult presence there. With other anticultists and countercultists, such as Tilman Hausherr and Roger Gonnet, Hein joined the group less for scholarly dialogue around NRMs than to challenge those who regarded such groups differently than he (cf. Introvigne 2000; Mayer 2000). Like Gonnet and Hausherr, Hein regularly ignored the academic nature of the list and used Nurel-l as another vehicle by which to denounce NRMs in favor of his own fundamentalist Christianity. Presenting himself on the list as an expert in countercult apologetics, Hein posted voluminously on any number of issues. As another emergent movement intellectual, though, another product of the movement's democratization and the new intellectual space created by the Internet, his postings gained him a measure of credibility within the countercult community. For a few years, he was both the comoderator of Rich Poll's AR-forum discussion lists, and one of their most frequent contributors. While hardly unanimous in their approbation—for example, a number Poll's other contributors regularly objected to Hein's portrayal of cult apologists—responses to his posts often either alluded or deferred to his "expertise" in apologetics.

Resource (http://members.aol.com/djrtx/resource.htm)

Finally, at the opposite end of the amateur Internet continuum is "Resource," an online ministry devoted to providing information about the International Churches of Christ (also known as the Boston Movement), and what it calls "other cultic organizations." It claims to include materials representing theological, sociological, and behavioral perspectives, as well as references on identifying cults, recovering from cult involvement and/or spiritual abuse, and postexit resources for former members, as well as their family and friends.

Aside from the statements of faith and purpose, it is primarily a layered set of link pages, with almost no original content on the site. Rather, it functions as a navigation platform for others' work. Updated irregularly, the "Announcements" link lists two events from November 1998. There are a number of links to resources for former ICC members, including an ex-members registry ("A safe way for former members to register, search, and locate old friends."); an ex-members email list (which does not exist); and a Web ring (Dance-Away) for sites published by former ICC members.

"Resource" attempts to appear as a serious information service on a sometimes very controversial religious movement. For example, on the page of "Links Related to the International Church of Christ," there is a section labeled "Sociological Perspectives." Of the two links there, one is listed as "Justin Cooke's Sociology Page on the International Churches of Christ," which is really Cooke's contribution to Jeffrey K. Hadden's Religious Movements Homepage project at the University of Virginia. The other is to a University of North Carolina (Chapel Hill) Ph.D. candidate's bibliography of ICC resources.

Despite its intentions and its very clean Internet appearance, "Resource" also epitomizes two of the major problems with the countercult Web presence. First, though hardly limited to the countercult, Internet Web sites can consume enormous amounts of time and energy, making them very difficult to update regularly—especially if sites depend on current events for their content. Second, because no information is provided about who the site operators are or what their background is, Internet navigators have no basis on which to assess their qualifications for countercult ministry and, consequently, how seriously their information ought to be taken by garden-variety visitors.

PLATFORM: "I CAN FINALLY SAY WHAT I THINK"

Ex-member testimony is as much a staple of the Christian countercult as it is of the secular anticult (see, e.g., Bromley, Shupe, and Ventimiglia 1983; Introvigne 1999). As noted in chapter 2, though, the fundamental difference is that, where ex-member testimony in the anticult is deployed in the service of extraction and exit, countercult testimony has the additional mandate to promote migration *from* the problem religious group *to* conservative Christianity. For the countercult on the Internet, ex-member testimony functions in three separate modes—catharsis, warning, and exemplar—all of which are related to this additional mandate. While, in practice, these modes are often less than entirely discrete, it is useful to differentiate them here.

Prior to the ready accessibility of the Internet, few former "cult" members had the resources to tell their stories to anyone other than close friends, family members, and perhaps a church group or two. Countercult material regularly includes ex-member testimony, carefully chosen and shaped by the author to serve his or her particular apologetic. While not all former members want to tell their stories, the ease with which information can be Web published today has made it much more common for those who do. One former member of the Boston Movement, for example, has uploaded a one-page Web site describing her story. She writes: "I wanted to get to know God better. I was not a bad person. I went to church, was reading my bible, was doing good in school, but I wanted to go to bible study and this seemed to fit in perfectly with my schedule."[5] Another former "cult" member, this one an ex-Mason, declares on his testimony page: "To make a long story short [Satan] helped me to join the lodge. I was made a Master Mason. . . . I thought I had found what I had been missing. But it was still the devil up to his old tricks."[6]

Marcia Montenegro's countercult ministry, "Christian Answers for the New Age" (http://cana.userworld.com) contains two separate pages devoted to her spiritual journey. A former astrologer whose accomplishments include passing "the 7-hour exam given by the Atlanta Board of Astrology Examiners" (a board she also claims to have chaired), Montenegro is now an independent missionary dedicated to helping people extract themselves from various aspects of the New Age. She describes how, as a teenage seeker from a dysfunctional family, she became more and more involved with New Age pursuits until "an unexplained compulsion to go to a church gripped me in the spring and summer of 1990." Her conversion experience led her to reject the New Age entirely and devote herself to her countercult ministry. Ex-Satanist Jeff Harshbarger (www.refugeministries.cc) tells a story not dissimilar to Montenegro's: a dysfunctional home life that led to involvement in the occult, and finally salvation in evangelical Christianity. And Timothy Campbell, a former Jehovah's Witness, suffered from such feelings of guilt and fear when he disaffiliated in the late 1970s, following the failure of the latest Watchtower prophecy about the end-times, that "in 1995 I decided that my feelings called for action, and so I started this Web site. I wanted to let other ex-Witnesses know that they are not alone, and that they are not bad people—no matter what the Watchtower Society says about those who leave the fold. In helping them, I believed I would also help myself."

In this first mode, the Internet functions as a platform for the cathartic articulation of personal experience, an electronic confessional unavailable even a few years ago.

Next, as warning speech, ex-member testimony serves as an anecdotal atrocity: this is how horrible things happened to me; don't let them happen to you. Rather than confession, here stress is laid on the negative aspects of recruitment by and experience within the NRM in a manner designed to alert site visitors to the alleged dangers of the group in question. Monica Pignotti, for example, a former member of the Church of Scientology, declares: "My purpose in writing this account of my experiences is to make people aware of how it feels to be a Scientologist."[7] "Word for the Weary" is a counter-LDS ministry that operates the Internet site www.answeringlds.org. Numerous testimonies there describe leaving the Mormon Church once the individual became convinced that it was racist (based on its exclusion of blacks from the priesthood), occultic (based on alleged similarities between Masonic and Mormon rituals), and fraudulent (based on denunciations of the character of Joseph Smith). All of these allegations serve to warn visitors—whether members or potential converts—of the dangers associated with particular groups.

Finally, as the corollary of warning speech, the exemplar mode functions as an anecdotal miracle. Here, the successful conversion from the NRM to conservative Christianity is emphasized, the triumphant migration from the false world to the true. Former Mormons, Jehovah's Witnesses, Scientologists, and Wiccans attribute their new life to leaving their former group and embracing evangelical—often fundamentalist—Christianity. These stories almost invariably contain a missionary, "if I can do it, you can too" quality. Ex-Wiccan Kathi Sharpe is now a fundamentalist Christian who operates "ExWitch Ministries" (www.exwitch.org). Although she does consider virtually everything from Ásatru to the Oddfellows Lodge related in some way to Witchcraft, Sharpe nevertheless presents a fairly positive picture of Wicca, divorcing it entirely from more sensationalist countercult presentations, such as those circulated by Constance Cumbey, Dave Hunt, and Bob Larson. She relates her own movement from Neopaganism to evangelical/fundamentalist Christianity as a function of divine healing. According to her testimony, God was able to heal her partial deafness when the Goddess was not.

Similar testimonies can be found on a number of avocational countercult sites. "Katina" tells of her involvement in Tarot and Ouija, and of the violent headaches she would experience whenever she tried to enter a church. "Sometimes people who have practiced Witchcraft end up getting a 'mind control' spirit attached to them," she writes. "I was experiencing the classic symptoms."[8] In a very common countercult pattern, salvation for Katina came when she repented of every sin she could think of—prior to and during her involvement in the occult—and accepted Jesus. Victoria Shephard relates a lengthy, similar testimony, during which a number of battles for her soul took place, and in which she eventually converted from Wicca to evangelical Christianity. In addition to her own Web site (http://webs-2-u.com/Newbirth), she also participates in an ex-occultists Web ring.

As a Web phenomenon, the chorus of voices represented by ex-member testimony not only stabilizes the construction of reality for those who actively participate in its creation—that is, those who place their stories on the Web— it also reinforces that construction for those seeking information on different NRM experiences, as well as for those looking merely to validate the superiority of their own religious position. Like the soapbox on Speaker's Corner, the Internet platform exists in the midst of the Internet community, a liminal public space that is neither defined by nor restricted to the physical boundaries of church or pew.

COMMUNITY: "THERE ARE OTHERS OUT THERE WHO THINK AS I DO"

In both secular anticult and Christian countercult domains, one common element in apostate testimony is the sense of social isolation members experience when they belonged to the group in question. Postexit, a concomitant sense of isolation arises from the perceived uniqueness of their NRM experience: no one understands what they've gone through. Thus, the capacity to socialize with former members, to learn that one's experience is not unique, to gather support for one's own perception of events, and to develop meaning thereby are extremely important components of the postexit construction of reality. This draws, of course, on key elements of social construction and symbolic interaction theories (cf. Berger 1967; Berger and Luckmann 1966; Blumer 1969; Denzin 1992; Prus 1996)—that is, meaning is never inherent in a situation, it is always constructed in the dialectic of ongoing conversation. Over the Internet, former members from around the world can now converse with each other, validating similar experiences, expanding the chorus of significant voices, and communicating through their own Web sites, on discussion boards, and by public and private email.

"Sword of the Lord Ministries," for example, provides audio, video, and printed interviews with ex-members of the Children of God (now The Family). The "Cult Awareness and Information Center" (CAIC) is operated by and for "Recovering Jehovah's Witnesses." Like "Resource" above, the CAIC includes hyperlinks to Web rings of similar sites. Although the International Churches of Christ Web ring is nonactive, at the time of writing the "Recovering Jehovah's Witnesses" Web ring listed over eighty separate sites in English, French, Italian, German, Spanish, and Slovenian. Exjws.net bills itself as "a community of survivors with years of experience," and provides, among other things, a search engine to locate former Jehovah's Witnesses worldwide. "Watchers of the Watch Tower World" is an Internet ministry run by former Witness Randall Watters (Watters 1987). Among the services he offers are Watchtower-related discussion boards and search engines for Witnesses, ex-Witnesses, and local ex-Witness support groups and conferences. Currently Watters lists more than fifty such support groups. "Recovery from Mormonism" has more than 130 apostate testimonies on site, as well as hyperlinks to email newsgroups and alt.-discussion boards designed specifically for ex-Mormons. The primary foci of the "Ex-Mormon" discussion group are to "discuss experiences with the Mormon church," and to "overcome the effects of having been a Mormon." The ground rules set by the group's moderator are simple: "Mormons are not allowed to 'defend the faith.' "

Several sites offer both open and time-specific chatrooms for former members. While not all links remain active, prior to the ready availability of the Internet this kind of international community establishment could scarcely be imagined. And because many of these forums specifically prohibit active group members from joining discussions "to bash and ridicule,"[9] the construction of meaning is restricted to an ongoing reinforcement and internalization of the negative NRM experience, the exit process, and the successful conversion to Christianity. Countervailing voices—for example, those for whom the NRM experience is not negative—are simply bounded out of the conversation.

As has been noted several times, when the Christian Research Institute experienced organizational trauma following the death of Walter Martin and the rise of Hank Hanegraaff as president, numerous staffers, some long-time employees, left under a variety of circumstances. Among these were Rich and Pamela Poll, a research resource manager and art director at CRI, respectively; Paul Carden, former senior researcher and *Bible Answer Man* cohost; and Ron Rhodes, former associate editor of the *Christian Research Journal*. While Carden and Rhodes are now involved in countercult ministries of their own (Centers for Apologetics Research, and Reasoning from the Scriptures Ministries), they have also joined with the Polls in creating "Apologia Report," an online educational ministry that surveys a wide variety of media and presents subscribers with distilled summaries of "the most valuable resources to aid Christians as they encounter competing truth claims and seek to wisely respond." The *Apologia Report*, a resource digest, which arrives in the form of an email and prints out at about eight pages, contains brief précis of both reviews and articles, all culled from popular magazines, Internet sources, and scholarly journals. As a secondary source for countercult apologists, the editors make no claim to reviewing primary source information, and a typical entry reads:

New Age Thinking: A Psychoanalytic Critique, by M. D. Faber (University of Ottawa Press, 1996)—described as an "openly contemptuous" and "ruthless critique" by an author who has reversed "his previously favorable interpretation of mystical experience." The brief review (con, not pro) does not indicate whether or not Faber has accounted for the various ways the phrase "New Age thinking" has been used over the history of the movement. Religious Studies Review, Oct '97 (rec'd Dec 5), p 369. (*Apologia Report* 1998)

However valuable the *Apologia Report* is or proves to be, though, Poll and his colleagues have contributed significantly to the democratization of the countercult through two Internet forums sponsored by his organization. AR-talk and AR-forum are subscription-based electronic mailing lists designed for the dissemination and discussion of apologetics resources. On AR-talk, subscribers are encouraged to post references to journal articles, conferences, books, or other material related to countercult evangelism and related issues of Christian apologetics. Here, though, while questions for clarification may be raised, Poll permits no further discussion of these resources. Since the nature of countercult resources—their usefulness, availability, often their theological orthodoxy—are of particular and enduring interest to list subscribers, however, Poll also offers AR-forum, a list on which such discussion may take place. Because he is trying to limit both the volume of posts and maintain a level of professionalism within the countercult community, Poll restricts posting privileges to "religion professionals and graduate students. All others will have read-only access"—a membership restriction that is more an ideal than a reality.

Like most Internet discussion lists, AR-forum begins with a particular post and often expands in a variety of directions as points within the original message catch the attention of other subscribers. A series of posts about the dangers of *Harry Potter*, for example, which emerged on the list soon after the 2001 release of the first Harry Potter film, serves to illustrate the tenor with which AR-forum discussions are often conducted.

In the face of evangelical protests over the film and the occasional picketing of theaters in which it was being shown, the countercult was divided on *Harry Potter*. Was it really a dangerous new inroad into the occult, as Richard Abanes, Douglas Groothuis, Marcia Montenegro, and others contended? Or was the countercult overreaction precisely that—much ado about nothing? Yet and again something spooky to get in a flap about. That *Harry Potter* was taken seriously by evangelical Christianity cannot be denied. Abanes (2001) was not the only evangelical to write condemning the film, the series, and, on occasion,

Harry's creator, J. K. Rowling (cf. McGee and Matriasciana 2001; Montenegro n.d., 2000, 2001; Neal 2001). AR-forum provided a microcosm of this larger evangelical discussion, both as a platform and as a community in which participants could air their views.[10]

Originally posting on AR-talk, John Morehead (of Watchman Fellowship and Evangelical Ministries to New Religions), ventured that the response of actual Wiccans to the books was mixed at best. Addressing Marcia Montenegro, who had uploaded two articles highly critical of the Potter books on her Web site, Morehead writes that "the Potter series contains little if any real magick, and that they [i.e., actual Wiccans] have not seen any type of interest as your research would indicate." In reply, Montenegro argued that the Potter books must contain real occultism, otherwise why would Wiccan sites feature them? "They don't do this with other books, except real occult books, that I am aware of." Ex-Wiccan Kathi Sharpe agreed, declaring "the Potter series DOES have a great deal of things in it that I used to do!!"

Because discussion was moving from the area of apologetic resource to a debate about the value of those resources and the relative dangers represented by the Potter books, the impending quarrel was moved to AR-forum. At this point, Richard Abanes weighed in, like Sharpe "not wanting to be contrary." He agreed with both Montenegro and Sharpe, suggesting to Morehead: "Could it be that your witch/occult contacts are not being very honest with you?" Abanes agreed, however, that there was a possibility the occult community was as divided over the Potter series as the Christian, some seeing it as a vindication of their religious views, others viewing it as a caricature, still others paying little or no attention at all.

At this point, the discussion was virtually taken over by Anton Hein, the forum's moderator, who posted a number of lengthy excerpts from various media sources to support the quite logical contention that "any increase reported now allegedly due to Harry Potter [sic] must in some way be documented in order to be validated." From here the exchange devolved into a dispute between Hein and Abanes over whether the so-called facts of the case had been fully established. Contending that Hein did not "want to be confused with facts" that he believed his book had already amply demonstrated, Abanes challenged Hein, writing that "I know you're on a one man crusade to legitimize and justify Harry Potter and distance it as far as possible from the occult." Rather than contend with the substance of Abanes's criticism, however, Hein responded instead to the caviling tone of Abanes's post. "Sigh," he wrote. "Richard, if you cannot hold a discussion with someone who does not view things the exact same way you do without resorting to those kind of comments, then you may find yourself in the dog house or penalty box."

The "dog house" and the "penalty box" are the two control measures instituted by Poll to ensure orderly conduct on the discussion lists. Both reduce the offender to "read-only" status, with posting privileges suspended, in the case of the "penalty box" until both an apology and a commitment to improved behavior are offered.

Protesting that his comments were not directed at Hein's unwillingness to agree with him, Abanes sought to return the argument to issues related to the Potter books themselves and declared that an "unwillingness to accept the fact that real world occultism is indeed in the Potter books is absolutely ludicrous." Since he had just published a book on this topic, and, like Morehead, Hein's remarks pointedly questioned the central thesis of that book, Abanes's rebuttal is hardly surprising. Once again, though, quoting lengthy portions of the AR-forum charter, Hein warned Abanes that he interpreted his posts as personal attacks and suggested to Abanes that "some balance in your approach to these issues would greatly increase your effectiveness and accuracy. Some people may consider it 'ludicrous' that you are seemingly unwilling or unable to acknowledge any other perspectives than your own on this issue." This provoked the penultimate post from Abanes, who pointed out that for Hein to accuse him of an unwillingness to acknowledge perspectives other than his own was "the pot calling the kettle black." He concluded the post with a quote from an article about Rowling: " 'You can lead a fool to a book but you can't make them think.' " With that, Hein closed the discussion and banished Abanes to the penalty box.

In terms of the both the countercult, and the countercult on the Internet, two things are worthy of note in this rather lengthy example: (1) this entire exchange took place over less than twenty-four hours, the final exchanges between Hein and Abanes in slightly more than three hours; and (2) it provides a good illustration of the internecine conflict that often occurs between competing movement intellectuals. Each side in the cyber-debate sought to defend the legitimacy of its position, even against those with whom on many (perhaps most) other issues they might agree entirely. Like the Web resources available for ex-members of different religious groups, the ability of countercult apologists from California (Abanes and Morehead) to Virginia (Montenegro), and from North Carolina (Sharpe) to the Netherlands (Hein) to engage each other in such a timely fashion could scarcely have been imagined even a decade ago.

THE DEMOCRATIZATION OF THE COUNTERCULT

As Swiss scholar Jean-François Mayer has noted, to this point, the Internet has served more fully the needs and agendas of the countercult than it has those of the new religious movements to which it is opposed (Mayer 2000). One obvious reason for this is that the cognitive praxis of the countercult is located precisely in its opposition to NRMs. On the other hand, if it happens at all, answering the claims and accusations of countercultists is rendered at best a subordinate agenda for most religious groups and movements. Thus, the cyber-politik of the countercult and the exclusivist ideology that drives it is foregrounded in cyberspace simply by virtue of primary intent. All of the countercult's energy is focused on its apologetic mission. With the exception of the Church of Scientology and the Local Church, very little, if any, energy is devoted by targeted religious groups to disputing the specific allegations raised by the countercult. As a result, Internet search engines often hit countercult sites first and more often than sites devoted to positive presentations of the religious groups concerned.

As well, because of the secular anticult's trajectory of development, from family and friends of NRM members organizing to effect the extraction of their loved ones to deprogramming professionalization as in the American Family Foundation, the old Cult Awareness Network,[11] the Council on Mind Abuse, and their current occupational incarnation as "exit counselors," the anticult has been primarily interventionist in orientation—certainly more interventionist than the countercult. And this is not a mode that is well supported by the Internet environment. Unless one exists in a "clockwork orange" scenario in which one is forced to view anticult Web sites, the interaction level is so low and so voluntary that an Internet presence could conceivably affect only those NRM members who are already looking for exit resources, or those family members who are seeking either data on or contact information for particular anticult groups. At this point in time, however much power computers may hold in our lives, proactive intervention in those lives through the Internet is still in the realm of science fiction.

On the other hand, the Internet supports very well both the conceptual model and the behavioral orientation of the countercult. With some few exceptions, the countercult throughout its history has been primarily information oriented. Following the biblical injunctions at 1 Peter 3:15 and Jude 3, its objective has been to provide Christians with the apologetic tools necessary (1) to counter the claims of competing worldviews and (2) effect the conversion of NRM members to conservative Christianity. Operating as a clearinghouse for countercult information, a platform for the articulation of countercult perspectives, a community for the ongoing maintenance and reinforcement of the countercult worldview, and a cyber-politik for the insertion of the countercult agenda into the marketplace of religious ideas, the Internet has significantly expanded and democratized the countercult's ability to realize its objective.

Absent a global computer meltdown, two things seem clear about the relationship between the Internet and the countercult. First, because the Internet now presents perhaps the quickest, least-complicated way to access information in the technological world, more and more people will seek their facts electronically, indeed using the Net like Polyfilla. It is naive to think the Christian countercult and those who depend on it for information about new and controversial religious groups will do less. Thus, second, the countercult presence on the Web will continue to grow—notably in its avocational and adjunct professional aspects. And, as Web authoring and server access become easier, the threshold of participation will lower even further, resulting in both the popular democratization and, I suspect, the intellectual degradation of these resources. Given that the quality of information available electronically "spans the entire spectrum from the readily demonstrable to the unconditionally fabricated," as Jeffrey Hadden and I have noted elsewhere (2000: 6, emphasis in the original), *"with decreased time . . . comes increased expectation."* The Net "encourages us to 'fill in the gaps' in such learning as we already possess, rather than take the time to gain a base of knowledge to which the information we acquire might contribute, and by which it can be evaluated."

Part III
Countercult Apologetics

From False Worlds to True, Part 1: Other Religions According to the Countercult

Perhaps the most fundamental tenet of symbolic interactionism is Herbert Blumer's oft-quoted dictum that actors respond to situations based on the meaning those situations have for them. Derivative dicta contend that meaning is constructed, maintained, reinforced, and modified through interaction with other actors, both those in support of one's construction of meaning and those who represent a challenge to it (Blumer 1969: 1–60). Meaning is constructed and maintained through an ongoing, interactive negotiation of symbolic capital (cf. Bourdieu 1977, 1991, 1998). Meaning varies both situationally and across the range of possible actors. Bearing in mind Mannheim's assertion (1936, 1952) that not all interpretations of meaning are available in every social situation and to every social actor, in a social situation where meaning is not anchored to an official, authorized interpretation, the fluidity of meaning is matched only by its potential for variation. An oxidation stain on the side of a building becomes for the faithful an image of the Virgin Mary, for others the result of rain water leaking through damaged gutters. What is for one person a random series of events with no discernible connection whatsoever is for another a carefully orchestrated series of plots within plots.

The control of meaning, then, the limitation and management of acceptable or authoritative meaning structures, and the mitigation or elimination of the ambiguity inherent in what might be called the "meaning flux," becomes of primary concern for those who seek to establish and maintain the unique correctness of their own particular meaning structure, as well as to repair that structure when it is faced with competition, challenge, and the potential for disconfirmation.

As I have noted throughout this book, although some members of the Christian countercult have advocated for programmatic confrontation and evangelization of adherents to new and controversial religious groups (i.e., a missiological approach), the majority of the material produced by and for the countercult community is directed toward the maintenance and reinforcement of the Christian worldview in the face of the challenge represented by these alternative religious choices (i.e., an apologetic approach). In an open religious economy, where the varieties of religious choice carry little or no social censure, control of the meaning structure becomes increasingly important. Definition of a situation is always an attempt to extend power over and within that situation (cf. Bourdieu 1977, 1991, 1998; Foucault 1965, 1977, 1978).

All of this intends toward the institution of an officially sanctioned aggregate of religious meaning: (1) establishing, maintaining, and reinforcing the meaning of particular religious situations in which actors find themselves; (2) limiting the number of "live options" (James [1902] 1985) for actors in terms of the authenticity, authority, and validity of their beliefs; and (3) determining and establishing the limits of officially sanctioned meaning in interreligious encounters. In this section, I discuss the countercult construction of meaning as it relates to particular religious groups and institutions, including aberrant Christianities, new religious movements, and the Roman Catholic Church.

"THE CULTS OF CHRISTIANITY": ABERRANT CHRISTIAN SECTS

While people may find the weekend approaches made by Mormon missionaries or Jehovah's Witness pioneers moderately annoying, depending on the nature of the activities these approaches have interrupted, many will not see them as more than a momentary distraction, a problem for no longer than the moment of intrusion. For the Christian countercult, however, these moments of intrusion are symptomatic of a much larger problem, a much more protracted battle taking place in the expanding religious economy and the concomitant struggle for the control of meaning within that economy. Authoritative meaning itself is at stake in this battle. In the countercult construction of reality, if either the Mormons or Jehovah's Witnesses are right—that is, if their cosmology, their conception of salvation history, and their interpretation of humankind's place within those have some measure of validity—then the religious meaning structure adhered to by the countercult must be incorrect to that extent. It is of paramount importance, therefore, to nihilate the worldviews adhered to by these so-called cults of Christianity.

The Church of Jesus Christ of Latter-day Saints

From 1877 to 1897, the Rev. Robert Gibson McNiece served as the pastor of First Presbyterian Church in Salt Lake City, Utah. Intimately acquainted with the growth of the Church of Jesus Christ of Latter-day Saints in that state, and claiming to have known church presidents from Brigham Young (1801–77) to Joseph F. Smith (1838–1918), McNiece contributed the essay on Mormonism to *The Fundamentals* collection. Criticizing the Mormon Church first on the basis of its ambiguous origins, McNiece deployed a theory of fictional origination for *The Book of Mormon* common in some counter-Mormon apologetics and polemics. In circulation since one of the first critiques of Mormonism, Eber D. Howe's *Mormonism Unvailed* ([sic] 1834), the so-called Rigdon-Spaulding theory asserts that *The Book of Mormon* could not have come from either the mind or the pen of Joseph Smith Jr. (1805–44), the founder of the church, whom McNiece characterized as "ignorant and illiterate, hardly able to read until after he was a grown man" ([1917] 1996: 132). Rather, the theory holds that it was the work of a Campbellite preacher and early convert to Mormonism, Sidney Rigdon, who allegedly plagiarized *The Book of Mormon* from an unpublished novel written by a man named Solomon Spaulding. Spaulding's manuscript told the fanciful story of the Israelite origins of the First Nations peoples in the Americas, a tale that bears some resemblance to the narrative history contained in *The Book of Mormon*. Vigorously denied by the Mormon Church, and despite the counterarguments of researchers such as Hansen (1981) and Brodie (1971), the Rigdon-Spaulding theory of Mormon origins still occurs regularly within the domain of the Christian countercult (e.g., Martin 1965, 1977, 1985, 1997; Spencer 1986).

McNiece saw three major flaws in Mormonism, which he characterized as a "crude, bogus, man-made system under the garb of Christian phraseology" ([1917] 1996: 132). First, "it is a strongly anti-American system" ([1917] 1996: 134) that sought to replace the "fundamental principles of our free, representative government" with a theocracy, the temporal power of which was located in the hands of its "tyrannical priesthood" ([1917] 1996: 134). Second, "the Mormon System is thoroughly anti-Christian" ([1917] 1996: 135). Here McNiece's concerns are similar to virtually every Christian condemnation of Mormonism: while appropriating the language and theological conceptualizations of Christianity, it imports into these such divergent understandings of the faith that the result is no longer recognizable as authentic. Third, "Mormonism is a deliberate counterfeit of the Christian religion, intended to deceive the ignorant" ([1917] 1996: 135).

"It is difficult for any one to study this Mormon system as a whole," writes McNiece in his concluding remarks ([1917] 1996: 148), "without coming to the conclusion that there is something in it beyond the power of man, something positively Satanic." Like Jan Karel van Baalen, who would write two decades later, McNiece saw the rise of the Latter-day Saints in Utah as "a reproach on the Christian churches of this country" ([1917] 1996: 148). And, with the election to federal government of Mormon politicians (according to McNiece in five states besides Utah), the problem of practical life represented by the Mormon Church was national, not simply local, and social, not simply religious. "The one important thing to be done," he concludes ([1917] 1996: 148), "is to double the Christian missionary forces in Utah, in order to bring deliverance to those who are in bondage."

"Of all the major cults extant in the melting pot of religions called American," wrote Walter Martin more than half a century later, "none is more subtle or dangerous to the unwary soul than The Church of Jesus Christ of Latter-day Saints" (1980: 63). In *The Maze of Mormonism*, he refers to the Mormon Church as "satanic polytheism" (1978: 78–80); in *The Kingdom of the Cults*, it was "a polytheistic nightmare of garbled doctrines draped with the garment of Christian terminology" (Martin 1985: 226). The Latter-day Saints under-standing of the Virgin Birth he terms "a blasphemous derivation from the mythology of Greece coupled with unmistakable signs of pagan sexual per-versions" (Martin 1976: 27).

While some writers are more charitable than Martin and consider Mormon-ism merely "inconsistent with genuine Christianity" (Tingle 1983: 133; cf. Scott 1990, 1994; Spencer 1984, 1986), other countercult apologists have been as critical or more. Decker and Hunt (1984) argue that Mormonism is actually an amalgam of "basic Hinduism and occultism," "a modified form of paganism which is so carefully camouflaged with a façade of Christian terminology that it deceives most Mormons" (1984: 20). Following the duelist conspiracism of the countercult, they conclude: "Careful investigation indicates that Joseph Smith was in touch with a suprahuman source of revelation and power that has been the common inspiration behind all pagan religions down through history" (Decker and Hunt 1984: 20). Marrs concurs, declaring that "the entire Mormon faith is thoroughly immersed in disguised satanism and heretical false teaching" (1990: 255). In another very common countercult argument, An-kerberg and Weldon (1991a: 13–56, 1992a: *passim*; 1999: 274–338) contend that the Mormon Church has deliberately lied about every one of its claims to represent biblical Christianity. Strongly suggesting a proactive deception on the part of the Latter-day Saints, they argue that "the church has misled the public concerning its true teachings" (Ankerberg and Weldon 1991a: 13).

Although this charge is made about any number of controversial religious groups, for the Christian countercult Mormonism presents a problem of prac-tical life that is fivefold, manifesting itself (1) ecclesiologically, (2) theologically, (3) sociologically, (4) politically, and (5) practically. Ecclesiologically, the claim of the Mormon Church to be the true, restored church of Jesus Christ presents an obvious challenge to the legitimacy and ultimacy of the evangelical coun-tercult worldview. If there is even a chance that the Latter-day Saints are correct in their ecclesiological assertions, much of the evangelical/fundamentalist con-struction of reality would collapse like a house of cards. Thus, these ecclesio-logical claims must be refuted if the countercult construction of reality is to remain intact. Next, like the institutional construction of reality in which the countercult participates, the theological claims of the Latter-day Saints rest on particular interpretations of the Bible and on Mormon extrabiblical revelation, most notably *The Book of Mormon*. Thus, for the countercult, Latter-day Saints claims about who God is, what God's purpose is for humanity, how humanity interacts with God, and the eschatology toward which that interac-tion tends must be answered as well. Sociologically, since the Mormon Church is one of the fastest growing faiths in the world—Rodney Stark, for example, believes that Mormonism stands "on the threshold of becoming the first major faith to appear on earth since the Prophet Mohammed rode out of the desert" in the seventh century (1984: 19)—it represents a significant demographic challenge to traditional Christianity. Politically, the wealth of the church, its positioning of church members in various levels of government, and its alleged commitment to the establishment of a theocratic society founded on Mormon principles (a "theocratic totalitarian communism," according to Decker and Hunt) all contribute to the countercult construction of Latter-day Saints evil (cf. Ankerberg and Weldon 1992a; Martin 1978). Described by Rhodes as the "mainstreaming agenda" of the cults (1994: 83–164), the countercult question posed to Mormons in positions of political power is not dissimilar to those raised during the presidential candidacy of John F. Kennedy, a Roman Catholic. If opponents wondered whether Kennedy's primary allegiance would be to Washington or to Rome, opponents of the Latter-day Saints ask whether a Mormon's first duty is to the Capitol or to the Tabernacle.

Finally, practically, some of the most serious—some might contend ludicrous—allegations have been made with regard to clandestine Latter-day Saints practices, notably blood atonement, satanic ritual abuse, and human sacrifice. While a number of countercult authors refer to the doctrine of blood atonement in the history of early Mormonism—specifically, the ritual murder of a Latter-day Saints member for so-called crimes ranging from intermarriage to apostasy (cf. Ankerberg and Weldon 1991a: 389–404; Geer 1986; Martin 1978: 237–64; for a Latter-day Saints interpretation, cf. McConkie 1966: 92–93; Scharffs 1989: 334–36)—and seek to assess its historicity and importance in the development of the tradition, Decker and Matrisciana (1993) maintain that there is a popular resurgence of the practice just below the veneer of modern public Mormonism. Citing the 1988 murders of four people in Texas, attributed in the media to the leaders of a "violent polygamist Mormon sect" in retribution for the victims' alleged apostasy (*Los Angeles Times,* June 28, 1988; cf. Melton 1992: 51–55),[1] Decker and Matrisciana contend that the horrific violence perpetrated by the Texas schismatics is a possibility just waiting to surface within mainstream Mormonism. Calling the murders "a sweet-smelling sacrifice to the god of Mormonism" (1993: 149), they contend that "the fruits of Mormon teaching at its purest level logically lead to these consequences" (Decker and Matrisciana 1993: 153).

In the sometimes inhospitable world of countercult apologetics, professional ex-Mormon J. Edward Decker often fares little better in his colleagues' esteem than do Constance Cumbey, Dave Hunt, or Texe Marrs. "Decker's name alone is enough to discredit a book," writes Carl Mosser, an evangelical scholar highly critical of the manner in which countercult apologetics has failed to keep pace with its Mormon counterpart (1998; Beckwith, Owen, and Mosser 2002; Mosser and Owen 1998; for a rebuttal to Mosser and Owen, see Ankerberg and Weldon 1999: 315–18). "Decker is infamous for the mistakes he makes describing Mormon doctrine, the sensationalist claims he has made about Mormon rituals and leaders, and the generally uncharitable attitude with which he conducts his ministry" (Mosser 1998). Former CRI researcher Robert Bowman concurs. "Decker's approach has been to portray Mormonism in the worst possible light, rather than in the most accurate light. That is, any accusation or criticism of Mormonism that appears to be useful to pull people out of the LDS church is seized upon by Decker (and not just by him, please note, but by *many* in the evangelical counter-LDS community) and used regardless of the accuracy of the charge" (Bowman 1998a). On the other hand, advertisements for his books in the *Christian Research Journal* describe Decker as "one of today's most-respected authorities on Mormonism," a prominent movement intellectual in the countercult community.

A faithful Mormon for nearly two decades, Decker was excommunicated by the church in 1976 when he converted to evangelical Christianity (Decker 1998). Two years later, working with others who had left the church and similarly converted, he began his countercult ministry, Ex-Mormons for Jesus Evangelistic Association, Inc., known colloquially as Saints Alive in Jesus (SAIJ). As a countercult apologist, Decker came to prominence in 1982 when he and fellow ex-Mormon Dick Baer produced (and appeared in) what is arguably the most influential of all countercult films, *The God Makers*, which SAIJ advertised as "the film that changed the way the world looks at Mormonism" (Saints Alive in Jesus 1994). Constructed around a dramatization of Decker and Baer approaching a law firm in hopes of bringing a class action suit against the Mormon Church, *The God Makers* is a mélange of dialogue, interviews, and narration, all supported by a cartoon that supposedly recounts Latter-day Saints theology and illustrates secret Mormon temple rituals.

According to the film, the lawsuit Decker and Baer sought to bring was for "fraud," "deliberate misrepresentation," and "causing family break-ups." In addition to Decker and Baer, five other interviewees claim that Latter-day Saints bishops counseled them to divorce their spouses. The "lawyers" ask whether it is the pair's contention that the Mormon Church pressures men and women to divorce and remarry when one spouse either questions Mormon doctrine or apostatizes; Baer nods, but the shot cuts away before a definitive or more qualified answer can be given (Decker 1982). Among the more specific charges made in the film are that an oath of total obedience is sworn by the woman to her husband, and that the temple ritual ridicules all Christian clergy (Decker 1982; for a rebuttal from the Latter-day Saints perspective, cf. Scharffs 1989).

At the time of its release, Karen Bossick, a reporter for *The Idaho Statesman* (Boise), wrote that "*The Godmakers* [sic], a 56-minute film produced by a group of former Mormons, has fueled claims of 'religious pornography,' as well as a wave of threats, harassment and violence in many of the places it has been shown, including Idaho where a fourth of the state's residents are Mormons" (1983: 5). While there are no statistics to substantiate her report, in Bossick's article Decker claims that *The God Makers* was "being shown more than a thousand times each month, with an average attendance of 2,500 people at each showing, or about 250,000 viewers per month" (1983: 6). Decker also alleged that, as a result of his work, "he and his members have been shot at, their cars burned, their doorsteps strewn with mutilated animals and their families exposed to obscene phone calls and death threats" (Bossick 1983: 7).

That mention of these events, however traumatic they must have been for Decker and his family, never appears again in SAIJ literature is, to say the least, curious. This is so especially since Decker was quite prepared to launch "a defamation of character suit against a television station general manager and a Mormon church official for public comments they made about *The Godmakers*" (*Journal-American* 1983). According to the news clipping reproduced in the *Saints Alive in Jesus Newsletter*, the remarks made by the defendants in the suit " 'were harmful to the reputation of the plaintiffs and the movie produced by the plaintiffs.' " The imbalance of response suggests that the claims made by Decker to Bossick should be more appropriately categorized as anecdotal atrocities.

In March 1984, the Arizona Regional Board of the National Conference of Christians and Jews (NCCJ; now the National Conference for Community and Justice) repudiated *The God Makers* in a decision entitled "Confronting Proselytization" (National Conference of Christians and Jews 1984). After an investigation lasting several months, the NCCJ made its feelings clear in a public letter. "The film does not—in our opinion—fairly portray the Mormon Church, Mormon history, or Mormon belief," they write, in a passage worth quoting at some length not least because it rehearses much of what one finds in countercult rhetoric.

It makes extensive use of "half-truths," faulty generalizations, erroneous interpretation, and sensationalism. It is not reflective of the genuine spirit of the Mormon faith. We find particularly offensive the emphasis in the film that Mormonism is some sort of subversive plot—a danger to the community, a threat to the institution of marriage, and is destructive to the mental health of teenagers. All our experiences with our Mormon neighbors provide eloquent refutation of these charges. We are of the opinion that *The Godmakers* relies heavily on appeals to fear, prejudice and other less worthy human emotions. We believe that continued use of this film poses genuine danger to the climate of good will and harmony which currently exists between Valley neighbors of differing faiths. It appears to us to be a basically unfair and untruthful presentation of what Mormons really believe and practice. (National Conference of Christians and Jews 1984: 3–4)

Those in favor of the film's widespread distribution responded to the NCCJ's report with a charge that the committee—and, indeed, the NCCJ Arizona Board of Directors as a group—was dominated by members of the Mormon Church, and therefore ineluctably biased.

The year 1984 also saw the publication of what has been, without question, Decker's most popular book, *The God Makers*, which was based on the film and which Decker co-authored with fellow apologist Dave Hunt (Decker and

Hunt 1984). Decker released two video sequels to *The God Makers* (1987, 1992), the latter of which (*The God Makers II*) was a significantly darker work. While much of that film concentrates on the financial holdings of the Mormon Church—the so-called subversive plot to which counter-Mormon polemicists at least since Ahmanson ([1876] 1984), McNiece (1898), and Combs (1899) have referred—a considerable portion focuses on Decker's perception of Mormon fundamentalism. In Decker's view, Mormon fundamentalists are those who would, allegedly, see the Latter-day Saints return to the public practice of polygamy and the ritual of blood atonement, which Decker and his colleagues interpret as legitimized murder within the Mormon community for sins considered too egregious to be cleansed in any other way. The perception left by this film is that a return to the practices of polygamy and religious vendetta is not reserved for a small fringe element within the Latter-day Saints but rather represents a cutting edge of Mormon revitalization.

At the other end of the counter-Mormon apologetic spectrum are two significant attempts to reduce the often pugnacious tension between evangelical Christians and Latter-day Saints. In 1997, setting aside the kind of polemic encountered in much of Christian countercult material on Mormonism, Craig Blomberg, a professor of New Testament at Denver Seminary, and Stephen Robinson, a professor of ancient Scripture at Brigham Young University, published an account of their efforts to sit down together and learn what were the real agreements and disagreements between their two religious traditions (Blomberg and Robinson 1997). Their effort, however, was not met with unanimous approbation among the Christian countercult, many of whom saw it as a direct attack on their vocation, or among members of the Mormon Church, who regarded it as an unwelcome compromise with their principal detractors. Professional anti-Mormon James White, for example, called it "one of the most disturbing and troubling books I have read in a very long time" (White 1997b; cf. Ankerberg and Weldon 1999: 318–20; White 1997a; for an extensive Latter-day Saints appraisal, see Hamblin and Peterson 1999).

About the same time, two evangelical doctoral students, Carl Mosser and Paul Owen (now an assistant professor of biblical studies and languages at Montreat College), published what is arguably one of the most significant pieces of evangelical scholarship on the Mormon Church in recent years. "Mormon Scholarship, Apologetic and Evangelical Neglect: Losing the Battle and Not Knowing It?" appeared first as a presentation to the Evangelical Theological Society, then in unofficial form on the Internet discussion list alt.religion.mormon, and finally in *Trinity Journal* (Mosser and Owen 1998). In their essay, Mosser and Owen called the evangelical community to account for the often polemical and anti-intellectual stance they have taken toward the Latter-day Saints. Of Ankerberg and Weldon (1992a), for example, they write that "in our estimation, *[Behind the Mask of Mormonism]* is among the ugliest, most unchristian, and misleading polemics in print. The authors constantly belittle their opponents—always questioning either their intelligence or integrity" (Mosser and Owen 1998: 203).[2] Their paper concludes with five recommendations, of which four read: "First, evangelicals need to overcome inaccurate presuppositions about Mormonism. Second, evangelical counter-cultists need to refer Latter-day Saints scholarship that is beyond their ability to rebut to qualified persons. Third, evangelical academicians need to make Mormonism, or some aspects of it, an area of professional interest. Fourth, evangelical publishers need to cease publishing works that are uninformed, misleading or otherwise inadequate" (1998: 180–81), which is to say, much of what has passed for counter-Mormon apologetic to date.

Jehovah's Witnesses

Conspiracies of world domination aside, eventually most critiques of alternative religious expression devolve into disputes over doctrine. In some cases, for example, such as the major world religions, these debates revolve around the nonacceptance of various Christian doctrines, especially the uniquely salvific nature of Jesus. In other cases, however, such as the Mormons, Christian Science, Seventh-Day Adventists, and Jehovah's Witnesses, heated disputes often take place over the correct *interpretation* of relevant doctrines. This was so in the early church, whether the venue was the Jerusalem Council and the issue the admissibility of Gentiles into the circle of nascent Christianity, or the various ecumenical councils leading to a final articulation of the traditional Trinitarian formula. At the center of the Reformation was the dispute between Martin Luther and the Roman Catholic Church over the nature of salvation—at its heart a doctrinal dispute. Four hundred years later, *The Fundamentals*, while written to protect so-called historic Christianity from the treble onslaught of higher criticism, Darwinism, and modernist theology, framed its defense in terms of the historic doctrines of the Church. Dispute over the correct interpretation of the Jesus event and the Christian movement that emerged and flourished following it has always generated both alternatives and monolithics, both challenges and commitments to the dominant order. Who was/is Jesus, and how is he to be understood for Christians—indeed, for all people—today? What is the nature of revelation, and is it ongoing or closed? What must one do to be saved, and ought something called "salvation" even be an issue?

In the case of the Watchtower Bible and Tract Society, known worldwide as Jehovah's Witnesses, two broad fields define the landscape of the dispute: (1) proactive denial by Jehovah's Witnesses of traditional Trinitarian dogma, and (2) the string of predictions made by the Watchtower about the return of Christ and the establishment of his eschatological kingdom. While the former is treated as a direct attack upon the "orthodox" Christian construction of reality, the latter is regarded as irrefutable evidence of the Watchtower's inability to claim legitimate prophetic status.

First, because Jehovah's Witnesses stand in the stream of Christian tradition that does not accept the traditional Trinitarian position, the first field is the doctrinal defense of that position. Indeed, Jehovah's Witnesses view the traditional Trinity as a perverse form of polytheism, one that makes sense neither doctrinally nor practically. It is important to note that by "traditional" I mean the Western (i.e., Roman Catholic) understanding of the Trinity, defined most fully in the Athanasian Creed. Though many evangelicals adopt (some might argue "co-opt") the term "orthodox" as a way of strengthening their position rhetorically, as though the doctrine of the Trinity were somehow inerrantly derived scripturally and immaculately determined historically, this usage is imprecise (cf. Pelikan 1990). As scholars of medieval church history recognize, one of the central disputes between the great Western and Eastern (Orthodox) branches of Christianity has been the precise nature of the Trinity. As opposed to the Orthodox, the Western (i.e., Athanasian) position is the one most often adopted by countercult opponents of Jehovah's Witnesses (e.g., Bowman 1989b: 11–15).

Often virulent ex-member polemics aside (e.g., Schnell 1956), defense of this Trinitarian position in the face of Witness denial constitutes much of the practical counter-Witness apologetic. Robert Bowman has written three books dealing with various aspects of the issue and provides a good example of counter-Witness apologetic conducted along this line. Until a conflict with current Christian Research Institute president Hank Hanegraaff resulted in his leaving the organization in 1992, Bowman was a staff member there. During his roughly seven years at the institute, he held various positions ranging from special projects editor to cohost of the institute's *Bible Answer Man* radio program. Unlike many of his countercult colleagues, however, including CRI founder Walter Martin, Bowman is reluctant to use the word "cult" as freely as others. "In my judgment," he writes in *Orthodoxy and Heresy* (Bowman 1992: 113–14), "the time has come to admit that using the word *cult* to refer to socially mainstream religious groups that espouse heresy is counterproductive. When referring to heretical religious groups, I prefer to call them heretical religions, or pseudo-Christian religions, or heretical sects. These labels are more descriptive and less prejudicial than the label of cult." Although precisely why the terms "heretical religion" or "heretical sect" are "less prejudicial" than "cult" remains unclear, Bowman is as unequivocal as other countercult apologists when it comes to the main cognitive boundary markers separating so-called true Christianity from the host of imposters seeking to force their way onto the stage.

Prior to leaving the Christian Research Institute, Bowman responded to a Witness tract, *Should You Believe in the Trinity?*, by publishing *Why You Should Believe in the Trinity: An Answer to Jehovah's Witnesses* (1989b). That same year, he also published *Jehovah's Witnesses, Jesus Christ, and the Gospel of John* (Bowman 1989a) to debate what is arguably the most oft-disputed scriptural text in counter-Witness apologetics, John 1:1, which Watchtower

literature (including their *New World Translation of the Holy Scriptures*) con-
cludes with "and the Word was a god." Finally, in *Understanding Jehovah's Witnesses: Why They Read the Bible the Way They Do*, Bowman wanted "to help evangelicals better understand Jehovah's Witnesses and also to help Jehovah's Witnesses better understand themselves" (1991b: 13). Concluding this analysis of Watchtower hermeneutics, however, Bowman writes: "My hope is that [Jehovah's Witnesses] will be challenged to abandon the unstable foundation of the Watchtower and build their faith on the sure foundation of the Scriptures" (1991b: 123).

In the prefatory material to each of these books, Bowman follows many of his countercult colleagues by carefully pointing out that his aim is neither to insult nor to denigrate Jehovah's Witnesses, but rather to point out where their views have led them into error. In *Understanding Jehovah's Witnesses*, in fact, he maintains that "actually, this is not really an 'anti-Witness' book. I am not an ex-Jehovah's Witness (and therefore am not an 'apostate') and am not writing this book to tear down the Witnesses" (Bowman 1991b: 7). For Bowman, these appear to be the only criteria by which an anti-Witness book is deter-
mined. One who is not an ex-Witness, and who at least claims not to be writing to "tear down the Witnesses," is by definition not writing "anti-Witness" material. He does point out, however, that "I do think evangelicals have the truth, and not Jehovah's Witnesses" (Bowman 1991b: 8).

Why You Should Believe in the Trinity was written specifically to answer the challenges presented in the Witness tract noted above. Although he is very clear that the *evangelical* understanding of the Trinity—indeed of all Christian doctrine—is the only correct understanding, Bowman's work is remarkably free from the anti-Witness polemic found in other countercult apologists (e.g., Martin and Klann 1974; Morey 1980; Schnell 1956; Watters 1987). "If the arguments of the JW booklet are sound," he begins (Bowman 1989b: 7), "the doctrine of the Trinity should be rejected by all Christians. However, if those arguments are not sound, the possibility ought to be considered that the Trinity is a biblical and Christian doctrine after all." Again, even though (1) Bowman has no intention of investigating the claims made by Jehovah's Witnesses, but seeks merely to refute them with the intent of nihilating the Watchtower construction of reality, thus encouraging them to transfer their allegiance to evan-
gelical Christianity, and even though (2) he does believe that the traditional Trinity is, indeed, the *only* biblical, Christian understanding, he does not assume a priori that refuting the Witness worldview automatically validates the traditionally Christian one.

In at least two places, however, Bowman does make his collateral biases abundantly clear. According to Watchtower doctrine, though hardly limited to Jehovah's Witnesses, shortly after the apostolic age there occurred a great apostasy, a great falling away from the true faith of Jesus, a faith that would remain hidden until Christ returned—which Witnesses believe took place "figura-
tively" in 1914. Bowman alledgedly refutes this Watchtower belief by sug-

gesting that the apostasy to which they refer "probably [applies] to different heresies and different periods of church history" (1989b: 45). Unfortunately, he elaborates on neither. Instead, he seems to negate the Witness argument on the grounds that these heresies took place long after the apostolic period. A bit further, he continues: "If the prediction of an apostasy has reference to a massive turning away from the truth by a large portion of the professing Christian church, the so-called Enlightenment stands out as the best candidate so far in recorded history. In the sixteenth and seventeenth centuries nearly all of the professing Christian culture was experiencing renewed faith in Christ and in the Bible as God's Word" (Bowman 1989b: 46).

Following this somewhat chimeric vision of a "professing Christian church," by which we can infer that he means the Protestant Reformation (elsewhere Bowman is critical of Roman Catholicism; see 1989b: 19), he points out how "this same culture largely abandoned even a profession of that faith as critical theories about the Bible's origin, skeptical denials of miracles, and the theory of naturalistic evolution changed the dominant worldview of the West from Christian to secular" (Bowman 1989b: 46). While he may be upset about these issues, Bowman avoids discussing the social and cultural context in the West during these times of "renewed faith in Christ and in the Bible as God's Word." Consider, among others, the various wars of religion in Europe, Luther's support for the violent suppression of the German peasants, French Catholic repression of the Huguenots, Calvin's theocratic tyranny in Geneva, or John Knox's virtually hysterical *The First Blast of the Trumpet against the Monstrous Regiment of Women* (1558).

Regarding the academic heirs of the Enlightenment, Bowman is equally willing to dismiss other challenges to his construction of reality that are raised by modern scholarship. In this, he even finds himself aligned with those he is criticizing. "What modern scholars think about the New Testament's teaching regarding Jesus is interesting," he writes, "but hardly decisive. Both JWs and evangelical trinitarians agree that modern critical biblical scholarship, with its denial of the inspiration and reliability of the Bible and its attempts to deny the supernatural, miracle-working Jesus of the Bible, is apostate and unreliable" (Bowman 1989b: 91). As with so many of his countercult colleagues, that which does not support, affirm, or participate in his religious construction of reality is anathema.

The second field on which counter-Witness apologetic is conducted is the prophetic. As those familiar with Witness history and theology are aware, various predictions of Christ's return have formed a major part of the development of the Watchtower Bible and Tract Society (cf. Beverley 1986; Botting 1993; Botting and Botting 1984; Penton 1998). Robert Morey's *How to Answer a Jehovah's Witness* (1980) provides a good example of the nihilative process based on the Watchtower's prophetic record (for similar treatments, see Abanes 1998b; Martin and Klann 1974; Rhodes 1993). As with Morey's treatment of Islam (see below), there is no attempt made to understand Jehovah's Witnesses beyond the information necessary to undermine and refute their worldview. Rather than prepared missiologues (e.g., Bjornstad 1979), Morey provides, among other things, reproductions of Witness literature with appropriate passages underlined. The book is divided into three sections: (1) "A manual on how to use these materials when witnessing to a Jehovah's Witness" (Morey 1980: 9–26); (2) "A witnessing notebook which contains the proof that the Watchtower is a false prophet" (Morey 1980: 27–90); and (3) "An inductive Bible study workbook on the deity of Christ" (Morey 1980: 91–106). According to Morey, taken together these constitute a complete therapeutic package whereby the worldview of the offending religion can be nihilated and that of the Christian validated.

"The [witnessing] notebook," he writes, "is laid out in a manner to lead a Witness to the conclusion that the Watchtower is a false prophet. This is the only function that the notebook has. You should avoid getting sidetracked to any other topic" (1980: 17). In his instructions on how to use the notebook, Morey suggests to the potential apologist that "the first step is to undermine the reliability of the New World Translation in the mind of a Witness" (1980: 19). If the Witness falls back on traditional Watchtower arguments, Morey instructs his readers: "First, remind him that he is repeating something he learned from a false prophet" (1980: 19). Morey's next suggestion is important in that it so clearly exemplifies the hubris by which countercult apologetics is so often marked.

Secondly, if he must have an answer to John 14:28; Col. 1:15, etc., tell him, "write down any verses you are concerned about and then AFTER we finish the workbook we will examine them." The main thing is not to get sidetracked into debating over Watchtower texts when he hasn't even had a chance to hear the arguments for the deity of Christ. Once he works through the notebook, he will not be so arrogant; rather, he should be more submissive in spirit. (Morey 1980: 19)

That is to say, the countercult apologist should specifically bound the debate such that only his or her point of view is allowed into the discussion; he or she should nihilate the Witness's worldview without allowing an opportunity for the Witness to respond.

Although it seems obvious, one point bears repeating here: understanding new religious movements—and religious movements that are, perhaps, not so new, but appear so on the landscape of North American experience—is a crucial task in a society of increasing religious plurality and a world of escalating geopolitical tension. Whereas once, a neighbor who was Buddhist, Hindu, or Muslim was an almost quaint oddity; he or she was an "other" that did not so much signal religious plurality by their presence as confirm the traditional religious demographic by their rarity. As Sullivan notes, however, and remembering that he is referring to religion in South America, we must strive to *understand* these new religions "if only because misunderstanding them shapes our reality. We face our world and reflect on our human condition by primping ourselves with illusions about others" (1988: 2).

In recounting the atrocities allegedly perpetrated by the Watchtower Society, Richard Abanes (1998b: 226) cites the oft-reported Watchtower ban on blood transfusion, contending that this practice "has led to countless Witness deaths over the years, including many children." As do many countercult apologists, Abanes here deploys the apparatus of scholarship (i.e., the endnote) in an attempt to support his claim. When the careful reader checks the note, however, looking perhaps for some statistical substantiation, he or she finds only a statistical conjecture based on 1980 Red Cross blood use figures that Abanes interprets to mean that "approximately 541,376 JWs need blood" (1998b: 302 n.2) in any given year. "No one has kept statistics on JW deaths due to the Watch Tower's ban on blood," he continues, "but the numbers must be staggering. Even if one out of every 10 JWs who needs a transfusion dies, this would add up to 54,137 deaths a year." What Abanes does not address, however, are critical issues raised by his analysis: (1) Is 10 percent an accurate mortality rate (note his use of an "if only" rhetorical device)? (2) How many of those who do die would have died regardless of a transfusion? (3) If his numbers are even close to accurate, how would the Watchtower possibly explain the loss to its community of the demographic equivalent of a medium-sized city *every year*? (4) Abanes neglects to mention that there are a growing number of persons who refuse blood transfusions for reasons other than religious (e.g., fear of HIV/AIDS, hepatitis, and immunologic reactions; cf. Dixon 1988). And finally, (6) he also neglects to mention that, while they may not be specific to transfusion, the Watchtower Society does maintain detailed membership statistics that list organizational growth by conversion as well as attrition due to death. Since his purpose is to present the most negative face possible, however, these are not discussed. Rather, the reader is left with the impression that the Watchtower Society knowingly presides over a substantial number of preventable deaths each year.

Although they have not attracted the same measure of opprobrium that is often leveled at the Latter-day Saints, Jehovah's Witnesses still figure prominently within the countercult purview. Noting the hostility with which Jehovah's Witnesses have often regarded Christian clergy—like Joseph Smith, Charles Taze Russell felt "they were making no effort to preach Christ's kingdom, were frequently influenced by higher criticism, or were teaching the God-dishonouring doctrines of hellfire and the immortality of the soul" (Penton 1998: 42–43)—Martin and Klann write that in "the history of cultism" few have rivaled Jehovah's Witnesses in their antipathy toward other religious traditions, who "literally 'make hate a religion' " (1974: 106). Unlike the Latter-day Saints, however, Jehovah's Witnesses do not control state legislatures or municipal governments; they do not maintain financial holdings nearly so vast as the Mormon church (cf. Ostling and Ostling 1999); and, while still impressive in the face of numerous failed prophecies (cf. Festinger, Riecken, and

Schachter 1956; Penton 1998; Stone 2000), their membership numbers have not increased quite as dramatically as have those of the Latter-day Saints. Where Mormon stake centers and temples are architecturally imposing, often dominating the landscape physically as well as metaphorically, Kingdom Halls are modest and utilitarian, announced only by small, rather unpretentious signs, the whole edifice often slipping the eye as one drives down the street on which it stands. Nevertheless, from within a few years of its beginnings in Pennsylvania to its more elaborate publishing interests in Brooklyn, Jehovah's Witnesses remain a major target of countercult apologetics.

WORLD RELIGIONS

The majority of the world is not Christian. Though this seems self-evident, in reading the cognitive praxis of the Christian countercult, it is often easy to lose sight of this simple fact. Though some countercult apologists (e.g., Walter Martin, Texe Marrs, and Dave Hunt) insist on calling the various world religions "cults," many avoid the term, preferring to deal with Buddhism, Hinduism, Islam, Judaism—as well as their various sectarian progeny—as so-called false religions. Not cults, perhaps, but no less dangerous to the soul.

Buddhism

In the first edition of *The Kingdom of the Cults*, Walter Martin referred to Zen Buddhism as "the second oldest of all the cult systems considered in this book (1965: 234). When *Kingdom*'s fourth edition was released in 1997, however, eight years after his death, many of the original chapters had been extensively rewritten to reflect what the publishers (Bethany House) called in their introduction "the best contemporary information about the onslaught of the cults in America and around the world today" (Martin 1997: 11). Such was the case with the chapter on Zen, which was written by former CRI researcher Richard Abanes and edited by Martin's long-time collaborator, Gretchen Passantino. At the beginning of the chapter, Passantino notes that "although Buddhism is a world religion, and thus not technically a 'cult' as defined in this book, it is included in this volume because of its strong presence in the United States and its importance as a foundation from which come some contemporary American religious movements that more closely fit this book's definition of 'cult' " (in Martin 1997: 301). That is, Martin's characterization notwithstanding, we know that Buddhism is not a cult, but we will treat it as though it is.[3]

Despite this somewhat ambiguous editorial disclaimer and the reasonably accurate précis of Buddhist origins that Abanes provides, it is clear that he still regards Buddhism as another invalid worldview to be repudiated in the face of evangelical Christianity. Like other countercult apologists who have written about Buddhism (e.g., Martin 1985; Weldon 1992; Yamamoto 1982, 1994a, 1994b, 1995a, 1995b, 1998), Abanes advises his readers that "actual evangelism

... may be accomplished not only by pointing out the philosophical errors and shortcomings of Buddhism but also by explaining the superiority of Christianity" (in Martin 1997: 318). One common aspect of this so-called superiority, for example, is belief in the historicity of Jesus as the final arbiter of religious validity and authenticity.

Of the Buddha, Abanes writes, "One might want to point out to Buddhists that their faith is built on a man about whom very little is known historically. In fact, there is a great deal of evidence that suggests many of the writings about Siddhartha are legends that sprang up over the course of many centuries. It is significant that four hundred years passed before anything about the Buddha was written" (in Martin 1997: 319). Betraying a Western bias for the primacy and authority of a written text, and a concomitant misconception about the nature of religious traditions that exist orally (cf., for example, Graham 1987; Richman 1991), Abanes ignores the fact that very little is known about *Jesus* historically, either. Rather, he simply repeats conventional evangelical assertions about the historical Jesus. Unlike Buddhism, Christianity "is built on the claims and actions of a historical person—Jesus of Nazareth— whose followers began transcribing accounts of his life within the lifetimes of his contemporaries and eyewitnesses. This means that the New Testament, which is authoritative for Christians, is much more reliable than the Buddhist scriptures" (Abanes, quoted in Martin 1997: 319). While Abanes does not say precisely what this "reliability" entails or how it follows necessarily from his statement (despite its regular deployment in countercult apologetics), he concludes: "The doctrines of Buddhism, like those found in all other world religions, promote beliefs that guide people into a Christless eternity" (in Martin 1997: 320).

To support the superiority of the Christian worldview over potential competitors, Abanes exploits another popular apologetic strategy—an appeal to the historical veracity of fulfilled biblical prophecy. "The Bible is not merely a collection of wise sayings, ancient beliefs, or spiritually transforming concepts," he writes. "It also contains history that is fully capable of being verified evidentially" (Abanes, quoted in Martin 1997: 318). He dismisses the possibility— some scholars would argue the certainty—that the written Christian Scriptures have been carefully managed and preserved to serve the requirements of a gradually emerging orthodoxy in the early church (cf., for example, Bauer 1971; Ehrman 1993; Lüdemann 1995; Lüdemann and Janssen 1997). He also dismisses the possibility of Buddhist prophecy. "In the eighth century," he writes at the close of the chapter, "a Tibetan Buddhist master named Padmasambhava allegedly prophesied, 'When the horses go on wheels, when the iron bird flies, my people shall scatter all over the world and my teachings shall come to the land of the red face' " (Abanes, quoted in Martin 1997: 320). In support of this, he cites a 1994 *Hinduism Today* article, "Is Buddha Awakening the U.S.?" Abanes admits that "Buddhist teachings have spread throughout America and continue to do so in this technologically advanced age. But a *seemingly fulfilled prophecy* by a Buddhist does not mean that we should embrace Buddhism. Scripture says that if someone makes a prophecy that comes to pass, they and their doctrines must still be rejected if their teachings lead people away from the true God" (in Martin 1997: 320; emphasis added). The interpretative calculus here is clear: Hebrew prophecy that Abanes believes has been fulfilled in Jesus is presented as having historical veracity; Buddhist prophecy is "alleged" and "seemingly fulfilled."

Worldwide, Buddhism embraces more than 360 million adherents. In *Larson's New Book of Cults*, Bob Larson discusses it in three brief sections totaling less than ten pages. Like Abanes, his account of Buddhist origins always presents Buddhism in the worst possible light. And, like Abanes, incidents in Buddhist history are always "alleged," and variant readings of Buddhist scripture taken as evidence of their inherent unreliability. He mistranslates certain words and phrases (e.g., *Tathāgata* he renders "Truth-Winner" [Larson 1989a: 77] as opposed to the more correct "thus-gone one" [Fischer-Schreiber, Erhard, and Diener 1991: 220]). Finally, he reduces the complexity of the world's many Buddhisms, presenting them all as if they were (or ought to be) a single coherent system, and then rejecting them because they are not.

Larson's characterizations of the various streams of Buddhism are similarly problematic. Of Mahāyāna, he writes that it "is more of a cult religion utilizing incense, magic, and occult rituals. Buddha figures are objects of deified worship" (1989a: 76). Of southern Buddhism, he declares that the "godless, virtually atheistic system of Theravada is worlds apart from the Mahayana school with its polytheistic legends of gods and goddesses" (Larson 1989a: 76). Tibetan Buddhism, he contends, was introduced into the region by "Padina Sambhava, a famed pagan exorcist" (Larson 1989a: 77) and "Tibetan Buddhists believe that the demons, spirits, and powers of witchcraft encountered in *The Book of the Dead* are real forces to be avoided and appeased" (Larson 1989a: 78). Indeed, regarding it as the "most openly occult of all non-Christian world religions" and deploring the recent interest shown in Tibetan Buddhism by its Western adherents and "dabblers," Larson believes that the views expressed by His Holiness the Dalai Lama "are of crucial concern to American evangelicals who [likewise] lament Buddhism's growing foothold in North America" (1989a: 79). Highlighting the countercult conspiracism endemic to his presentation of world religions, he concludes that "perhaps the demonic forces behind Tibetan Buddhism have deliberately prolonged [the Dalai Lama's] exile as a means of exporting this ancient, shamanistic faith" (Larson 1989a: 79).

Islam

While the Christian countercult may be able to make the claim that Buddhism presents less of a challenge by virtue of its textual history or the historicity of its founder, such is not the case with Islam, the fastest growing religion worldwide and one that some members of the countercult have come to regard with significant trepidation. The first two editions of Martin's *The Kingdom of the Cults* (1965, 1977) contained chapters only on "The Black Muslim Cult" (i.e., The Nation of Islam), which Martin regarded as "propelled by a fervent nationalistic spirit on the part of Negroes," "the most disconcerting feature of which is the fact that it has capitalized upon the Christian church's apparent reticence in some quarters to support vigorously the rights of blacks guaranteed under the constitution" (1977: 259). By 1985, however, Martin had dropped any reference to the "Black Muslim Cult" but did include a very brief chapter on Islam itself (1985: 364–67). Like Buddhism, Martin noted that "Islam is not a cult, but a major world religion distinctly different from Christianity" (1985: 364). However, because "the West has experience an unanticipated invasion" of Islam (1985: 364), Martin felt constrained to include a chapter in later editions of *Kingdom*. A much longer, remarkably balanced presentation[4] was prepared by Richard Mendoza for the 1997 edition (1997: 608–31), which once again included a short section on The Nation of Islam. As she did for Buddhism, though, Gretchen Passantino notes that Islam was included in the book because of its growing presence and influence on the American religious landscape. That is, it too has become a problem of practical life for evangelical Christians in North America.

While Robert Morey, a popular though sometimes controversial countercult apologist, wrote *The Islamic Invasion* in 1992, on September 11, 2001, the rhetoric of invasion took on a significance in the United States unknown in its history. That morning, of course, two hijacked airliners crashed into the World Trade Center towers in lower Manhattan, a third into the Pentagon, and a fourth in the Pennsylvania countryside as passengers sought to wrest control of the plane from its hijackers. Nearly 4,000 people died in the attacks, and for months the United States conducted a bombing campaign of Afghanistan in an effort to force the ruling Taliban to surrender Saudi dissident Osama bin Laden, the man believed by the U.S. government to be responsible. Whether bin Laden is actually guilty still remains to be determined, and while the mainstream U.S. media was unusually circumspect in its treatment of Islam during the first few weeks of the crisis, countercult apologists such as Dave Hunt and Robert Morey saw this tragedy as little more than vindication for the anti-Islamic views they have held for years.

In the online bookstore for Morey's ministry, Faith Defenders, *The Islamic Invasion* (hereafter *Invasion*) is offered for sale as "the definitive work on Islam"; Morey claims both to have been awarded a doctor of divinity degree in Islamic studies for "groundbreaking research on the pre-Islamic origins of Islam," and to have read each of the more than seven thousand volumes on Islam in the Library of Congress (Beverley 1997: 13). What he produces, however, is little more than anti-Islamic propaganda, written with no intention to inform his readers about Islam, but to reinforce in them the very worst stereotypes of the world's second largest religious faith.

Like other countercult apologists, however (e.g., Decker and Hunt 1984), Morey states at the beginning of *Invasion* that "it is not our intent in this book to offend devout Muslims. We are not trying to hurt their feelings or to embarrass them in any way" (1992: 7). The rest of his book, though, is replete with rhetoric about Islam's "inherent" violence; its "far-fetched" nature; its "subtle form of racism"; his contention that "Allah is merely a revamped and magnified Arabian pagan moon deity"; and his "refutations" of Islam's various religious claims, all of which Morey contends are conducted according to the rigors of academic discourse. Indeed, in this Morey exemplifies a common countercult appeal to academic authority. If it can be shown that a so-called scholar has said a particular thing, or if elements of the apparatus of scholarship (which usually means copious endnotes) can be employed in the prosecution of one's argument, then that lends legitimacy to the countercult apologist's case. Throughout *Invasion*, Morey makes this appeal, citing various scholars in support of his position. Few, if any, however, are given sufficient context to judge the value of their contribution; most are identified simply as "scholars," without mention that a number of these sources are explicitly evangelical in nature and some well over a century old. He cites, for example, "McClintock and Strong's well-known encyclopedia on religion" (Morey 1992: 23) but does not acknowledge that, while well-regarded in its day, the multivolume work was originally published between 1868 and 1888 and can hardly be considered a reliable source for Islamic studies at the close of the twentieth century. Similarly, he quotes Gibb's *Encyclopedia of Islam* (1913), Hughes's *Dictionary of Islam* (1885), Henry Preserved Smith's *The Bible and Islam* (1897), and Samuel Marinus Zwemer's *The Muslim Doctrines of God* (1905), which Morey also neglects to mention was published by the evangelical American Tract Society.

For Morey, "freedom of religion" means, essentially, the freedom to criticize religions with which he disagrees (1992: 8, 10, 72, 132). In his sweeping criticisms of Islam, he consistently equates "Muslim" and "Arab," and either ignores or is unaware of the fact that most Muslims are not Arab, nor are all Arabs Muslim. In an attempt to explain why "Westerners sometimes feel uneasy about the mass migration of Arab Muslims" (1992: 9), a rhetorical device that supports his overarching invasion metaphor, Morey offers up one so-called case in point. He cites a 1991 *USA Today* poll (published February 6, during the height of the U.S.-led saturation bombing of Iraq), noting that "When asked, 'Are you willing to have your son or daughter fight for the United States in this war?' 82 percent of American Arab Muslims said no." From this figure, Morey concludes: "Only 18 percent of those surveyed were willing to back America in the war against Iraq!" (1992: 9). Morey omits, however, the survey's finding that nearly half the Muslims polled *would* be willing to fight for the United States in what they considered a just war against an Arab nation (Hall 1991). As the article made clear, the issue for respondents was not Islam, but their conviction that the war against Iraq was both hypocritical and opportunistic on the part of the United States and served only to maintain American hegemony in the Persian Gulf region (Hall 1991)—a conclusion reached by not a few scholars as well. Morey's conclusion, however, was radically different. "For all practical purposes," he writes, "this survey revealed that many Arab Muslims have not been assimilated into the melting pot of American culture" (Morey 1992: 10).

Despite his repeated protestations that "our intent is not to offend but to inform" (1992: 73–74), and that his "discussions should not be viewed as a personal attack or slur" (since they are "carried out in an objective and scholarly manner"; 1992: 132), even the most cursory reading of Morey's material reveals his aim is to present Islam in an unrelentingly negative light. Considered unreliable by some countercult apologists as well as secular academics,[5] Morey is still heartily recommended by others as a significant movement intellectual.[6] In the wake of the September 11 attacks, Morey offered "Will Islam Cause WW III" (1999) for download on his Web site (www.faithdefenders.com). Claiming to have written the tract two years prior, "Will Islam Cause WW III" contains some of Morey's most troubling rhetoric.

"It is time to launch a new Crusade against Islam," he writes (1999), declaring quite unequivocally that Islam augurs the rise of a new Nazism, "a clear and present danger to the peace of the world." In the face of this peril, Morey considers himself one of "those few soldiers of the cross who are brave enough to stand up to Islam with courage and boldness" (1999). Not surprisingly, Morey is particularly critical of *jihad*, perhaps the most misunderstood and misrepresented aspect of Islam. According to Morey, *jihad*, the "holy war," is "the second most important duty in Islam" (1999). According to Harvard Islamicist Annemarie Schimmel, however, *jihad* was never made a pillar of the Islamic faith. It is a word that has many meanings in the context of Islam (cf. Schimmel 1992: 39–40; on *jihad*, see Ramadan al-Bouti 1995; Firestone 1999; Peters 1996); defense or propagation of the faith is only one of these. Of all the peoples, language groups, beliefs, practices, and geographies Islam encompasses, though, the most prejudicial interpretation of *jihad* is the one Morey chooses.

The blood lust of Islam is thus rooted in a perverted religious impulse to kill and mutilate in the name of Allah. This is what makes it so insidious and wicked. The killing of innocent men, women, and children in the name of Islam becomes a thing of praise and a badge of honor. The more you kill, the more Allah is honored. The greater the destruction, the greater the glory of Islam. Listen carefully to what the most influential leaders of Islam have said. (Morey 1999)

Among these "most influential leaders" are the Ayatollah Khomeini, Sheik Omar Abdel Rahman, and Ramzi Yousef, who was convicted of carrying out the 1993 attack on the World Trade Center at the behest of Abdel Rahman. Morey also includes in this list "Muslim mobs in Egypt, Iran, Iraq, etc." (1999).

In the face of this threat, and while he is hardly alone in this sentiment, Morey warns that "top priority must now be given to converting Muslims."

As well, U.S. military action must be taken against Islamic countries; indeed, to this end, "now is not the time to disarm our military." Rather, "our missiles must be reprogrammed to hit Baghdad and Kabul instead of Moscow and Kiev," and the "Star Wars" defense system must be completed to protect the United States from Islamic missiles.

Unfortunately, in the days and weeks following the destruction of the World Trade Center towers and the attack on the Pentagon, inflammatory rhetoric such as Morey's found fertile ground in North America. Fortunately, it is not Morey's intent "to offend devout Muslims. We are not trying to hurt their feelings or offend them in any way" (1992: 7). Others, such as Jay Howard, director of the Association for Theological Studies (and its Web site "Focus on the Faulty"), do not harbor the same misgivings. Shortly after September 11, Howard mused on AR-talk that the attacks "could be classified as the worst mass murder/suicide of a cult group in history" (October 12, 2001), that the training regimes allegedly employed by followers of Osama bin Laden look "more and more like common cult tactics," and "if it looks, walks and acts like a cult it's . . ." (October 13, 2001; ellipses in the original). Finally, Howard opined that he has "yet to see much discussion of the possible demonic aspect that underlies the Islamic religion" (October 31, 2001). While Howard agrees that other discussions of Islam have merit in an effort to understand the crisis generated by the September 11 attacks, he wonders if it "isn't important also to discuss the Satanic component of Islam. I have seen us discuss at length the demonic when it comes to cults and certainly the occult without hesitation. Maybe we believe it is so obvious that it need not be broached" (October 31, 2001).

In the months following September 11, the question of al-Qaeda as a cult was raised not infrequently by countercult apologists. Given its ability as a floating signifier to explain even the most violent events, its use in this instance should not surprise. Once labeled as the actions of a cult, or the result of demonic interference, the search for any further explanation for the attacks is obviated. We now know all we need to know. While this explanation gained little currency beyond the countercult, that apologists sought to shape the meaning of September 11 in this way is an extreme example of the "Othering" process that is central to the construction of a social movement's cognitive praxis.

From False Worlds to True, Part 2: Cults, the Occult, and the New Age Rage

When Irving Hexham, a noted Canadian scholar of new religious movements, completed his M.A. in 1971 with a thesis on the New Age movement in Britain (Hexham 1972), potential publishers for his research were few and far between. "I approached several Evangelical publishers with a proposal for a book on the New Age," he writes (1992: 152). "Without exception they told me that my subject was obscure and of no significance." While Hexham was finally able to publish his work, the situation for the New Age has changed considerably. In *Fast Facts on False Teachings*, for example, Ron Carlson and Ed Decker declare little more than twenty years later: "So much has been said and written lately about the New Age movement that you almost need a directory to sort out all the material. A recent article in one of the national magazines said that books and articles dealing with the New Age accounted for approximately half of all Christian bookstore sales in the early 1990s!" (1994: 181). While we might forgive them their hyperbole about the commercial value represented by the New Age, that it has caught the attention of the Christian countercult in such a significant way cannot be denied.[1] Because they illustrate both a range of approaches to the problem and several of the mechanisms deployed in countercult apologetics, I limit discussion in this chapter to three movement intellectuals: Constance Cumbey, Douglas Groothuis, and Dave Hunt.

But first, a caveat. In his review of *New Religions as Global Culture* (Hexham and Poewe 1997), Ronald Enroth complains that "unfortunately, it is Dave Hunt and Constance Cumbey who are cited by Hexham and Poewe as representative of Christian anticult writers" (1997). Whether this is an accurate reflection of Hexham and Poewe's work or not (and presumably Enroth will have similar concerns here), as I have argued throughout this book, between Cumbey, Hunt, Larson, Marrs, and more "legitimate" countercult apologists the difference is merely one of degree, not of kind; they all exist along kindred continua bounded by similar concerns, beliefs, and proposed resolutions to the problems represented by phenomena such as the New Age. They differ primarily in the minutiae of their interpretations, and the extremity of the claims they make based on those interpretations. In his review, however, Enroth demonstrates the very internecine questioning of legitimacy and authority that exists within the Christian countercult community itself (and that is considered in greater depth in chapter 12).

Cumbey's work may have the least historical, literary, or theological merit of any surveyed here, but it has had a distribution and an impact that far exceeds its value in these regards. While he quite correctly cites a number of faults with her *Hidden Dangers of the Rainbow* and does not regard her work as the best critique of the New Age, Cumbey's is still one of the few books Groothuis recommends for further reading in *Unmasking the New Age* (1986: 189). Although he recognizes Dave Hunt's propensity for overstatement, Groothuis still considers him "a good researcher" who is "on top of the New Age movement. Even those who don't agree with his end-times emphasis and connection of the New Age movement with Nazism will benefit from his work" (1986: 189). And, while Groothuis regards Hunt and McMahon's *The Seduction of Christianity* (1985; see chapter 12) as "sometimes too heavy-handed," it is, nevertheless, a "well-documented study of how unbiblical New Age ideas are infiltrating the church" (1986: 192). On the other hand, in print and in film Caryl Matrisciana both applauds and reiterates the "thorough and exhaustive research, paralleling New Age with Nazi philosophy" done by Cumbey and Hunt (1985: 216).

That the New Age is perceived as a problem by the countercult has been evident for many years; what kind of a problem it is, however, seems less clear. One of the difficulties facing all researchers of the loose mélange of new religious movements, instrumental spiritualities, alternative healing practices, religious parapsychologies, perennial philosophies, and self-indulgent middle-class mysticisms that have become known collectively as "the New Age" is that a systematic definition is decidedly elusive. Secular scholars (e.g., Hanegraaff 1996; Heelas 1996; Saliba 1999; York 1995) concede that the wide variety of practices and beliefs that have been collected under the New Age rubric hamper the articulation of any coherent, parsimonious, analytical framework—though, unable to escape their own academic instincts, many still try to impose one on their research. Largely responsible for this analytic confusion is the diversity of sources, beliefs, and practices in the New Age—many of which are diametrically opposed to one another—and the utter lack of a governing *ecclesia* or *magisterium*.

As with the concept "cult," though, the problem of definition and identification is considerably less troublesome for the Christian countercult than for secular academics. In the past few years, in fact, cults, the occult, the growth of Eastern religious practices, as well as more recognizable aspects of the New Age, have often been subsumed under the New Age umbrella. As Hunt and McMahon declare, "The church needs to recognize that cults are only part of a much larger and more seductive deception known as the New Age movement" (1985: 7).

HIDDEN DANGERS AND WELL-PLANNED DECEPTIONS: CONSTANCE E. CUMBEY

From countercult organizations to academic analyses, the person who is most frequently credited with bringing the New Age to evangelical awareness is Constance E. Cumbey, a Detroit-area lawyer and the author of *Hidden Dangers of the Rainbow* (1983) and *A Planned Deception* (1985), two of the first books to situate the New Age as a problem of practical life with which Christians must deal, and which have set the tone for many of the different works that have followed (cf. Hexham 1992; Miller n.d.; Saliba 1999; SCP Staff 1987). Cumbey's work, however, is not without controversy. Not only did *Hidden Dangers* raise Cumbey to dubious prominence among the community of countercult apologists, according to a review in the *Christian Research Journal*, it also caused considerable consternation in the evangelical and fundamentalist community for the irresponsibility of a number of her claims (cf. Miller n.d.).

The epigram with which she begins reads: "It is the contention of this writer that for the first time in history there is a viable movement—the New Age Movement—that truly meets all the scriptural requirements for the antichrist and the political movement that will bring him on the world scene" (Cumbey 1983: 7). In Cumbey's opinion that political movement is Nazism. Like Hunt and Matrisciana (who both rely on her work), Cumbey contends that "for all practical purposes, the New Age Movement appears to qualify as a revival of Nazism" (1983: 99). To support her contention, she provides a five-page comparison chart that details the alleged "equivalences between Nazism and the New Age" (Cumbey 1983: 114; see 114–20). Consider these few of the many "correlations" Cumbey offers. "The Nazis believed in the Law of Karma and reincarnation," she writes, and "the New Agers believe in the Law of Karma and Reincarnation" (Cumbey 1983: 116). As well, "Nazis operated free maternity homes in the interests of breeding a master race"; this she supposedly correlates with "the New Agers have an operation known as The Farm in Tennessee which has a free maternity home and women are told they can leave their babies for as short or as long a period as they like" (Cumbey 1983: 117). Finally, mistranslating the title of Hitler's *Mein Kampf* as "My Plan" (1983: 118), Cumbey correlates this with the claim that "New Agers call their scheme to take over 'The Plan' " (1983: 118).

In describing her own countercult apologetic, Cumbey often exhibits the same mixture of suspicion and hubris displayed by other apologists when they ascribe a measure of solipsistic significance to themselves and their work. "Many of the readers of this book," she writes, referring to *A Planned Deception*, "no doubt watched the 'roasting' I endured on the John Ankerberg program. There two Walter Martin associates Gretchen Passantino and Chet

Lackey hurled both ridicule and abuse up on me" (Cumbey 1985: 53). That she is about doing God's business, though, like Bob Larson a lone soldier on the watchtower, is evident throughout her work. "Time after time as I would confront the critics," she writes, invoking an anecdotal miracle, "I would discover that I in packing my briefcase for a lonely and often harsh encounter far from home, had included the exact documentation needed for what was thrown at me. Out of a library of several thousand books, I do not need to tell you how statistically improbably that was" (Cumbey 1985: 3).

A good portion of her own ire Cumbey reserves for former Dominican (now Episcopalian) priest and theologian Matthew Fox, the popularizer of Creation Spirituality, to whom she devotes one of the longest chapters in *A Planned Deception*. While she admits that there are other New Age problems around, Fox's writings "dominate a vast field of religious filth," little of which "approaches the deliberate perversions of [this] imaginative Dominican priest" (Cumbey 1985: 129, 130). Two facets of her argument against Fox (which itself is dominated by *ad hominem* attacks and *ignoratio elenchi* polemics) are of particular interest. First, Cumbey regards the wide distribution Fox's work has enjoyed as evidence of the depths to which the New Age movement has been able to infiltrate even the Christian church and evangelical book distribution network. She is particularly appalled by the availability of Fox over her own work. "One Seattle area evangelical bookstore," she writes, declining either to name the shop or to provide any supporting evidence, "sells *The Hidden Dangers of the Rainbow* under the counter in a plain brown bag, stapled shut and enclosed with a critical review from *Christianity Today*. However, Matthew Fox was accorded generous open shelf-space—over the counter!" (Cumbey 1985: 131).

Second, Cumbey takes issue with Fox's name. Born Timothy Fox, he took the name Matthew upon entering the Dominican order in 1960 (cf. Fox 1996: 18; Cumbey 1985: 130). On this, Cumbey is worth quoting at length.

Second Thessalonians clearly told us we would not know the antichrist's identity until the 'restrainer' was taken out of the way. However, Revelations 13 just as clearly said it was OK to guess. It may be sheer coincidence, and it must be remembered that 'Matthew' is an assumed name, but no matter what one does to Matthew Fox's names using either the occult system of numerology or the Greek/Hebrew system, or mixing them up, using his first name, his last name, or his nickname, Matthew Fox adds up to a perfect 666. (Cumbey 1985: 145)

While she has been both applauded and criticized for her views along the various countercult continua, as a movement intellectual her work has had an impact both within and beyond the countercult community. Dave Hunt, Caryl Matrisciana, and such online countercult ministries as "The Cutting Edge" all applaud the work that she has done; Douglas Groothuis and the Christian Research Institute are ambivalent, unwilling either to endorse her wholeheartedly or to dismiss her entirely. Her writings and radio broadcasts have been influential in domains beyond merely the Christian countercult. Consider her effect on one small Tennessee community.

When court recessed for the final time following the 1925 trial of John Scopes, many believed that the battle over fundamentalist control of public education was coming to an end. Nearly sixty years later, though, the battle erupted anew in Hawkins County, on the border between Tennessee and Virginia. In a series of actions that brought national attention to the county and its inhabitants, provoked the involvement of organizations such as the ACLU, Norman Lear's People for the American Way, and Beverly LaHaye's Concerned Women for America, and brought the litigants finally before the Sixth U.S. Circuit Court of Appeals, "Scopes II" raised the issue once again of whether personal religious beliefs would be allowed to bound the limits of public education.

In *Battleground: One Mother's Crusade, the Religious Right, and the Struggle for Our Schools* (1993), Stephen Bates chronicles the 1983–84 battle waged in Hawkins County, Tennessee, against school textbooks whose content challenged the religious views of Christian fundamentalists. Such challenges are hardly new (see, e.g., Martin 1996; Numbers 1992; Provenzo 1990). In Hawkins County, however, the teachings of Constance Cumbey played a not insignificant role in engendering the challenge. One of the principal protagonists in the case was Vicki Frost, a Hawkins County housewife who, according to Bates, "worked tirelessly to insulate her family from everything contrary to Scripture" (1993: 17). A devoted fan of religious radio broadcasting, Frost had been sensitized to issues she believed threatened her ability to protect her family through "an eight-part lecture about secular humanism, telepathy, and the one-world government" given by Constance Cumbey (Bates 1993: 19). Both she and fellow litigant, Jennie Wilson, had read *Hidden Dangers,* often sharing "juicy tidbits" from their reading like recipes (Bates 1993: 19). Following Cumbey's radio lecture series, which had been presented under the auspices of the fundamentalist Southwest Radio Church in Bethany, Oklahoma, Frost remarked, "She is the one that brought these things to my heart and mind" (Frost, quoted in Bates 1993: 19). What, though, were those "things"?

Helping her daughter with homework one evening, Frost became alarmed by what she perceived to be depictions of mental telepathy and ESP in her child's school reader. From reading and listening to Constance Cumbey, coupled with the reinforcement provided by her friend Jennie Wilson and the various radio preachers they listened to together, Frost knew that telepathy and ESP were signs of the New Age and were to be avoided at all costs (Bates 1993: 18–19). As Bates puts it, "this new textbook, *Riders on the Earth,* seemed to be proselytizing ungodliness. After instructing Rebecca to stop working on the questions, Frost hurriedly phoned Wilson. "It's here, Jennie," she reported. "Humanism in Hawkins County" (1993: 9). That telephone call began the legal battle to ban the readers, along with several other books from the school library. Eventually, in July 1986, the battle reached the Sixth U.S. Circuit Court as

Mozert v. Hawkins County Board of Education, though it was quickly dubbed "Scopes II" by the media (Bates 1993: 233–67).

While *Mozert v. Hawkins County* was an initial victory for Frost and her fellow plaintiffs, the decision was overturned on appeal to the Circuit Court. The U.S. Supreme Court refused to hear it. While the case has been discussed from vantage points as prestigious as the Columbia and Harvard law reviews (cf. Fish 1997; Stolzenberg 1993 respectively) to online college term paper mills, the debate usually (and understandably) focuses on constitutional issues of religious freedom. How the case came to be, however, and the parts played by radio preachers in Oklahoma, fundamentalists in Georgia (i.e., Charles Stanley), and a countercult lawyer from Detroit, Michigan, are not without significance.

UNMASKING, CONFRONTING, AND REVEALING: DOUGLAS R. GROOTHUIS

Few if any countercult apologists do not consider the New Age problematic, and countercult interpretations of it range across a continuum from the evangelistic to the conspiratorial, and from those that seek to take an academic approach to others that engage in the most simplistic reductionism. While he has not published on the New Age in several years (though it still figures prominently in apologetics classes he teaches at Denver Seminary), when *Unmasking the New Age* (1986) and its sequel, *Confronting the New Age* (1988), were written, Douglas Groothuis was considered by many to be among the foremost evangelical thinkers addressing the problem. According to Gordon Lewis, he "has clearly revealed the terminal disease at the heart of the New Age movement" (Lewis, quoted in Groothuis 1986: 9). In his foreword to *Confronting the New Age,* the venerable Walter Martin called Groothuis "a dedicated, philosophically oriented Christian scholar and apologist" (Martin, quoted in Groothuis 1988: 10). Evangelical novelist Frank Peretti calls Groothuis's *Revealing the New Age Jesus* "an ideal resource for any open-minded seeker of truth" (Groothuis 1990: front cover promotional comment), while D. James Kennedy dubs it "a brilliant and exhaustive analysis" (Groothuis 1990: back cover promotional comment).

A campus minister for twelve years, and now an associate professor of philosophy of religion and ethics at Denver Seminary, Groothuis was educated at the Universities of Wisconsin and Oregon. Like Bob Larson, he is something of a wunderkind in the countercult community, publishing his first book, *Unmasking the New Age*, through InterVarsity Press at the age of twenty-nine. He followed that two years later with *Confronting the New Age*, and two years after that with *Revealing the New Age Jesus.*

While the various essential components of the New Age vary from researcher to researcher, for Groothuis (following the intellectual leadership of Francis Schaeffer [1968], James Sire [1976], and Gordon Lewis), all New Age

phenomena converge under the overarching worldview of "pantheistic monism," a conflation of the theory that God is everything and the concept that
all reality is ultimately of one piece.[2] Like Jan Karel van Baalen's apologetic
opposition between Christianity and "autosoterism," and Dave Hunt's argument that there are basically only two religions in the world—Christianity and
Hinduism—"pantheistic monism" is Groothuis's antithetical rubric. While
there are certainly aspects of these phenomena that could be described as monistic, with little or no supporting data and no differentiation between the
philosophical positions that could variously be described as monistic, Groothuis
reduces all New Age phenomena— "from holistic health to the new physics,
from politics to transpersonal psychology, from Eastern religions to the occult"
(1986: 18)—to this essential monism. A reductivism that is fundamental to the
argument many countercult apologists make against the New Age, Groothuis
continues: "Monism, then, is the belief that all that is, is one, all is interrelated,
interdependent, and interpenetrating. Ultimately there is no difference between God, a person, a carrot or a rock. They are all part of one continuous
reality that has no boundaries, no ultimate divisions" (1986: 18). Groothuis
illustrates this concept through an interpretation of the Jim Henson children's
film *The Dark Crystal*, which he calls "a fairy tale of monism" (1986: 19).
From this, he concludes that "monism, the basic premise of the New Age
movement, is radically at odds with a Christian view of reality" (Groothuis
1986: 19).

The next element in Groothuis's New Age equation is that "once we admit
that all is one, including god, then it is a short step to admitting that 'all is
god.' This is pantheism" (1986: 20). And, from here Groothuis's theological
calculus extends with predictable certainty: All is one; all is God; therefore,
humanity is God (1986: 21–22). Both Groothuis and his mentor, James Sire,
locate their theological difficulty with pantheistic monism in the east (punning
Herman Hesse, Sire titles his chapter on the subject "Journey to the East");
and, since it is the influx of so-called Eastern influences into the North American religious economy that Groothuis seeks to highlight, this makes good
sense. However, the dispute over pantheism and monism is a philosophical
debate that has been ongoing since at least the Enlightenment.

In *Unmasking the New Age*, Groothuis recognizes that the differences between the New Age and Christianity (however either is conceived) "come down
to a clash of worldviews" (1986: 165). He continues that "as Christians we
must reject any practice or belief that contradicts our faith" (Groothuis 1986:
165). Fair enough as far as it goes. One would hardly expect an Orthodox Jew
to accept the practice of eating pork, or an observant Muslim the practice of
eating anything before sundown during Ramadan, or an observant Buddhist
the practice of killing a sentient being in order to eat at all. Where Groothuis's
understanding differs from these is that, for him, not only must Christians
reject the practices he considers contradictory to faith, *everyone* must ulti-

mately reject them if they wish to participate in the divine plan of salvation. If they do not, the very future of Christian culture may be at stake.

Writing of the possibility of a New Age apocalypse, a planetary "cleansing" allegedly prophesied by some of those involved in the New Age, Groothuis concludes that "these kinds of predictions have led some Christians to believe that New Agers have a secret plan to eradicate Christians and other obstinate monotheists" (1988: 204–205).[3] While he admits that the number of "New Agers" who might advocate the proactive removal of "obstinate monotheists" is small, to those who do he attributes almost philanthropic reasons. Relying heavily on Texe Marrs (1987: 157–58), Groothuis conjectures two New Age rationalizations for this allegedly lethal altruism. First, the wholesale murder of Christians might be justified on the grounds that in the New Age, "death is unreal"; rather than an end, it is seen as "a vehicle for 're-education' in another life." Second, in the karmic balance of the universe, Christians "are thought to have brought it all on themselves." "Granted," he concludes, "this is mostly speculation on my part, but the foundational beliefs for this kind of thinking are in place" (Groothuis 1988: 205).

In all his work, Groothuis demonstrates what Karl Mannheim called "the sociological 'unmasking' of an ideology," a nihilation that he differentiated from "the 'unmasking' of a lie as such" (1952: 140). For Mannheim, one of the major factors that allowed for the development of a sociology of knowledge was the Enlightenment contribution of a "phenomenon that one may call the 'unmasking turn of mind' " (1952: 140). Predicated on thinking that is calculated to challenge the legitimacy of whole systems, whether theological, political, or economic, "this is a turn of mind which does not seek to refute, negate, or call into doubt certain ideas, but rather to *disintegrate* them, and that in such a way that the whole world outlook of a social stratum becomes disintegrated at the same time" (Mannheim 1952: 140). While Mannheim locates the general development of this unmasking function in the Enlightenment, it has made appearances far earlier than that. For example, Gerd Lüdemann notes that in "the second book [of *Unmasking and Refutation of the Gnosis Falsely So Called*] Irenaeus sets himself the aim of 'refuting their whole system by means of lengthened treatment' (Preface 2)" (1995: 15). In his dispute with the Gnostics, Irenaeus did not set out to disprove certain points of difference between Christianity and Gnosticism, but to disintegrate, to refute the latter's entire construction of reality.

So it is with Groothuis. This rationalist unmasking informs his critique of whatever religious phenomenon is under discussion. Specifically, he criticizes the New Age for its apparent inability to "adequately anchor the world view in objective reality" (Groothuis 1986: 163). He points out, quite correctly in many cases, that for those involved in the New Age, the "idea of an objective revelation from a higher, divine authority is replaced by the search within" (Groothuis 1986: 163), a distinction similar to that made by Heelas (cf. 1996: 18–20). As noted in chapter 4, Groothuis depends on an external authority, one to which reference and appeal can be made apart from concern for the problems of social construction and cultural interpretation. "Along with being holistic," he writes, "Christianity is also objective, providing a standard beyond and above the created world by which to evaluate all of life. Truth is not based on subjective experience but one God's revelation of himself through the Bible and through Christ" (Groothuis 1986: 170).

Quite apart from his debatable use of the term "objective"—how things actually are, as opposed to how they might appear—the construction of reality in which Groothuis and his countercult colleagues participate obviates the need to acknowledge that the faith with which one invests divine revelation in order even to call it *objective* is itself *subjective*, open to interpretation, and liable to all the dialectical exigencies of reality-construction. Following a sociology of knowledge, it is no more than a different subjective construction of reality to which one gives assent and within which one chooses to reside. In this, they become *ideologies*, succeeding, as Doyle McCarthy suggests, "by repressing the constructive function of knowledge, by hiding the social histories and circumstances from which ideas and systems of knowledge derive their logics" (1996: 7).

In many instances, countercult argumentation devolves into an extended exercise in hyperbole, often building on a single, simple comment and importing into it far more menace than it ought reasonably be expected to hold. In much of his writing on the New Age, Groothuis is no exception. Consider, for example, his foreword to Richard Abanes's *Harry Potter and the Bible: The Menace Behind the Magick* (2001; see chapter 8). Into the midst of "Pottermania," writes Groothuis, Abanes, to whom he refers as a "well-published expert in cults and the occult," provides "a rare voice of sanity, reason, and biblical discernment" (in Abanes 2001: x, ix). What bothers Groothuis about the books is that "the Potter series is steeped in a thinly disguised occultism; it favors morally flawed, egocentric characters who lie with impunity, practice occultic techniques, use profanity and refuse to repent; and it frequently depicts gratuitous violence" (in Abanes 2001: x). Arguably an overstatement, but hardly indictable. More problematic, however, is his reference to a lengthy *New York Times* review of the Potter novels by Stephen King. According to Groothuis, King wrote "that the Potter series, which he loves, would provide children with a good introduction to his own gruesome and demonic horror novels when they are old enough to read them" (cited in Abanes 2001: x). The original review (King 1997) is just under 2,000 words long, most of it a witty consideration of Harry Potter and his enormous popularity. Although hardly a stranger to the self-promotion required by the modern publishing industry, King refers to his own work only in the final sentence: "And if these millions of readers are awakened to the wonders and rewards of fantasy at 11 or 12 . . . well, when they get to age 16 or so, there's this guy named King" (King 1997). Groothuis exaggerates (one might say, "with impunity") this virtual throwaway comment by King to serve his own countercult agenda and that of Abanes.

Again, hardly indictable, but problematic nonetheless, and indicative of the manner in which many countercult apologists handle their material.

BEARING FALSE WITNESS?: DAVE HUNT

It is as though there are two Dave Hunts. On one hand is Dave Hunt the wounded spirit, an ardent Christian believer excommunicated from his Plymouth Brethren congregation for preaching and teaching heresy—in this case, the ongoing manifestation of charismatic gifts in the modern Christian church (Hunt 1972). On the other hand is Dave Hunt as he appears in 1980 with *The Cult Explosion* and as he continues to this day—a harsh critic of any form of Christianity that differs in even the slightest measure from his own, an exemplar of some of the most problematic aspects of the Christian countercult movement. Living and working now in Bend, Oregon, there is no question that in the ongoing development of the countercult's cognitive praxis, Hunt is a significant movement intellectual. He is a prolific writer, a sought-after conference speaker, and the founder of The Berean Call, his own countercult ministry.

Similar to many of the countercult apologists considered here, in Hunt's analysis, cults, the occult, and the "New Age rage" constitute a single problem of practical life that is located within both his fundamentalist construction of reality and his own particular dispensational eschatology. Whereas Walter Martin identifies "the rise of the cults" as an existential and theological threat to Christianity, Hunt sees them *both* as that *and* as an integral part of a Satanic plot to bring about a one-world government and a one-world religion. Whereas Douglas Groothuis wants his readers to make a rational choice for Christianity based on his presentation of what he believes is simply better evidence for the veracity of the Christian faith and his nihilation of worldviews that conflict with it, Hunt presents his readers with a scenario in which all the above phenomena play indispensable roles in a predestined, end-times melodrama.

Born in 1926, Hunt was raised in a Plymouth Brethren family and, according to biographical information available on his Web site (www.thebereancall.org), "enjoyed the advantages of a Godly upbringing." In the mid-1960s, while serving as a preaching elder in Brethren churches near his home, Hunt began to experience charismatic manifestations of the Holy Spirit. Since the official denominational position is that the manifest gifts of the Spirit ceased following the apostolic age, these experiences brought him into conflict with other Brethren. In 1966, the Plymouth Brethren with whom he had been worshipping and among whom he had been serving for several years officially withdrew their fellowship from him. In Hunt's words, he had been excommunicated (1972: 175–82).

Since entering the often turbulent waters of countercult apologetics with *The Cult Explosion* (1980), Hunt has been alternately admired and castigated for his work, used as a reliable source by some,[4] and questioned about his reliability by others (cf. Hexham 1992). Some countercult apologists, even those who consider Hunt a friend and regard much of his work with favor, express concerns about the substandard quality of his research skills and logical inferences. Others think his books so poorly written that they are not worth the time to read. Steve Van Natten, the editor of the Balaam's Ass countercult Web site, is even less equivocal, writing that Hunt "has not graduated. He has corrupted God's Word, added to it, and thrown in his lot with Christ haters. Dave WILL quickly repent, or we must consider him a pagan—an agent provocateur from Satan and possibly the Jesuits" (1998; emphasis in the original). Apparently, though, with all due respect to Van Natten, other countercult apologists, and Hunt's alleged Jesuit controllers, large numbers of other evangelical and fundamentalist Christians think otherwise.

According to the publisher's notes on the revised edition of *The God Makers* (Decker and Hunt 1994), Hunt's twenty plus books have been translated into more than twenty-five languages and have combined sales in excess of four million copies. A very respectable figure by anyone's standards. His ministry newsletter, *The Berean Call,* claims a subscription list of over 120,000 in both print and electronic formats. While other countercult apologists may not consider him a scholar, Hunt is marketed by his publisher, Harvest House, as a world authority on new religious movements and Christian apologetics, and as an "internationally recognized cult expert." Regardless of the respect or contempt in which he is held, though, Hunt's writings provide numerous examples of the way information is managed and manipulated in the service of the countercult movement's cognitive praxis. Among these are antipathetic language, sophistic logic and fallacious arguments, the unsubstantiated deployment of conventional pieties, the privileged use of apostate testimony, questionable scholarship, false or incomplete witness, and the specific bounding of debate.

While some countercult apologists are scrupulous about citing primary sources from the religious traditions they critique, others use few if any such sources to substantiate claims about the groups, practices, or individuals under consideration. In many cases, though, countercult apologists make copious use of the particular tools of the academic trade. The most common of these is the humble endnote, some apologists including scores for each chapter. When the Christian Research Institute issued an official statement about Dave Hunt and claimed that although they considered him a "brother in Christ," they did not regard him as a credible scholar, Hunt reacted with outrage. "I'm not a scholar? How is that defined? In spite of the more than 800 footnotes in *A Woman Rides the Beast,* I'm not thorough in my research?" (Hunt 1995: 3). *Occult Invasion* (1998) contains nearly 1,500 endnotes. That countercult apologists employ the apparatus of scholarship is, of course, not the issue; how those apparatus are employed is. What are the sources and are they reliable? Are they quoted fairly and correctly? The mere use of scholarly apparatus in no way ensures the reliability of the information provided.[5]

Often, for example, Hunt uses tautological endnotes, which simply restate information contained in the text. The impression, though, for those who do not check the endnote, is that an authority of some kind is being cited. In *Global Peace and the Rise of Antichrist*, Hunt notes that "One writer points out . . . ," then proceeds to quote a lengthy passage deploring the fact that Roman Catholicism has not been listed in what the "writer" considers a prominent book on cults (1990: 137). The endnote, however, lists neither the writer's name nor the work from which Hunt is quoting. Instead, it reads: "The current deafening silence concerning criticism of the Catholic Church may have less to do with one's courage than with the practical concern that to oppose Rome severely limits one's audience" (Hunt 1990: 312 n.3). Given Hunt's feelings about Roman Catholicism, it is not inconceivable that the unnamed writer here is Hunt himself. Similarly, in *A Woman Rides the Beast*, his premier anti-Catholic book (1994), Hunt writes:

There is an all-out effort by Catholic apologists to refute the errors and inadequacies in evangelicalism. Thomas Howard's book describing his journey to Rome was titled *Evangelical Is Not Enough*. Tapes and books of this type are offered freely by Christian distributors and are carried without objection in most Christian bookstores. Yet many of these same distributors and bookstores which handle Catholic material refuse to stock books or tapes that are in any way critical of Catholicism, even though they present the truth. (Hunt 1994: 416)

Here, one cannot help but be reminded of Cumbey's complaint that her books were kept beneath bookstore counters, available only by request and then only in a sealed, plain brown bag. Aside from Hunt's reference to Thomas Howard, however, a prominent evangelical scholar of literature who converted to Roman Catholicism in the early 1980s, none of the other materials that comprise Rome's "all-out effort" to refute evangelicalism are identified. Rather, Hunt's endnote for the passage reads: "We could give a long list of stores and distributors but will refrain from naming them in the hope that they may change their policies" (1994: 539 n.12).

"Thou shall not bear false witness against thy neighbor," reads the ninth of the Ten Commandments (Ex. 20:16, Dt. 5:20, KJV). Ex. 23:1 expands the pentateuchal statute, further enjoining the adherent: "Thou shalt not raise a false report: put not thine hand with the wicked to be an unrighteous witness." While Hunt might argue that this applies only to witnesses in a civil suit, the plain sense of the text is clear: bearing false witness—whether lying outright about someone or something, or selectively omitting part of the case in order to promote or protect one's own interests—is condemned by God. That this ought to be of more concern to countercult apologists than it often appears is evident from the use Hunt hopes readers will make of his work. "We are not simply a source of 'information,' " he writes in a 1992 newsletter. "We earnestly desire to join together tens of thousands of concerned believers who will not only be informed but who will *act* upon the information we provide" (Hunt

1992: 1). Recalling Decker and Hunt's declaration that in their consideration of the Mormon Church, they would make their case "avoiding bare assertions and ridicule," the nature of the "information" countercult apologists provide becomes of considerable interest.

As noted elsewhere, *The God Makers* has been the target of substantial criticism for its numerous inaccuracies and fabrications (cf. Brown and Brown 1995; Scharffs 1989). For example, quoting an unnamed government study drawn from *The Denver Post*, Decker and Hunt write that Mormon " 'church members take more non-barbiturate sedatives, tranquilizers, antidepressants, stimulants, pep pills, heroin, cocaine, and LSD' than non-Mormons" (1984: 19). Taken seriously, this would seem to indicate that the state of Utah has all the makings of a junkie paradise. While much of Scharffs's rebuttal of *The God Makers* is dedicated to reactive argument, and offers less refutation of Decker and Hunt's data than a different interpretation of it, to this particular charge he responds directly:

I was told by Attorney Arthur M. Wood that when he asked the *Denver Post* authors to document this statement they claimed they obtained the material from Leonard J. Arrington and Davis Bitton, *The Mormon Experience*, p. 287. However, on that page it says, 'There are to our knowledge no accurate figures indicating consumption of such products [marijuana, LSD, and other drugs] by Mormons.' The *Denver Post* authors (whom *The God Makers'* authors quote) did not quote their source accurately. (Scharffs 1989: 75)

Elsewhere, writing of the "accelerating explosion of Satanism worldwide" (1990: 44), Hunt makes a number of unsubstantiated claims. "Satanists have their own chaplains in the U.S. Armed Forces," he declares, "and are protected under freedom-of-religion laws" (Hunt 1990: 44). Theoretically, *all* religious expression in the United States is protected by constitutional fiat unless that expression violates the rights of others or contravenes U.S. legal statutes. Thus, technically, Hunt is correct; Anton LaVey's Church of Satan has the constitutional right to exist and enjoys legal protection in the United States. This is not to say that certain of what are alleged to be Satanic *practices* may not be proscribed under particular federal and/or state laws, but their protection as a religious institution is ensured. Indeed, this is the sine qua non of a religiously plural society. Accessing the popular fear that mention of the word "Satanism" often generates, though, Hunt's claim that Satanic *chaplains* either exist in or are sanctioned by the U.S. military is quite simply false. While there is sensitivity to the varied religious beliefs held by members of the military (e.g., the Military Pagan Network), officially recognized chaplains in the U.S. Armed Forces are currently restricted to Christianity, Judaism, and Islam, with provision underway to add Buddhism and Hinduism.

Similar prevarication obtains in Hunt's treatment of other individuals and institutions as well. Criticizing Agnes Sanford, for example, a writer and pioneer in charismatic healing ministry whose books he contends "are so blatant in their occultism that their acceptance stands as an indictment of the entire charismatic movement" (1998: 503), Hunt points to Sanford's citation of paleontologist and "Jesuit priest Pierre Teilhard de Chardin as her authority." Of Teilhard, he continues: "Declared a heretic even by the Roman Catholic Church, Chardin was known as the father of the New Age movement" (Hunt 1998: 121). While Hunt never divulges just who labeled Teilhard "the father of the New Age movement" (the phrase appears repeatedly in his references to Teilhard), his claim that the Jesuit was declared a heretic by Rome is also false.

On "holistic health cults," Hunt notes that "voodoo and witchcraft are among the folk remedies now studied by candidates for a bachelor's degree in nursing at the University of Alabama. These are only a few of the indications that medical science is turning back to its occult origins" (1980: 118). Nowhere in either the core or elective curricula at University of Alabama's Capstone College of Nursing is folk medicine of the type described by Hunt (or, indeed, of any type) mentioned at all. Dr. Donna Packa, the associate dean at Capstone, suggests that, while there may have been lectures in which different religious traditions were discussed in the context of sensitivity and managing client care, these religious traditions—such as Voodoo and witchcraft—would never have been cast in a medically active role. She remarks that there "is a very strong religious culture down here and that would simply not have been the case" (Packa 1998).

Finally, in *America: The Sorceror's New Apprentice*, Hunt and co-author T. A. McMahon (president and executive director of The Berean Call, and co-founder of Ex-Catholics for Christ) describe the Afro-Caribbean religion of Santería as "one of the fastest growing witchcraft cults in America, with an estimated 100 million adherents worldwide" (Hunt and McMahon 1988: 90). They offer no data to support their claim, despite the fact that this many adherents would make Santería less a "witchcraft cult" than an emergent world religion (on Santería, cf. Brandon 1993; Marks 1974). Currently, for example, the energetically missionary Latter-day Saints, which Rodney Stark regards as the nearest competitor for the status of a new world religion, has a little over eleven million members. However, Hunt and McMahon continue that "while most of its practitioners would deny any involvement in human sacrifices, that side of Santeria was depicted in *The Believers*, one of the most horrifying feature films to come out of Hollywood in 1987" (1988: 90). Here, they are correct in two regards: a film called *The Believers* was released in 1987, and the Afro-Caribbean religion of Santería played a not insignificant role in the plot. Hunt and McMahon claim, however, that Santería is the religious tradition responsible for the ritual murders around which the central narrative is built. In fact, the opposite is the case. The film's characters who are portrayed as authorities on Santería go to great lengths to point out in the narrative that it is *not* their tradition that is being practised in the murders; rather, it is *brujería*, "bad magic." The issue here is not whether the film's depiction of

Santería is accurate. Rather, it is that Hunt and McMahon falsified their description of its depiction *in the film* in order to cast it in as dark a light as possible. The question is how many of the target audience for whom Hunt and McMahon write would be willing to rent the video in order to ensure the accuracy of their description? Since Hunt explicitly wants "to join together tens of thousands of concerned believers who will not only be informed but who will *act* upon the information we provide" (1992: 1), the reliability of that information becomes of critical concern—especially when dealing with factual claims that are open to immediate and conclusive disconfirmation.

The Countercult against Christianity: The Case of Rome

While the countercult is by no means completely agreed on these, a number of Christian theological positions have been declared too irregular to be included within the domain of legitimate Christianity. Among these are Oneness Pentecostalism, the Word Faith movement, Fourth Wave Pentecostalism (the "laughing revival"), and, for some, the largest Christian denomination in the world, Roman Catholicism.

The Word Faith movement, for example, characterized by well-known Pentecostals and televangelists such as Kenneth Hagin, Kenneth and Gloria Copeland, Morris Cerullo, Benny Hinn, Earl Paulk, David (Paul) Yonggi Cho, and Oral Roberts, is among the most recent incarnations of "Positive Confession" theology, popularized in the early twentieth century by E. W. Kenyon (1867–1948) and William M. Branham (1909–65). Known variously as the "Health and Wealth Gospel," the "Gospel of Prosperity," and "Name-It-and-Claim-It" teachings, its fundamental principle is that God wants believers to have all the riches and blessings of material life as a sign of their favored status with the divine. The emphasis on "positive confession" refers to the spoken nature of its primary religious practice. Adherents confess with their mouths those things they wish to manifest in their lives, believing that they can literally speak such things into existence. Not surprisingly, these doctrines have come under considerable criticism from a number of countercult apologists (cf., for example, Barron 1987; Bowman 2001c; Farah 1982; Hanegraaff 1993; Horton 1990; Hunt 1987; Hunt and McMahon 1985; McConnell 1988).

Richard Abanes, for example, who wrote the chapter on Word Faith for the fourth edition of *The Kingdom of the Cults,* declares that "rarely has Christianity felt an unbiblical influence as all-pervasive as the Word Faith movement" (1997b: 495). D. R. McConnell, himself a "confirmed, unapologetic" charismatic, notes that its critics have called the movement " 'heresy,' 'cultic,' 'gnostic,' and 'a work of Satan' " (1988: xvii)—assessments with which McConnell largely agrees. Consistent with the argument they make in other books, in *The Seduction of Christianity*—which itself generated considerable controversy in the evangelical community (see chapter 12), and on which McConnell largely relies for his analysis—Hunt and McMahon interpret Word Faith as yet another sign of the rapidly approaching end-times and regard it as nothing less than the wholesale acceptance of "sorcery" by the Christian church. Finally, Hank Hanegraaff, whose own problems with the Word Faith movement are not limited to its doctrines but include controversy surrounding the book he published condemning it, wrote that Kenneth Copeland "learned enough from [Kenneth] Hagin to establish his own cult. To say his teachings are heretical would be an understatement" (1993: 33).

As pervasive as Abanes thinks Word Faith is in the Christian church, as dangerous as all these authors believe it to be, it exists primarily as a small, idiosyncratic segment of conservative Protestantism. Roman Catholicism, on the other hand, accounts for over sixty million adherents in the United States alone, and around one billion worldwide. It is for this reason, primarily, that I spend the rest of this chapter considering countercult reaction to this, the largest Christian denomination in the world.

THE COUNTERCULT AGAINST ROME

Anti–Roman Catholic propaganda is hardly new, having appeared with some regularity and varying degrees of vitriol since well before the Protestant Reformation. Geoffrey Chaucer (1340?–1400), for example, poked often not-so-gentle fun at various clergy in *The Canterbury Tales*. Anti-Catholic pamphleteering and pulpiteering was well known during the decades of the Reformation and beyond. Two centuries after Luther nailed his Ninety-five Theses to the door of the castle church at Wittenberg, Voltaire (1694–1778) declared acerbically that the Roman Catholic Church was from its inception the enemy of reason. In *La Religieuse*, Voltaire's contemporary Denis Diderot (1713–84) described the physical and emotional misfortunes of Suzanne Simonin, a young woman committed to a convent by a family unable to provide suitable dowry for her. And, invariably, the worst of the libertine villains imagined by the Marquis de Sade (1740–1814) were Roman Catholic clergy— whether simple priests or princely ecclesiastics—a tradition continued by his young contemporary Matthew Lewis (1775–1818) in *The Monk*.

In the nineteenth century, anti-Catholic polemic plumbed new depths, building on the lurid fiction of Sade and Lewis, and replacing Voltaire's more articulate sarcasm with simple invective and invention. Of these accounts, arguably the most well known (and notorious) is titled in good Victorian fashion, the *Awful Disclosures of Maria Monk, as Exhibited in a Narrative of Her Sufferings during Her Residence of Five Years as a Novice and Two Years as a Black Nun in the Hotel Dieu Nunnery, at Montreal, Ont* (Monk 1876). Published first in 1836, the book purports to tell the story of the novitiate and truncated religious career of a woman known to the reader only as "Maria Monk." According to her story, among other atrocities committed at the Hotel Dieu Convent, monks and nuns regularly engaged in orgiastic sex, and the children born of these unholy unions were killed and buried in cellar graves.

In fact, Maria Monk (1816–49) was a young woman whose promiscuity and periodic mental derangement eventually brought her to an asylum for prostitutes that was administered by the Roman Catholic Church. Discharged in 1834 when it was discovered she was pregnant, she formed an alliance with a virulent anti-Catholic preacher named William Hoyt. Hoyt took Maria to New York and together they produced what became one of the most popular pieces of anti-Catholic literature of the nineteenth century. Selling more than 300,000 copies before the Civil War, the *Awful Disclosures of Maria Monk* remains in print to this day. Literary fame, however, was short-lived for Maria herself. Imprisoned for picking the pocket of a customer in the Philadelphia bordello where she was living, she died in the alms-house on Blackwell's Island at the age of thirty-three.

Putative conventual memoirs by Maria Monk, Edith O'Gorman (1871), and Rebecca Reed (1835), polemical novels such as *The Convent and the Manse* (Hyla 1853) and *Stanhope Burleigh: The Jesuits in Our Homes* (Dhu 1855), and miraculous tales of lay and clerical escape from the clutches of Rome (e.g., Chiniquy 1886; Fresenborg 1904; Weiss 1854) all both benefited from and contributed to a social undercurrent of anti-Catholicism that resulted in, among other tragedies, the 1834 burning of Mount Benedict, an Ursuline convent and women's school in Charlestown, Massachusetts (Schultz 2000). Almost half a century later, Charles Chiniquy (1809–99), a Canadian priest who converted late in life to Protestantism and whose accounts of Catholic church life rival those of *Maria Monk*, wrote in *The Priest, The Woman and the Confessional:*

There are two women who ought to be constant objects of the compassion of the disciples of Christ, and for whom daily prayers ought to be offered at the mercy-seat—the Brahmin woman, who, deceived by her priests, burns herself on the corpse of her husband to appease the wrath of her wooden gods; and the Roman Catholic woman, who, not less deceived by her priests, suffers a torture far more cruel and ignominious in the confessional-box, to appease the wrath of her wafer-god. (Chiniquy 1880: 21)

Post–World War II, according to Robert Lockwood, former editor of the Catholic *Our Sunday Visitor* newspaper, "anti-Catholicism is the last refuge of acceptable bigotry in the United States" (2000: 53). From the kinds of anti-Catholicism described above to anti-Catholic weekly newspapers such as *The Menace*, from the modern media caricature of the Roman Catholic Church as backward, antidemocratic, totalitarian, and the last religious refuge of ignorant dupes (Lockwood 2000), to the often spiteful portrayals of the church in evangelical countercult apologetics, other Catholics argue that as "one of the few forms of bigotry socially acceptable in the America, [it] is quite possibly the nation's original sin" (Baldwin 2000: 55; cf. Welter 1987). And, it is to this legacy that Jack T. Chick is heir.

Anti-Catholicism as Hate Speech

"Does Jack Chick hate Catholics?" is the first question asked in the "Common FAQs on Roman Catholicism" section of Chick's online bookstore (www.chick.com). Not surprisingly, the cartoonist who has built a career self-publishing some of the most hostile anti-Catholic tracts in the modern era answers, "No!" In fact, in an issue of his ministry newsletter, *Battle Cry*, while Chick admits "there are those who call Chick literature 'hate literature,' " he maintains that "they do not know the true meaning of hate. True hatred hides the Gospel in beautiful words that upset no one, and therefore bring no conviction of sin. True hatred stands in selfish silence as hell's population grows" (Chick 1996). Over a decade earlier, in a manner not dissimilar to that of Constance Cumbey, Ed Decker, and Texe Marrs, Chick wrote in the introduction to *Smokescreens*, a book claiming to expose "the Vatican's intent to stamp out religious freedom and rule the world," that "there has been a multi-million dollar campaign made through the media to convince people that I am a bigoted, anti-Catholic, hate-literature publisher" (1983: 5). To this accusation Chick responds, "The truth is, I love the Catholic people enough to risk my life and my business to reach them with the gospel of Christ to pull them out of the false religious system they're now serving" (1983: 5).

Regardless of Chick's sincerity or insincerity, the fine distinction eludes him that one does not have to hate in order to be hateful, just as one does not have to hate in order to promote hatred. As Catholic apologist Karl Keating notes:

> Chick is generally regarded as the king of the anti-Catholic publishers. He has received more attention in the Catholic press since 1980 than all other professional anti-Catholics combined, and his rantings against the Church have inspired even Protestant publications, such as *Christianity Today*, to investigate his operation. His ideas are so perverse, his hate mongering so outlandish, that even some anti-Catholics shun him. If the average Catholic has heard anything about the recent revival of anti-Catholic prejudice, he has heard about Jack Chick. (Keating 1988: 107)

Indeed, if anyone has heard about Chick, it is probably through finding one of his dozens of small comic strip tracts in elevators, hotel room bedside tables, or tucked into a wide variety of books in libraries, bookstores, or magazine racks. Each issue of *Battle Cry* includes the best of "Tract Passing Tips" sent in by Chick supporters. Some insert tracts in envelopes with their monthly bill payments; others include them in chain letters before sending those letters on to the next layer of unsuspecting recipients. One particularly inventive anti-evolutionist tract-passer always leaves a copy of "Big Daddy" (Chick's most popular anti-Darwinian tract) in the spare tire compartment of rental cars when he returns the vehicles. "Someone will find it while changing a tire when they probably need a spiritual lift," he reasons.

Chick self-publishes a wide range of these tracts, as well as full-color comic books and his own editions of traditional anti-Catholic books such as Chiniquy's *Fifty Years in the Church of Rome* (which is also available in comic form as "The Big Betrayal") and L. H. Lehmann's *Out of the Labyrinth.* "Last Rites," for example, is a comic tract in which a devout Catholic learns after death that all his devotion to the church has been for naught. Purgatory is a myth, and without reprieve, he is destined for hell (Chick 1994). In "The Death Cookie" readers learn that over the course of its history the Roman Catholic Church has added to the faith a number of other "Jesuses" expressly to confuse Christians, the most dangerous of which is the "cookie god." A calumny of the Eucharistic host similar to Chiniquy's "wafer-god," Chick insists that the "IHS" often found either inscribed or in bas-relief on the host "stands for Isis, Horus, and Seb, the gods of Egypt" from which Chick claims Satan gave the wafer to the Catholic Church (Chick 1988).

In a fundamentalist conspiracism that rivals those offered by Cumbey, Hunt, or Marrs, Chick believes the Roman Catholic Church has been behind every major world event since its "creation" by Constantine the Great, whom Chick mischaracterizes as "the first pope" (1982: 7). According to Chick, Constantine "tried to pull the Romans and Christians together by mixing Satanic Baal worship with the teachings of Christ. What came out of this mess was the godless Roman Catholic system" (1982: 7). Established and maintained by Satan, the Vatican has been directly responsible for, among other things, the rise of Nazism, Communism, and Islam, all of which were calculated to subdue different religious competitors. The broad reach of this conspiracy he describes most fully in *The Godfathers,* one of the "Alberto" series of full-color anti-Catholic comic books.[1]

Although this kind of conspiracism is hardly unique to Chick, he believes that since the seventeenth century, the leaders of this global conspiracy have been members of the Society of Jesus (cf. Dhu 1855; Martin 1987; Paris 1983). A survey of modern history from Chick's point of view illustrates the simple elegance of his explanation. In their writing of *The Communist Manifesto,* for example, Karl Marx and Friedrich Engels were explicitly instructed and carefully controlled by Jesuit priests. In fact, the Communist Party was created by the Jesuits with one goal in mind—the destruction of the Czar, the protector of the Russian Orthodox Church, Rome's principal competitor in continental Europe (Chick 1982: 10). When that did not occur, and "the power of the Orthodox Church was spreading into Rumania, Bulgaria, Greece, the European part of Turkey, and Serbian Yugoslavia" (Chick 1982: 11), the Vatican realized it had to eliminate religious competition in the East once and for all. "The solution was simple," Chick declares. "The Jesuits would set up World War 1" (1982: 11). While the slaughter that was the First World War progressed, however, the Jesuits were busy on a number of other fronts. They were already planning the Second World War, which would be required to eliminate the Jews. Responsible for the anti-Semitic *Protocols of the Elders of Zion,* they fomented the Bolshevik Revolution of 1917 and the Russian civil war that followed. No plan, it seems, was too vile for Ignatius Loyola's long black line.

Like Marrs, Chick often places his most problematic contentions and conjectures in the mouth of a third party—in this case, the alledged ex-Jesuit
Alberto Rivera. Along with Rivera, much of this putative history Chick alleges
came directly from Augustin Cardinal Bea (1881–1968), a Jesuit theologian,
ecumenist, and confessor to Pope Pius XII. "In our long and careful preparation
for the Russian revolution," Bea supposedly told Rivera and his Jesuit colleagues during one of their periodic "briefings," "Jesuits worked closely with
Marx, Engels, Trotsky, Lenin and Stalin. We believed that soon our enemy
would be destroyed and Communism would rise up as a strong new daughter
of the Vatican!" (Chick 1982: 12). Not everything could be left to the vagaries
of civil war, however. In the midst of the revolution, while Russians were killing
Russians in the streets of Moscow and Petrograd, Jesuits posing as members
of the Ural Regional Soviet murdered the Czar, his family, and several servants
in the basement of a whitewashed stone house in the Ural city of Ekaterina-
burg. Contrary to Chick's version, however, Harvard scholar Richard Pipes
argues that "although it has been the undeviating practice of Communist authorities then and since to lay responsibility for the decision to execute the
Imperial family on the Ural Regional Soviet, this version, made up to exonerate
Lenin, is certainly misleading" (1990: 770). It is the beauty of Chick's conspiracism, however, that even this inaccuracy does little damage to his thesis, since
Chick regards Lenin as a Jesuit dupe as well.

Between the wars the Jesuits swept Mussolini into power in Italy and Hitler
in Germany. Mussolini's campaign against Ethiopia, Chick claims, had both a
papal blessing and official designation as a "catholic crusade" (1982: 18). De-
spising both Protestantism and democracy, the Jesuits also had to stop the
emerging Weimar Republic. "The stage was being set for Germany's new Roman Catholic star," Chick writes. "His name . . . Adolf Hitler. A priest was
busy writing a book for Hitler called '**MEIN KAMPF.**' The writer was the Jesuit
father, Staempfle. **This book was the master plan of the Jesuits for Hitler's
take-over of Germany**" (1982: 91; all emphases in the original). According to
"Rivera"/"Bea," during the course of the Second World War, "one of Hitler's
greatest sources of military intelligence came through the Vatican *via the Roman Catholic confessionals all over the world*" (Chick 1982: 23; all emphases
in the original).

Postwar, the Roman Catholic Church has continued its reign of terror. Vatican II, according to Chick, "almost destroyed Protestantism in the U.S. and
Europe" (1982: 31). Geopolitically, the Vatican's new "favorite boy" is Fidel
Castro, "a faithful Catholic and a well-trained Jesuit under oath" (Chick 1982:
31). In the United States, the Ku Klux Klan, which Chick contends was formed
following the Civil War by Roman Catholic Confederate officers, is now "led
by Jesuits," "growing stronger every day," and "is another masterpiece of the
Jesuits" (Chick 1982: 31). Today, the Vatican maintains a massive database
containing the name of every Protestant clergyperson and every church member, whether Roman Catholic or otherwise. When, in the fulfillment of biblical

prophecy, the church rises to the level of a satanic "superchurch," all non-Catholics will be eliminated (Chick 1979: 20; see below on Hunt's interpretation of Rome as the "Whore of Babylon").

Few in the Western world do not rightly despise Nazism and have not been educated to condemn Communism similarly. Thus, to associate a particular group with either of these ideologies—especially Nazism—is arguably to promote hatred against them. Note well that Chick is not saying that the Roman Catholic Church either supported the Third Reich or turned a blind eye to Nazi atrocities. Numerous authors, both popular and scholarly, all unconnected to the Christian countercult, have made a variety of similar claims (cf., for example, Bergen 1996; Conway 1968; Cornwell 1999; Hoffmann 1996; Lewy 1964; Lutzer 1995; Passelecq and Suchecky 1997; Reitlinger 1957), and the court of history has yet to render its full decision on the relationship between the Vatican and the Reich. Rather, drawing on a conspiracism that dates to at least the Revolutionary War (cf. Baldwin 2000), Chick argues that the Vatican—through the Jesuits, who are the true power behind the throne of Peter—actually organized the Nazi party in Germany; ghostwrote *Mein Kampf* for Hitler; masterminded the Second World War as an elaborate pretext for, among other objectives, the annihilation of the Jews; and, through the SS (which Chick believes was in reality a Jesuit suborder), planned and implemented the Final Solution.

As numerous others have pointed out, Chick's work is the darkest kind of conspiracism and, in proffering his alleged explanations for atrocity, misfortune, and tragedy, appeals to the basest of human prejudice. Since he does not, in fact, present an argument—either in the form of hypotheses or propositions derived from historical events, the coherence and validity of which may be checked against those events, or by means of credible witnesses (putative ex-priest Alberto Rivera included)—how should his work be evaluated? While spending more than the minimum scholarly energy refuting Chick's absurdities may seem a waste of time for both researcher and reader, what makes Chick important is precisely that he is *not* a lone voice crying in the wilderness. Though he is something of a pariah in the countercult community, and few Christian bookstores will stock his tracts and comic books, like Cumbey, Larson, and Marrs, Chick is not a discrete countercult entity, but merely the far end of a particular discriminate continuum.

How then ought his material—and other material like it—be regarded? Does it constitute hate speech or hate propaganda? If so, what if anything ought society do? I suggest that those who label Chick publications "hate speech" and "hate propaganda" are both intuitively and demonstrably correct. Does it follow, though, that its publication, advertisement, and dissemination constitute what legal scholars such as Jacobs and Potter (1998: 84–86) call a "low-level hate crime"?

As noted earlier, a number of freedoms collide in the context of the Christian countercult. Within the larger evangelistic imperative of Christ's Great Commission, many countercult apologists interpret the freedom of religion to include permission to point out where any worldview different from theirs is flawed, and its adherents morally and spiritually deficient. While hardly limited to Christianity, this dynamic obtains in any conflict between competing exclusive religious claims. Chick, on the other hand, exemplifies the freedom to express one's beliefs (in this case, that the Jesuits are Satan's willing pawns in a deadly game of world domination) in conflict with protection from ridicule, condemnation, and outright slander.

For those who would advocate some measure of proactive censure, two problems obtain, one conceptual, the other legal. First, is it an "outright lie," no matter how egregious or absurd the claim, if the one who makes the claim actually believes it? While certainly *untrue* in a historical sense, are conspiracist pronouncements like Chick's on the same level as lies consciously told? Is Chick's hatred, if not necessarily for Catholics per se, then certainly for the Roman Catholic Church, protected by virtue of its being integrally grounded in his religious faith? And is his expression of that hatred, briefly demonstrated here, protected as both a free expression of his religion and of his right to free speech? As Jacobs and Potter point out (1998: 112), while "the impulse to ban 'offensive' speech runs deep in every society," the Constitution has been consistently interpreted to preclude prosecution on the basis of content alone.

Second, if there is no specific incitement to violence, no so-called fighting words, then the only real prohibitive avenue open is through a charge of group libel. This is difficult for two reasons. One, since there are no laws prohibiting offensive ideas, group libel is only possible when the accused disseminates material that is "knowingly false"—an extremely difficult proposition to prove in cases of religious or political ideology. Two, since the early 1960s, group libel cases cannot be brought simply because one is a member of the group attacked; "an individual bringing a libel suit [must] prove the libelous statement was directed *at the individual,* personally, *and not simply at a group to which the individual belongs*" (Jacobs and Potter 1998: 116, emphasis in the original). In the case of Chick's conspiracist history of the Jesuits, perhaps the only person who might have had a case was Augustin Cardinal Bea, dead more than a decade before Chick published the first of his "Alberto" series of comic books (Chick 1979).

Anti-Catholicism as Countercult Boundary-Maintenance

By and large, with the exception of Chick's nineteenth-century-style anti-Catholicism, modern countercult opposition to the Church of Rome is located in two general domains, one heretical, the other prophetic. For apologists such as James R. White and Ron Rhodes, the Catholic Church represents a doctrinal box illegitimately shaped and foisted onto a largely unsuspecting population as though it contained the genuine gospel, which, according to them, it does not. For countercult writers such as Dave Hunt, on the other hand, the Roman

Catholic Church is an essential component in the imminent unfolding of the eschaton. Here, I consider first the doctrinal domain, followed by the prophetic.

Doctrinally, a number of issues combine in the countercult apologetic against Roman Catholicism: whether the Apocrypha ought to be regarded as a legitimate part of the Bible[2]; the question of *sola scriptura* versus the authority of church tradition; papal infallibility and the teaching *magisterium* of the church; sacramentalism and the grace of God; the sacrifice of the Mass; and the differences between Roman Catholic biblical hermeneutics (read: "Scripture twisting") and that of evangelical Protestants (read: "biblical Christianity").

Of all the various aspects of Roman Catholicism that offend evangelical apologists, though, what Rhodes calls the "exaltation of Mary" is arguably the most prominent. On one hand, from the countercult perspective Mary has replaced Jesus as the vehicle by which human salvation is achieved. In fact, as far as Hunt is concerned, Mary is more important to Catholics than God, and "when Mary commands even God obeys" (1994: 435, 446).[3] On the other hand, the veneration of Mary challenges both the evangelical conception and logical inevitability of the doctrine of substitutionary atonement. In *Reasoning from the Scriptures with Catholics,* Rhodes (2000) devotes more space to Mary than to any other aspect of doctrine, and almost double what he spends on the doctrines of *sola scriptura* and papal infallibility combined. White (1998) felt the issue sufficiently important to warrant an entire book, *Mary—Another Redeemer?*, the cover of which declares "What you should know about the controversial movement to name Mary as Co-Redeemer with Christ."

All of this is *not* to say that there are not Roman Catholics who are extraordinarily devoted to Mary, even to the virtual exclusion of Jesus from the framework of their popular piety. The millions who have visited Marian shrines—whether the famous such as Medjugorje, Fatima, or Lourdes, or the less well known, even extemporaneous (e.g., the appearance of the Virgin on the side of a building, or a backyard shrine visited by friends and neighbors)—certainly attest to the reverence with which Mary is regarded. Even Catholic historian Thomas Bokenkotter, who cherishes his own memory of being in St. Peter's Square when Pius XII officially defined the dogma of the Assumption of the Blessed Virgin Mary in 1950, points out that Marian devotion "often degenerated into superstition." Citing the example of the famous Franciscan preacher Bernard of Siena (1380–1444), Bokenkotter continues: "Mary actually did more for God than God did for man, [Bernard] dares to say. If at this level such excesses could occur, one is not surprised at the absurdities that became the common coin of Marianists and led inevitably to the Protestant reaction" (1986: 129). A reaction that continues in apologists such as Hunt, Rhodes, and White.

In building their arguments, countercult apologists often ahistoricize and decontextualize Roman Catholicism by means of a reductivist reading of Catholic doctrinal history—for example, reading the dogma of papal infallibility as though it had been in place much longer than the century and a half since Pius

IX had the doctrine defined and pronounced at Vatican I. In fact, they often impose on Roman Catholicism a linearity and uniformity that ignores the many social and cultural influences responsible for the evolution of doctrine. Using only the voices of a few Marian devotionalists such as St. Alphonsus de Liguori (Alphonsus de Liguori 1852) and modern proponents of Mary Mediatrix such as Mark Miravalle (Miravalle 1993, 1997, 2000), for example, they ignore modern Catholic theologians and historians who point out that the development of Marian devotion is anything but linear. Hans Küng, arguably one of the most significant theologians of the Vatican II era, lists a number of these influences on Marian devotionalism, including cultural reaction to "the cult of Near Eastern mother divinities," "theological rivalries," "ecclesio-political antagonisms," and the "sometimes very personal intervention by churchmen." Here, Küng cites "Cyril of Alexandria's large-scale manipulation of the Council of Ephesus in 431 and his definition of 'God-bearer' before the arrival of the other, Antiochene party at the Council" (1974: 459). To this list could easily be added such names as Pius IX, Pius XII, and John Paul II.

Conversely, Dave Hunt reduces the history of the Catholic doctrinal development and misrepresents *Munificentissimus Deus,* the Apostolic Constitution of Pius XII (1954) that defined the dogma of Mary's assumption into heaven, declaring "the pope claimed that the dogma of the assumption had been unanimously believed in the Church from the very beginning and that it was fully supported by Scripture" (1994: 443). On the one hand, this is not what the Pope wrote; indeed, the actual document says quite the opposite—that while certain writers have argued for Mary's bodily assumption, the dogmatic declaration was the result of piety and investigations that had increased in both scope and clarity in the present era of the Catholic Church (*Munificentissimus Deus* §§3, 8). On the other hand, in presenting the Apostolic Constitution as though it self-evidently condemns all of Roman Catholicism for a rampant and continual Mariolatry, Hunt as well ignores such Catholic theologians and historians as Küng, Bokenkotter, and McBrien.

In *On Being A Christian,* for example, Küng writes: "The Second Vatican Council deliberately refrained from defining further dogmas, regarded as logically following on what was already defined (mediatrix, co-redemptrix), integrated its (moderately traditional) Mariology as the closing chapter in its teachings on the Church and unmistakably condemns the excesses of Marianism" (1974: 461; cf. *Lumen Gentium* ch. 8; McBrien 1994). Küng concludes: "During the time after the Council this exaggerated Marian cult has completely lost its force also in theology and the life of the Church" (1974: 461–62). For Hunt, Rhodes, and White, though, it appears that any Marianism is excessive.

On Being a Christian's very brief section on Mary—a section significant for its brevity in comparison with the mass of material devoted to the topic by countercult apologists—demonstrates that Marian devotionalism has generated considerable controversy within the Catholic Church itself, and that, contrary to the way in which apologists such as these portray it, Marian devotion has never been "the subject of any universally binding dogmatic definition" (Küng 1974: 457).[4] Indeed, only two aspects of this devotion does Küng consider grounded in Scripture: that Mary is the mother of Jesus, and that she "is the example and model of Christian faith" (1974: 459). If there is to be any ecumenical agreement with regard to Mary's place within the structure of the wider Christian faith—a possibility that appears solidly rejected by evangelical apologists such as Chick, Hunt, Rhodes, and White, but that is important here to illustrate aspects of the Marian debate, which are explicitly ignored in the formulation of their countercult apologetic—Küng suggests two conciliatory dynamics, one each for Catholics and for Protestants. For the Roman Catholic Church, he writes:

There must be a more decisive attempt than formerly to follow the guidelines of the biblical evidence and not to fear an honest, critical examination of the recent two Marian and papal dogmas, which in various respects form a unity and which are not substantiated in a universally convincing way either in Scripture or in tradition, or by "intrinsic reasons" (= theological postulates); in any case ranking very low in the "hierarchy of truths." (Küng 1974: 462)

"On the *Protestant* side," Küng continues, both referring to three centuries of anti-Catholic propaganda and presaging the kind of rhetoric encountered in Rhodes, Hunt, and White, "a purely apologetic and polemical attitude is not sufficient. . . . Poetical statements in the Catholic tradition (songs, hymns, prayers) and forms of piety which suit individuals or nations must be distinguished from the strictly theological or still more official dogmatic utterances of the Church" (1974: 462, emphasis in the original). Put differently, whereas Marian Catholics must become less attached to a pietism that has little grounding in the historical records and practices of the church, Protestants such as the countercult apologists must acknowledge that the Roman Catholic Church is not the hidebound monolith they often portray, that Catholic dogma does not destine for perdition those who refuse to worship Mary, and that the "Mother of God" has in no way supplanted either God the Son or God the Father.

While Jack Chick makes his position abundantly clear, lest anyone have to "hunt and search or make a wild guess about the 'thesis statement' " in *The Fatal Flaw* (1990: 19), James White proclaims: "The Roman Catholic Church's teachings on the work of Jesus Christ (specifically, His atonement) is anti-Biblical and false; hence, the Roman Catholic Church is not in possession of the Gospel of Jesus Christ, and cannot, therefore, be considered a Christian church." Like White, Ron Rhodes declares that nothing more than evangelical concern lies at the heart of his staunch opposition to the world's largest Christian denomination. "What is of particular concern," he writes (Rhodes 2000: 17), "is that today there are nearly 945 million Catholics in the world. That means that almost 18 percent of the world's total population has bought into a works-oriented system of salvation"—which is to say, they are not Christians,

and therefore not "saved." Of these three apologists, though, Dave Hunt is the
least equivocal:

For decades evangelicals have diligently and faithfully attempted to identify, analyze
and warn the church against *cults* . . . . Yet the most seductive, dangerous and largest
cult (many times larger than the rest of them combined) is not included in the list!
Most cult experts refuse to identify this horrendous cult as such! Instead, they accept
it as "Christian." Worst of all, this cult (which preaches a *false gospel* that is sending
hundreds of millions into a Christless eternity) is now embraced as a partner in "evangelizing the world" by many groups which preach the biblical gospel. (Hunt 1991: 1,
emphasis in the original)

   To this, Hunt concludes, "I solicit your help in providing church leaders with
the facts they need to identify this cult—facts of which I myself was ignorant
years ago when I, too, failed to identify the Roman Catholic Church as the cult
it is" (1991: 1).
   As party to this sham, Hunt accuses a number of well-known evangelicals
and countercultists. Were the Reformers "alive today," he writes (1991: 1),
"they would denounce Roman Catholicism as the largest and most dangerous
cult on earth! Yet the Christian Research Institute (and other countercult
groups) refuse to classify it as a cult." Likewise, he names individuals such as
Bob and Gretchen Passantino, James Sire (editor-in-chief at InterVarsity Press),
and Michael Horton (whom Hunt claims simply reprises many of the arguments from his own *Seduction of Christianity*; cf. Horton 1990; Hunt and
McMahon 1985), as well as prominent evangelical parachurch ministries such
as Campus Crusade for Christ, Youth with a Mission, and the Billy Graham
Evangelistic Association.
   Though their arguments are framed in the context of salvation,[5] much more
complex apologetic dynamics are actually at work. Each aspect of the countercult critique of Catholicism reveals the same concerns for boundary-
maintenance as with so-called false religions. If Roman Catholics are permitted
the legitimacy of their convictions, if they are allowed the prima facie authenticity of their beliefs (as is implied, at least, in such efforts at Evangelical–
Roman Catholic rapprochement as the 1994 document "Evangelicals and
Catholics Together," to which Hunt refers as "the most significant event in
nearly 500 years of church history" [1994: 5]), then the entire structure of
Christian reality as these apologists believe it constituted is threatened. Therefore, no rapprochement is possible, no dialogue available. Roman Catholicism
must be demonstrated theologically deficient, doctrinally deviant, and ecclesiologically apostate—that is to say, *heretical.*
   In order for this construction of reality to succeed, Catholicism must be
presented as authoritarian, monolithic, and merciless in the prosecution of its
heretical doctrines—features Hunt declares "the primary mark of a cult," continuing that "no cult demands surrender of mind and conscience more fully or
arrogantly than Roman Catholicism" (1991: 1). In his opening "word to the

Christian reader," James White implies something equally sinister: "The evil of Roman Catholicism lies in a system, not, by and large, the individuals who are part of it. Only a small percentage of Roman Catholics are actively involved in promulgating falsehood. The vast majority," he concludes, "are simply deceived" (1990: 190). And, in his introductory material on "Evangelizing Catholics," Ron Rhodes makes clear that he understands that Roman Catholicism embraces a wide variety of theological positions, popular and liturgical pieties, as well as social and cultural contexts. "Roman Catholics cannot be lumped together into one big bucket," he declares, immediately prior to doing virtually that. "There are some Roman Catholics," he continues, "who *do* believe what is taught in the Bible about grace and justification and are, in fact, saved" (Rhodes 2000: 15, emphasis in the original). In his note on "methodology," Rhodes states that "it is not my goal in this book to simply quote what other Protestants have said about Roman Catholicism. Rather, I intend to quote or cite directly from key representative Roman Catholic sources" (2000: 21), among these, the *Catechism of the Catholic Church*.

Of the over 450 endnotes Rhodes provides, however, less than half are to Roman Catholic sources, official or otherwise. And only twenty-eight of these reference the *Catechism*. Among the most oft-cited of Rhodes's Catholic sources are *Fundamentals of Catholic Dogma* (Ott 1954), the *Pocket Catholic Dictionary* (Hardon 1985), and *The Essential Catholic Handbook* (1997). Of these, the first is significantly pre–Vatican II, the second an abridged, popular edition of Hardon's magisterial *Modern Catholic Dictionary* (1980), and the third bills itself as "a compact guide to the basic tenets of the Catholic faith." Hardly a catalogue of "key representative Roman Catholic sources," despite the regard with which both Ott and Hardon are held in the Church. On the other hand, almost forty percent of his references are to evangelical Protestant sources, including such explicitly anti–Roman Catholic writers as James White (1996, 1998) and James McCarthy (1995, 1997).

Even though Rhodes insists that there is a spectrum of belief, practice, and piety within Roman Catholicism, like Hunt and White his construction of reality, the foundation upon which his apologetic rests, virtually requires that he "lump them together in one big bucket." Describing the importance of the *Catechism*, for example, and encouraging those who would evangelize Catholics to "digest its contents," Rhodes points out quite correctly that it "cites heavily from pontifical documents (which are considered authoritative by Catholics), from Roman Catholic canon law, from Roman Catholic liturgy (also considered authoritative), and from Thomas Aquinas's *Summa Theologica* (held in very high esteem by Catholics)" (2000: 22). However, Rhodes does not say to which species of pontifical documents he refers, nor what he means by "authoritative." Does he mean "infallible"? Not all pontifical documents, which range from *ex cathedra* apostolic constitutions to encyclicals, apostolic exhortations, and *motu proprio* (documents originating from the Pope's own office), carry the same authoritative weight. As well, not all Catholics regard papal proclamations of whatever species with equal respect and deference. This is easily established by even a brief review of the cognitive praxes of traditionalist, sedevacantist, and third-world liberationist movements, as well as the varied response among Roman Catholics to such initiatives as *Novus Ordo Missae* (1969) and encyclicals such as *Humanae Vitae* (1968).

Rather than entering into a debate with the many different voices crying to be heard in the Catholic communion, Rhodes and other anti-Catholic apologists rely on a reduced and simplified version of the faith—a straw church, if you will, one stripped of complexity and nuance. This manner of reality construction underpins much of the countercult apologetic, and Rhodes, in particular, accomplishes it in three ways: (1) a classic straw man argument, in which Catholic sources are used to refute questions those sources are neither asking nor attempting to answer[6]; (2) modern sources (e.g., Ott 1954), which are quoted without appropriate context, thus manipulating the sense of the text; and (3) simply misrepresenting sources, whether through selective omission, imported meaning (eisegesis), or oversimplification. Consider the following examples from Rhodes's use of Catholic dogmatic theologian Ludwig Ott and Ott's classic text, *Fundamentals of Catholic Dogma* (1954).

In his treatment of "sola scriptura versus tradition," Rhodes contends that, with respect to 2 Tim. 2:2 and quoting Ott (1954: 7), "Roman Catholics often argue that this verse supports the idea of a separate oral tradition" (2000: 81). Besides Ott, no other Catholic writers—official or otherwise—are cited. When the original reference is checked, however, one finds that, while Ott does cite the biblical text (along with four others), he is discussing the early church fathers and their battle with those they considered heretics. Specifically, Ott is referring to Irenaeus and Tertullian contesting Gnostic claims to possession of secret knowledge or new revelations unavailable to other Christians. There is nothing in Ott's original text that even remotely supports Rhodes's use of the passage. Indeed, elsewhere Rhodes deploys the same biblical text and the same reference in Ott to support another unrelated, otherwise unattested, straw man argument: "Some Roman Catholics say that the idea of entrusting doctrine to faithful men to be passed onto others supports apostolic succession" (2000: 119). Once again, there is nothing in Ott's text to support this reading. In fact, in the very next paragraph, Rhodes writes that "Roman Catholics are reading something into the verse that is not there. There is virtually no mention of apostolic succession here" (2000: 119–20). Yes, exactly—any mention of it has been imported by Rhodes himself.[7] Finally, in the midst of three chapters devoted to a question-by-question elaboration of the controversy over forensic versus meritorious justification, Rhodes states that Roman Catholics often cite James 2:21 "with a view to proving that final justification before God is not by faith alone but requires works" (2000: 147). Here he references but does not quote Ludwig Ott (1954: 264). Once again, though, in Ott's original text no mention is made of either the argument Rhodes is attempting to make, or the biblical text with which he is trying to make it. Similar examples could be multiplied across the body of Rhodes's countercult work, from *The Culting of America* (1994) to *Reasoning from the Scriptures with Masons* (2001b).

Another way in which he is able to construct his reductivist version of Roman Catholicism is through the selective omission of pertinent information from the sources he is quoting. Once again, his use of Ott is instructive. Referring to Jesus's gift to Peter of the "keys of the Kingdom of Heaven," Rhodes quotes Ott (1954: 416) that the "person who possesses the power of the keys has the full power of allowing a person to enter the empire of God or to exclude him from it [and] . . . the power to forgive sins must also be included in the power of the keys" (2000: 108–9; both gloss and ellipses in Rhodes). In a curiously wrought argument for someone who wants to deny any arrogation of soteriological power to human beings, and one for which there is considerably less textual support than the Roman Catholic interpretation he purports to refute, Rhodes maintains that the biblical passage actually "relates to witnessing and evangelism by the apostles" and that *all* the apostles "were given the power to grant or deny access into the Kingdom of God based on how people respond to the gospel message" (2000: 109). It is the lacuna, though, that is of particular interest here. Rhodes's argument is predicated on the arrogation of soteriological power by the Catholic Church, in particular the See of Peter and its occupant. His use of Ott makes it appear as though entry into the "empire of God" is at the sole (and perhaps arbitrary) discretion of the Pope—the one who holds the keys of Peter. Rather than a pontifical whim, though, Ott makes it very clear in the brief but crucial bit of text omitted by Rhodes that "it is precisely sin which hinders this entry into the Empire of God in its perfection" (1954: 416). Presumably, that sin would prevent someone from entering the Kingdom is not a theological principle with which Rhodes would disagree, yet his construction of Roman Catholic inadequacy requires that Ott's use of it be deleted.

At a number of points, Rhodes quotes Ott—or rather, Ott's text—but leaves out crucial contextual references required to understand what Ott is actually saying. In most instances, the reader is left with the impression that it is Ott himself speaking, and that Ott's word is somehow officially authoritative for the Church in these matters. Of the controversy over Mary's perpetual virginity, for example, Rhodes writes: "Catholic theologian Ludwig Ott says that 'Mary gave birth in miraculous fashion without opening of the womb and injury to the hymen, and consequently also without pains' " (2000: 260). And, this is exactly the passage as it is found in Ott (1954: 203). What Rhodes omits, however, is that Ott is describing some of the developmental stages through which the doctrinal concept of Mary's perpetual virginity passed. More importantly, what Rhodes does not tell his reader is that it is not Ott who is speaking, but again the early church fathers and medieval scholastics, who argued that virginal integrity was contingent on "non-injury to the hymen" (1954: 203), and so taught that doctrine. Ott himself goes on to make an entirely different argument. Dispute over the state of Mary's virginity continues, though, when Rhodes states that "some Roman Catholics take [Luke 1:34] to mean that Mary 'had taken the resolve of constant virginity on the ground of special Divine enlightenment' " (2000: 297). His source? Ott (1954: 205). However, again Ott is quoting selected patristic authors, in this case Augustine. And, once again, Rhodes's prose leaves the reader with the distinct impression that this is immutable and quite uncontroversial dogma that reflects current and ordinary Catholic thought on the matter. Any acknowledgment of these omissions, of course, would seriously weaken the rather simplistic construction of Roman Catholic uniformity on which Rhodes's argument ultimately depends.

Anti-Catholicism as Eschatological Fulfillment

Finally, with apologists such as Jack Chick and Texe Marrs, Dave Hunt is convinced that the Roman Catholic Church is destined by God to play a pivotal role in the imminent unfolding of the eschaton. Confident that we are living in the end-times predicted by Protestant fundamentalists since the nineteenth century, Hunt locates the Roman Catholic Church at the very center of the Antichrist's rise to power and his ultimately doomed bid for earthly domination. Put differently, the Roman Catholic Church is the ecclesial platform for a "revived Roman Empire," a staple of fundamentalist end-time conspiracism that is required to fulfill some of the more troublesome passages in the books of Daniel and Revelation, two of the primary texts for dispensationalist Christians.

In Hunt's interpretation of end-time events, the Biblical *Antichrist* is cast as a pretender to the throne of Christ, an imposter rather than a straightforward opponent as other dispensationalists have suggested. It is on this reading of the biblical witness that the rest of Hunt's argument depends. "Since the Antichrist pretends to be Christ," he continues, "his followers must be 'Christians' and his world religion must be a perverted form of Christianity" (Hunt 1990: 104). And, to the Antichrist's "false Christ," the leader of this false church would be the "False Prophet." For Hunt, the false prophet's identity is clear. "The false prophet must be the head of the World Church identified in Revelation 17 as 'mystery Babylon,' " he writes. "Even Catholic apologist Karl Keating admits that Babylon signifies Rome. The current Pope, John Paul II, is working feverishly to merge all faiths. He obviously understands that not only Protestants and Catholics but all mankind must unite in a new religion" (Hunt 1990: 98).

Beyond Hunt's declaration, however, there is no indication that John Paul II believes anything of the sort. As well, Hunt misrepresents Keating's identification of Rome with Babylon. Keating uses the equation to argue that it is not impossible that the apostle Peter had been in Rome and contends (with Eusebius Pamphilias, the first so-called church historian) that, in 1 Pet. 5:13, Peter used "Babylon" as a codeword for "Rome" for security reasons. This "unusual trope" (Eusebius) would have been easily understood by the letter's intended recipients, but obscure enough not to condemn Peter himself were the letter to fall into the wrong hands (cf. Keating 1988: 199–201, 2000: 146–48). Keating certainly does *not* intend the equation to suggest that the modern city of Rome is the eschatological Babylon required by Hunt's apocalyptic dispensationalism.

In both *Global Peace and the Rise of Antichrist* (1990) and *A Woman Rides the Beast* (1994), Hunt reserves some of his harshest language for the Roman Catholic Church. Like Chick and Marrs, he presents the darkest possible version of Roman Catholic history, laying responsibility squarely at Rome's door for, among other things, the rise of Nazism in Germany (elsewhere, he claims Hinduism is responsible; cf. Hunt 1983); the implementation of the Final Solution (Hunt 1994: 265–93); and the Ustaschi (Croat) massacres of Yugoslavian Serbs in the early 1940s (Hunt 1994: 297–307). For Hunt, as for Chick, the syllogism is simple: Because there were at least nominal Catholics involved in these atrocities, therefore the Roman Catholic Church as an institution supported and encouraged their actions—a convenient, monocausal explanation for these various atrocities.

Today, he writes, one "finds every shade of New Age, occult, and mystical belief inside the Roman Catholic Church" (Hunt 1994: 480). And, according to his definition of these core concepts, he is technically correct. Since, in Hunt's construction of reality, mysticism *is* the occult, which *is* the New Age, evidence of any one demonstrates the existence of them all. Guilt by association is leveled as a result of the Pope John Paul II's friendship with the fourteenth Dalai Lama who "proposes to bring global peace through a heavily demonic Yoga visualization technique" (Hunt 1990: 268). Referring to the Dalai Lama's presentation of the *kalachakra* ceremony, Hunt writes that this "forerunner of the Antichrist continues to be feted by the Roman Catholic Church, which previously gave Hitler its blessing" (1990: 268).

While he is certainly not alone in this interpretation, for Hunt there is no doubt that the Roman Catholic Church plays a pivotal role in the end-times drama. She is the "Great Whore of Babylon," allegedly prophesied in the Revelation to St. John (17:3–6)—the "woman who rides the beast." For Hunt, as well, there is no doubt why it is a *woman* who rides the beast.

Worldwide, today's women are asserting themselves as never before in history. Contrary to popular opinion, "women instigate more domestic violence [and] hit men more frequently and more severely [than men hit them]" and violence is far more frequent in lesbian relationships than between husband and wife. Women are taking over what were once men's jobs, and there is a growing acceptance of women at the highest levels of leadership in business, government, and religion. Only God could have given John, 1900 years ago, a vision that so fits our day—a *woman* in control. From current trends, it seems inevitable that a *woman* must ride the beast. (Hunt 1994: 456; glosses and emphasis in the original)

There are two points of interest here, one methodological, the other substantive. First, while arguments like this surface from time to time, Hunt's takes his citation of domestic violence statistics from *USA Today* (June 29, 1994; Hunt 1994: 541 n.20) rather than a recognized research source. In addition, as is often the case, Hunt misrepresents the reference he does use. On that date, *USA Today* published three articles related to domestic violence—none of which contain the statistics Hunt cites, and two of which contain information in direct contradiction to it. Second, one is led to wonder about Hunt's thinly veiled misogynism, given that his chief candidate for the Whore of Babylon is a church that has yet to ordain its first woman priest.

Whereas White and Rhodes object to Catholic veneration of Mary on theological grounds, Hunt sees in the Mother of God one of the crucial components of eschatological fulfillment. Classification of these various components, and their correlation with current events, is a staple of dispensationalist hermeneutics. "That the 'last-days' Babylon is described as a *woman*," he writes, "again identifies her as the Roman Catholic Church, for whom a *woman*—the 'Virgin Mary'—is the dominant deity. Though many Catholics would deny it, she has taken the place of God and Christ" (1990: 120, emphasis in the original). His discussion of Marian apparitions illustrates the lengths to which he will go to ensure this identification.

At Fatima, for example, both Mary and Jesus "were betrayed as masquerading demons by the heresy they taught" (Hunt 1990: 123). Here, Hunt quotes from the Pontevedran apparition to Lucia dos Santos (December 10, 1925), during which the Holy Child says to Lucia, who was by then a young woman living cloistered, "Have pity on the Heart of your Most Holy Mother. It is covered with thorns with which ungrateful men pierce it at every moment, and there is no one to remove them with an act of reparation" (1990: 123; cf. 1994: 462–63).[8] For Hunt, though it is not entirely clear why, the apparent heresy was that Mary had usurped the salvific prerogative of both God and Christ.[9] This he condemns as "blasphemy of the worst kind. It would never be uttered by the real Mary or by Jesus" (Hunt 1994: 463). While Hunt's definition of the Fatima messages as heresy is intriguing, even more so is his response to a reader's question in *The Berean Call*, in which he gives his primary reasons for identifying the mother and child as "masquerading demons."

The satanic delusion is undeniable. A "child Jesus" sometimes appears (at Fatima, etc.) with "Mary." Jesus was a mature man when he died for our sins; and is resurrected and glorified at the Father's right hand. . . . Obviously, then, the appearance of any "child Jesus" is demonic. For Catholics, however, millions of wafers are each simultaneously Christ, whom they ingest into their stomachs—so it is easy to believe that He can appear as a baby or a child. (Hunt 1999: 4; see also Hunt 1994: 463)

That is, since Jesus died as an adult, any appearance he makes as a child is, ipso facto, demonic. Similarly, since Jesus was a single human being, the belief that he can be simultaneously present in "millions of wafers" is also a demonic delusion. As I have noted elsewhere in this book, the elegance of countercult conspiracism is that no matter what happens in the world—war or peace, apparitions or prayer meetings, concern for the ecology of the planet or concern only for the state of one's bank account—all can be accommodated within the eschatological framework.

THE ENFORCEMENT OF EVANGELICAL ORTHODOXY

In *A Woman Rides the Beast*, Hunt summarizes the position of many anti-Catholic apologists: "Salvation is through obeying the church, not on the basis of the finished work of Christ on the cross" (1994: 351). Conversely, it could also be argued that for Hunt and other evangelicals, salvation is "not on the basis of the finished work of Christ on the cross," but through the ritualized precepts of a conscious, volitional process of recognition, repentance, and reception—the archetypal acceptance of Jesus as one's personal Lord and Savior. Epitomizing the apologetic hubris of orthodoxy discussed earlier (see chapter 4), Hunt continues that "it is an insult to God to suggest that He can forgive sins because someone prays the Rosary or goes to Mass or does something else which the Church has prescribed. *God can only forgive sins and save the soul on the basis of Christ having paid the full penalty demanded by God's justice*" (1994: 360, emphasis in the original). Once again, one wonders if it could not be argued that it is an insult to God to suggest that God can forgive only those who have completed a particular ritual process as described by Christian fundamentalists, that is, the "Sinner's Prayer"? Moreover, while few evangelicals or fundamentalists would deny the omnipotence of God, the thought that it might be considered an insult to God to suggest that God is *prohibited* from doing just about anything God wants never enters the discussion. In condemning the Roman Catholic Church on the grounds of what anti-Catholic apologists believe the Church says it *can* do, however, Hunt and his colleagues display their own arrogance through repeated declarations of what God *cannot* do. In fact, the parallels between their own position and that of which they accuse the Roman Catholic Church often escape them.

While the specific meaning of the phrase has changed for the Church over the centuries, both Roman Catholicism and the Christian countercult have their own version of *extra ecclesiam nulla salus*, their own understanding of "beyond the church there is no salvation." What constitutes the particular *ecclesia*, what authorizes entry into that *ecclesia*, and what determines ongoing membership within it, though, is the manner in which each attends to the relevant gospel evidence and what questions each brings to that attendance. Jack Chick, Dave Hunt, Ron Rhodes, and James White anathematize those who disagree with their subjective construction of theological reality no less severely than Rome. While Hunt (1987: 242, emphasis in the original) warns his readers about "the teaching that only an elite few know the true *interpretation*" of the Bible, the anti-Catholic apologists discussed here have merely established a different category of theological elitism, predicated on the authority of biblical interpretations that *they* hold true.

"Gittin' Thar Fustest with the Mostest": Antipathy, Authority, and Apologetics

That danger to the Christian faith lurks everywhere is the countercult's controlling paradigm, and a perception it seeks to mediate to the Christian church at large. Jan Karel van Baalen regarded Jehovah's Witnesses as "the deadliest and most fierce enemies of the Christian religion" (1960: 266). Walter Martin believed the Mormon Church "constitutes an immense threat to the church of Jesus Christ in our era" (1955: 63). "Aggressive, well-funded, and deceptive cults and aberrant sects pose a present or potential danger in virtually every place the gospel is preached," writes Paul Carden (1998: 147), a former Christian Research Institute staff member and now director of the Centers for Apologetics Research. For Richard Abanes (1997a: 334, emphasis in the original), the New Age "is much more than just an isolated system of religious beliefs and practices"; it "is literally a *movement* . . . that encompasses countless groups seeking to direct the path of society." Indeed, from Bob Larson's Buddhist and Hindu "demonism" to the billion or more souls lost in the satanic maw of the Roman Catholic Church, it appears there is no spiritual or religious movement that does not represent something of a clear and present danger to the Christian faith, and thus provide grist for the countercult mill.

Danger to the countercult witness appears from other directions as well, however. On the one hand are the aforementioned "cult apologists," whose work often implicitly (or explicitly) challenges the reliability and validity of countercult apologetics. On the other hand, internecine conflicts within the countercult community itself often pit apologist against apologist, splitting their witness and weakening their apologetic.

THE COUNTERCULT BATTLEGROUND

Setting aside the recurring problem of which came first, the heretical egg or the orthodox chicken, in the past two decades countercult apologists have grown increasingly critical not only of each other, but of various aspects of the

Christian church itself. In response to this, at least some in the countercult community have suggested that these attacks might be less than completely reasonable and have sought to call their colleagues to account (cf. Bowman 1991a; DeMar and Leithart 1988; Grady 1995; Passantino and Passantino 1990b; Paulk 1987; Reid et al. 1986; Spencer 1993; Wise et al. 1986). In *Witch Hunt,* for example, Bob and Gretchen Passantino (1990b) criticize fellow apologists for many of the same reasons these individuals and ministries are critiqued in this work—fallacious logic, speculation and hyperbole offered as fact and certainty, and the condemnation of particular groups on the thinnest of presented evidence. Reviewing *Witch Hunt,* however, Robert Bowman (1991a) also critiqued the Passantinos for similar transgressions.

Although the Passantinos do briefly consider Texe Marrs, most of *Witch Hunt's* criticism is reserved for Dave Hunt and Constance Cumbey. Cumbey, they contend, has accused the Spiritual Counterfeits Project, *Cornerstone Magazine,* and the Christian Research Institute variously of being fronts for the New Age, of suppressing the New Age involvement of other ministries, and of being ill informed or insufficiently concerned about the threat represented by the New Age. Rather than substantive disagreements over the nature of the New Age or the threat that it allegedly represents, however, while Cumbey's sense of persecution by those who disagree with her is amply annotated by the Passantinos (1990b: 220–27), their criticisms—and the official Christian Research Institute response written by Elliot Miller (1988)—suggest that deep-seated interpersonal issues are actually closer to the heart of the conflict. Few critics have failed to comment on Cumbey's obsession with the New Age, her ability to see its conspiracy everywhere, and her dismissal of those who do not so perceive it as either dupes or collaborators. Although they do detail some of the problems with Cumbey's analysis, the overall tenor of the Passantinos' defense and of Miller's reply is that her most serious infraction was questioning Walter Martin's commitment to countercult ministry. Since Martin's role as a movement intellectual has rendered him, to return to Eyerman and Jamison's conceptualization, "a role model . . . an inspirational figure of almost mythological proportions" (1991: 113), criticizing him has become verboten in much of the countercult community.

Three years later, James Spencer, "a recognized expert on religious cults" (Spencer 1993: 158), published *Heresy Hunters: Character Assassination in the Church* (1993), in which he took both the Passantinos and *Cornerstone* to task for their criticism of, among others, Bob Larson. Spencer protested the ridicule both parties had heaped upon Larson for his obsession with Satanism and satanic ritual abuse, objecting particularly to Gretchen Passantino's biting *Cornerstone* lampoon of Larson, "Tickets to Nowhere: Another Counter-Cult Apologist Adventure." It is important to note, however, that Spencer neither defends Larson against the substantive criticisms of the Passantinos and *Cornerstone,* nor does he suggest that their critique is altogether unwarranted (cf. Parks 2002). Rather, objecting to what he regards as the ungracious manner and caviling tone of the attacks, he calls into question the un-Christian quality of their criticism. While Spencer acknowledges both Larson and his critics as fellow Christians, he does wish they could avoid fighting with each other when there is an enemy common to both who is so much more deserving of their reproach.

"I know," he concludes (Spencer 1993: 139), "that both I and the heresy hunters will one day sheathe our swords for good. The time is coming when we will make war no more. Until that day, I pray they will gain the wisdom to turn from attacking the body and join the real battle we must all wage together against the forces of darkness." On the one hand, Spencer's call for solidarity in the face of a common enemy might be regarded as commendable. On the other hand, his apparent willingness to overlook the often egregious claims made by some of his countercult colleagues in the name of that solidarity virtually ensures that such heresy hunting will continue.

Aside from a disagreement with the Passantinos over the "Biblical Counseling Movement," a dispute in which he misrepresents the Passantinos' position (cf. Hunt 1998: 480; Passantino and Passantino 1995a, 1995b, 1995c, 1995d), Dave Hunt has repeatedly criticized the Christian Research Institute for its stand on Roman Catholicism, specifically its refusal to name the Catholic Church as the world's largest cult—whatever else, a not impolitic decision on the institute's part. In response to a reader's question in the October 1993 *Berean Call*, though, Hunt summarizes their differences: "I have pleaded with CRI, no matter what they call Catholicism, to state clearly that its counterfeit gospel is sending hundreds of millions to hell. Instead, CRI has defended Catholicism on radio and in its *Journal*, while its 'criticism' has been so vague as to leave one wondering what was meant. The perception of numerous people who have contacted us is that CRI is more concerned with defending Catholicism than opposing it"(1993b: 3). The Christian Research Institute, on the other hand, publishes a standard statement to queries about its relationship with Hunt, reading in part that "CRI fully supports [Hunt's] commitment to the gospel of Christ and to testing all things by the biblical record. . . . This does not mean, however, that we are in complete agreement with the conclusions of his studies. Hunt teaches that Roman Catholicism is a cult. . . . He also denounces Christian psychology as teaching a false gospel. CRI disagrees with him on these issues" (Christian Research Institute 1996).

The Christian Research Institute's qualified support notwithstanding, no countercult apologist has generated more controversy and criticism among the Christian community—and among fellow apologists—than Hunt, most particularly for *The Seduction of Christianity*, which he co-authored with T. A. McMahon (1985), and which became one of the bestselling books on the evangelical market during the 1980s. "We have written this book reluctantly," Hunt and McMahon begin, "yet knowing it had to be done. We have no desire to cause controversy or division; our sole purpose is to expose a seduction that is gathering momentum and is no respecter of persons" (1985: 7). While hindsight may seem omniscient, *Seduction* is the logical extension of books Hunt had been writing since 1980 (cf. Hunt 1980, 1983) and that he and McMahon would continue to write following *Seduction*'s release (cf. Hunt 1987, 1990, 1998; Hunt and McMahon 1988). Its basic premise is eschatological—specifically that prior to Christ's return a "great apostasy" must take place within the Christian church to prepare the way for the coming of the Antichrist. Hunt and McMahon's contention is that that apostasy is already well underway. Reducing "all pagan/occult practices" to a single rubric, they argue that "sorcery" has entered the gates of the church like a trojan horse, an "unrecognized enemy" in the house of God (Hunt and McMahon 1985: 12–14).

While many Christians reading *Seduction*'s first few pages might have initially nodded their heads in grave agreement, it is safe to say that a fair number were stunned when Hunt and McMahon began to name names. Among those singled out for their often harsh criticism were well-known evangelicals Robert Schuller, Norman Vincent Peale, and Paul (David) Yonggi Cho—all of whom had apparently come under the influence of the "heretical and deeply occult" teachings of Napoleon Hill, author of the self-motivation bestseller *Think and Grow Rich* (Hunt and McMahon 1985: 27). Other targets included Seattle pastors Richard Romney and Casey Treat; Crystal Cathedral copastor Bruce Larson; missionary and former head of the World Evangelization Crusade Norman Grubb; Word Faith preachers Charles Capps, Kenneth and Gloria Copeland, Kenneth Hagin, and Robert Tilton; popular Christian authors Richard Foster, Calvin Miller, and Morton Kelsey; and, finally, charismatic renewal preachers Robert Wise, Dennis and Rita Bennett, and John Wimber.

All of these and more Hunt and McMahon accused of either wittingly or unwittingly promoting a revival of "sorcery," "shamanism," and "idolatry" in the evangelical Christian church. Careful to point out that they are not "suggesting that the Christian leaders who promote these ideas are knowingly cooperating with the spirit of Antichrist," they conclude that "our concern has been to show that there is a growing pattern of seduction pointing in a particular direction prophesied in the Scriptures, and that none of us is immune from being deceived and deceiving others" (Hunt and McMahon 1985: 213).

That disclaimer notwithstanding, *The Seduction of Christianity* generated four book-length rebuttals (DeMar and Leithart 1988; Paulk 1987; Reid et al. 1986; Wise et al. 1986), reviews in the Christian press that ranged from open adulation to outright denunciation, and innumerable sermons from evangelical pulpits. Thomas Reid, for example, a Full Gospel pastor and president of the Association of Church-Centered Bible Schools, writes that *Seduction* was "a book that I personally believe is doing more to divide the Body of Christ than any other single event of modern history" (1986: 1). Reid's colleague, Alan Langstaff concurs, arguing that *Seduction* was not dangerous because it was entirely and completely wrong, but precisely because it wasn't (Langstaff 1986). William De Arteaga, an inner-healing minister, called the book "a case study in Christian Phariseeism" (1986b: 48), while the most detailed and often

erudite criticism came from Christian Reconstructionists Gary DeMar and Peter Leithart (1988), who dispute both Hunt's premillennialism and his association of postmillennial Dominion Theology with the New Age. Like so many
of Hunt's critics, though, it is important to note that DeMar and Leithart do
not dismiss him out of hand; they do not underestimate either the depth of
Hunt's commitment or the size of his audience. On the contrary, they regard
him as "an entirely orthodox Christian," who is "generally calling for a return
to a sound biblical Christianity" (1988: 13). What they object to is Hunt's
insistence on inspecting every phenomenon, whether secular or religious,
through the lens of his own premillennial dispensationalism, and then making
the results of that inspection the standard of an unassailable orthodoxy. Two
years after *Seduction*'s release, Hunt followed it with a sequel, *Beyond Seduction* (1987), which begins, somewhat disingenuously: "Such strong reactions
[to *Seduction*] caught me by surprise."

At the Christian Research Institute (CRI), internecine struggles since the
death of Walter Martin in 1989 have revolved generally around (1) lawsuits
filed by over thirty former CRI employees (the Group for CRI Accountability)
against Hank Hanegraaff, accusing Hanegraaff of numerous counts of wrongful
termination, financial mismanagement, and abuse of managerial authority; (2)
occasional questions regarding the legitimacy of Hanegraaff's claims to ordination; (3) more serious charges of plagiarism leveled against Hanegraaff by
former CRI staff members; and (4) recent allegations that, despite what he has
claimed for more than a decade, Hanegraaff was not hand-picked by Martin to
succeed him as president of CRI but simply assumed the mantle in the vacuum
left by Martin's death. Here, in the interests of space, we consider only the
issue of plagiarism.

In the eyes of many in the countercult community, since Hanegraaff took
over management of CRI the Christian Research Institute has become little
more than a clearinghouse for "Hank Hanegraaff, Inc.," a multimedia commercial platform from which he can merchandise his own writings and persona
as a preeminent countercult apologist. Hanegraaff's face, sometimes thoughtful
and serious, other times smiling and jovial, is abundantly displayed on both
print and electronic CRI advertising material. There are "Letters from Hank,"
and "Hank's Resource of the Month" available; "Hank Hanegraaff Resources"
occupies its own shelf in CRI's online bookstore. And, he is the lead host for
the organization's flagship medium, the daily radio program *Bible Answer
Man*, the final arbiter on issues that arise during the show. However, it is
Hanegraaff's Personal Witness Training program (PWT) and Memory Dynamics material that have generated the most controversy in terms of his alleged
misappropriation of other's time, ideas, intellectual property, and published
work.

In late 1995, *On the Edge*, a photocopied newsletter that claims to be "a
controversial yet supremely accurate publication dealing with religious hypoc-
risy and scandal in ministry," yet which appears to focus primarily on the

various scandals at CRI, published a report stating that "high-level sources close to Hanegraaff" had reported that the CRI president had plagiarized much of his Personal Witness Training material from evangelist D. James Kennedy's extremely popular *Evangelism Explosion* (Sardasian 1995). The charges were serious, ranging from Hanegraaff's alleged appropriation of *Evangelism Explosion*'s basic witnessing philosophy, to the general organization of the material, to simply copying text and illustrations from Kennedy's work and passing them off as his own. If Sardasian's obscure, often ranting newsletter were the only source of accusation, no further mention need be made of the charges. In more than five years, though, the allegations have continued, and the chorus of accusers has grown to include a former senior CRI researcher, Walter Martin's daughter and widow, and D. James Kennedy himself.

Prior to the publication of Sardasian's report, a copy was faxed to former CRI researcher Robert Bowman (Bowman 1998b). Initially skeptical, Bowman asserts that his interest in the matter was "piqued" when Hanegraaff associates Bob and Gretchen Passantino declared unequivocally that the charges were groundless and, according to Bowman, Web published an open letter attacking him for his concerns, accusing him of "libel and/or slander, and encouraging Christians to avoid us" (Bowman 2001b). Rather than "accept the secondhand research of anonymous critics," Bowman continues (1998b), "I decided to investigate the matter for myself." Once he had completed his own review, and wanting to follow a biblical pattern of conflict resolution (i.e., Matt. 18), he wrote to Hanegraaff, with whom he had not been on good terms since his strained departure from CRI three years before,[1] and asked his former employer about the plagiarism charges and the similarities his own investigation had revealed. "The letter was returned unopened" (Bowman 1998b). Other attempts to discuss the matter with Hanegraaff yielded similar results, including a third-party offer to meet to consider Bowman's "grievances," but from which issues of plagiarism were to be explicitly excluded. Finally, feeling that he had shown due diligence to the biblical injunction, Bowman sent the report, entitled *Is the Good News Bear a Copycat? Hank Hanegraaff and Plagiarism*, "to a senior editor at CRI, to the members of the Board of CRI, and to the members of the Board of the Evangelical Ministries to New Religions" (Bowman 1998b). Once again, Bowman received no official reply.

Bowman's review of the Hanegraaff material, and his side-by-side comparison of it with Kennedy's *Evangelism Explosion*, is an excellent example of plagiarism research. He notes that, while later editions of *Personal Witness Training* do contain a vague acknowledgment of the intellectual debt Hanegraaff owed Kennedy, this acknowledgment is absent in early editions of the material. As well, in Bowman's opinion, Hanegraaff simply copied the *Evangelism Explosion* logo—a fish symbol with the word *ichthus* inside—replacing *icthus* with "PWT." Apparently, Hanegraaff then had the temerity to trademark his version of the logo. After a lengthy columnar comparison, Bowman concludes, among other points, that (1) "six of 'the seven pillars of *PWT*' are taken directly from pages 2–5 of *EE*. The concepts, biblical proof texts, lines of reasoning, and even some of the illustrations are the same"; (2) "the instructions for sharing one's personal testimony are the same in *PWT* as in *EE*, including the same three essential elements of a testimony and giving the same counsel on the fine points"; and (3) "*PWT* uses the same strategy for handling objections as *EE*, and presents this strategy using much of the same wording as in *EE*" (Bowman 1998b; cf. Bowman 2001a, 2001b). While Bowman admits that there are differences, he insists that they "do not diminish the significant similarities between the two works, nor do they undermine the case for plagiarism."

Like Sardasian's broadside, Bowman's critique of Hanegraaff's work could be dismissed as the carping of a disgruntled ex-employee were it not for the fact that Bowman never actually accuses Hanegraaff of plagiarism and publicly acknowledges that he will repent if any evidence is brought to demonstrate that his analysis is flawed. Rather, he builds what he believes is a solid case for plagiarism, then urges others—specifically the directorial boards of CRI and Evangelical Ministries to New Religions—to evaluate his case on its merits. Since the CRI regards itself as "the largest, most effective apologetics ministry in the world" (www.equip.org) the charges leveled against Hanegraaff are serious indeed. Yet, to date, no official reply has been forthcoming.

THE STRUGGLE FOR DOMINANCE

An entire book could be devoted to the social histories and internecine conflicts of various organizations in the Christian countercult. In keeping with the theoretical orientation of this work, however, just a few remarks are in order. First, at the core, these battles are about hubris and power, specifically, as discussed in chapter 4, the apologetic hubris of orthodoxy, and a concomitant arrogation of the power to determine who fits that orthodoxy and who does not. The Passantinos begin *Witch Hunt*, for example, stating that "without knowing what is orthodox, we cannot know the difference between what is genuinely heretical and what has been labeled falsely as heresy" (1990b: 39). They then spend a chapter detailing what they regard as the substance of orthodoxy—for them, a standard fundamentalist kerygma, supplemented with subscription to the historic creeds of the church. Similarly, DeMar and Leithart's first chapter in response to Hunt is entitled "Orthodoxy: Setting the Record Straight" and also argues for a return to credal formularies as the canon of orthodoxy. In each of these, the protocol is the same. The clear establishment of one's own orthodox credentials is considered a necessary prelude to the public criticism of another Christian. Taking a different tack, Reid and his collaborators bring *A Biblical Response* to Hunt and McMahon, implying that the latter's effort fell somewhat short of the scriptural mark. And Bishop Earl Paulk, pastor of the Chapel Hill Harvester megachurch in Atlanta, Georgia, and another of *Seduction*'s targets, pleads for Christian unity through what he regards as appropriate scriptural mandate. Rather than establish their authority with reference to Scripture through the historic creeds, in response to the accusations of Hunt and McMahon these critics (especially Reid et al.) weave together a pastiche of biblical texts they believe support their position.

Second, in a manner similar to the Evangelical Ministries to New Religions's *Manual of Ethical and Doctrinal Standards* (1997), the standards of conduct to which countercult ministries are held by their peers are quite conspicuously *not* applied when the target groups are not Christian. Wise quite accurately critiques Hunt and McMahon, for example, stating that "while their books appear to be scholarly and researched, much of the material is taken out of context and in some instances material is used in a deceptive manner" (1986: 40). Similarly, Wise's colleague William De Arteaga declares that "one of the primary errors on *The Seduction of Christianity* is an attitude of spiritual arrogance and failure to properly measure the works and people it examines— that is, by their fruits" (1986a: 45). However, although they are accurate in many of their criticisms, they do not raise comparable concerns when these practices are employed against non-Christian religious groups. One can look in vain among the responses generated by *The Seduction of Christianity* for similar denunciations of Hunt and McMahon's "spiritual arrogance" toward Hinduism, for similar criticism of their decontextualization and deceptive rhetoric when the target is Buddhism, or for similar censure of their problematic claims regarding any number of other religious groups (e.g., "Scientology is very similar to Mormonism" [1985: 68]—a statement that would outrage not a few on both sides of the equation).

Even though the Passantinos make an attempt at such criticism in *Witch Hunt*, it too is problematic. In rather a straw man fashion, they contend that *"we cannot honestly and fairly claim to represent the God of truth—the God whom we claim to serve—by accusing anyone unfairly,"* and point out that "it would be *unfair* to accuse Mormons of thinking that the Holy Spirit is not a person and is not God"; similarly, "it would be *unfair* to accuse Jehovah's Witnesses of thinking that they can become gods" (1990b: 14; emphases in the original). The fact that no one seems to be making these mistakes notwithstanding, their reasoning is obvious: it would be unfair to condemn one for the doctrinal sins of the other. "Understand this," though, they disclaim, lest they be accused of going soft on cults, "both Mormonism and Jehovah's Witnesses are cultic, heretical, unbiblical, and non-Christian" (Passantino and Passantino 1990b: 15). Apparently, no similar unfairness obtains in this characterization. Like Wise and his colleagues, while the Passantinos call their countercult colleagues on the carpet for "slandering" such evangelical luminaries as James Dobson, Robert Schuller, or John Wimber, no such outrage is expended on Jack Chick, Dave Hunt, or James White for their often egregious distortions of Roman Catholicism, very little on John Ankerberg, John Weldon, or Ed Decker for their misrepresentations of Mormonism and Freemasonry, and none on Caryl Matrisciana or Bob Larson for their hostile portrayals of Hinduism and

Buddhism. The reason for this particular lacuna seems clear: by and large, when it comes to non-Christian religious groups, with a few exceptions, other countercult apologists do not substantively disagree with these more sensationalist authors.

THE PROBLEM OF AUTHORITY AND CREDIBILITY

Robert Wise begins his critique of *The Seduction of Christianity* in what seems an obvious, if often overlooked, place: who are Dave Hunt and Thomas Aloysius McMahon? Noting that "Hunt and McMahon define truth in a way peculiar to themselves," Wise continues: "We are never told who Hunt and McMahon are nor what credentials they have. Apparently Hunt is a self-certified authority on cults" (1986: 40). DeMar and Leithart complain similarly: "That Dave Hunt, a man with a bachelor's degree in mathematics, is now the most prominent theologian of the dispensationalist movement . . . indicates the extent of the crisis" (1988: xvii). Comparable questions obtain across the various countercult continua. While both the Passantinos and William Alnor claim to be "award winning investigative journalists," each accuses the other of transgressions ranging from knowingly publishing false reports (the Passantinos about Alnor) to lying about their journalistic and countercult credentials (Alnor about the Passantinos). Accusing each other of bad journalism, they implicitly indict each other for bad faith. These sorts of charges highlight the problem of authority, credentialing, and credibility in the Christian countercult.

Avocational apologists such as Anton Hein may not consider it important in any official capacity, but authority and credentialing do matter in the world of social discourse. In the occasional book review Hein contributes to Web sites such as Amazon.com, for example, he lists himself as "Publisher, Apologetics Index," itself an appeal to some measure of authority. Put simply, though, if one has the authority to speak on a particular subject, if one is credentialed in a particular area, it is not unreasonable to expect that one's comments in that area will be taken more seriously than those of a person with no discernible experience or education, or, in the context of new religious movements, whose only qualification appears to be his or her status as an ex-member. On the other hand, if credibility were unimportant, the collection of laudatory comments on bookflaps, back covers, and publisher's promotional material would not be so prominent in the countercult marketing process. Such, however, is not the case.

Bob and Gretchen Passantino are listed in promotional copy as "experts in cult research"—though there is no indication what qualifies them as experts. Richard Abanes is "a highly regarded authority on cults" (Abanes 1998a: front cover); promotional material on the back of *End-Time Visions* (1998a) lists among those who endorse his work agencies as diverse as the Simon Wiesenthal Center and the Bureau of Alcohol, Tobacco, and Firearms. Dave Hunt is "an internationally known author and lecturer" (e.g., Hunt 1994: back cover)—

a claim not unsupported by the qualified manner in which other countercult apologists often acclaim his writings. As noted above, though, some countercult claims are quite obviously hyperbolic. Robert Morey maintains that he has read every one of the more than seven thousand volumes on Islam in the Library of Congress, a claim at least some apologists are still willing to defend on Morey's behalf.[2] Finally, in addition to his alleged expertise in Mormonism, former CRI researcher John Weldon is touted as "perhaps the most qualified living Christian authority on the occult" (Miller 1988)—a claim for which there is no empirical evidence, and one that Bob Larson, at least, might be inclined to dispute.

Given that it is a decentralized, increasingly democratized social phenomenon with no established magisterium or institutional structure, authority and credentialing in the Christian countercult is a murky business at best. In fact, this circumstance presents another discriminate continuum according to which the countercult can be typologized. At one end are those, such as Beckwith, Blomberg, Bowman, Gomes, Groothuis, Hawkins, Lewis, Mosser, Owen, and Rhodes, who have (or are pursuing) degrees relevant in some way to the apologetic enterprise, and that were (or will be) granted by recognized and accredited institutions. For others, such as Ankerberg, Martin, Weldon, and White, some dispute exists about the caliber of the institutions from which they claim relevant degrees, and, by implication, the actual legitimacy of the degrees themselves. Still others, such as Cumbey, Hanegraaff, Hunt, and Marrs, have degrees in fields unrelated to countercult apologetics. Finally, with the expanding democratization of the countercult, many now entering the field have no discernible academic credentials whatsoever. Of these, a number—for example, Abanes, Baer, Decker, McCarthy, Montenegro, Scott, and Spencer—have felt called to countercult ministry out of their own involvement in new or controversial religious movements. While some, such as Montenegro, may pursue academic training as a result of these decisions, the principal authority is a self-credentialing based on personal experience.

This is not to say that an academic degree is the ultimate cachet, and that only those who are academically trained in a particular area can speak with authority. Relevant academic training does, however, provide a basis for discourse *about* the authoritative voice. Ex-members participate differently in that discourse than do secular academics, and it is important to be able to recognize that difference. Similarly, an ex-member with no theological education functions differently as a movement intellectual than an academically trained apologist such as Douglas Groothuis, who grew up in an evangelical church.

The issue becomes even more complicated when those who do self-credential often do not restrict themselves to the movements in which they were involved, those about which they might legitimately claim to speak with some authority. While Richard Abanes was a member of The Way International for a time, he now speaks and writes on virtually any topic that takes his interest. *Cults, New Religious Movements, and Your Family* (Abanes 1998b), for example, is subtitled *A Guide to Ten Non-Christian Groups Out to Convert Your Loved Ones*. The fact that at least one of the groups he considers does not proactively recruit notwithstanding, the question of what qualifies Abanes, as a former member of one group, to speak with authority on all these others is left unanswered. In the case of Satanism, at least, it seems all that is required is a passing familiarity with evangelical literature on the subject. While he does quote from two of Anton LaVey's published writings, the majority of Abanes's sources on Satanism are from established countercult sources. He very briefly cites one scholar of new religious movements—J. Gordon Melton—but ignores the growing body of nonevangelical scholarship on the topic. Even the extensive quotes from LaVey are used mainly as fodder for a columnar comparison with passages from the Bible. Montenegro, on the other hand, claims to have been so thoroughly immersed in all aspects of the New Age that she is qualified to speak to all of them. While one might question aspects of her description, she does not, however, venture outside her alleged area of experience.

The issue in all of this, of course, is the ability to speak with perceived authority and credibility, to be recognized as a reputable, significant voice in the countercult chorus. While Walter Martin's credentialing difficulties were discussed in chapter 5, in recent years, other countercult apologists—John Ankerberg, John Weldon, and James White—have come under criticism for the legitimacy of their various academic degrees.

Conferred in 1998, White's Th.D. is from Columbia Evangelical Seminary (CES), where he now serves as professor of apologetics and which advertises on its Web site (www.ColumbiaSeminary.org) that its "curriculum has been designed for self-paced learning by Mentorship Study"—a euphemism for correspondence courses. That same year, Latter-day Saint Gary Novak questioned the quality of White's CES degree on his Web site, "Worst of the Anti-Mormon Web" (now archived at www.shields-research.org/Novak).[3] Among the issues Novak raised were whether White ever took classes from anyone other than his mentor, Rick Walston (president of CES), whether anyone but Walston served on a dissertation committee for White, and whether White completed either doctoral comprehensive examinations or a dissertation defense. When White discovered Novak's charges, a lengthy Internet correspondence ensued— Novak doggedly asking the same questions, White steadfastly insisting that his work at CES was actually more lengthy and more rigorous than at a normal, accredited institution, and that he should be judged by the quality of his published work in the evangelical marketplace. Time and again, Novak reiterated that he was utterly uninterested in White's published works, rather only in the academic legitimacy of his doctoral degree. At the conclusion of his Web site page, Novak writes:

Does James White have a genuine doctorate? Here is what we know. The degree is granted by an unaccredited correspondence school. There are no set course syllabi; students write their own syllabi. CES has no library, student services or bookstore. The

school has no curriculum committees and no course review procedures. There appears
to have been no committee and no thesis or dissertation defense; the only signature in
James White's Masters Thesis is that of CES president, Rick Walston. White's "con-
tract" was also with Rick Walston. Does James White have a genuine doctorate? What
do you think? (Novak n.d. [a]; cf. Novak n.d. [b])

This passage is reposted in one of White's lengthy online replies to the
charges. Responding, though, he disputes only one aspect of Novak's assessment: "If Mr. Novak put the last statement in its only meaningful form," he
writes, "we would not have any problems: if he would replace the word 'genuine' with 'governmentally accredited,' all would be well" (White 2001b; cf.
White 2001a, 2001c), which is, of course, precisely Novak's argument, although
White contends (along with Walston) that "government accreditation" is more
an issue of approval for funding than an assessment of academic rigor and
credibility.[4]

A review of the Columbia Evangelical Seminary's *Student Handbook*, however, indicates that Novak's concerns are not entirely without foundation. Dis-
sertations are "approved" only by the student's mentor, and are "reviewed by
a Seminary representative," although there is no indication of the nature of
this review, nor who undertakes to conduct it on behalf of the seminary. Once
approved, a "Declaration of Authenticity" is included in the final dissertation
copy, the online example of which lists the name of the advisor (who has
"reviewed and accepted" it), and the seminary representative (who appears to
serve purely an administrative function). Again, though, what is meant by
"authenticity" is left unclear. No committee guides the dissertation, and there
is no indication that either doctoral comprehensive examinations or a dissertation defense takes place. Indeed, the student handbook contains no references
to examinations of any kind (cf. www.ColumbiaSeminary.org). Promotional
material for the seminary lists Walston as an expert in distance learning, and,
in response to the somewhat thorny question of accreditation, he concludes:
"Columbia Evangelical Seminary is not accredited. However, as stated above,
if you do not absolutely need a degree from an accredited school, why spend
the extra money earning one when a degree from a non-accredited school may
serve your purposes just as well?"

Depending on what one's purposes are, why indeed?

Similar questions pursue John Ankerberg and John Weldon. In his review
of *Behind the Mask of Mormonism*, which he regards as "bigoted, intolerant,
ugly, incompetent, and dishonest" (1996), Latter-day Saint and Brigham Young
University professor Daniel Peterson points out that according to promotional
material on the back covers of their various books, both Ankerberg and Weldon
claim a confusing variety of degrees. Ankerberg "holds advanced degrees in
theology and philosophy, including two master's degrees and a doctorate"; Weldon "has three master's degrees and two doctorates, one each in comparative
religion and contemporary religious movements." Of these, we consider only

Ankerberg in depth here (see Peterson 1996 for a similar evaluation of Weldon).

According to author information in *Cult Watch* (Ankerberg and Weldon 1991a: 379), Ankerberg has an M.A. in "Church History and the History of Christian Thought" and an M.Div., both from "Trinity Seminary," and a "doctorate degree from Bethel Theological Seminary." According to online information, however, Ankerberg claims to have completed his B.A. in 1972, and both his M.A. and M.Div. degrees ("with high academic honors in both") in 1973, barely a year later, this time not from Trinity Seminary but from "Trinity Evangelical Divinity School." These are very different institutions, and the distinction is crucial from the perspective of credentialing and authority. Like Columbia Evangelical Seminary above, Trinity Seminary is unaccredited and advertises that all degrees may be earned through home study. On the other hand, Trinity Evangelical Divinity School (now part of Trinity International University) is an accredited, well-respected evangelical institution, offering a number of Association of Theological Schools (ATS)–approved graduate degrees. From which institution did Ankerberg obtain his? ATS accreditation guidelines for a Master of Divinity degree stipulate that the minimum program duration is "three academic years of full-time work or its equivalent" (www.ats.edu), not the one year Ankerberg's own Web site declares he devoted to the task. Moreover, Ankerberg also claims a concurrent Master of Arts degree, for which ATS requires "two academic years of full-time study or the equivalent." Additionally, Trinity Seminary offers a degree very similar in nomenclature to the one described by Ankerberg—Master of Arts in Christian Thought; Trinity Evangelical Divinity School does not. Given this, the timelines involved, and his numerous published acknowledgments of Trinity Seminary, it seems likely that this is the institution from which Ankerberg gained his Master's degrees, not Trinity Evangelical Divinity School.

Virtually identical problems obtain with his doctoral degree. In various biographical sketches (e.g., Ankerberg and Weldon 1992a, 1996a, 1999), Ankerberg lists either a "doctorate" or a "doctorate degree." On his ministry Web site and in other publications (Ankerberg and Weldon 1991a, 1996b), this is listed as a "doctor of ministry," conferred by Luther Rice Seminary in 1991. Biographical information in *Cult Watch*, however, which was published in 1991, lists his "doctorate degree" as coming from Bethel Theological Seminary (Ankerberg and Weldon 1991a: 379). That same year, Ankerberg and Weldon also published *One World: Bible Prophecy and the New World Order*, in which Ankerberg is listed as "a candidate for the doctoral degree from Bethel Theological Seminary" (1991b: 5). The ambiguity of the nomenclature in this instance notwithstanding—Ankerberg does not disclose what manner of doctorate he is pursuing, a professional or an academic degree—as an ATS – accredited institution, Bethel's standards for admission to the Doctor of Ministry program require a Master of Divinity or equivalent from another accredited school. Unaccredited by the ATS, Luther Rice Seminary does not make such a stipulation.

Though speaking only of Weldon, Peterson (1996) quite correctly notes that "it is not at all clear how a D.Min. degree would qualify Weldon to research and write on either 'comparative religions' or 'cultic theology.' " While a similar concern certainly obtains with regard to Ankerberg, the confusion does not end there. The dates according to which Ankerberg claims his doctoral degrees—and, indeed, which doctoral degrees he claims—are also somewhat bewildering. Instead of the D.Min., author information on at least two of his publications (e.g., Ankerberg and Weldon 1989, 1992b) claims that Ankerberg has a Ph.D. from Luther Rice Seminary, a degree that is not offered at that institution and was apparently conferred at least two year prior to the D.Min. he claims variously from Luther Rice and Bethel. Even eliminating the use of the Ph.D. as an unfortunate oversight on the part of the publisher does not solve the problem. Indeed, other credibility blurbs (e.g., Ankerberg and Weldon 1988, 1993, 1996b) do list his degree as a "D.Min. from Luther Rice Seminary." Here the problem is that Ankerberg claimed the degree as early as 1988, now at least three years before he elsewhere admits to being either a recipient or a candidate. While it is, of course, possible that Ankerberg's publisher has updated his biographical information for later printings of earlier material, this still does not clarify Ankerberg's educational claims. Finally, in his investigation, Peterson (1996) notes that there is no record of a doctoral dissertation, either submitted by John Ankerberg or submitted from Luther Rice Seminary, in any of the standard scholarly compendia.

Two central questions obtain in these brief explorations: (1) First is the issue of traditional versus nontraditional modes of graduate education, or, put differently, the validity of accredited resident programs as opposed to those completed through largely unaccredited correspondence, home study, or distance education courses—hardly a debate that is limited to the Christian countercult. As Peterson (1996) asks, "do graduate degrees earned via correspondence represent the same quality of training as those attained through close work with graduate faculty advisors and research in graduate libraries?" And (2), the more important issue is whether some countercult apologists actually have the degrees they claim. That the perception of these credentials is important to countercult apologists is obvious; that the Evangelical Ministries to New Religions's *Manual of Ethical and Doctrinal Standards* saw fit to include a section specifically addressing the issue under its section on "Self-Representation"—in particular whether academic degrees had "been legitimately earned at an institution requiring in-class instruction or through an accredited 'distance education' facility" (Evangelical Ministries to New Religions 1997)—indicates that the countercult community clearly recognizes the potential both for self-misrepresentation and for the damage that could inflict on the legitimacy and integrity of the countercult witness as a whole. Consider, for example, the countercult's not infrequent use of trial transcripts in which Watchtower founder Charles Taze Russell was forced to admit his own misrepresentation of academic training (cf., for example, Martin 1965: 38–40, 1997: 83–86; Martin and Klann 1974: 21–23; van Baalen 1960: 267). Following this trail of credential claims is important because it contributes to the information consumers of countercult material have access to and on the basis of which they make purchasing decisions. As a movement intellectual, these advertisements credential Ankerberg as an authority but disguise the fact that his preparation for the task at hand may be less than as advertised.

"FUSTEST WITH THE MOSTEST": RESOURCE MOBILIZATION AND COUNTERCULT APOLOGETICS

Even given the wide variety of groups and individuals who have created the countercult over the past several decades, even accounting for both the internecine theological differences and the idiosyncratic variations in the specifics of their apologetic, why is the overall countercult landscape so similar? Even conceding that the Internet democratization of the countercult has resulted in an occasional "dumbing down" of the arguments presented, the root epistemology of those arguments is not appreciably different from that which informs more academic apologetic efforts. Finally, even recognizing the efforts of apologists such as Craig Blomberg, John Morehead, Carl Mosser, and Paul Owen to raise the intellectual bar for their colleagues, there exists little practical regard for a higher science of countercult apologetics.

In August 2000, an online conversation on AR-vent (now AR-forum) developed a somewhat simpler argument over the practical value of an academically informed and reflective countercult epistemology from which effective apologetics might proceed, versus the often blunt pragmatics of so-called street-level witnessing and conversion. Put differently, whether one's goal is proactive evangelism or religious boundary-maintenance, what resources can be most easily and effectively delivered in order to achieve that objective? Conceptualized in this way, it is readily apparent that resource mobilization favors precisely the kind of material one finds abundant in the modern countercult—that which is simple, simplified, and frequently, in the end, simplistic.

In the AR-vent discussion, Joe Paskewich, a pastor with a Connecticut affiliate of the Calvary Chapel (and formerly with Vineyard Christian Fellowship), chided another contributor for suggesting that the pool of countercult resources most easily available was both epistemologically shallow and often theologically naive. The original contributor, Carl Mosser, had lamented that "people usually want resources they can find on the Web or at their local Christian bookstore," and opined that the unsophisticated nature of these resources might account for the "uncharitable," "mean-spirited," and "accusatory" manner in which countercult apologetics is often carried out. "What's wrong with looking for resources on your desktop computer if they are available?" replied

Paskewich, recalling one of Walter Martin's initial visions for the Christian Research Institute. "Who can blame them? Available, free, quick information is preferable to difficult to find, time burdened material." Preferable perhaps, but, recalling also Wright's suggestion to "use the Net like Polyfilla and fill the gaps in your knowledge with ready-made, instant info bites," not necessarily more accurate or more reliable. Practical apologetics, it seems, in a dictum attributed to Confederate General Nathan Bedford Forrest, is driven by a need to "git thar fustest with the mostest."

Paskewich, however, using a "naive housewife" as an example, states quite candidly that "most of the people that are leading cultists to the Lord are ladies with a Women's Devotional Bible and the Left Behind Series as the sum total of their theological library." While one might question both the validity of his claim and the merit of the resources he cites, for Paskewich the pragmatic, evangelistic value of readily available and easily understood countercult material is clear. Paskewich concludes: "The 'naive' believer equipped only with another lady friend that has a copy of the 'Godmakers' brings it over and the lady Mormon gets upset and gives her heart to Jesus. Her husband who she sleeps with now has to deal with this new weirdness and this strange neighbor and as well. The neighbor, her church and now his wife are praying for him. That's the way conversions are happening in Mormonism" [sic].

Another participant in the discussion, an occasional contributor to the AR-talk lists who identified herself as "a housewife, though, I think, not utterly naive," supported Paskewich's position. "I appreciate the simpler resources and tools out there to counter false doctrine," she writes. "Most folks know diddly-squat about philosophy and research," which was, of course, precisely Mosser's original point.

Protesting the lack of scholarship and epistemological reflection—discussion comoderator Anton Hein's declaration that "the AR-talk lists are scholarly forums" notwithstanding—Mosser complains, perhaps somewhat unfairly but not entirely without empirical grounds: "I know it's hard to get you [i.e., Hein] or most anyone else on this list to read anything that doesn't come off the Web or from Bethany or Harvest House publishers." Mosser's point is well taken, though perhaps not for the reasons he imagined. It is not the case that people purchase and make use of countercult material produced by Bethany and Harvest House and ignore other, more academically sophisticated apologetics. The reality is that there is a veritable flood of the former and a definite dearth of the latter. The majority of commercial countercult publication is concentrated in a very few companies similar in theological orientation to Bethany and Harvest House (who count among their stable of authors many of the countercult apologists considered here, including Ankerberg, Decker, Groothuis, Hanegraaff, Hunt, Martin, Matrisciana, McCarthy, Morey, Rhodes, Weldon, and White). Little of the material produced by these houses—and even less of that available on the Internet—rises to the level of serious scholarship for which Mosser called.

More important in this regard, though, is the issue of resource mobilization. More and more evangelical publishers are willing to produce and promote material in the countercult arena. And, there are good reasons why the less sophisticated material about which Mosser complains is the most popular, and why the entirely unregulated flow of information through the Internet is daily increasing in popularity. First, whether oriented toward mission or boundary-maintenance, this material is written with what might be called a first-order practicality in mind. In the vast majority of cases, complexity, nuance, and variation between or within competitor religions, as well as attention to the controversial development of Christian doctrine and belief, are subsumed to the overriding principle of countercult apologetics and evangelism. Once that principle is firmly established, any need for further understanding of either controversial groups or the historical development of one's own faith virtually disappears. In the cognitive praxis of the countercult movement, the evangelical worldview has been, as Gunter Remmling puts it, "hypostasized as an ontological absolute" (1973: 16).

Second, since both the target consumer of countercult material and the producer share this same subjective construction of reality, a first-order practicality requires less intellectual and ethical rigor of both. Based on testimonial evidence from the newsletters and Web sites of numerous countercult apologists, it is clear that consumers such as the "naive housewife" above are already predisposed to accept at least the general framework of the arguments made by the producer and have purchased or accessed these material because they present that information in the quick, effective, and efficient manner Paskewich suggests. Because of these predisposing conditions, much of the countercult material can then be rendered in the form of conventional pieties. Countercult authors begin from the assumption that religious group or teaching "X" is heretical, and then simply mine such resources as are available—whether primary, secondary, or tertiary—to prove that conclusion. Since the turn of the twentieth century, for example, no one in either the nascent or the more intentional countercult has begun a book on the Latter-day Saints or Jehovah's Witnesses with the honest question, "Is what this group teaches *really* wrong?" Rather, *that* they are wrong is understood a priori; what remains is simply that fact's satisfactory demonstration. As a result, the ordinary rigors of scholarship—for example, sound argument, triangulated references, credible sources—are simply not required. Indeed, an argument could be made that if they were employed, these rigors would seriously impede the process of popular countercult apologetics as it is currently constituted.

This brings us to the third point: the vast majority of countercult material is produced for—and, in not a few cases, by—people who have little or no academic, theological training. They are quite simply not interested in a product that does not serve the needs of first-order apologetic or evangelistic practicality. Surveying the now voluminous scholarly literature on alternative religious movements—never mind reading it in depth—would be a prodigious undertaking for someone who only wants to know how to prove to their Mormon neighbor just who's going to hell and who isn't, or to defend themselves and their faith against the eight A.M. door-knockers from the local Kingdom Hall. As well, because much of the social scientific literature would not support either their evangelistic or apologetic objectives, but would only confuse issues that require a certain measure of reductivist clarity if the migration from false world to true is to be effected, it would actually be detrimental to the cause. The requirement is for simple, relatively unsophisticated, easily managed apologetic material. Thus, as long as the countercult apologist says what the target audience expects to hear, issues of credibility, authority, and reliability become somewhat moot.

CONCLUDING THOUGHTS

Over the course of writing, as aspects of this research have filtered out into the countercult community, the criticism has been often made that I have not drawn a clear enough distinction between so-called pop apologists and more academically oriented, responsible apologists. That distinction, however, is one that I have endeavored to make throughout the book, although perhaps not in those precise terms or to the degree desired by the countercult—both of which conditions, I think, serve more the needs of apologists who want to be distanced from others such as Cumbey, Hunt, Larson, and Marrs, than they do an accurate assessment of the countercult phenomenon itself. For example, while numerous countercult apologists cite Douglas Groothuis as the model of a more respectable, academic apologist, the problem remains that in Groothuis's two most popular books, which are undoubtedly *Unmasking the New Age* (1986) and *Confronting the New Age* (1988), he in fact uses both Hunt and Marrs as reliable sources. Further, *Confronting the New Age* (which, with the possible exception of *Deceived by the Light* [1995], is arguably his *least* academic book) remains in popular circulation and is either required or recommended reading in a number of graduate-level apologetics courses across the United States, including Groothuis's own courses at Denver Seminary.

Thus, the basic problem is not that any distinction among the various countercult continua is not made here; rather, it is that the Christian community at large doesn't make the distinction. Admittedly, in the grand sweep of Protestant evangelicalism, the countercult is not large. All tolled, it includes a few hundred apologists, with fewer than fifty publishing commercially and consistently. In that sense, it is something of a fringe movement, but a fringe movement with appeal well beyond its meager numbers. As I noted in the opening chapter, few if any evangelical Christian bookstores do not have some shelves, perhaps even an entire section, devoted variously to "Cults and Sects," "False Religions," "Cult Apologetics," or some other rubric. And, by and large, it is the movement intellectuals, the apologists considered in this book, who populate those shelves. Douglas Groothuis's books are stacked cheek-by-jowl with those of Dave Hunt; Bob Larson and Robert Morey vie for front-facing space with Walter Martin and Texe Marrs. Obviously, this situation doesn't speak to the relative merits of these books; rather it points out both the lack of ability and the unwillingness in the evangelical community at large to discern any significant difference between them. The argument that I have tried to make here is that, while apologists such as Groothuis, Hawkins, Martin, or Rhodes might not make the same kind of extreme claims or sensational appeals as Cumbey, Hunt, Larson, or Marrs, in terms of epistemology and methodology, there is very often little to choose between them. While they may occupy different points on the various countercult continua, that they operate within a shared cognitive praxis and with similar methodological tools is clear.

That there are more rigorously academic countercult apologists is also clear, although they have yet to really make their appearance on the field. As emergent movement intellectuals, for example, Carl Mosser and Paul Owen are making something of a name for themselves in evangelical–Latter-day Saints apologetics. Graduate students when they wrote "Mormon Scholarship, Apologetics and Evangelical Neglect: Losing the Battle and Not Knowing It?" (1998), whether they will continue as countercult apologists is anyone's guess. I suspect, though, that the primary reason they have not yet begun to make their mark is that they counsel a very different, considerably more difficult epistemological course for the countercult than has heretofore been the case. They urge apologists at all levels not simply to read evangelical material about target groups, but to read material produced by the groups themselves. They argue that, because it almost invariably presents a skewed vision of the group under discussion, reading only evangelical countercult material is perhaps the most fundamental mistake made by the Christian countercult. Even if the vision is not skewed in its actual description, it is weighted by virtue of its intent: the conversion of target adherents. Thus, the only indication the countercult consumer has of what those adherents believe comes from the arguments and descriptions of those who seek to refute and convert them. As well, as has been demonstrated here, while many countercult apologists may appear to cite primary sources, they are very often citing them from the writings of other countercult apologists—stripped of context and dependent on those who went before them to have rendered the material accurately. The result? If the only material countercult apologists read is that produced by other countercult apologists— who may themselves have read and worked from the original, but whose research is diluted through generational extension and democratization—then the movement becomes locked in a progressively deteriorating epistemic loop, the intellectual rigor of which will continue to degrade over time. Put differently, it becomes a tail-chasing exercise in boundary-maintenance—everyone quoting each other in hopes of supporting their shared worldview.

Mosser and Owen, on the other hand, encourage apologists not to read only Walter Martin on the Mormons, and certainly not to read Ankerberg, Decker, Hunt, or Weldon; instead, go to a Mormon bookstore and read what Latter-day Saints have to say about themselves, about their tradition, and about their beliefs—not what other people very often misrepresent about them. These are, to my mind, valuable contributions to the epistemology and methodology of the countercult effort.

Whether this more rigorous apologetic effort will be successful is unclear. First, if one of the basic principles of apologetics as it is currently constituted is "gittin' thar fustest with the mostest," and by implication, with apologetic tools of first-order practicality, realistically speaking, this means apologetic tools that are easily put to use by a rapidly democratizing countercult with little or no formal theological training. The kind of rigor for which Mosser and Owen call is not conducive to this kind of apologetic or missiologic effort; it introduces significantly more complexity and nuance than the apologetic market will bear. It is the same reason, essentially, that countercult apologists— whether lay or professional—do not appear particularly interested in reading the work of academic sociologists and historians of religion. While not ignored entirely (Carden 1998; Mosser and Owen 1998; Pettit 1998), the kind of work these academics do does not well serve—or is not perceived to serve—the cognitive praxis of the Christian countercult, which is to present simple, refutative arguments in a readily digestible and deployable form. The abysmal retention rates of the Unification Church, for example, which were well documented by Eileen Barker in *The Making of a Moonie* (1984), do not serve the countercult perception of the Moonies as a dangerous, inexorable cultic force.[5] The voluminous anecdotal evidence that there are millions upon millions of people who quite happily inhabit religious universes different from the evangelical Christian does not serve the countercult contention that anyone not an evangelical is, perforce, a "slave to sin" (Evangelical Ministries to New Religions 1997).

Second, in times past, it was not uncommon for foreign missionaries to spend a considerable period preparing for the mission field. Diligently learning the language, the customs, the beliefs, the ways of the people among whom they would work, missionaries often (though certainly not always) lived with and among those people, sharing their hardships, participating in their celebrations, gaining their trust, and endeavoring to show them that the way of Christianity was superior to the way in which they had been worshiping. With a few exceptions, this kind of missiologic, which implies a more authentic commitment to the people evangelized than the rhetoric of concern so common in the introductions and conclusions of any number of the works considered here, is conspicuously absent from modern countercult apologetics. It must be very difficult for the average Latter-day Saint, or Roman Catholic, or Jehovah's Witness to believe that countercult apologists care about them at all when, from their perspective, those apologists have taken so little time and expended so little effort in actually getting to know what it is they believe. That the attempts of Blomberg and Robinson (1997) and Mosser and Owen (1998) to do precisely this were not met with overwhelming approbation in the countercult only underscores my point. Rather, by approaching religionists with an a priori attitude that they have the only authentic vehicle of truth, countercult apologists demonstrate a remarkable *lack* of concern for their subjects. To reiterate, it must be difficult to believe that countercult apologists truly care when what they do write is so often inaccurate, biased, and objectionable. Consider, for example, Anton Hein's consistent portrayal of the Church of Scientology as a "hate group," and his adamant resistance to anything that might suggest otherwise. Whatever the reality of the situation, Hein's characterization notwithstanding, such an approach is not conducive to winning the hearts and minds of Scientologists.

Rather than a carefully prepared missiologic enterprise, as it is currently constituted, modern American countercult apologetics is more like the tent evangelism of the past three centuries—recurrent appeals to people whose worldview is not dissimilar from those of the evangelists themselves. Because of this, in the grand scheme of things I believe it will remain largely a fringe function of the broader boundary-maintenance mechanisms open to the evangelical community writ large. This is not to say that countercult apologists and apologetic organizations will not post conversions; obviously, they will. They will not, however, gain the kind of ground on the open religious economy their missiologic suggests they intend and indeed demands. As an evolving cognitive praxis within the evangelical community, however, the Christian countercult will undoubtedly continue to influence the manner in which new and emergent religions are regarded.

Notes

CHAPTER 2

1. See, for example, Appel 1983; Barker 1982, 1984; Beckford 1982; Bromley and Richardson 1983; Bromley and Shupe 1981, 1987; Clay 1987; Conway and Siegelman 1979; Freed 1980; Giambalvo 1995; Hassan 1990, 2000; Keiser and Keiser 1987; Maloney 1988; Patrick 1976; Richardson 1980; Shupe and Bromley 1980, 1981, 1985, 1994, 1995; Shupe, Bromley, and Oliver 1984; Shupe and Darnell 2000, 2001; Shupe, Spielmann, and Stigall 1977; Singer and Lalich 1995; Tobias and Lalich 1994; Zablocki 1997, 1998.

2. The Christian Research Institute considers a wide variety of nontraditional religious groups to be cults. Those discussed over the years include the International Society for Krishna Consciousness (ISKCON), the Church of Jesus Christ of Latter-day Saints, Christian Science, Jehovah's Witnesses, the Unification Church, the Children of God (now The Family), and Oneness Pentecostalism. *The Kingdom of the Cults* included chapters on the Theosophical Society, Buddhism, Eastern religions ("Rajneeshism," ISKON, and Transcendental Meditation), Scientology, Baha'i, and the Church Universal and Triumphant.

3. For a devastating critique of the old Cult Awareness Network and its activities in this regard, see Shupe and Darnell 2000, 2001.

CHAPTER 3

1. On Marrs as conspiracist, see also his ministry Web site www.conspiracyworld. com.

2. In almost identical fashion, fundamentalist pastor and countercult apologist Robert Morey challenges the claims of Muslims to exclusive divine revelation. "Muslim: 'the Quran is without error.' Non-Muslim: 'Why is this true?' Muslim: 'Because the Quran says so.' Non-Muslim: 'But why is the Quran true?' Muslim: 'Because the Quran is without error'" (1992: 130–31).

3. Much of this chapter in *The Kingdom of the Cults* it appears Martin took from a December 19, 1960, editorial in *Christianity Today*, entitled "The Challenge of the

Cults" (reprinted in Lindsell et al. 1961: 74–80). With only the most minor changes in terminology—for example, "Roman Catholicism" in the original became "Jesuit scholars" in Martin's version—Martin simply copied the editorial and expanded it into his program for cult evangelism. Is it a case of plagiarism? Perhaps. At the time, theologian Carl F. H. Henry was the editor of *Christianity Today,* and evangelist Billy Graham's father-in-law, L. Nelson Bell, the executive editor; Martin's name appears nowhere in the extensive list of contributing editors.

4. Similarly, in *The Complete Book of Bible Answers,* Ron Rhodes states that "though I can't be dogmatic about this, it seems to me that there are several good reasons that point to the likelihood of there being no life on other planets" (1997: 313; Rhodes 1998: 38–41). Rhodes's disclaimer notwithstanding, the first reason he gives for denying the possibility of extraterrestrial life is that "though atheist scientists would scoff at this, Scripture points to centrality of planet earth and gives no hint that life exists elsewhere" (1997: 313). Other countercultists, notably Dave Hunt, Bob Larson, and William Alnor, deploy similar logic to deny the possibility that life exists beyond Earth.

5. Included in Wanda Marrs's list are media mogul Ted Turner; Senator Claiborne Pell (D-R.I.), to whom she refers as "perhaps the most avid, some would say fanatical New Ager in the U.S. Congress"; Sirhan Sirhan, the assassin of Robert Kennedy, according to Marrs a Rosicrucian at the time of Kennedy's death; Jonas Salk, discoverer of the polio vaccine; former Senator Gary Hart; retired astronaut Edgar Mitchell; James Park Morton, pastor of New York's St. John the Divine Episcopal Cathedral; filmmaker George Lucas; singers Tina Turner and Cher; actresses Marsha Mason, Sharon Gless, and Linda Evans; science fiction author Michael Crichton and (then) Senator Al Gore. The list continues (W. Marrs 1989: 40–50).

6. See, for example, Bainbridge 1978, 1997; Barker 1984; Bromley and Hammond 1987; Bromley and Shupe 1981; Dawson 1998; Greer 1995; Hanegraaff 1996; Heelas 1996; Hexham and Poewe 1997; Hutton 1999; Lewis 1995, 1996a, Lewis and Melton 1992; Luhrmann 1989; Palmer and Hardman 1999; Richardson, Best, and Bromley 1991; Saliba 1995; Stark and Bainbridge 1985; York 1995.

CHAPTER 5

1. On the history and development of *The Fundamentals,* see Ammerman 1991; Boyer 1992; Dollar 1973; Marsden 1980; Numbers 1992; Russell 1976; Sandeen 1970.

2. Moorehead's figures came from the title page of Russell's *Studies in the Scripture,* which " 'bound in cloth, embosed in silver,' sell for the ridiculously small sum of $2.25—37 1/2 cents each!" Moorehead recorded the distribution figures as: "Series I. 3,358,000 edition. Series II. 1,132,000 edition. Series III. 909,000 edition" ([1917] 1996: 110).

3. Another earlier attempt was Gaius Glenn Atkins's *Modern Religious Cults and Movements* (1923). Atkins spent most of his time discussing Christian Science and the rise of New Thought churches, but did so in a manner much more sympathetic to emergent movements as a whole. Presaging much that postwar scholars from Braden (1949) to Stark and Bainbridge (1985) would suggest about the formation of new religious movements, Atkins argued that human understanding of God is not fixed and immutable, and that, therefore, religion itself "must be plastic and changing" (1923:

339). New and emergent religious traditions are examples of that change and plasticity; they are "aspects of the creative religious consciousness of the age" (1923: 338).

4. On the other hand, consider Buddhism in North America as presented by Bob Larson: "If consumer laws of full disclosure were applied to the 'sale' of religions, Buddhism would probably be left on the shelf" (Larson 1989a: 72); or Hinduism, which Texe Marrs considers the result of an "avalanche of Hindu gurus and swamis [who] invaded the United States in the 1960s and 1970s" (Marrs 1990: 216); or Islam, currently the fastest growing religion in the world, but which Robert Morey claims most Westerners "have a difficult time comprehending . . . because they fail to understand that it is a form of cultural imperialism in which the religion and culture of seventh-century Arabia have been raised to the status of divine law" (Morey 1992: 19).

5. While van Baalen expressed concern about the influx of emergent religions into what he perceived as an essentially monoreligious culture, at the far end of the counter-cult spectrum is the alarm evident in such apologists as Bob Larson and Texe Marrs. Lacking van Baalen's theological and historical acumen, Larson and Marrs rely instead on sensationalism, conspiracism, and what often amounts to simple prevarication. "Dear friend," writes Larson in a May 1996 fundraising letter, "Satanists have an evil agenda to take over America and kill all Christians! . . . For years I've known about this agenda, and I've tried my best to warn Christians. Some didn't want to believe it!" Similarly, in "Agents of Disinformation," Marrs writes: " 'Certain powerful forces have targeted Texe Marrs and Living Truth Ministries for destruction,' a reliable source warned us recently. 'Your message of truth is getting through to so many millions of people, and the word has gone out, Texe Marrs must be stopped' " (1997a).

6. An abbreviated text of Martin's memorial service, including excerpts from the numerous eulogies, is available online at www.waltermartin.org/memorial.html, a site operated by Martin's daughter, Jill Martin Rische, as a way of continuing his apologetic legacy.

7. As a result of a name infringement suit, California Western University was forced in 1981 to change its name to California Coast University (Brown and Brown 1986: 303–308). At the time Martin claimed to have been enrolled, institutional officials admit that "it is entirely possible that this school offered a degree in Comparative Religion in '76; however, we have no record of this" (Welty 1981, in Brown and Brown 1986: 52). According to their own Web site, California Coast University was founded in 1974, only two years before Martin claimed to have been granted his Ph.D. Currently, California Coast University remains unaccredited and offers off-campus, self-directed (i.e., correspondence) programs in Administration and Management, Engineering, Behavioral Science, and Education.

8. The Browns' work, *They Lie in Wait to Deceive: A Study in Anti-Mormon Deception*, has been published in several volumes. Each concentrates on different personalities in the world of professional anti-Mormonism and, with Scharffs (1989), ought to be considered among the first sustained critiques of professional countercult polemics from the perspective of the target community—in this case, the Latter-day Saints. Though amateur researchers, the Browns make compelling cases for the manner in which "professional anti-Mormons work to obstruct and distort the truth" (Brown and Brown 1986: front cover). Besides Walter Martin, among those considered by the Browns are Dee Jay Nelson, a "renowned Egyptologist" whom the Browns claim "completely misrepresented his credentials" (Brown and Brown 1981: vi); the Rigdon-Spaulding "caper" and its modern proponents (Brown and Brown 1984); anti-Mormon

apologists Jerald and Sandra Tanner, whom the Browns accused of distorting Latter-day Saints literature (Brown and Brown 1981: 155–64; 1995: 152–57); professional anti-Mormons Ed Decker and Richard Baer, producers of *The God Makers*, one of the most popular (and notorious) anti-Mormon films, and whom the Browns contend must accept personal responsibility for the film's "inaccuracies and misrepresentations" (Brown and Brown 1995: 3).

9. Similar criticisms have been made regarding Martin's ordination. Ordained in 1951 in the General Association of Regular Baptists, as the Browns demonstrate, this ordination was revoked two years later when "the ordination council learned in 1953 of his **second** marriage" (Brown and Brown 1986: 41, emphasis in the original). Martin had been divorced by his first wife, Patricia Toner Martin, in 1950, the former Mrs. Martin alleging "extreme mental cruelty." "Although the ordination council seemed to frown on ordaining a divorced man to the ministry, he was ordained in July 1951 **'with the understanding with Walter that if he ever re-married, we would have to revoke his ordination'** " (Brown and Brown 1986: 3, emphasis in the original). Martin was, in fact, married twice more.

10. For an interesting discussion of Jehovah's Witnesses in Alberta, Canada, and the exodus from the Witnesses of the "Penton group," see Beverley 1986; for Penton on the Witnesses, see Penton 1998.

11. Braden's definition corresponds rather well to that suggested by Rodney Stark and William Sims Bainbridge; cults (and sects) are "religious movements in a high state of tension with their surrounding sociocultural environment" (Stark and Bainbridge 1985: 24; cf. Dawson 1998: 29–40; Stark and Bainbridge 1987: 155–93). In *Religion, Deviance, and Social Control*, Stark and Bainbridge refine this definition somewhat, conforming it even more closely to that of Braden: "As we define them, cults are religious groups outside the conventional religious tradition(s) of a society. They may or may not impose stricter demands on their adherents, but their primary form of religious deviance does not concern being too strict, but being too different" (1997: 104).

CHAPTER 6

1. When Larson's book, *UFOs and the Alien Agenda: Uncovering the Mystery behind UFOs and the Paranormal* (1997), was published, Larson sent out a fundraising letter headlined: "Aliens have landed to take over our planet!" The letter began: "Dear Friend, That headline isn't true yet, but I believe it will be soon. That's why God has called me to take on the biggest spiritual fight of my life. And I desperately need your help. . . . I must have at least 500 people who will share a gift of $50 or more to help me fight back this alien invasion." "I'll take the demons behind this UFO craze head-on and cast them out in the name of Jesus!" he continued, concluding: "Thank you for being one of the 500 who will share a gift of $50 or more to keep me on radio and TV to launch a counterattack against the evil aliens of UFOs."

2. I was in the audience at this seminar, seated just a few feet from where Larson and the young woman stood. Though not a big man physically, the volume of Larson's voice, his rapid-fire delivery and utter unwillingness to consider her stammering answers, and his physical proximity appeared to have quite intimidated her.

3. *Cornerstone Magazine* is a publication of the Jesus People USA community, and has been involved in uncovering a number of incidents of fraud among high-profile

evangelicals. Their most notable case was Mike Warnke, a Christian comedian whose routines included reference to a fictitious career as a pimp, drug dealer, Satanist high priest (in 1972, Warnke published an extremely successful book entitled *The Satan Seller*), as well as spurious experiences as a Marine Corps medic in Vietnam (cf. Warnke, Balsiger, and Jones 1972). For an excellent example of evangelical journalism and self-regulation in exposing Warnke, see Hertenstein and Trott 1993.

4. Citing overburdening due to the birth of their third child, *Talk Back with Bob Larson* aired last on December 14, 2001.

5. The Web site for Living Truth Ministries, *Flashpoint,* and *Power of Prophecy* newsletters can be accessed at www.texemarrs.com. It offers a complete online archive of past issues.

6. During the final editing of this manuscript, the remains of Chandra Levy were discovered in Rock Creek Park. The investigation into her disappearance and death continues.

CHAPTER 7

1. Consider, for example, the words of these few of the nation's founders on religion. "The question before the human race is, whether the God of nature shall govern the world by his own laws, or whether priests and kings shall rule it by fictitious miracles" (Adams [1815] 1959: 445). "Millions of innocent men, women, and children, since the introduction of Christianity, have been burnt, tortured, fined, imprisoned; yet we have not advanced one inch toward uniformity. What has been the effect of coercion? To make one-half the world fools and the other half hypocrites" (Jefferson, quoted in Seldes 1983: 363). "During almost fifteen centuries has the legal establishment of Christianity been on trial. What has been its fruits? More or less, in all places, pride and indolence in the clergy; ignorance and servility in the laity; in both, superstition, bigotry and persecution" (Madison [1785] 1973: 301). Other similar examples could easily be multiplied.

2. In his course on "Religious Pluralism," for example, Douglas Groothuis prepares his class to meet the core competencies required of Denver Seminary students. "By comparing and contrasting other religions with Christian truth," reads the course syllabus, "we will labor to show the intellectual superiority of the Christian message"; and, "by analyzing world religions, we will try to learn how to reach those in other religions for Christ." In this course, Groothuis includes as recommended reading both *Unmasking the New Age* (1986) and *Confronting the New Age* (1988). In courses more directly aimed at apologetics, he requires *Confronting* as a text.

CHAPTER 8

1. According to Hein, "a cult apologist is someone who consistently or primarily defends the teachings and/or actions of one or more movements considered to be cults—as defined sociologically and/or theologically. Note that the term 'cult apologist" is technical, and not (as some of them claim) derogatory. . . . Alternative terms used include: 'cult defenders,' 'cult sympathizers' " (www.gospelcom.net/ apologeticsindex/ c11.html). The current author is also included in this company.

2. Anton Hein; www.gospelcom.net/apologeticsindex/about.html.

3. Anton Hein; www.gospelcom.net/apologeticsindex/apologetics.html#freedom.

4. Anton Hein; www.gospelcom.net/apologeticsindex/m08.html.

5. Angel; www.fortunecity.com/campus/medicine/364/.

6. Chuck Helton; www.ephesians5–11.org/ex_masons_for_jesus/helton.htm.

7. Monica Pignotti; www.caic.org.au/stories/monica-p.htm.

8. Katina; www.christian-faith.com/testimonies/katina-witchcraft.html.

9. "Helping Mormons Reach Perfection"; www.helpingmormons.org/Support_Group.htm.

10. All posts are reproduced precisely as they appeared on AR-talk and AR-forum; individual posts are identified here only by contributor. AR-talk's charter states that "individual posts to AR-talk are considered public domain at the time of their release to the list. Subscribers are therefore free to reproduce individual AR-talk posts without permission, as long as they are properly credited and are not modified" (Poll 2001). Unfortunately, Poll has not yet had time to archive this valuable resource.

11. In 1996, the Cult Awareness Network, an information clearinghouse and referral agency for coercive deprogrammers (Shupe and Darnell 2000) collapsed in a bankruptcy precipitated by a multimillion dollar lawsuit filed by a victim of coercive deprogramming. In the ensuing proceedings, the name "Cult Awareness Network," as well as all the old Cult Awareness Network files, were purchased by agents of the Church of Scientology, who now operate it under the auspices of the Foundation for Religious Freedom.

CHAPTER 9

1. In March 1997, Aaron LeBaron, son of the sect's founder, Ervil LeBaron, was convicted of the murders and sentenced to forty-five years in prison.

2. In a review of *Behind the Mask of Mormonism*, published in the *FARMS Review of Books*, Latter-day Saint and Brigham Young University professor Daniel Peterson (1996) describes it as "a stupefyingly bad book," "one of the most uncharitable and unpleasant things I have ever read," "worse by far even than most other anti-Mormon writing," "unrelentingly negative, unremittingly hostile, and not overly scrupulous in its methods of attack"; it is, Peterson concludes, "bigoted, intolerant, ugly, incompetent, and dishonest" (cf. Peterson and Ricks 1992).

3. For a fuller discussion of evangelical countercult response to Buddhism, see Cowan 2000a.

4. For example, while Mendoza does list many of the atrocities that have been attributed to Islam, particularly in the Ottoman Empire and the Uganda of Idi Amin Dada, he also points out the Christian oppression of Muslims in Chad and Ethiopia under Haile Selassie II, the massacres in "predominantly Roman Catholic Rwanda," and other atrocities for which the Christian church was directly responsible (e.g., the Crusades, the witch burnings, the Inquisition). And, while he goes on to argue why Islam is a false religion in comparison with Christianity, unlike other countercult apologists (and much of North American mainstream media [cf., for example, Cowan forthcoming [a]; Ghareeb 1983; Kamalipour 1997; Said 1997]) he rightly points out that one ought not judge the quality of another's religious faith by the atrocities committed historically in the name of that faith. In this regard, one could also point to what is

recorded in the Biblical record as the wholesale slaughter of competing Canaanite tribes by the emerging Israelites in the post-Exilic period.

5. Those few secular academics who have paid any attention to Morey have been even more critical. In a letter to the editor of *The Washington Report on Middle East Affairs*, University of Québec librarian Gerald Parker, who has prepared an extensive dossier on Morey, calls him a "demagogue" and an "arch-mountebank," whose newsletter, *The Truth Seeker*, he considers a "hate-rag of a magazine" (Parker 1999; cf. Ally 1996).

6. According to his Web site, Morey's ministry has been recommended by, among others, Walter Martin, D. James Kennedy, John Ankerberg, John Weldon, Tim LaHaye, "and many other nationally known Christian leaders."

CHAPTER 10

1. See, for example, Ankerberg and Weldon 1991a; Baer 1989; Chandler 1988; Cumbey 1983, 1985; DeMar and Leithart 1988; Groothuis 1986, 1988, 1990, 1995; Hoyt and Yamamoto 1987; Hunt 1980, 1983, 1998; Hunt and McMahon 1985, 1988; T. Marrs 1987, 1989b, 1992; W. Marrs 1989; Martin 1989; Matrisciana 1985; Miller 1989; Paulk 1987; Reid et al. 1986; Winkler 1994; Wise et al. 1986.

2. Wouter Hanegraaff, on the other hand, argues that there is an inherent tension in the New Age movement between a monistic understanding of reality and an idealistic understanding. The former begins with matter and seeks the salvation of spirit; the latter finds its origins in spirit but must explain the existence of matter. Cf. Hanegraaff 1996: 180–81.

3. In an endnote to this passage, Groothuis writes simply, "Texe Marrs documents these kinds of claims in his book *Dark Secrets of the New Age*" (1988: 215 n.16). As far as Marrs is concerned, "documents" may be overstating the case. The chapters to which Groothuis refers are entitled "The Dark Secret: What Will Happen to Christians?" and "New Age Zeal . . . New Age Aggression." The former begins: "Only one thing stands in the way of Satan and his Plan today: the true Church of Jesus Christ. Up to now God has not allowed Satan to move aggressively to destroy the earth's Christian believers. But leaders of the New Age see their coming triumph over traditional Christianity as inevitable" (Marrs 1987: 136). In the latter, Marrs writes: "New Age leaders tell the average New Age believer that it is only the negativity of devout Christians and Jews that prevents the world from being magically transformed into the New Age Kingdom. The New Age believer is told, 'You could be God in the next instant if only those horrible Christians weren't around with their poisonous attitudes" (1987: 153). While he provides no evidence to support his claims, as a result of this "New Age indoctrination," Marrs believes the world can expect "the wholesale massacre of Christians" (1987: 158).

4. In *Larson's New Book of Cults*, while he points out that *The Cult Explosion* "does not deal with the cults individually or in a systematic way," Bob Larson endorses Hunt's work as " a thoroughly scriptural, psychological, and sociological perspective on the rise of the cults" (1989a: 484).

5. For similar examples, some of which are at least as problematic as those of Hunt, see Groothuis 1986: 21–22; Rhodes 1994: 25–26, 41, 54–57, 84–85, 119.

CHAPTER 11

1. Alberto Rivera, Chick's model of apostate testimony, claims to have been a secret Jesuit operative, trained since early childhood for one mission: the overthrow of Protestantism. For information on Rivera as a fraud, see Keating 1988: 107–15; Metz 1981.

2. Rhodes, for example, is careful to avoid the mistake made by other anti-Catholic writers that the Deuterocanonical books were *added* by the Council of Trent (cf. Boettner 1962: 80–84), as opposed to affirmed as Scripture by that Council in the face of their deletion from the biblical canon by the Reformers. He does, however, ahistoricize the Tridentine decision and write as though the anathema pronounced on those who do not accept the deuterocanonicals is still in force nearly five centuries later. With no historical contextualization—that is, that the Council of Trent was called explicitly to meet the threat of the burgeoning Protestant Reformation and the various dogmatic challenges it represented—Rhodes declares simply, "Those who reject the Apocrypha are considered accursed" (2000: 33).

3. In support of this, Hunt cites St. Alphonsus de Ligouri (1696–1787), the founder of the Redemptorist Order and patron saint of moral theologians, and claims that it "is implicit throughout the entire teaching of calling upon Mary from whom help is obtained more quickly than by calling upon God or Christ directly" (1994: 541 n.23).

4. Bokenkotter (1986) concurs. "The doctrine of Mary's Immaculate Conception," he writes, "was very slow to win general acceptance." (1986: 128). Noting that Marian apparitions, "while officially approved by the Church," "are not obligatory matters of faith for Catholics"; he continues, "the impact of [Vatican II] on Marian devotion and theology within the church has been tremendous. Devotion to Mary declined precipitously as old forms of piety disappeared with little replacement" (Bokenkotter 1986: 132, 136). While this may be the case at the institutional level, in certain parts of the world popular Marian devotionalism remains an integral part of Catholic life (cf., for example, Carroll 1986; Martin 1998; Miravalle 1997; Rey 1999; Warner 1983).

5. For an excellent discussion of the differences between the evangelical understanding as salvation as a personal possession and that of the Roman Catholic Church, see Keating 1988: 164–76.

6. This technique is common in Rhodes's work. In each of his books and on his ministry Web site, he asks and answers what he maintains are "common questions" among his readers. For example, on his Web site (http://home.earthlink.net/~ronrhodes), the first "commonly asked question" is "Can God's face really be seen?" Others include "Does 1 Corinthians 10:14 forbid Christians to wear a cross?"; "Why did Solomon have so many wives?"; and "Why couldn't Jesus do miracles in His hometown?"

7. The danger of eisegesis is a constant refrain in Rhode's criticism of Roman Catholicism, and his construction of its theological and doctrinal inadequacy. Elsewhere, quite un-self-consciously, he points out that, "eisegesis can make a verse say virtually anything" (Rhodes 2000: 203).

8. In *A Woman Rides the Beast*, Hunt basically reprints the Fatima material from *Global Peace and the Rise of Antichrist*. Such changes as are made, however, lend to his prose a heightened sense of outrage. "On several occasions the 'child Jesus' accompanies its mother 'Mary' when she appeared as 'Our Lady of Fatima'" (Hunt 1990: 122), for example, becomes "The false gospel of salvation through Mary is even endorsed by a demon posing as Jesus who accompanies Mary" (Hunt 1994: 462).

9. In *Mary in Our Life*, Fr. William Most (1959: 56, emphasis in the original), a theologian and Marian scholar, discusses the "necessity and extent of devotion to

Mary." The question of the relative devotion due the Mother as opposed to the Son is the first question with which Most deals. "Good Catholics sometimes wonder how much attention they ought to give to Mary in their prayers and other religious practices. They do not put the question so mathematically as to ask what percentage of a holy hour, for example, should be devoted to prayers to Mary, for if the question were stated in that way it might imply that prayers to Mary are said at the expense of devotion to her Son—which would be ridiculous. *If our devotion to Mary were to take away anything from devotion to Him, it would have to be rejected.*"

CHAPTER 12

1. In an open letter to Gretchen Passantino, Bowman (2001a) states that he was "fraudulently laid off [from the Christian Research Institute], most likely due to my unwillingness to ghostwrite books for Hank Hanegraaff."

2. In response to criticism of Morey's claim on the grounds of simple arithmetic (i.e., number of books divided by time available), for example, Jeff Downs, a B.S. student at Lancaster Bible College and director of the Resource Center for Apologetics Research, a ministry that highlights resources available to the apologetic community, argued on the AR-forum discussion list that, while Morey's feat may seem "incredible," "who's to say he didn't?"

3. For a Latter-day Saint review of White's anti-Mormon apologetic, see Norwood 1993.

4. The accrediting agency for free-standing theological colleges and seminaries is the Association of Theological Schools. Contrary to White and Walston's claims, accreditation is a significantly more serious issue than simply the ability to apply for government funding and demands substantially more of potential candidates in terms of academic and institutional rigor. Both general and program standards related to the process of accreditation are available from the Association of Theological Schools Web site (www.ats.edu). That notwithstanding, however, even if the only issue were government funding, it renders White and Walston's argument no more compelling.

5. One reader's review on Amazon.com, for example, declares: "Eileen Barker seems to spend most of this book apologising for the cult's behavior and practices and every turn rather than telling parents what they can do to help their troubled children. Barker should have spent more time listening to former members, and less time talking to the cult leaders."

References

Abanes, Richard. 1996. *American Militias: Rebellion, Racism, and Religion*. Downers Grove, Ill: InterVarsity Press.

———. 1997a. "The New Age Movement." In *The Kingdom of the Cults*, 4th ed., by Walter R. Martin, gen. ed. Hank Hanegraaff, 333–49. Minneapolis: Bethany House.

———. 1997b. "The Word Faith Movement." In *The Kingdom of the Cults*, 4th ed., by Walter R. Martin, gen. ed. Hank Hanegraaff, 495–516. Minneapolis: Bethany House.

———. 1998a. *End-Time Visions: The Doomsday Obsession*. Nashville, Tenn.: Broadman & Holman.

———. 1998b. *Cults, New Religious Movements, and Your Family: A Guide to Ten Non-Christian Groups Out to Convert Your Loved Ones*. Wheaton, Ill.: Crossway Books.

———. 2001. *Harry Potter and the Bible: The Menace behind the Magick*. Camp Hill, Pa.: Horizon Books.

Adams, John Quincy. [1815] 1959. "Letter to Thomas Jefferson, June 20." In *The Adams-Jefferson Letters: 1812–1826*, ed. Lester J. Capon, 445–46. Chapel Hill: University of North Carolina Press.

Ahmanson, John. [1876] 1984. *Secret History: An Eyewitness Account of the Rise of Mormonism*, trans. Gleason L. Archer. Wheaton, Ill.: Moody Press.

Ally, Shabir. 1996. *Robert Morey's Moon-god Myth and Other Deceptive Attacks on Islam*. Toronto: Islamic Information & Da'wah Centre International.

Alnor, William M. 1992. *UFOs in the New Age: Extraterrestrial Messages and the Truth of Scripture*. Grand Rapids, Mich.: Baker Books.

———. 1998. *UFO Cults and the New Millennium*. Grand Rapids, Mich.: Baker Books.

Alphonsus de Ligouri. 1852. *The Glories of Mary*. New York: E. Dunigan & Brother.

Ammerman, Nancy T. 1990. *Baptist Battles: Social Change and Religious Conflict in the Southern Baptist Convention*. New Brunswick, N.J.: Rutgers University Press.

———. 1991. "North American Protestant Fundamentalism." In *Fundamentalisms Observed*, eds. Martin E. Marty and R. Scott Appleby, 1–65. The Fundamentalism Project, Vol. 1. Chicago and London: University of Chicago Press.

Ankerberg, John, and John Weldon. 1988. *Facts on the New Age Movement*. Eugene, Oreg.: Harvest House.

———. 1989. *Facts on the Masonic Lodge*. Eugene, Oreg.: Harvest House.

———. 1991a. *Cult Watch*. Eugene, Oreg.: Harvest House.

———. 1991b. *One World: Bible Propecy and the New World Order*. Chicago: Moody Press.

———. 1992a. *Behind the Mask of Mormonism*. Eugene, Oreg.: Harvest House.

———. 1992b. *Facts on Jehovah's Witnesses*. Eugene, Oreg.: Harvest House.

———. 1993. *The Facts on Creation vs. Evolution*. Eugene, Oreg.: Harvest House.

———. 1996a. *Encyclopedia of New Age Beliefs*. Eugene, Oreg.: Harvest House.

———. 1996b. *The Facts on the King James Only Debate*. Eugene, Oreg.: Harvest House.

———. 1999. *Encyclopedia of Cults and New Religions*. Eugene, Oreg.: Harvest House.

Apologia Report. 1998. "Book Review of *New Age Thinking*, by M. D. Faber." 3 (6): February 9.

Appel, Willa. 1983. *Cults in America: Programmed for Paradise*. New York: Holt, Rinehart and Winston.

Atkins, Gaius Glenn. 1923. *Modern Religious Cults and Movements*. New York: Fleming H. Revell.

Baer, Randall N. 1989. *Inside the New Age Nightmare*. Shreveport, La.: Huntingdon House.

Bainbridge, William Sims. 1978. *Satan's Power: A Deviant Psychotherapy Cult*. Berkeley and Los Angeles: Unversity of California Press.

———. 1997. *The Sociology of Religious Movements*. New York: Routledge.

Baldwin, Lou. 2000. "Pious Prejudice: Catholicism and the American Press over Three Centuries." In *Anti-Catholicism in American Culture*, ed. Robert P. Lockwood, 55–87. Huntingdon, In.: Our Sunday Visitor.

Barker, Eileen. 1982. "Glossary." In *New Religious Movements: A Perspective for Understanding Society*, ed. Eileen Barker, 331–58. Studies in Religion and Society, Vol. 3. New York and Toronto: Edwin Mellen Press.

———. 1984. *The Making of a Moonie: Choice or Brainwashing?* London: Basil Blackwell.

Barker, Jason. 1998a. "Christians and Interreligious Dialogue." *Watchman Expositor* 15 (4): 4–8.

———. 1998b. "The Key to Effective Religious Dialogue." *Watchman Expositor* 15 (4): 9–12.

———. 1998c. "New Religious Movements and Interreligious Dialogue." *Watchman Expositor* 15 (4): 13–15.

———. 1999. "Heresies: Then and Now." *Watchman Expositor* 16 (1). Available online at www.watchman.org/reltop/heresiesthenandnow.htm.

Barron, Bruce. 1987. *The Health and Wealth Gospel*. Downers Grove, Ill.: InterVarsity Press.

Barthes, Roland. 1982. *A Barthes Reader*, ed. Susan Sontag. New York: Hill and Wang.

Bates, Stephen. 1993. *Battleground: One Mother's Crusade, the Religious Right, and the Struggle for our Schools*. New York: Owl Books.

Bauer, Walter. 1971. *Orthodoxy and Heresy in Earliest Christianity*, 2d ed., trans. Philadelphia Seminar on Christian Origins; eds. Robert A. Kraft and Gerhard Krodel. Mifflintown, Pa.: Sigler Press.

Beckford, James A. 1982. "Beyond the Pale: Cults, Culture and Conflict." In *New Religious Movements: A Perspective for Understanding Society,* ed. Eileen Barker, 284–301. Studies in Religion and Society, Vol. 3. New York and Toronto: Edwin Mellen Press.

———. 1994. "The Media and New Religious Movements." In *From the Ashes: Making Sense of Waco,* ed. James R. Lewis, 143–49. Lanham, Md.: Rowman & Littlefield.

Beckwith, Francis, Paul Owen, and Carl Mosser. 2002. *The New Mormon Challenge: Responding to the Latest Defenses of a Fast-Growing Movement.* New York: Zondervan.

Bedell, Ken. 2000. "Dispatches from the Electronic Frontier: Explorations of Mainline Protestant Use of the Internet." In *Religion on the Internet: Research Prospects and Promises,* eds. Jeffrey K. Hadden and Douglas E. Cowan, 183–203. London: JAI/Elsevier.

Bergen, Doris L. 1996. *Twisted Cross: The German Christian Movement in the Third Reich.* Chapel Hill: University of North Carolina Press.

Berger, Peter L. 1967. *The Sacred Canopy: Elements of a Sociological Theory of Religon.* New York: Doubleday Anchor.

Berger, Peter L., and Thomas Luckmann. 1966. *The Social Construction of Reality: A Treatise on the Sociology of Knowledge.* Harmondsworth, Middlesex, U.K.: Penguin Books.

Berlinerblau, Jacques. 2001. "Toward a Sociology of Orthodoxy, Heresy, and *Doxa.*" *History of Religions* 40 (4): 327–51.

Beverley, James A. 1986. *Crisis of Allegiance: A Study of Dissent among Jehovah's Witnesses.* Burlington: Welch Publishing Company.

———. 1997. "Muhammed: A prophet for the church?" *Faith Today* 15 (4): 13.

Bjornstad, James. 1979. *Counterfeits at Your Door.* Ventura, Ca.: Regal Books.

Blakeney, Richard P. 1911. *Protestant Catechism, or Popery Refuted and Protestantism Established by the Word of God.* Edinburgh, Scotland: Hope Trust.

Blomberg, Craig L., and Stephen E. Robinson. 1997. *How Wide the Divide? A Mormon and an Evangelical in Conversation.* Downers Grove, Ill.: InterVarsity Press.

Blumer, Herbert. 1969. *Symbolic Interactionism: Perspective and Method.* Berkeley and Los Angeles: University of California Press.

Boa, Kenneth D., and Robert M. Bowman Jr. 2001. *Faith Has Its Reasons: An Integrative Approach to Defending Christianity.* Colorado Springs, Colo.: NavPress.

Boettner, Loraine. 1962. *Roman Catholicism.* Philadelphia: Presbyterian and Reformed Publishing House.

Boff, Leonardo. 1978. *Jesus Christ Liberator: A Critical Christology for Our Times,* trans. Patrick Hughes. Maryknoll, N.Y.: Orbis Books.

Bokenkotter, Thomas. 1986. *Essential Catholicism: Dynamics of Faith and Belief.* Garden City, N.Y.: Image Books.

Borovoy, A. Alan. 1988. *When Freedoms Collide: The Case for Our Civil Liberties.* Toronto: University of Toronto Press.

Bossick, Karen. 1983. "*The God Makers:* Film Produced by Ex-Mormons Draws Crowds and a Lot of Controversy." *The Idaho Statesman* (Boise), December 11. Photocopy reproduced in *Saints Alive in Jesus Newsletter* (January/February 1984): 5–10.

Botting, Gary. 1993. *Fundamental Freedoms and Jehovah's Witnesses.* Calgary: University of Calgary Press.

Botting, Gary, and Heather Botting. 1984. *The Orwellian World of Jehovah's Witnesses.* Toronto: University of Toronto Press.

Bourdieu, Pierre. 1977. *Outline of a Theory of Practice,* trans. Richard Nice. Cambridge: Cambridge University Press.

———. 1991. *Language and Symbolic Power,* ed. John B. Thompson, trans. Gino Raymond and Matthew Adamson. Cambridge: Harvard University Press.

———. 1998. *Practical Reason: On the Theory of Action.* Stanford, Calif.: Stanford University Press.

Bowman, Robert M. Jr. 1989a. *Jehovah's Witnesses, Jesus Christ, and the Gospel of John.* Grand Rapids, Mich.: Baker Books.

———. 1989b. *Why You Should Believe in the Trinity: An Answer to Jehovah's Witnesses.* Grand Rapids, Mich.: Baker Books.

———. 1991a. "Of Definitions and Discernment: An Open Letter Review of Bob and Gretchen Passantino's Book, *Witch Hunt.*" Available online at www.gospelcom.net/apologeticsindex/cpoint8–1.html.

———. 1991b. *Understanding Jehovah's Witnesses: Why They Read the Bible the Way They Do.* Grand Rapids, Mich.: Baker Books.

———. 1992. *Orthodoxy and Heresy: A Biblical Guide to Doctrinal Discernment.* Grand Rapids, Mich.: Baker Books.

———. 1998a. E-mail communication to ar-talk@xc.org, electronic discussion group, March 1.

———. 1998b. "Is the Good News Bear a Copycat? Hank Hanegraaff and Plagiarism," rev. ed. Available online at www.atlantaapologist.org/COPYCAT.html.

———. 2001a. Letter to Gretchen Passantino, June 29. Available online at www.waltermartin.org/passentino.pdf.

———. 2001b. Letter to Hank Hanegraaff, June 29. Available online at www.waltermartin.org/hanegraaff.pdf.

———. 2001c. *The Word-Faith Controversy: Understanding the Health and Wealth Gospel.* Grand Rapids, Mich.: Baker Books.

Boyer, Paul. 1992. *When Time Shall Be No More: Prophecy Belief in American Culture.* Cambridge: Harvard University Press.

Braden, Charles Samuel. 1949. *These Also Believe: A Study of Modern American Cults and Minority Religious Movements.* New York: The Macmillan Company.

Branch, Craig. 1990. "Destructive Cultism and the Constitution." *Watchman Expositor* 7 (4). Available online at www.watchman.org/cults/destcult.htm.

Brandon, George. 1993. *Santeria from Africa to the New World: The Dead Sell Memories.* Bloomington: Indiana University Press.

Bratt, James D. 1984. *Dutch Calvinism in Modern America: A History of a Conservative Subculture.* Grand Rapids, Mich.: William B. Eerdmans Publishing.

Brodie, Fawn M. 1971. *No Man Knows My History: The Life of Joseph Smith,* 2d ed. New York: Borzoi Books.

Bromley, David G. 1998. "Listing (in Black and White) Some Observations on (Sociological) Thought Reform." *Nova Religio: The Journal of Alternative and Emergent Religions* 1 (2): 250–66.

———. 2001. "A Tale of Two Theories: Brainwashing and Conversion as Competing Political Narratives." In *Misunderstanding Cults: Searching for Objectivity in a Controversial Field,* eds. Benjamin Zablocki and Thomas Robbins, 318–48. Toronto: University of Toronto Press.

Bromley, David G., and Phillip E. Hammond, eds. 1987. *The Future of New Religious Movements*. Macon, Ga.: Mercer University Press.

Bromley, David G., and James T. Richardson, eds. 1983. *The Brainwashing/Deprogramming Controversy: Sociological, Psychological, Legal, and Historical Perspectives*. Studies in Religion and Society, Vol. 5. New York and Toronto: Edwin Mellen Press.

Bromley, David G., and Anson D. Shupe Jr. 1981. *Strange Gods: The Great American Cult Scare*. Boston: Beacon Press.

———. 1987. "The Future of the Anticult Movement." In *The Future of New Religious Movements*, eds. David G. Bromley and Phillip E. Hammond, 221–334. Macon, Ga.: Mercer University Press.

Bromley, David G., Anson D. Shupe Jr., and J. C. Ventimiglia. 1983. "The Role of Anecdotal Atrocities in the Social Construction of Evil." In *The Brainwashing/Deprogramming Controversy: Sociological, Psychological, Legal, and Historical Perspectives*, 139–60. Studies in Religion and Society, Vol. 5. New York and Toronto: Edwin Mellen Press.

Brown, Harold O. J. 1988. *Heresies: Heresy and Orthodoxy in the History of the Church*. Peabody, Mass.: Hendrickson Publishers.

Brown, Robert L., and Rosemary Brown. 1981. *They Lie in Wait to Deceive: A Study in Anti-Mormon Deception*, Vol. 1, ed. Barbara Ellsworth. Mesa, Az.: Brownsworth Publishing.

———. 1984. *They Lie in Wait to Deceive: A Study in Anti-Mormon Deception*, Vol. 2, ed. Barbara Ellsworth. Mesa, Az.: Brownsworth Publishing.

———. 1986. *They Lie in Wait to Deceive: A Study in Anti-Mormon Deception*, Vol. 3, ed. Barbara Ellsworth. Mesa, Az.: Brownsworth Publishing.

———. 1995. *They Lie in Wait to Deceive: A Study in Anti-Mormon Deception*, Vol. 4, ed. Barbara Ellsworth. Mesa, Az.: Brownsworth Publishing.

Carden, Paul. 1998. "The Threat of the Cults on the Mission Fields of the World." *International Journal of Frontier Missions* 15 (3): 147–55.

Carlson, Ron, and Ed Decker. 1994. *Fast Facts on False Teachings*. Eugene, Oreg.: Harvest House.

Carroll, Michael P. 1986. *The Cult of the Virgin Mary: Psychological Origins*. Princeton, N.J.: Princeton University Press.

Chandler, Russell. 1988. *Understanding the New Age*. Dallas, Tex.: Word.

Chick, Jack T. 1979. *Alberto*. Chino, Calif.: Chick Publications.

———. 1982. *The Godfathers*. Chino, Calif.: Chick Publications.

———. 1983. *Smokescreens*. Chino, Calif.: Chick Publications.

———. 1988. *The Death Cookie*. Chino, Calif.: Chick Publications.

———. 1994. *Last Rites*. Chino, Calif.: Chick Publications.

———. 1996. "Is This Hate?" *Battle Cry* (May/June): 8.

Chiniquy, Charles. 1880. *The Priest, The Woman and the Confessional*. New York: Fleming H. Revell.

———. 1886. *Fifty Years in the Church of Rome*. New York: Fleming H. Revell.

Christian Research Institute. 1993. "Does Dr. Walter Martin Have a Genuine Earned Doctor's Degree?" CRI Statement DM100. Available at www.equip.org/free/DM100.htm.

———. 1996. "Dave Hunt." CRI Statement 4.102.

Clark, David K., and Norman L. Geisler. 1990. *Apologetics in the New Age: A Christian Critique of Pantheism.* Grand Rapids, Mich.: Baker Books.

Clark, Elmer T. 1949. *The Small Sects in America,* rev. ed. New York: Abingdon.

Clay, Colin. 1987. *No Freedom for the Mind: A Study of the Cult Phenomenon from a Canadian Perspective.* Burlington, Ont.: Trinity Press.

Cobb, John B. Jr. 1985. "Beyond Dialogue." In *Readings in Christian Theology,* eds. Peter C. Hodgson and Robert H. King, 375–80. Philadelphia: Fortress Press.

Combs, George Hamilton. 1899. *Some Latter-day Religions.* Chicago: Fleming H. Revell.

Conway, Flo, and Joe Siegelman. 1979. *Snapping: America's Epidemic of Sudden Personality Change.* New York: Delta Books.

Conway, J. S. 1968. *The Nazi Persecution of the Churches, 1933–45.* London: Weidenfeld and Nicolson.

Cornwell, John. 1999. *Hitler's Pope: The Secret History of Pius XII.* New York: Penguin Books.

Coughlin, Paul T. 1999. *Secrets, Plots, and Hidden Agendas: What You Don't Know about Conspiracy Theories.* Downers Grove, Ill.: InterVarsity.

Cowan, Douglas E. Forthcoming (a). "Religion and the Mass Media: The Case of Islam before and after September 11."

———. Forthcoming (b). *The Remnant Spirit: Conservative Reform in Mainline Protestantism.* Forthcoming from Westport, Conn.: Praeger.

———. 1990. "Christian Apologetics or Christian Hate Literature?" Paper presented at the American Academy of Religion Annual Regional Meeting (Pacific Northwest Region), Seattle, Washington.

———. 1996. "Jack's Buddhism: A Dharma Walk with Jack Kerouac." *Journal of Buddhist and Tibetan Studies* 2: 38–91.

———. 1998. "Too Narrow and Too Close: Some Problems with Participant Observation in the Study of New Religious Movements." *Method and Theory in the Study of Religion* 10: 391–406.

———. 2000a. "No Harmony: Some Notes on Evangelical Christian Response to Buddhism." *Religious Studies and Theology* 19 (2): 17–52.

———. 2000b. "Religion, Rhetoric, and Scholarship: Managing Vested Interest in E-Space." In *Religion on the Internet: Research Prospects and Promises,* eds. Jeffrey K. Hadden and Douglas E. Cowan, 101–24. London: JAI/Elsevier Science.

———. 2001. "From Parchment to Pixels: The Christian Countercult on the Internet." Paper presented to the International Conference of CESNUR, London, England. Available online at http://religiousmovements.lib.virginia.edu/cesnur/cowan.html.

Cumbey, Constance E. 1983. *Hidden Dangers of the Rainbow: The New Age Movement and Our Coming Age of Barbarism,* rev. ed. Lafayette, La.: Huntingdon House.

———. 1985. *A Planned Deception: The Staging of a New Age "Messiah."* Detroit: Pointe Publishing.

Cuneo, Michael W. 1997. *The Smoke of Satan: Conservative and Traditionalist Dissent in Contemporary American Catholicism.* Baltimore: Johns Hopkins University Press.

———. 2001. *American Exorcism: Expelling Demons in This Land of Plenty.* New York: Doubleday.

Dawson, Lorne L. 1998. *Comprehending Cults: The Sociology of New Religious Move-ments.* Oxford: Oxford University Press.

De Arteaga, Bill. 1986a. "Errors in *The Seduction of Christianity.*" In *The Church Divided: The Holy Spirit and a Spirit of Seduction,* eds. Robert Wise et al., 44–55. South Plainfield, N.J.: Bridge Publishing.

———. 1986b. "In Defense of Inner Healing." In *Seduction?? A Biblical Response,* 48–49. New Wilmington, Pa.: Son-Rise.

Decker, Ed. 1982. *The God Makers.* Jeremiah Films, VHS 33001.

———. 1987. *Temple of the God Makers.* Jeremiah Films, VHS 40001.

———. 1990. *The Mormon Dilemma.* Eugene, Oreg.: Harvest House.

———. 1992. *The God Makers II.* Jeremiah Films, ISBN 1-878993-37-2.

———. 1998. "Out of Mormonism: Ed Decker's Story." Available online at www.saint-salive.com/mormonism/edstestimony.htm.

Decker, Ed, and Dave Hunt. 1984. *The God Makers.* Eugene, Oreg.: Harvest House.

———. 1994. *The God Makers,* rev. ed. Eugene, Oreg.: Harvest House.

Decker, Ed, and Caryl Matrisciana. 1993. *The God Makers II.* Eugene, Oreg.: Harvest House.

DeMar, Gary, and Peter Leithart. 1988. *The Reduction of Christianity: A Biblical Re-sponse to Dave Hunt.* Ft. Worth, Tex.: Dominion Press.

Denzin, Norman K. 1992. *Symbolic Interactionism and Cultural Studies: The Politics of Interpretation.* Oxford and Cambridge: Blackwell.

Dhu, Helen. 1855. *Stanhope Burleigh: The Jesuits in Our Homes.* New York: Stringer & Townsend.

Dixon, J. Lowell. 1988. "Blood: Whose Choice and Whose Conscience?" *New York State Journal of Medicine* 88: 463–64.

Doerksen, Linda J. 1995. Book review of *New Age Cults* by Texe Marsden [sic]. *Hecate's Loom* 29 (Lammas): 37–38.

Dollar, George W. 1973. *A History of Fundamentalism in America.* Greenville, S.C.: Bob Jones University Press.

Duncan, Homer. n.d. *Secular Humanism: The Most Dangerous Religion in America.* Lubbock, Tex.: Missionary Crusader.

———. 1981. *Humanism in the Light of Holy Scripture.* Lubbock, Tex.: Missionary Crusader.

Eadie, Betty, with Curtis Taylor. 1992. *Embraced by the Light.* Placerville, Calif.: Gold Leaf Press.

Ehrman, Bart D. 1993. *The Orthodox Corruption of Scripture: The Effect of Early Christological Controversies on the Text of the New Testament.* New York: Ox-ford University Press.

Engelsma, David J. 1996. "An Introduction to Henry Danhof's 'The Idea of the Cove-nant of Grace.' " *Protestant Reformed Theological Journal* (April). Available online at www.prca.org/prtj/apr96d.html.

Enroth, Ronald. 1977. *Youth, Brainwashing, and the Extremist Cults.* Grand Rapids, Mich.: Zondervan.

———. 1979. *The Lure of the Cults.* Chappaqua, N.Y.: Christian Herald Books.

———. 1997. "The Kingdom of the Cult-Watchers." *Books and Culture* 3 (6) (Novem-ber/December): 36.

Evangelical Ministries to New Religions. 1997. *Manual of Ethical and Doctrinal Stan-dards.* Available online at www.emnr.org/emnrmeds.htm.

Eyerman, Ron, and Andrew Jamison. 1991. *Social Movements: A Cognitive Approach.* University Park: Pennsylvania State University Press.

Farah, Charles. 1982. *This Cancer Kills: A Critical Analysis of the Roots and Fruits of 'Faith-Formula Theology.'* Portland, Oreg.: Charis Life.

Festinger, Leon, Henry W. Riecken, and Stanley Schachter. 1956. *When Prophecy Fails: A Social and Psychological Study of a Modern Group That Predicted the Destruction of the World.* New York: Harper Torchbooks.

Fields, Rick. 1992. *How the Swans Came to the Lake: A Narrative History of Buddhism in America,* 3d ed. Boston: Shambhala.

Finke, Roger, and Laurence R. Iannoccone. 1993. "Supply-Side Explanations for Religious Change in America." *The Annals* 527: 27–39.

Finke, Roger, and Rodney Stark. 1992. *The Churching of America, 1776–1990: Winners and Losers in Our Religious Economy.* New York: New Brunswick, N.J.: Rutgers University Press.

Firestone, Reuven. 1999. *Jihad: The Origin of Holy War in Islam.* Oxford: Oxford University Press.

Fischer-Schreiber, Ingrid, Franz-Karl Erhard, and Michael S. Diener. 1991. *The Shambhala Dictionary of Buddhism and Zen,* trans. Michael S. Kohn. Boston: Shambhala Publications.

Fish, Stanley. 1997. "Mission Impossible: Settling the Just Bounds between the Church and State." *Columbia Law Review* (December): 2255–2333.

Foster, J. M. [1917] 1996. "Rome, the Antagonist of the Nation" In *The Fundamentals: A Testimony to the Truth,* eds. R. A. Torrey, A. C. Dixon, et al., 3: 301–14. Grand Rapids, Mich.: Baker Books.

Foucault, Michel. 1965. *Madness and Civilization: A History of Insanity in the Age of Reason,* trans. Richard Howard. New York: Vintage Books.

———. 1977. *Discipline and Punish: The Birth of the Prison,* trans. Alan Sheridan. New York: Vintage Books.

———. 1978. *The History of Sexuality: Vol. 1, An Introduction,* trans. Robert Hurley. New York: Vintage Books.

———. 1980. *Power/Knowledge: Selected Interviews and Writings, 1972–1977,* ed. Colin Gordon, trans. Colin Gordon, Leo Marshall, John Mepham, and Kate Soper. New York: Pantheon Books.

Fox, Matthew. 1983. *Original Blessing: A Primer in Creation Spirituality Presented in Four Paths, Twenty-Six Themes, and Two Questions.* Santa Fe, N. Mex.: Bear.

———. 1991. *Creation Spirituality: Liberating Gifts for the People of the Earth.* New York: HarperCollins.

———. 1996. *Confessions: The Making of a Post-Denominational Priest.* New York: HarperCollins.

Freed, Josh. 1980. *Moonwebs: Journey into the Mind of a Cult.* Toronto: Dorset Publishing.

Fresenborg, Bernard. 1904. *"Thirty Years in Hell" or "From Darkness to Light."* St. Louis, Mo.: North-American Book House.

Geer, Thelma. 1986. *Mormonism, Mama, and Me.* Chicago: Moody Press.

Geisler, Norman. 1976. *Christian Apologetics.* Grand Rapids, Mich.: Baker Books.

Geisler, Norman L., and Ron Rhodes. 1997. *When Cultists Ask: A Popular Handbook on Cultic Misinterpretations.* Grand Rapids, Mich.: Baker Books.

Ghareeb, Edmund, ed. 1983. *Split Vision: The Portrayal of Arabs in the American Media*. Washington, D.C.: American-Arab Affairs Council.

Giambalvo, Carol. 1995. *Exit Counseling: A Family Intervention*. Bonita Springs, Fla.: American Family Foundation.

Gomes, Alan W. 1998. *Truth and Error: Comparative Charts of Cults and Christianity*. Zondervan Guide to Cults and Religious Movements. Grand Rapids, Mich.: Zondervan.

Grady, J. Lee. 1995. "Does the Church Need Heresy Hunters?" *Charisma* (May): 47–50, 52.

Graham, William A. 1987. *Beyond the Written Word: Oral Aspects of Scripture in the History of Religion*. Cambridge: Cambridge University Press.

Gregg, Robert C., and Dennis E. Groh. 1981. *Early Arianism: A View of Salvation*. Philadelphia: Fortress Press.

Greer, Mary K. 1995. *Women of the Golden Dawn: Rebels and Priestesses*. Rochester, Vt.: Park Street Press.

Groothuis, Douglas R. 1986. *Unmasking the New Age*. Downers Grove, Ill.: InterVarsity.

———. 1988. *Confronting the New Age: How to Resist a Growing Religious Movement*. Downers Grove, Ill.: InterVarsity.

———. 1990. *Revealing the New Age Jesus: Challenges to Orthodox Views of Christ*. Downers Grove, Ill.: InterVarsity.

———. 1995. *Deceived by the Light: A Biblical Response to Mega-Bestseller* Embraced by the Light. Eugene, Oreg.: Harvest House.

Guazzo, Franceso Maria. [1608] 1988. *Compendium Maleficarum: The Montague Summers Edition*, trans. E. A. Ashwin. New York: Dover.

Gutierrez, Gustavo. 1973. *A Theology of Liberation: History, Politics, and Salvation*, trans. John Eagleson. Maryknoll, N.Y.: Orbis Books.

Hadden, Jeffrey K., and Douglas E. Cowan. 2000. "The Promised Land or Electronic Chaos? Toward Understanding Religion on the Internet." In *Religion on the Internet: Research Prospects and Promises*, eds. Jeffrey K. Hadden and Douglas E. Cowan, 3–21. London: JAI/Elsevier Science.

Hall, Mimi. 1991. "Arab-Americans Speak Out. Poll: Most Support U.S. in Gulf war." *USA Today*, February 6, 1A.

Hamblin, William J., and Daniel C. Peterson. 1999. Review of *How Wide the Divide? A Mormon and an Evangelical in Conversation*, by Craig L. Blomberg and Stephen E. Robinson. *FARMS Review of Books* 11 (2): 178–209.

Hanegraaff, Hank. n.d. "M-A-P-S to Guide You through Biblical Reliability." CRI Statement DB011. Available at www.equip.org/free/DB011.htm.

———. 1993. *Christianity in Crisis*. Eugene, Oreg.: Harvest House.

Hanegraaff, Wouter J. 1996. *New Age Religion and Western Culture: Esotericism in the Mirror of Secular Thought*. Leiden, Netherlands: E. J. Brill.

Hansen, Klaus J. 1981. *Mormonism and the American Experience*. Chicago History of American Religion. Chicago: University of Chicago Press.

Hardon, John A. 1980. *Modern Catholic Dictionary*. New York: Doubleday.

———. 1985. *Pocket Catholic Dictionary*. New York: Doubleday.

Hall, John R. 1999. *Cultures of Inquiry: From Epistemology to Discourse in Sociohistorical Research*. Cambridge: Cambridge University Press.

Hassan, Steven. 1990. *Combatting Cult Mind Control*. Rochester, Vt.: Park Street Press.

———. 2000. *Releasing the Bonds: Empowering People to Think for Themselves.* Somerville, Mass.: Freedom of Mind Press.

Hawkins, Craig S. 1996. *Witchcraft: Exploring the World of Wicca.* Grand Rapids, Mich.: Baker Books.

———. 1998. *Goddess Worship, Witchcraft and Neo-Paganism.* Zondervan Guide to Cults and Religious Movements. Grand Rapids, Mich.: Zondervan.

Heelas, Paul. 1996. *The New Age Movement: The Celebration of the Self and the Sacralization of Modernity.* Oxford: Blackwell.

Hein, Anton. n.d. "Apologetics and Religious Freedom/Tolerance." Available online at www.gospelcom.net/apologeticsindex/r04.html.

———. 2000. "The Church of Scientology." Available online at www.gospelcom.net/apologeticsindex/s04.html.

Henderson, John B. 1998. *The Construction of Orthodoxy and Heresy: Neo-Confucian, Islamic, Jewish, and Early Christian Patterns.* Albany, N.Y.: SUNY Press.

Hertenstein, Mike, and Jon Trott. 1993. *Selling Satan: The Evangelical Media and the Mike Warnke Scandal.* Chicago: Cornerstone Press.

Hexham, Irving. 1972. "Some Aspects of the Contemporary Search for an Alternative Society." Master's thesis, University of Bristol, U.K.

———. 1981. "Calling the Kettle Black: The Spiritual Counterfeits Project and the Cults." University of Manitoba. Photocopy of typescript.

———. 1992. "The Evangelical Reponse to the New Age." In *Perspectives on the New Age*, eds. James R. Lewis and Gordon Melton, 152–63. Albany, N.Y.: SUNY Press.

Hexham, Irving, and Karla Poewe. 1997. *New Religions as Global Culture: Making the Human Sacred.* Boulder, Colo.: Westview Press.

———. 1999. " 'Verfassungsfeindlich': Church, State, and New Religions in Germany." *Nova Religio: The Journal of Alternative and Emergent Religions* 2 (2): 208–27.

Hill, D. G. 1980. "Defining the Problem." In *New Religions and Mental Health: Understanding the Issues*, ed. Herbert Richardson, 3–6. New York and Toronto: Edwin Mellen Press.

Hoffmann, Peter. 1996. *The History of German Resistance, 1933–1945*, 3d ed., trans. Richard Barry. Montréal and Kingston: McGill-Queen's University Press.

Horton, Michael, ed. 1990. *The Agony of Deceit: What Some TV Preachers Are Really Teaching.* Chicago: Moody Press.

House, H. Wayne. 1997. "With an Apology to Arius: When and How Should We Deal with Heresies and Heretics?" *Journal of Christian Apologetics* 1 (1): 29–47.

Howard, Jay, with Timothy Fink and Nathan Unseth. 1990. *Confronting the Cultist in the New Age.* Old Tappan, N.J.: Power Books.

Howe, Eber D. 1834. *Mormonism Unvailed.* Painesville, Ohio: Author.

Hoyt, Karen, and J. Isamu Yamamoto, eds. 1987. *The New Age Rage.* Old Tappan, N.J.: Power Books.

Hunt, Dave. 1972. *Confessions of a Heretic.* Plainfield, N.J.: Logos.

———. 1980. *The Cult Explosion.* Eugene, Oreg.: Harvest House.

———. 1983. *Peace, Prosperity, and the Coming Holocaust: The New Age Movement in Prophecy.* Eugene, Oreg.: Harvest House.

———. 1986. " 'Christian Psychology': Part X." *The Berean Call* (July): 1–2.

——. 1987. *Beyond Seduction: A Return to Biblical Christianity.* Eugene, Oreg.: Harvest House.

——. 1990. *Global Peace and the Rise of Antichrist.* Eugene, Oreg.: Harvest House.

——. 1991. "A Cult Is a Cult." *The Berean Call* (June): 1–2.

——. 1992. "Heeding the Berean Call." *The Berean Call* (April): 1–6.

——. 1993a. *How Close Are We?* Eugene, Oreg.: Harvest House.

——. 1993b. "Q & A." *The Berean Call* (October): 3–4.

——. 1994. *A Woman Rides the Beast: The Catholic Church and the Last Days.* Eugene, Oreg.: Harvest House.

——. 1995. "Q & A." *The Berean Call* (July): 3–4.

——. 1996. *In Defense of the Faith: Biblical Answers to Challenging Questions.* Eugene, Oreg.: Harvest House.

——. 1998. *Occult Invasion: The Subtle Seduction of the World and Church.* Eugene, Oreg.: Harvest House.

——. 1999. "Q&A." *The Berean Call* (March): 3–4.

Hunt, Dave, and T. A. McMahon. 1985. *The Seduction of Christianity: Spiritual Discernment in the Last Days.* Eugene, Oreg.: Harvest House.

——. 1988. *America, The Sorcerer's New Apprentice: The Rise of New Age Shamanism.* Eugene, Oreg.: Harvest House.

Hutton, Ronald. 1999. *Triumph of the Moon: A History of Modern Pagan Witchcraft.* Oxford: Oxford University Press.

Hyla. 1853. *The Convent and the Manse.* Boston: John P. Jewett.

Iannaccone, Laurence R. 1990. "Religious Practice: A Human Capital Approach." *Journal for the Scientific Study of Religion* 29 (2): 297–314.

——. 1994. "Why Strict Churches Are Strong." *American Journal of Sociology* 99: 1180–1211.

——. 1995. "Voodoo Economics? Reviewing the Rational Choice Approach to Religion." *Journal for the Scientific Study of Religion* 34 (1): 76–89.

Introvigne, Massimo. 1993. "Strange Bedfellows or Future Enemies?" *Update and Dialog on New Religious Movements* 3: 13–22.

——. 1995a. "L'évolution du 'mouvement contres les sectes' chrétien 1978–1993." *Social Compass* 42 (2): 237–47.

——. 1995b. "The Secular Anti-Cult and the Religious Counter-Cult Movement: Strange Bedfellows or Future Enemies?" In *New Religions and the New Europe,* ed. Robert Towler, 32–54. RENNER Studies on New Religions. Aarhus, Denmark: Aarhus University Press.

——. 1998. "Religious Liberty in Western Europe." Presentation to the Commission on Security and Cooperation in Europe and the House International Relations Committee. Available at: www.cesnur.org/testi/Washington2.htm.

——. 1999. "Defectors, Ordinary Leave-takers, and Apostates: A Quantitative Study of Former Members of New Acropolis in France." *Nova Religio: The Journal of Alternative and Emergent Religions* 3 (1): 83–99.

——. 2000. " 'So Many Evil Things': Anti-Cult Terrorism via the Internet." In *Religion on the Internet: Research Prospects and Promises,* eds. Jeffrey K. Hadden and Douglas E. Cowan, 277–306. London: JAI/Elsevier Science.

Irvine, William C. 1935. *Heresies Exposed: A Brief Critical Examination in the Light of the Holy Scriptures of Some of the Prevailing Heresies and False Teachings of Today.* New York: Loiseaux Bros.

Jacobs, James B., and Kimberly Potter. 1998. *Hate Crimes: Criminal Law and Identity Politics.* Oxford: Oxford University Press.

James, William. [1902] 1985. *The Varieties of Religious Experience.* Cambridge: Harvard University Press.

Journal-American. 1983. "Filmaker [*sic*] Files Suit against Mormon Official, TV Exec." May 21. Photocopy reproduced in "Having done all, to stand." *Saints Alive in Jesus Newsletter* (May/June, 1983): 22.

Kamalipour, Yahya R., ed. 1997. *The U.S. Media and the Middle East: Image and Perception.* Westport, Conn.: Praeger.

Keating, Karl. 1988. *Catholicism and Fundamentalism: The Attack on 'Romanism' by 'Bible Christians.'* San Francisco: Ignatius Press.

———. 2000. *The Usual Suspects: Answering Anti-Catholic Fundamentalists.* San Francisco: Ignatius Press.

Keiser, Thomas W., and Jacqueline L. Keiser. 1987. *The Anatomy of Illusion: Religious Cults and Destructive Persuasion.* Springfield, Ill.: Charles C. Thomas Publisher.

King, Stephen. 1997. "Wild about Harry." *New York Times,* July 23, Sec. 7, 13.

Knox, John. 1558. *The First Blast of the Trumpet against the Monstrous Regiment of Women,* ed. Edward Arber. Westminster, G.B.: A. Constable, 1895.

Kraft, Robert A. 1975. "The Development of the Concept of 'Orthodoxy' in Early Christianity." In *Current Issues in Biblical and Patristic Interpretation,* ed. Gerald F. Hawthorne, 47–59. Grand Rapids, Mich.: Eerdmans.

Kramer, Heinrich, and James Sprenger. [1484] 1971. *The Malleus Maleficarum,* trans. Montague Summers. New York: Dover.

Küng, Hans. 1974. *On Being a Christian,* trans. Edward Quinn. Garden City, N.Y.: Doubleday.

Kurtz, Lester R. 1983. "The Politics of Heresy." *American Journal of Sociology* 88 (6): 1085–1115.

Langone, Michael. 1995. "Secular and Religious Critiques of Cults: Complementary Visions, Not Irresolvable Conflicts." *Cultic Studies Journal* 12 (2): 166–86.

———. 1999a. "Cults 101: Aren't the Marines a Cult by Your Definition?" Available online at www.csj.org/infoserv_cult101/marine_def.htm.

———. 1999b. "Cults 101: Checklist of Cult Characteristics." Available online at www.csj.org/infoserv_cult101/checklis.htm.

Langstaff, Alan. 1986. "A Reply to *The Seduction of Christianity.* In *Seduction?? A Biblical Response,* 7–14. New Wilmington, Pa.: Son-Rise.

Larson, Bob. 1969. *Hippies, Hindus and Rock and Roll.* McCook: Author.

———. 1989a. *Larson's New Book of Cults,* rev. ed. Wheaton, Ill.: Tyndale House.

———. 1989b. *Satanism: The Seduction of America's Youth.* Nashville, Tenn.: Thomas Nelson.

———. 1991. *Dead Air.* Nashville, Tenn.: Thomas Nelson.

———. 1993. *Abaddon.* Nashville, Tenn,: Thomas Nelson.

———. 1996. *In the Name of Satan.* Nashville, Tenn.: Thomas Nelson.

———. 1997. *UFOs and the Alien Agenda: Uncovering the Mystery behind UFOs and the Paranormal.* Nashville, Tenn.: Thomas Nelson.

———. 1998a. "First Ever Live Public Exorcism in Calgary." Seminar presented at the Sheraton-Cavalier Hotel, Calgary, Alberta, August 7.

———. 1998b. "Let Me Help You Demon-Proof Your Life!" Fundraising letter (May).

———. 1999. *Larson's Book of Spiritual Warfare.* Nashville, Tenn.: Thomas Nelson.

Levack, Brian P. 1995. *The Witch-Hunt in Early Modern Europe,* 2d ed. London: Longman.

Lewis, Gordon R. 1966. *Confronting the Cults.* Phillipsburg, N.J.: Presbyterian and Reformed Publishing.

Lewis, James R., ed. 1995. *The Gods Have Landed: New Religions from Other Worlds.* Albany, N.Y.: SUNY Press.

———. 1996a. *Magical Religion and Modern Witchcraft.* Albany, N.Y.: SUNY Press.

———. 1996b. "Works of Darkness: Occult Fascination in the Novels of Frank E. Peretti." In *Magical Religion and Modern Witchcraft,* ed. James R. Lewis, 339–50. Albany, N.Y.: SUNY Press.

Lewis, James R., and Gordon Melton. 1992. *Perspectives on the New Age.* Albany, N.Y.: SUNY Press.

Lewy, Guenter. 1964. *The Catholic Church and Nazi Germany.* New York: De Capo.

Lindsell, Harold. 1976. *The Battle for the Bible.* Grand Rapids, Mich.: Zondervan.

Lindsell, Harold, et al. 1961. *The Challenge of the Cults: A* Christianity Today *Symposium.* Grand Rapids, Mich.: Zondervan.

Lockwood, Robert P. 2000. "The Evolution of Anti-Catholicism in the United States." In *Anti-Catholicism in American Culture,* ed. Robert P. Lockwood, 15–53. Huntingdon, In.: Our Sunday Visitor.

Lucas, Phillip. 1995. "From Holy Order of MANS to Christ the Savior Brotherhood: The Radical Transformation of an Esoteric Christian Order." In *America's Alternative Religions,* ed. Timothy Miller, 141–48. Albany, N.Y.: SUNY Press.

Lüdemann, Gerd. 1995. *Heretics: The Other Side of Early Christianity,* trans. John Bowden. Louisville, Ky.: Westminster John Knox.

Lüdemann, Gerd, and Martina Janssen. 1997. *Suppressed Prayers: Gnostic Spirituality in Early Christianity,* trans. John Bowden. Harrisburg, Pa.: Trinity Press International.

Luhrmann, T. M. 1989. *Persuasions of the Witch's Craft: Ritual Magic in Contemporary England.* London: Picador.

Lutzer, Erwin W. 1995. *Hitler's Cross: The Revealing Story of How the Cross of Christ Was Used as a Symbol of the Nazi Agenda.* Chicago: Moody Press.

Lyons, Gene. 1985. "Let There Be Books." *Newsweek,* August 5, 65.

Madison, James. [1785] 1973. "Memorial and Remonstrance." In *The Papers of James Madison,* Vol. 8, eds. Robert A. Rutland et al., 298–304. Chicago: University of Chicago Press.

Maloney, H. Newton. 1988. *Brainwashing, Coercive Persuasion, Undue Influence, Mind Control: A Psychologist's Point of View.* Pasadena, Calif.: Integration Press.

Mannheim, Karl. 1936. *Ideology and Utopia: An Introduction to the Sociology of Knowledge.* New York: Harcourt Brace.

———. 1952. "The Problem of a Sociology of Knowledge." In *Essays on the Sociology of Knowledge,* ed. Paul Kecskemeti, 134–90. International Library of Sociology and Social Reconstruction. London: Routledge and Kegan Paul.

Marks, Morton. 1974. "Uncovering Ritual Structures in Afro-American Music." In *Religious Movements in Contemporary America,* eds. Irving I. Zaretsky and Mark P. Leone, 60–134. Princeton, N.J.: Princeton University Press.

Marrs, Texe. 1987. *Dark Secrets of the New Age: Satan's Plan for a One World Religion.* Wheaton, Ill.: Crossway Books.

————. 1989a. *Mega Forces: Signs and Wonders of the Coming Chaos.* Austin, Tex.: Living Truth Publishers.

————. 1989b. *Ravaged by the New Age: Satan's Plan to Destroy Our Kids.* Austin, Tex.: Living Truth Publishers.

————. 1990. *Texe Marrs Book of New Age Cults and Religions.* Austin, Tex.: Living Truth Publishers.

————. 1992. *Dark Majesty: The Secret Brotherhood and the Magic of A Thousand Points of Light.* Austin, Tex.: Living Truth Publishers.

————. 1993. *Big Sister Is Watching You: Hilary Clinton and the White House Feminists Who Now Control America—And Tell the President What to Do.* Austin, Tex.: Living Truth Publishers.

————. 1996. *Project L.U.C.I.D.: The Beast 666 Universal Human Control System.* Austin, Tex.: Living Truth Publishers.

————. 1997a. "Agents of Disinformation." *Flashpoint: A Newsletter Ministry of Texe Marrs* (April): 3.

————. 1997b. "Australia Confiscates Firearms—We're Next!" *Flashpoint: A Newsletter Ministry of Texe Marrs* (June): 3.

————. 1997c. "Devil Companies, Devil Products, Devil Logos?" *Flashpoint: A Newsletter Ministry of Texe Marrs* (December): 1–2.

————. 1997d. "The Pope, the Devil, and the Masonic Lodge." *Flashpoint: A Newsletter Ministry of Texe Marrs* (July): 1–3.

————. 1998a. "IRS Muzzles Free Speech." *Flashpoint: A Newsletter Ministry of Texe Marrs* (December): 1–2.

————. 1998b. "ORPM Stalled—Continued Vigilance Necessary." *Flashpoint: A Newsletter Ministry of Texe Marrs* (November): 1–2.

————. 1999. "New Ministry Launched—Praise God!" *Power of Prophecy* (January): 1–2.

————. 2001a. "The Mysterious Riddle of Chandra Levy." *Power of Prophecy* (November): 1–2.

————. 2001b. "Was Chandra Levy Sacrificed to Satan?" *Power of Prophecy* (November): 3.

Marrs, Wanda. 1989. *New Age Lies to Women.* Austin, Tex.: Living Truth Publishers.

Marsden, George M. 1980. *Fundamentalism and American Culture: The Shaping of Twentieth-Century Evangelicalism, 1870–1925.* Oxford: Oxford University Press.

Martin, John. 1998. *Roses, Fountains, and Gold: The Virgin Mary in History, Art, and Apparition.* San Francisco: Ignatius Press.

Martin, Malachi. 1987. *The Jesuits: The Society of Jesus and the Betrayal of the Roman Catholic Church.* New York: Touchstone.

Martin, Paul R. 1993. *Cult-Proofing Your Kids.* Grand Rapids, Mich.: Zondervan.

Martin, Walter R. 1955. *The Rise of the Cults: An Introductory Guide to the Non-Christian Cults.* Grand Rapids, Mich.: Zondervan.

————. 1965. *The Kingdom of the Cults: An Analysis of the Major Cult Systems in the Present Christian Era.* London: Marshall, Morgan & Scott.

————. 1976. *Mormonism.* Minneapolis: Bethany House.

————. 1977. *The Kingdom of the Cults: An Analysis of the Major Cult Systems in the Present Christian Era,* rev. ed. Minneapolis: Bethany House.

————. 1978. *The Maze of Mormonism,* 2d ed. Santa Ana, Calif.: Vision House.

————. 1980. *Rise of the Cults: A Quick Guide to the Cults,* 3d ed. Santa Ana, Calif.: Vision House.

————. 1985. *The Kingdom of the Cults,* 3d rev. ed. Minneapolis: Bethany House.

————. 1989. *The New Age Cult.* Minneapolis: Bethany House.

————. 1997. *The Kingdom of the Cults.* 4th rev. ed., ed. Hank Hanegraaff. Minneapolis: Bethany House.

Martin, Walter, and Norman Klann. 1974. *Jehovah of the Watchtower,* rev. ed. Minneapolis: Bethany House.

Martin, Walter, and Gretchen Passantino, eds. 1980. *The New Cults.* Santa Ana, Calif.: Vision House.

Martin, William. 1996. *With God on Our Side: The Rise of the Religious Right in America.* New York: Broadway Books.

Matrisciana, Caryl. 1985. *Gods of the New Age.* Eugene, Oreg.: Harvest House.

Mayer, Jean-François. 2000. "Religious Movements and the Internet: The New Frontier of Cult Controversies." In *Religion on the Internet: Research Prospects and Promises,* eds. Jeffrey K. Hadden and Douglas E. Cowan, 249–76. London: JAI/Elsevier Science.

McBrien, Richard P. 1994. *Catholicism: A New Study,* rev. ed. New York: HarperSanFrancisco.

McCarthy, E. Doyle. 1996. *Knowledge as Culture: The New Sociology of Knowledge.* London: Routledge.

McCarthy, James. 1995. *The Gospel According to Rome.* Eugene, Oreg.: Harvest House.

————. 1997. *Conversations with Catholics.* Eugene, Oreg.: Harvest House.

McConkie, Bruce. 1966. *Mormon Doctrine.* Salt Lake City, Utah: Bookcraft.

McConnell, D. R. 1988. *A Different Gospel: A Historical and Biblical Analysis of the Modern Faith Movement.* Peabody, Mass.: Hendrickson.

McDowell, Josh, comp. 1979. *Evidence That Demands a Verdict: Historical Evidences for the Christian Faith,* rev. ed. San Bernardino, Calif.: Here's Life Publishers.

————. 1981. *More Evidence That Demands a Verdict: Historical Evidences for the Christian Scriptures,* rev. ed. San Bernardino: Here's Life Publishers.

McDowell, Josh, and Don Stewart. 1983. *Handbook of Today's Religions.* San Bernardino: Here's Life Publishers.

McGee, Robert S., and Caryl Matrisciana. 2001. *Harry Potter: Witchcraft Repackaged.* Jeremiah Films, HPWV101.

McNiece, R. G. 1898. *Present Aspects of Mormonism.* New York: League for Social Service.

————. [1917] 1996. "Mormonism: Its Origin, Characteristics, and Doctrines." In *The Fundamentals: A Testimony to the Truth,* eds. R. A. Torrey, A. C. Dixon, et al., 4: 131–48. Grand Rapids, Mich.: Baker Books.

Medhurst, T. W. [1917] 1996. "Is Romanism Christianity?" In *The Fundamentals: A Testimony to the Truth,* eds. R. A. Torrey, A. C. Dixon, et al., 3: 288–300. Grand Rapids, Mich.: Baker Books.

Melton, J. Gordon. 1992. *Encyclopedic Handbook of Cults in America,* rev. ed. New York: Garland Publishing.

————. 1999. Brainwashing and the Cults: The Rise and Fall of a Theory." Available online at www.cesnur.org/testi/melton.htm.

————. 2000. "Emerging Religious Movements in North America: Some Missiological Reflections." *Missiology: An International Review* 28 (1): 85–98.

Metz, Gary. 1981. "Jack Chick's Anti-Catholic Comic Book Is Exposed as a Fraud." *Christianity Today* (March 13): 50–53.

Michaelson, Johanna. 1989. *Like Lambs to the Slaughter: Your Child and the Occult*, 2d ed. Eugene, Oreg.: Harvest House.

Midelfort, H. C. Erik. 1972. *Witch Hunting in Southwestern Germany, 1562–1684: The Social and Intellectual Foundations*. Stanford, Calif.: Stanford University Press.

Miller, Elliot. n.d. "A Summary Critique: The Hidden Dangers of the Rainbow." Available online at www.equip.org/free/dc925.htm.

———. 1988. "A Reply to Constance Cumbey's Charges against Walter Martin and CRI." Available online at www.equip.org/free/dc825.htm.

———. 1989. *A Crash Course on the New Age Movement*. Grand Rapids, Mich.: Baker Books.

Miravalle, Mark, ed. 1993. *Mary: Coredemptrix, Mediatrix, Advocate*. Santa Barbara, Calif.: Queenship Publishing.

———. 1997. *Introduction to Mary: The Heart of Marian Doctrine and Devotion*. Santa Barbara, Calif.: Queenship Publishing.

———. 2000. *Contemporary Insights on a Fifth Marian Dogma*. Santa Barbara, Calif.: Queenship Publishing.

Missler, Chuck, and Mark Eastman. 1997. *Alien Encounters: The Secret behind the UFO Phenomenon*. Coeur d'Alene, Idaho: Koinonia House.

Modica, T. A. 1996. *Overcoming the Power of the Occult*. Milford, Ohio: Faith Publishing.

Monk, Maria. 1876. *Awful Disclosures of Maria Monk, as Exhibited in a Narrative of her Sufferings during Her Residence of Five Years as a Novice and Two Years as a Black Nun in the Hotel Dieu Nunnery, at Montreal, Ont.*, rev. ed. New York: The Truth Seeker.

Montenegro, Marcia. n.d. "The Harry Potter Movie." Available online at http://cana.userworld.com/cana_pottermovie.html.

———. 2000. "Harry Potter, Sorcery and Fantasy." Available online at http://cana.userworld.com/cana_harrypotter.html.

———. 2001. "Harry Potter: A Journey to Power." Available online at http://cana.userworld.com/cana_morehpotter1.html.

Moorehead, William G. [1917] 1996. "Millennial Dawn: A Counterfeit of Christianity." In *The Fundamentals: A Testimony to the Truth*, eds. R. A. Torrey, A. C. Dixon, et al., 4: 109–30. Grand Rapids, Mich.: Baker Books.

Morehead, John W. 2000. "Tired of Treading Water: Rediscovering and Reapplying a Missiological Paradigm for 'Countercult' Ministry." Paper presented at the annual meeting of Evangelical Ministries to New Religions, New Orleans, Louisiana.

———. 2002. "Moving Together beyond the Fringes: A Paradigm for EMNR's Viability in an Age of Religious Pluralism." Paper presented at the annual meeting of Evangelical Ministries to New Religions, Louisville, Kentucky.

Morey, Robert A. 1980. *How to Answer a Jehovah's Witness*. Minneapolis: Bethany Fellowship.

———. 1992. *The Islamic Invasion: Confronting the World's Fastest Growing Religion*. Eugene, Oreg.: Harvest House.

———. 1999. "Will Islam Cause WW III?" Available online at www.faithdefenders.com/wwiii.html.

Mosser, Carl. 1998. E-mail communication to ar-talk@xc.org, electronic discussion group, February 28.

Mosser, Carl, and Paul Owen. 1998. "Mormon Scholarship, Apologetics and Evangelical Neglect: Losing the Battle and Not Knowing It?" *Trinity Journal*, Fall: 179–205.

Most, William G. 1959. *Mary in Our Life*, 3d ed. New York: P. J. Kenedy and Sons.

National Conference of Christians and Jews. 1984. *Programs in Pluralism* (March/April).

Neal, Connie. 2001. *What's a Christian to Do with Harry Potter?* Colorado Springs, Colo.: Waterbrook Press.

Newport, John P. 1998. *The New Age Movement and the Biblical Worldview: Conflict and Dialogue*. Grand Rapids, Mich.: William B. Eerdmans.

Norwood, L. Ara. 1993. "*Ignoratio Elenchi:* The Dialogue That Never Was." Book review of *Letters to a Mormon Elder*, by James R. White. *FARMS Review of Books* 5. Available online at http://farms.byu.edu/free/review/5.

Novak, Gary. n.d. (a) "Worst of the Anti-Mormon Web Special Edition: Does James White Have a Genuine Doctorate?" Available online at www.shields-research.org/Novak/james.htm.

———. n.d. (b). "Of James White and the Salt River: Or, 'Dr.' White Leads an Excursion in the Art of *Non-Sequitur* and *Ad Hominem* and in Which Piglet Nearly Meets a Hefalump." Available online at www.shields-research.org/Novak/james2.htm.

Numbers, Ronald L. 1992. *The Creationists: The Evolution of Scientific Creationism*. Berkeley and Los Angeles: University of California Press.

O'Gorman, Edith. 1871. *Trials and Persecutions of Edith O'Gorman, Otherwise Sister Teresa de Chantal, of St. Joseph's Convent, Hudson City, N.J.* Hartford: Connecticut Publishing.

Ostling, Richard N., and Joan K. Ostling. 1999. *Mormon America: The Power and the Promise*. New York: HarperSanFrancisco.

Ott, Ludwig. 1954. *Fundamentals of Catholic Dogma*, ed. James Canon Bastible, trans. Patrick Lynch. St. Louis, Mo.: B. Herder.

Packa, Donna. 1998. Personal communication with author. July 6.

Palmer, Susan Jean. 1995. "Women in the Raëlian Movement: New Religious Experiments in Gender and Authority." In *The Gods Have Landed: New Religions from Other Worlds*, ed. James R. Lewis, 105–35. Albany, N.Y.: SUNY Press.

Palmer, Susan J., and Charlotte E. Hardman, eds. 1999. *Children in New Religions*. New York: Routledge.

Paris, Edmund. 1983. *The Secret History of the Jesuits*. Chino, Calif.: Chick Publications.

Parker, Gerald. 1999. "Letter to the Editor." *Washington Report on Middle East Affairs* (October/November): 95.

Parks, Steven. 2002. "The Devil Is in the Details: An Examination of the Teachings of Bob Larson." *Christian Research Journal* 24 (2): 22–25, 42–46.

Passantino, Bob, and Gretchen Passantino. 1990a. "What Is a Cult?" Available online at http://answers.org/CultsAndReligions/What_Is_A_Cult.html.

———. 1990b. *Witch Hunt*. Nashville, Tenn.: Thomas Nelson.

———. 1995a. "Psychology and the Church (Part One): Laying a Foundation for Discernment." *Christian Research Journal* 17 (3), Winter, 20–3, 35–8.

———. 1995b. "Psychology and the Church (Part Two): The 'Biblical Counseling' Alternative." *Christian Research Journal* 17 (4), Spring, 24–30.

———. 1995c. "Psychology and the Church (Part Three): Can Psychotherapy Be Integrated with Christianity?" *Christian Research Journal* 18 (1), Summer, 16–24, 39.

———. 1995d. "Psychology and the Church (Part Four): The High Cost of Biblical Compassion and Commitment." *Christian Research Journal* 18 (2), Fall, 18–23, 42–3.

———. 1997. "Critiquing Cult Mind-Control Model." In *The Kingdom of the Cults*, 4th ed., ed. Hank Hanegraaff, 49–78. Minneapolis: Bethany House.

Passelecq, Georges, and Bernard Suchecky. 1997. *The Hidden Encyclical of Pius XI: The Vatican's Lost Opportunity to Oppose Nazi Racist Policies That Led to the Holocaust*, trans. Stephen Rendall. New York: Harcourt Brace.

Patrick, Ted. 1976. *Let Our Children Go!* New York: Ballantine Books, 1976.

Paulk, Earl. 1987. *That the World May Know: Clearing the Air after* The Seduction of Christianity: *A Plea for Unity through Scriptural Mandate*. Atlanta: K Dimension Publishers.

Pelikan, Jaroslav. 1990. "Fundamentalism and/or Orthodoxy? Toward an Understanding of the Fundamentalist Phenomenon." In *The Fundamentalist Phenomenon: A View from Within, a Response from Without*, ed. Norman J. Cohn, 3–21. Grand Rapids, Mich.: William B. Eerdmans.

Pement, Eric. 1999. "A History of Evangelical Ministries to New Religions." *EMNR Quarterly Update* 3 (1): 4.

Penton, M. James. n.d. "Phoney Scholarship, False Orthodoxy, and Commercialized Hate Peddling." Photocopy of typescript.

———. 1998. *Apocalypse Delayed: The Story of Jehovah's Witnesses*. 2d ed. Toronto: University of Toronto Press.

Peretti, Frank E. 1986. *This Present Darkness*. Wheaton, Ill.: Crossway Books.

———. 1989. *Piercing the Darkness*. Westchester, Ill.: Crossway Books.

———. 1995. *The Oath*. Dallas, Tex.: Word.

Peters, Rudolph. 1996. *Jihad in Classical and Modern Islam: A Reader*. Princeton, N.J.: Markus Weiner.

Peterson, Daniel C. 1996. "Constancy amid Change." Book review of *Behind the Mask of Mormonism*, by John Ankerberg and John Weldon. *FARMS Review of Books* 8 (2). Available online at http://farms.byu.edu/free/review/8_2.

Peterson, Daniel C., and Stephen D. Ricks. 1992. *Offenders for a Word: How Anti-Mormons Play Word Games to Attack the Latter-day Saints*. Provo, Utah: Foundation for Ancient Research and Mormon Studies.

Pettit, Bryce A. 1998. "New Religious Movements: An Historical Overview." *International Journal of Frontier Missions* 15 (3): 125–33.

Pipes, Daniel. 1997. *Conspiracy: How the Paranoid Style Flourishes and Where It Comes From*. New York: Free Press.

Pipes, Richard. 1990. *The Russian Revolution*. New York: Vintage.

Poll, Rich. 2001. "AR-talk Charter and FAQ." Available online at www.apologia.org/chartertalk.html.

Pollock, Algernon J. [1917] 1996. "Modern Spiritualism Briefly Tested by Scripture." In *The Fundamentals: A Testimony to the Truth*, eds. R. A. Torrey, A. C. Dixon, et al., 4: 166–82. Grand Rapids, Mich.: Baker Books.

Provenzo, Eugene F. Jr. 1990. *Religious Fundamentalism and American Education: The Battle for the Public Schools*. Albany, N.Y.: SUNY Press.

Prus, Robert. 1996. *Symbolic Interaction and Ethnographic Research: Intersubjectivity and the Study of Human Lived Experience.* Albany, N.Y.: SUNY Press.

Ramadan Al-Bouti, Muhammed Said. 1995. *Jihad in Islam: How to Understand and Practice It.* n.p.: Dar Al-Fikr.

Reed, Rebecca Therese. 1835. *Six Months in a Convent, or, the Narrative of Rebecca Theresa Reed, Who Was under the Influence of the Roman Catholics about Two Years, and an Inmate of the Ursuline Convent on Mount Benedict, Charlestown, Mass., Nearly Iix Months, in the Years 1831–2. With Some Preliminary Suggestions by the Committee of Publication.* Boston: Russell, Odiorne & Metcalf.

Reid, Thomas F. 1986. "Critique of *The Seduction of Christianity.*" In *Seduction?? A Biblical Response,* 1–6. New Wilmington, Pa.: Son-Rise.

Reid, Thomas F., et al. 1986. *Seduction?? A Biblical Response.* New Wilmington, Pa.: Son-Rise.

Reitlinger, Gerald. 1957. *The SS: Alibi of a Nation.* New York: De Capo.

Remmling, Gunter, ed. 1973. *Towards the Sociology of Knowledge: Origin and Development of a Sociological Thought Style.* London: Routledge and Kegan Paul.

Rey, Terry. 1999. *Our Lady of Class Struggle: The Cult of the Virgin Mary in Haiti.* Lawrenceville, N.J.: Africa World Press.

Rhodes, Ron. 1993. *Reasoning from the Scriptures with the Jehovah's Witnesses.* Eugene, Oreg.: Harvest House.

———. 1994. *The Culting of America.* Eugene, Oreg.: Harvest House.

———. 1995. *Reasoning from the Scriptures with Mormons.* Eugene, Oreg.: Harvest House.

———. 1997. *The Complete Book of Bible Answers.* Eugene, Oreg.: Harvest House.

———. 1998. *Alien Obsession: What Lies behind Abductions, Sightings, and the Attraction to the Paranormal.* Eugene, Oreg.: Harvest House.

———. 2000. *Reasoning from the Scriptures with Catholics.* Eugene, Oreg.: Harvest House.

———. 2001a. *The Challenge of the Cults and New Religions.* Eugene, Oreg.: Harvest House

———. 2001b. *Reasoning from the Scriptures with Masons.* Eugene, Oreg.: Harvest House.

Richardson, H., ed. 1980. *New Religions and Mental Health: Understanding the Issues.* New York and Toronto: Edwin Mellen Press.

Richardson, James T. 1995. "Manufacturing Consent about Koresh: A Structural Analysis of the Role of Media in the Waco Tragedy." In *Armageddon in Waco: Critical Perspectives on the Branch Davidian Conflict,* ed. Stuart A. Wright, 153–76. Chicago: University of Chicago Press.

Richardson, James T., and Barend van Driel. 1997. "Journalists' Attitudes toward New Religious Movements." *Review of Religious Research* 39 (2): 116–36.

Richardson, James T., Joel Best, and David G. Bromley, eds. 1991. *The Satanism Scare.* New York: Aldine de Gruyter.

Richman, Paula, ed. 1991. *Many Rāmāyanas: The Diversty of a Narrative Tradition in South Asia.* Berkeley and Los Angeles: University of California Press.

Roberts, R. Philip. 2000. "Are Evangelism, Apologetics, and Missions a Hate Crime?" *Watchman Expositor* 17 (2). Available online at www.watchman.org/reltop/hatecrime.htm.

Robinson, Thomas A. 1988. *The Bauer Thesis Examined: The Geography of Heresy in the Early Christian Church.* Lewiston: Edwin Mellen Press.

Russell, C. Allyn, ed. 1976. *Voices of American Fundamentalism: Seven Biographical Studies.* Philadelphia: Westminster Press.

Said, Edward W. 1997. *Covering Islam: How the Media and the Experts Determine How We See the Rest of the World,* rev. ed. New York: Vintage Books

Saints Alive in Jesus. 1994. Product catalog.

Saliba, John A. 1995. *Understanding New Religious Movements.* Grand Rapids, Mich.: William B. Eerdmans Publishing.

―――. 1999. *Christian Responses to the New Age Movement: A Critical Assessment.* New York: Geoffrey Chapman.

Sandeen, Ernest R. 1970. *The Roots of Fundamentalism: British and American Millenarianism, 1800–1930.* Grand Rapids, Mich.: Baker Books.

Sardasian, Gunther. 1995. "CRI Prez under Fire." *On the Edge* (October). Available online at www.geocities.com/ote3/ote1.html.

Schaeffer, Francis A. 1968. *The God Who Is There: Speaking Historic Christianity into the Twentieth Century.* Downers Grove, Ill.: InterVarsity.

Scharffs, Gilbert W. 1989. *The Truth about "The God Makers,"* 2d ed. Salt Lake City, Utah: Publishers Press.

Schimmel, Annemarie. 1992. *Islam: An Introduction.* Albany, N.Y.: SUNY Press.

Schnell, W. J. 1956. *Thirty Years a Watchtower Slave: The Confessions of a Converted Jehovah's Witness.* Grand Rapids, Mich.: Baker Books.

Schultz, Nancy Lusignan. 2000. *Fire and Roses: The Burning of the Charlestown Convent, 1834.* New York: Free Press.

Scott, Latayne C. 1990. *Why We Left Mormonism: Eight People Tell Their Stories.* Grand Rapids, Mich.: Baker Books.

―――. 1993. *Why We Left a Cult: Six People Tell Their Stories.* Grand Rapids, Mich.: Baker Books.

―――. 1994. *After Mormonism, What? Reclaiming the Ex-Mormon's Worldview for Christ.* Grand Rapids, Mich.: Baker Books.

SCP Staff. 1987. "The Final Threat: Cosmic Conspiracy and End Times Speculation." In *The New Age Rage,* eds. Karen Hoyt and J. Isamu Yamamoto, 185–201. Old Tappan, N.J.: Power Books.

Seldes, George, comp. 1983. *The Great Quotations.* Secaucus, N.J.: Citadel Press.

Shupe, Anson D. Jr., and David G. Bromley. 1980. *The New Vigilantes: Deprogrammers, Anti-Cultists, and the New Religions.* Sage Library of Social Research, Vol. 113. Beverly Hills and London: Sage Publications.

―――. 1981. "Apostates and Atrocity Stories: Some Parameters in the Dynamics of Deprogramming." In *The Social Impact of New Religious Movements,* ed. Bryan Wilson, 176–216. New York: Rose of Sharon Press.

―――. 1985. *A Documentary History of the Anti-Cult Movement.* Arlington: Center for Social Research, University of Texas at Arlington.

―――, eds. 1994. *Anti-Cult Movements in Cross-Cultural Perspective.* New York and London: Garland Publishing.

―――. 1995. "The Evolution of Modern American Anticult Ideology: A Case Study in Frame Extension." In *America's Alternative Religions,* ed. Timothy Miller, 411–16. Albany, N.Y.: SUNY Press.

Shupe, Anson D. Jr., David G. Bromley, and D. L. Oliver. 1984. *The Anti-Cult Movement in America: A Bibliography and Historical Survey.* New York: Garland Publishing.

Shupe, Anson D., and Susan E. Darnell. 2000. "CAN, We Hardly Knew Ye: Sex, Drugs, Deprogrammers' Kickbacks, and Corporate Crime in the (Old) Cult Awareness Network." Paper presented to the annual meeting of the Society for the Scientific Study of Religion, Houston, Texas.

———. 2001. "Agents of Discord: The North American-European ACM Connection." Paper presented to the International Conference of CESNUR, London, England.

Shupe, Anson, and Jeffrey K. Hadden. 1995. "Cops, News Copy, and Public Opinion: Legitimacy and the Social Construction of Evil in Waco." In *Armageddon in Waco: Critical Perspectives on the Branch Davidian Conflict,* ed. Stuart A. Wright, 177–202. Chicago: University of Chicago Press.

Shupe, Anson D. Jr., R. Spielmann, and S. Stigall. 1977. "Deprogramming: The New Exorcism." In *Conversion Careers: In and Out of the New Religions,* ed. James T. Richardson, 145–60. Sage Contemporary Social Science Issues 47. Beverly Hills, Calif.: Sage Publications.

Silk, Mark. 1997. "Journalists with Attitude: A Response to Richardson and van Driel." *Review of Religious Research* 39 (2): 137–43.

Singer, Margaret, and Janja Lalich. 1995. *Cults in Our Midst.* San Francisco: Jossey-Bass.

Sire, James. 1976. *The Universe Next Door: A Basic Worldview Catalog.* Downers Grove, Ill.: InterVarsity.

———. 1980. *Scripture Twisting: 20 Ways the Cults Misread the Bible.* Downers Grove, Ill.: Intervarsity Press.

———. 1997. *The Universe Next Door: A Basic Worldview Catalog,* 3d ed. Downers Grove, Ill.: InterVarsity.

Slick, Matt. 1998. "Cults!" Available online at www.carm.org/cults/cultic.htm.

———. 2001. "Cesnur Knocks CARM." Available online at www.carm.org/features/counter_cult.htm.

———. 2002. *Right Answers for Wrong Beliefs.* Tonbridge, U.K.: Sovereign World.

Sobrino, Jon. 1993. *Jesus the Liberator: A Historical-Theological Reading of Jesus of Nazareth,* trans. Paul Burns and Francis McDonagh. Maryknoll, N.Y.: Orbis Books.

Spencer, James R. 1984. *Beyond Mormonism: An Elder's Story.* Grand Rapids, Mich.: Chosen Books.

———. 1986. *Have You Witnessed to a Mormon Lately?* Grand Rapids, Mich.: Chosen Books.

———. 1991. *Hard Case Witnessing: Winning the "Impossibles" for Christ.* Tarrytown, N.Y.: Chosen Books.

———. 1993. *Heresy Hunters: Character Assassination in the Church.* Lafayette, La.: Huntingdon House.

Stark, Rodney. 1984. "The Rise of a New World Faith." *Review of Religious Research* 26 (1): 18–27.

Stark, Rodney, and William Sims Bainbridge. 1985. *The Future of Religion: Secularization, Revival, and Cult Formation.* Berkeley and Los Angeles: University of California Press.

———. 1987. *A Theory of Religion.* New Brunswick, N.J.: Rutgers University Press.

———. 1997. *Religion, Deviance, and Social Control.* New York: Routledge.

Stark, Rodney, and Roger Finke. 2000. *Acts of Faith: Explaining the Human Side of Religion.* Berkeley and Los Angeles: University of California Press.

Stolzenberg, Nomi Maya. 1993. "'He Drew a Circle That Shut Me Out': Assimilation, Indoctrination, and the Paradox of a Liberal Education." *Harvard Law Review* (January): 582–667.

Stone, Jon, ed. 2000. *Expecting Armageddon: Essential Readings in Failed Prophecy.* New York: Routledge.

Sullivan, Lawrence E. 1988. *Icanchu's Drum: An Orientation to Meaning in South American Religion.* New York: Macmillan.

Swidler, Leonard. 1983. "The Dialogue Decalogue: Ground Rules for Interreligious Dialogue." *Journal of Ecumenical Studies* 20 (1): 1–4.

Tamez, Elsa. 1982. *Bible of the Oppressed,* trans. Matthew J. O'Connell. Maryknoll, N.Y.: Orbis Books.

Taylor, A. J. P. 1985. *Introduction to* The Communist Manifesto *(1888), by Karl Marx and Friedrich Engels,* trans. Samuel Moore. Harmondsworth, Middlesex, U.K.: Penguin Classics.

Tingle, Donald S. 1983. "Latter-day Saints (Mormons)." In *A Guide to Cults and New Religions,* ed. Ronald Enroth, 117–34. Downers Grove, Ill.: InterVarsity.

Tipton, Steven M. 1982. *Getting Saved from the Sixties: Moral Meaning in Conversion and Cultural Change.* Berkeley and Los Angeles: University of California Press.

Tobias, Madeleine Landau, and Janja Lalich. 1994. *Captive Hearts, Captive Minds: Freedom and Recovery from Cults and Abusive Relationships.* Alameda, Calif.: Hunter House.

Torrey, R. A. [1917] 1996. "Preface." In *The Fundamentals: A Testimony to the Truth,* eds. R. A. Torrey, A. C. Dixon, et al., 4 vols. Grand Rapids, Mich.: Baker Books.

Toumey, Christopher P. 1994. *God's Own Scientists: Creationists in a Secular World.* New Brunswick, N.J.: Rutgers University Press.

Trott, Jon. 1993. "Bob Larson's Ministry under Scrutiny." *Cornerstone* (100). Available online at www.cornerstonemag.com/features/iss100/larson.htm.

van Baalen, Jan Karel. 1938. *The Chaos of Cults: A Study in Present-Day Isms.* Grand Rapids, Mich.: Wm. B. Eerdmans.

———. 1948. *Our Christian Heritage: An Exposition of the Apostolic Creed, the Ten Commandments, and the Lord's Prayer.* Grand Rapids, Mich.: Wm. B. Eerdmans.

———. 1960. *The Chaos of Cults: A Study in Present-Day Isms,* 3d ed. Grand Rapids, Mich.: Wm. B. Eerdmans.

van Driel, Barend, and James T. Richardson. 1988. "Categorization of New Religious Movements in American Print Media." *Sociological Analysis* 49 (2): 171–83.

Van Natten, Steve. 1998. "Off the Deep End with Dave Hunt." Available online at www.balaams-ass.com/journal/warnings/davehunt.htm.

Walker, James K. 2000. "Conspiracy to Commit Evangelism." *Watchman Expositor* 17 (2). Available online at www.watchman.org/reltop/conspiracyevangelism.htm.

Walvoord, John F. 1990. *Armageddon, Oil and the Middle East Crisis: What the Bible Says about the Future of the Middle East and the End of Western Civilization,* 3d rev. ed. Grand Rapids, Mich.: Zondervan.

Warner, Marina. 1983. *Alone of All Her Sex: The Myth and Cult of the Virgin Mary.* New York: Random House.

Warnke, Mike, David Balsiger, and Les Jones. 1972. *The Satan Seller*. Plainfield, N.J.: Logos.

Watchman Fellowship. 2000. "Intolerance, Apologetics, and Evangelism." *Watchman Expositor* 17 (2). Available online at www.watchman.org/reltop/evangintol.htm.

Watters, Randall. 1987. *Refuting Jehovah's Witnesses*. Manhattan Beach, Calif.: Bethel Ministries.

Weiss, Charles M. 1854. *Weiss's Great History of the French Protestant Refugees*, 2 vols. New York: Stringer & Townsend.

Weldon, John. 1992. "Nichiren Shoshu Buddhism: Mystical Materialism for the Masses." *Christian Research Journal* 15 (2): 8–13.

Wells, George A. 1999. *The Jesus Myth*. Chicago: Open Court.

Welter, Barbara. 1987. "From Maria Monk to Paul Blanschard: A Century of Protestant Anti-Catholicism." In *Uncivil Religion: Interreligious Hostility in America*, eds. Robert Bellah and Frederick Greenspahn, 43–72. New York: Crossroad.

Welty, R. D. 1981. Letter to Robert L. Brown, December 3. Photocopy in Robert L. Brown and Rosemary Brown, *They Lie in Wait to Deceive: A Study in Anti-Mormon Deception*, Vol. 3. ed. Barbara Ellsworth (Mesa, Az.: Brownsworth Publishing, 1981), 52 .

White, James R. 1990. *The Fatal Flaw: Do the Teachings of Roman Catholicism Deny the Gospel?* Southbridge, Mass.: Crowne Publications.

———. 1996. *The Roman Catholic Controversy*. Minneapolis: Bethany House.

———. 1997a. *Is the Mormon My Brother? Discerning the Differences between Mormonism and Christianity*. Minneapolis: Bethany House.

———. 1997b. Review of *How Wide the Divide?* by Craig L. Blomberg and Stephen E. Robinson. *Christian Research Journal* 20 (2). Available online at www.equip.org/free/DM388.htm.

———. 1998. *Mary—Another Redeemer?* Minneapolis: Bethany House.

———. 2001a. "Of Doctorates and Eternity." Available online at www.aomin.org/CrEd.html.

———. 2001b. "Of Gary Novak and the Columbia River." Available online at www.aomin.org/Novak1.html.

———. 2001c. "A Test of Scholarship." Available online at www.aomin.org/Offenders1.html.

Wilber, Ken. 1993. *The Spectrum of Consciousness*, 2d ed. Wheaton, Ill.: Quest Books.

Williams, B. 1997. *The ABC of Cults*. Ross-shire, U.K.: Christian Focus Publications.

Williams, Rowan. 1987. *Arius: Heresy and Tradition*. London: Darton, Longman and Todd.

Wimbish, David. 1990. *Something's Going On Out There*. Old Tappan: Fleming H. Revell.

Winkler, Eldon K. 1994. *The New Age Is Lying to You*. St. Louis, Mo.: Concordia Publishing House.

Wise, Robert. 1986. "Could This Be Occult?" In *The Church Divided: The Holy Spirit and a Spirit of Seduction*, by Robert Wise et al., 40–43. South Plainfield, N.J.: Bridge Publishing.

Wise, Robert, et al. 1986. *The Church Divided: The Holy Spirit and a Spirit of Seduction*. South Plainfield, N.J.: Bridge Publishing.

Wolfe, Alan. 1999. *One Nation, after All: What Americans Really Think about God,*

Country, Family, Racism, Welfare, Immigration, Homosexuality, Work, the Right, the Left and Each Other. New York: Penguin USA.

Wright, S. 2000. "Instant Genius! Just Add the Net. *.net* (June): 50–58.

Wright, Stuart A. 1997. "Media Coverage of Unconventional Religion: Any 'Good News' for Minority Faith?" *Review of Religious Research* 39 (2): 101–15.

Wuthnow, Robert. 1995. "Old Fissures and New Fractures in American Religious Life." In *Religion and American Culture: A Reader,* ed. David G. Hackett, 369–81. New York: Routledge.

Yamamoto, J. Isamu. 1982. *Beyond Buddhism: A Basic Introduction to the Buddhist Tradition.* Downers Grove, Ill.: InterVarsity.

———. 1994a. "The Arrival of Theravada: Southeast Asians Bring Their School of Buddhism to America." *Christian Research Journal* 17 (2): 8–15.

———. 1994b. "The Buddha and What He Taught." *Christian Research Journal* 17 (1): 8–15, 33–34.

———. 1995a. "Zest for Zen: North Americans Embrace a Contemplative School of Buddhism." *Christian Research Journal* 17 (3): 8–15.

———. 1995b. "Tibetan Buddhists: Exiled from Their Homeland, Extolled in the West." *Christian Research Journal* 17 (4): 8–15, 31.

———. 1998. *Buddhism, Taoism, and Other Far Eastern Religions.* Grand Rapids, Mich.: Zondervan.

York, Michael. 1995. *The Emerging Network: A Sociology of the New Age and Neo-Pagan Movements.* Lanham, Md.: Rowman & Littlefield.

Young, Lawrence A., ed. 1997. *Rational Choice Theory and Religion: Summary and Assessment.* New York: Routledge.

Zablocki, Benjamin D. 1997. "The Blacklisting of a Concept: The Strange History of the Brainwashing Conjecture in the Sociology of Religion." *Nova Religio: The Journal of Alternative and Emergent Religions,* 1 (1): 96–121.

———. 1998. "Reply to Bromley." *Nova Religio: The Journal of Alternative and Emergent Religions,* 1 (2): 267–71.

Zablocki, Benjamin, and Thomas Robbins, eds. 2001. *Misunderstanding Cults: Searching for Objectivity in a Controversial Field.* Toronto: University of Toronto Press.

Zito, George V. 1983. "Toward a Sociology of Heresy." *Sociological Analysis* 44 (2): 123–30.

Index

Abanes Richard, 40, 128, 191, 199–201;
   on biblical prophecy, 148–49; on
   Buddhism, 147–49; on *Harry Potter*,
   126–28, 163–64; on Jehovah's
   Witnesses, 146; on Word Faith
   movement, 171–72
Abdel Rahman, Sheik Omar, 152
Alnor, William, 8, 10, 59, 79, 199, 214
al-Qaeda, 153
American Family Foundation (AFF), 15,
   25–26, 129
American Transcendentalists, 66
Anecdotal atrocities, 83, 104, 113, 123,
   139, 174; miracles, 83, 113, 123, 158
Ankerberg, John, 37, 45, 47, 49–50, 76,
   157, 206; countercult colleagues on,
   198; educational credentials of, 113,
   200, 202–4; and First Amendment,
   100–101; on the Latter-day Saints,
   136; Mosser and Owen on, 140–41,
   209
Ankerberg Theological Research
   Institute, 100, 117–18
Anti-Catholicism, 65, 89, 166, 172–89; as
   eschatological fulfillment, 186–89; as
   hate speech, 174–78. *See also* Roman
   Catholic Church
Antichrist, 41, 79, 88–90, 92, 157–58,
   166, 194; Roman Catholic Church as
   platform for, 186–90
Anticult movement, secular, 9, 15–28,
   116, 122, 124, 129

Apologetics Index, 96, 117, 118, 119–21,
   199. *See also* Hein, Anton
Apologia Report, 96, 125–26. *See also*
   Poll, Rich
Apostate testimony. *See* Ex-member
   testimony
AR-forum, 121, 126–28, 205–6, 218,
   221; AR-talk, 126–28, 153, 218
Arius, 57–58
Ásatru, 77, 123
Astrology, 122–23
Atkins, Gaius Glenn, 214

Baer, Dick, 138, 200, 215
Baha'i, 73, 213
Bainbridge, William Sims, 29, 214, 216
Barker, Eileen, 27, 119, 210, 221
Barker, Jason, 108–10
Barthes, Roland, 34
Bates, Stephen, 159–60
Bea, Augustin Cardinal, 176, 178
Beckwith, Frank, 87, 200
Bedell, Ken, 117
Bennett, Dennis and Rita, 194
Berean Call, The, 12, 95, 164–65; and
   EMNR, 111. *See also* Hunt, Dave
Berger, Peter, 5–7, 29, 43, 45–46, 47–48,
   52, 69, 116–17
Bethany House Publishers, 206
Bible: alleged twisting of by cults and
   new religious movements, 58, 179; as

countercult boundary marker, 31–38, 49–51, 68, 74–76; divine inspiration of, 30–31, 64; inerrancy of, 31–38, 39, 45, 49–51, 64, 93; interpretation of, 50–51, 59; prophecy in, 32, 38, 92–93, 148–49; Southern Baptist Convention and, 52–53
Biederwolf, William, 104
Bjornstad, James, 33, 98, 110
"Black Muslim Cult, The," 74
Blavatsky, Helena Petrovna, 66
Blomberg, Craig, 140, 200, 205, 210
Blumer, Herbert, 133
Boespflug, Lori, 85–86
Bokenkotter, Thomas, 179, 180, 220
Book of Mormon, The, 51, 135, 136
Borovoy, Alan, 101
Boston Movement (International Churches of Christ), 121–22
Bowman, Robert M., 17, 49, 138, 192, 200; definition of cult, 142; on Hank Hanegraaff, 196–97, 221; on Jehovah's Witnesses, 142–44
Braden, Charles S., 74, 214, 216
Brainwashing, 16, 18, 21–22, 23, 26, 27, 77. *See also* Deprogramming; Thought control hypothesis
Branch Davidians, 76, 90
Branham, William M., 171
British Israelism, 74
Bromley, David G., 26, 119
Brown, Harold O. J., 55–56, 58
Brown, Robert and Rosemary, 72–73, 215–16
Buddhism, 9, 53, 54, 66, 77, 117, 167, 198; as cult, 40–41, 81, 213; as "false religion," 20, 34, 147–49, 215, 218; Tibetan Buddhism, 77; Zen Buddhism, 39, 73, 102, 120

Capps, Charles, 194
Carden, Paul, 125, 191
Carlson, Ron, 155
Cathars, 60
Caven, William, 64
Cerullo, Morris, 171
Chaucer, Geoffrey, 172

Chick, Jack T., 173–78, 181, 186, 187, 189, 198
Children of God (The Family), 76, 125, 213
Chiniquy, Charles, 173
Cho, Paul (David) Yonggi, 171, 194
Christadelphianism, 118
Christian Apologetics and Research Ministry (CARM), 96, 113, 118–19. *See also* Slick, Matt
Christian Identity, 118
Christian Research Institute (CRI), 17, 27, 100, 182, 192; countercult criticisms of, 112; and countercult professionalization, 95, 97; cults, according to, 20, 118, 213; on Dave Hunt, 165, 193; and Evangelical Ministries to New Religions (EMNR), 111; and Hank Hanegraaff, 102, 142; internecine conflicts at, 195–97; and Walter Martin, 50–51, 72–73, 75–76, 102–6. *See also* Hanegraaff, Hank; Martin, Walter
Christian Research Journal, 138, 157
Christian Science, 63, 65, 74, 76, 118, 141, 213, 214
Church of Jesus Christ of Latter-day Saints (LDS), 40, 52, 67, 123, 134–41, 213. See also *Book of Mormon, The*; Latter-day Saints
Church Universal and Triumphant, 213
Clark, David, 63
Clinton, Bill, 89
Clinton, Hilary Rodham, 90
Cognitive praxis: Bible as anchor for, 31; countercult, 29, 82–83, 93, 101, 108, 147, 164–65; definition of, 10–13; function of in countercult apologetics, 93, 95, 103–4, 128, 210; Internet and, 116–30; as mode of analysis, 27; "othering" process in, 34, 43, 153, 207 and worldview-maintenance, 48. *See also* Movement intellectuals
Columbia Evangelical Seminary, 201–2
Combs, George Hamilton, 63–64, 76–77, 140
Common grace controversy, 67

Communism, as Roman Catholic conspiracy, 175–76
Communist Manifesto, The, 56, 175
Condit, Gary, 90–91
Conspiracism, 38–41, 79, 87–92, 100, 149, 157–58, 175–78, 213
Copeland, Gloria, 171, 194
Copeland, Kenneth, 171–72, 194
Cornerstone Magazine, 85, 192, 216–17
Cosmology: countercult, 27, 29, 34, 75–76; dualistic/duelistic nature of, 24, 38–41, 46
Council on Mind Abuse, 129
Countercult apologetics, 5–7, 23, 24–25, 26, 35, 43, 49, 95; appeal to academic authority in, 146, 151–52, 165–66, 183–86, 219; biblical mandate of, 9, 66, 129; cognitive boundary markers of, 10, 36–38, 49–51, 64, 68, 96, 142; democratization of, 95–99; as evangelical boundary-maintenance, 28, 98, 106, 110, 178–86, 210; as hate speech, 107, 174–78, 219; "negative," 51, 54, 70; reductivism in, 34–35; 75, 101, 161, 179–81, 183–86, 194, 205–8, 210 self-representation in, 113–14
Countercult movement: avocational, 5, 97, 99, 116; democratization of, 115–30; as evangelical fringe movement, 208–9; internecine conflict within, 155–56, 191–200; and the Internet, 115–30; problem of authority and credibility in, 199–205; professionalization of, 5, 97–99, 103–14; resource mobilization and, 205–8
Creeds, 69, 197–98
Cult apologist, 119–21, 191, 217
Cult Awareness Network (old), 129, 213, 218
Cults: definition of, 18–21, 69, 114, 142; as part of the New Age movement, 156–57, 164. *See also* New religious movements (NRMs)
Cumbey, Constance, 47, 93, 123, 166, 174, 177, 200; countercult colleagues on, 112, 137, 156–58, 192; as countercult extremist, 5, 27, 88,

208–9; on Matthew Fox, 158; as movement intellectual, 155–56; on the New Age movement, 40–41, 157–60, on Walter Martin, 192

De Arteaga, William, 194–95, 198
De Chardin, Teilhard, 168
Decker, J. Edward, 83, 174, 200, 206, 216; countercult colleagues on, 137–38, 198, 209; on the Latter-day Saints, 136–41, 167; on the New Age movement, 155. *See also* Saints Alive in Jesus (SAIJ)
DeMar, Gary, 195, 197, 199
Deprogramming, 16, 24, 25, 27, 218. *See also* Exit counseling
De Sade, Marquis, 172
Diderot, Denis, 172
Dobson, James, 198
Downs, Jeff, 113, 221

Eadie, Betty, 33
Eckankar, 118
Eddy, Mary Baker, 63, 68
Emerson, Ralph Waldo, 66
Enroth, Ron, 21, 39, 71, 110, 155–56
est, 77
Evangelical Ministries to New Religions (EMNR), 71, 95, 196–97; as coalition movement, 110–14; *Manual of Ethical and Doctrinal Standards (MEDS)* of, 110–13, 198, 204
Exit counseling, 24, 25–26, 129. *See also* Deprogramming
Ex-member testimony, 26, 122–25, 199; as catharsis, 122–23; as exemplar, 123; and postexit community, 124–25; as warning, 123–24, 220
Eyerman, Ron, 10–11, 13, 43, 47, 96, 104, 192. *See also* Jamison, Andrew

False witness, 165, 166–69. *See also* Countercult apologetics, reductivism in
Finke, Roger, 29
Forster, J. M., 65
Foster, Richard, 194
Foucault, Michel, 7

Fox, Matthew, 158
Freedom of religion, 27, 29, 53, 93,
    99–101, 151, 160, 167, 178, 217; and
    interreligious dialogue, 107–9. *See
    also* Religious economy; Religious
    pluralism
Frost, Vicki, 159–60
Fundamentalism, 36, 58, 64–66, 108,
    159–60; fundamentalists, 186, 189
Fundamentals, The, 64–66, 77, 134–35,
    141, 214

Gates, Bill, 88
Geisler, Norman, 54, 63, 71
Gnosticism, 60
God, character of; triune nature of,
    57–58, 70
God Makers, The, 138, 165, 167, 206,
    215; Bossick on, 138–39; National
    Conference of Christians and Jews on,
    139. *See also* Decker, J. Edward; Hunt,
    Dave
Gomes, Alan, 34, 200
Graham, Billy, 89
Groothuis, Douglas, 24, 33, 50, 113, 155,
    200, 206, 208–9; on countercult
    colleagues, 156, 158; evangelism as
    spiritual warfare, 22, 45–46; on *Harry
    Potter*, 126, 163–64; on "negative
    apologetics," 25, 51, 54, 70; on the
    New Age movement, 44, 76, 160–64,
    219; on religious pluralism, 47, 217
Grubb, Norman, 194

Hadden, Jeffrey K., 119, 121, 130
Hagin, Kenneth, 171–72, 194
Hanegraaff, Hank, 17, 51, 85, 89, 206,
    221; accused of plagiarism, 195–97;
    and Christian Research Institute, 102,
    125, 142, 195–97; educational
    credentials of, 113, 200; on Word Faith
    movement, 172. *See also* Christian
    Research Institute (CRI)
Hare Krishnas, 29, 34, 77, 117, 213. *See
    also* International Society for Krishna
    Consciousness (ISKON)
Harry Potter, 126–28, 163–64
Harvest House Publishers, 206

Hawkins, Craig S., 33, 200
Heaven's Gate, 8. *See also* Unidentified
    flying objects (UFOs)
Hein, Anton, 96, 101, 119–21, 128, 199,
    206, 217–18; on *Harry Potter*, 127–28;
    on Scientology, 211. *See also*
    Apologetics Index; Cult apologist
Heresy, 23, 51–52, 54–60, 74, 115,
    142–44, 171, 182, 197; Marian
    apparitions as, 188–89. *See also*
    Orthodoxy
Hexham, Irving, 67, 71, 119, 120–21,
    155–56
Hill, Napoleon, 194
Hinduism, 109, 161, 198; as
    "demonism," 80, 81–83, 191; as
    "Eastern cult," 40–41, 215; as "false
    religion," 20, 34, 147; Mormonism
    described as, 136; Nazism described as,
    187; as signifier of religious pluralism,
    9, 53, 54, 60, 66, 77, 145, 167
Hinn, Benny, 51, 171
Hitler, Adolf, 88, 157, 176–77, 187. See
    also *Mein Kampf*; Nazism and Neo-
    Nazism
Holy Order of MANS, 76–77
Honeywell, 88
Horton, Michael, 182
House, H. Wayne, 55–60
Howard, Jay, 21, 40; on Islam, 153
Howard, Thomas, 166
Howe, Eber D., 135
Hoyt, William, 173
Hunt, Dave, 12, 22–23, 36–38, 39, 47,
    81, 147, 155, 158, 161, 199–200,
    208–9; anti-Catholicism of, 38,
    178–82, 186–90, 193; on biblical
    prophecy, 32, 59, 93; on the Christian
    Research Institute, 193; on countercult
    apologetics, 3, 23, 76; countercult
    colleagues on, 112, 137, 156, 164–65,
    192–95, 197–98, 209, 219; as
    countercult extremist, 5, 88, 123, 175;
    disfellowshipping of, 164; false witness
    of, 27; on Hinduism, 161; on Islam,
    150; on the Latter-day Saints, 136–37,
    139; misogyny of, 187–88; on the New
    Age movement, 41, 157, 164–69, 214;

The Seduction of Christianity, and, 193–95; on Word Faith movement, 172. *See also* Berean Call, The

Illuminati, 91
International Churches of Christ. *See* Boston Movement
International Society for Krishna Consciousness (ISKCON), 74, 213. *See also* Hare Krishnas
Internet, 11, 17, 27, 96–97, 98, 100–101, 104, 113; and countercult democratization, 115–30, 205–7
Intolerance, 75–76
Introvigne, Massimo, 15, 119, 120
Islam, 81, 91, 118, 161, 200, 213, 215; as "false religion," 20, 53, 54, 74, 147, 149–53, 218; as Roman Catholic conspiracy, 175; as signifier of religious pluralism, 107, 145, 167

Jamison, Andrew, 10–11, 13, 43, 47, 96, 104, 192. *See also* Eyerman, Ron
Jehovah's Witnesses, 65, 70, 73, 75, 106, 117, 118, 134, 141–47, 207; ban on blood transfusion, 146; countercult and, 25, 33, 35, 50, 97, 98–99, 106, 118, 210; denial of Trinity by, 51–52, 141–43; designated as "cult," 40, 70, 191, 213; eschatological predictions of, 141, 144–47; ex-member testimony and, 108, 116, 123, 125; as Millennial Dawn, 65; Passantinos on, 198; and "Penton group," 216; Richard Abanes on, 146; Robert Bowman on, 142–44; Robert Morey on, 144–45; as signifier of religious pluralism, 4, 8, 63, 67, 74, 76; as Watchtower Bible and Tract Society, 63, 102, 104, 123, 141, 144
Jesuits, 32, 165, 168, 173, 178; as conspiratorial cabal, 175–76; Fidel Castro as, 176; and Ku Klux Klan, 176; Nazi SS as suborder of, 177
Jesus Christ, 141; divinity/deity of, 35, 36–38, 70; historicity of, 37, 148; substitutionary atonement of, 36, 64, 70, 107, 179; virgin birth of, 35, 36–38, 64, 136

Jihad, 152
Jobs, Stephen, 88
John Paul II, Pope, 89, 186, 187
Judaism, 107, 147, 167

Keating, Karl, 174, 186–87
Kelsey, Morton, 194
Kennedy, D. James, 160, 196
Kenyon, E. W., 171
Khomeini, Ayatollah, 152
King, Stephen, 163–64
Kingdom of the Cults, The, 20, 71–72, 74–75, 102–6, 118, 136, 147–49, 150, 171–72, 213. *See also* Martin, Walter R.
Knox, John, 144
Küng, Hans, 180–81

Langone, Michael, 15, 18–19, 22
Langstaff, Alan, 194
Larson, Bob, 160, 200, 219; on Buddhism, 149, 191, 198–99, 215; conspiracism of, 87, 88, 92, 177, 215; countercult colleagues on, 192–93, 198; as countercult extremist, 47, 90, 123, 155, 158, 208–9, 217; definition of "cult," 21, 39–40; disclaimer by publisher, 85; exorcism and, 80, 84, 216; ghost-writing and, 85–86; on Hinduism, 81–83, 191, 198–99; plagiarism and, 86; spiritual warfare and, 46, 80, 83–84, 99; on UFOs, 214, 216
Larson, Bruce, 194
Latter-day Saints, 8, 60, 63, 75–76, 98–99, 102, 106, 146–47. *See also* Church of Jesus Christ of Latter-day Saints (LDS); Mormonism, Mormons
Leithart, Peter, 195, 197, 199
Levy, Chandra, 90–91, 217
Lewinsky, Monica, 89
Lewis, Gordon, 25, 71, 110, 113, 160, 200
Lewis, James, 120
Lewis, Matthew, 172
Lockwood, Robert, 173
Lucent Technologies, 88

Luckmann, Thomas, 5, 7, 10, 43, 46–48, 52, 116–17
Lüdemann, Gerd, 55, 162
Luther, Martin, 141, 144, 172

Mannheim, Karl, 10, 31–32, 133, 162
Maria Monk, 65, 172–73
Marrs, Texe, 47, 147, 162, 200, 217; alleged attacks on ministry of, 88, 215; anti-Catholicism of, 89, 186, 187; antisemitism of, 89; conspiracism of, 31, 44, 86–93, 100, 174–76, 213, 215; countercult colleagues on, 137, 192, 219; as countercult extremist, 5, 27, 155, 177, 208; on Hinduism, 215; on the Latter-day Saints, 136
Marrs, Wanda, 40, 87, 214
Martin, Walter R., 3, 5, 32–33, 47, 85, 110, 157, 160, 164, 209, 213–14; on Black Muslims, 150; and Christian Research Institute, 17, 51, 102–6, 116, 125, 195–96, 206; Constance Cumbey on, 192; definition of cult, 19–20, 73–76, 118, 142, 147; descent from Brigham Young of, 72; educational credentials of, 71–73, 113, 201, 215; on Islam, 150; on Jehovah's Witnesses, 146; on the Latter-day Saints, 135–36, 191; memorial service of, 71, 215; as movement intellectual, 19, 71–77, 192, 219; ordination of, 71, 75, 216; on Zen Buddhism, 102, 147. *See also* Christian Research Institute (CRI)
Marx, Karl, 56
Mary: miraculous appearances of, 188–89, 220; Mother of Jesus, 35, 179–81; perpetual virginity of, 185–86; popular devotion to, 179–81, 220–21
Masonic Lodge, 25, 83, 91, 122
Matrisciana, Caryl, 40, 47, 137, 156, 157, 158, 198, 206
Mayer, Jean-François, 128
McCarthy, E. Doyle, 163
McCarthy, James, 183, 200, 206
McMahon, T. A., 12, 168, 193–95, 197–98. *See also* Berean Call, The
McNiece, Robert Gibson, 134–35, 140
Medhurst, T. W., 65

Mein Kampf, 157, 176–77. *See also* Hitler, Adolf
Melton, J. Gordon, 15, 119, 120, 201
Michaelson, Johanna, 79
Microsoft, 88, 115
Millennial Dawn. *See* Jehovah's Witnesses, as Millenial Dawn
Miller, Calvin, 194
Missiology, 5, 6, 23, 26, 102–6, 112, 210–11; and interreligious dialogue, 108–10
Missler, Chuck, 79
Montenegro, Marcia, 113–14, 122–23, 128, 200–201; on *Harry Potter*, 126
Moorehead, William, 65, 214
Morehead, John, 27, 87, 127–28, 205
Morey, Robert, 34–36, 98, 206, 219, 221; on Islam, 150–53, 200, 209, 213, 215; on Jehovah's Witnesses, 144–45; recommends military action against Islam, 153
Mormonism, 63, 65, 68, 70, 74, 76, 107, 118, 134–41, 167; doctrine of blood atonement in, 137; ex-member testimony and, 123, 125; Mormons, 25, 33, 70, 107, 117, 208; Passantinos on, 198
Mosser, Carl, 27, 87, 136–37, 140–41, 200, 205–6, 209–10
Movement for the Restoration of the Ten Commandments of God, 120
Movement intellectuals, 23, 96–97, 128, 155, 208; Ankerberg as, 205; Cumbey as, 158; Decker as, 138; defined, 5, 10–13; function of, 43–48; Groothuis as, 200, 217; Hunt as, 164; and the Internet, 115–17, 119, 121; Larson as, 82, 86; Martin as, 73, 103–4, 192; Morey as, 152; Mosser as, 209; Owen as, 209. *See also* Cognitive praxis
Mozert v. Hawkins County Board of Education, 160. *See also* Scopes Trial (1925), "Scopes II"

Nazism and Neo-Nazism, 88, 90; Islam as, 152; New Age movement as, 156, 157; as Roman Catholic conspiracy, 175, 177, 187

Near-death experiences (NDEs), 33
Neopaganism, 29, 33, 53, 77, 87, 112–13, 124. *See also* Wicca; Witchcraft
New Age movement, 6, 39–41, 63, 77, 79, 95, 106, 118, 126, 155–69, 219; Abanes on, 191; Alnor on, 8; Cumbey on, 40–41, 156–60, 192; definition of, 156–57, 219; Groothuis on, 22, 25, 33, 44, 46, 76, 160–64, 208, 217; Hunt on, 164–69, 187, 195; Marrs on, 87–90, 214, 219; Montenegro on, 113–14, 122–23, 201; Roman Catholic Church and, 187
New religious movements (NRMs), 8–9, 38–39, 71, 75, 93, 100, 105, 114, 134, 145, 207; *See also* Cults
New Thought churches, 63
Newport, John, 6
Novak, Gary, 201–2

Occult, 25, 79, 99, 123–24, 153, 156; Buddhism as, 149; Cumbey on, 158; Groothuis on, 161, 163–64; *Harry Potter* and, 126–28, 163–64; Hunt on, 34, 136, 168, 187, 194; Larson on, 84, 149, 200; Marrs on, 91; Mormonism as, 136; Rhodes on, 40; Roman Catholic Church and, 187; UFOs as, 8; Weldon on, 200
Olcott, Henry Steel, 66
Orr, James, 64
Orthodoxy, 21, 48, 51, 65–66, 68, 93, 126, 141–42, 148, 191; according to Martin, 19–20, 71, 73; according to van Baalen, 68–70; Bauer thesis of, 55–56; creeds as charters for, 68–69; Eastern, 108, 142, 175; evangelical hubris of, 54–60, 189, 197. *See also* Heresy
Ott, Ludwig, 183–86
Owen, Paul, 87, 140–41, 200, 205, 209–10

Palmer, Susan Jean, 86
"Pantheistic monism," 161
Paskewich, Joe, 205–6, 207
Passantino, Bob and Gretchen, 147, 150, 157–58, 182, 193, 199, 221; criticism

of counter cult colleagues, 112, 114, 192, 196, 197–99; definition of "cult," 20; on Jehovah's Witnesses, 198; on Mormonism, 198
Paul VI, Pope, 89
Paulk, Earl, 171, 197–98
Peale, Norman Vincent, 194
Pement, Eric, 110
Pentecostalism, 171
Penton, M. James, 73, 216
Peretti, Frank, 84, 160
Personal Freedom Outreach (PFO), 97
Peterson, Daniel C., 202–4, 218
Pipes, Richard, 176
Poewe, Karla, 67, 71, 155–56
Poll, Rich, 17, 121, 125–27, 218; Pamela, 125. *See also* Apologia Report; AR-forum, AR-talk
Positive confession, 171–72

Qabalah, 77, 79

Reality: maintenance of, 5–7, 9, 23, 26, 30, 41, 43–60, 98, 120; perception of, 5, 163; *See also* Universe-maintenance; Worldview, maintenance
Reebok International, 88
Reid, Thomas, 194, 197
Religious economy, 8, 19, 23, 29–30, 67, 69, 71, 76–77, 93, 102, 108, 134, 210
Religious pluralism, 29, 47–48, 53, 60, 63, 145, 167, 217
"Resource," 121–22
Rhodes, Ron, 45, 46, 47, 53–54, 98, 200, 206, 209; anti-Catholicism of, 178–86, 188, 189, 220; on the Bible, 59, 81, 214; and Christian Research Institute, 17, 125; on countercult apologetics, 24–25, 38, 40, 50–51; on the "culting of America," 53–54, 137; questionable scholarship of, 183–86, 220; on UFOs and extraterrestrial intelligence, 81, 214
Rigdon, Sidney, 135, 215
Rivera, Alberto, 176–77, 220
Roberts, Oral, 171
Roberts, R. Philip, 107–8
Robinson, George, 64

Robinson, Stephen, 140, 210
Roman Catholic Church, 36, 65, 134, 141, 168; as "Great Whore of Babylon," 187–88; and Nazism, 175, 177, 187; Roman Catholicism, 166, 171–90; "Romanism," 65. *See also* Anti-Catholicism
Romney, Richard, 194
Russell, Charles Taze, 65, 68, 146, 205, 214
Russian revolution, as Jesuit conspiracy, 176

Saints Alive in Jesus (SAIJ), 3, 83, 95, 97, 138; and EMNR, 111. *See also* Decker, J. Edward
Sanford, Agnes, 167–68
Santería, 168–69
Satan, 22, 24, 27, 38–40, 46, 76, 79, 80–81, 84, 87, 122, 165, 171, 175; Church of, 29, 40, 167
Satanism, 79, 81–82, 87–91, 100, 164, 167, 201; Islam as, 153; Satanists, 99, 100, 123, 167, 215
Scharffs, Gilbert, 167
Schimmel, Annemarie, 152
Schnell, W. J., 104
Schnoebelen, Bill, 79
Schuller, Robert, 194, 198
Scientology, 54, 74, 117, 120, 210, 213; Church of, 8, 40, 60, 77, 123, 129, 218
Scopes Trial (1925), 159; "Scopes II," 159–60
Secular humanism, 30
September 11 attacks, 91, 150, 152–53
Seventh-Day Adventism, 70, 141
Sharpe, Kathi, 123, 127
Shupe, Anson D., 26, 119
Singer, Margaret, 18
Sire, James, 161, 182
Slick, Matt., 96, 113, 118–19, 120; definition of cult, 118–19. *See also* Christian Apologetics and Research Ministry (CARM)
Smith, Joseph, Jr., 135, 136, 146
Social Construction of Reality, The, 5–6, 43, 124. *See also* Berger, Peter; Luckmann, Thomas

Sociology of knowledge, 69, 162–63
Southern Baptist Convention, 52–53, 75
Spaulding, Solomon, 135, 215
Spencer, James, 51, 54, 112, 114, 200; on countercult colleagues, 192–93
Spiritual Counterfeits Project (SCP), 17, 27, 95, 97, 112, 118, 192; and EMNR, 111
Spiritual warfare, 22, 38–39, 46, 55, 70, 83, 103
Spiritualism, 63, 66; "spiritism," 73
Stark, Rodney, 29–30, 136–37, 168, 214, 216
Sullivan, Lawrence, 145–46
Swidler, Leonard, 108–9
Symbolic interactionism, 133

Tanner, Jerald and Sandra, 3, 216
Tarot, 77
Taylor, A. J. P., 56
Thaipusam, 82–83
Theosophy, 66, 74
Thoreau, Henry David, 66
Thought control hypothesis, 16, 18, 21–22, 23
Tilton, Robert, 194
Torrey, R. A., 64
Treat, Casey, 194
Trott, Jon, 27. See also *Cornerstone Magazine*

Unidentified flying objects (UFOs), 7, 8, 39, 79, 81, 86, 214, 216
Unification Church, 27, 109, 117, 210, 213
Unity School of Christianity, 74, 118
Universe-maintenance, 70; therapeutic model of, 47–54. *See also* Reality, maintenance of; Worldview, maintenance
Utah Lighthouse Ministry (ULM), 3, 95; and EMNR, 111

Van Baalen, Jan Karel, 66–71, 74, 76–77, 135, 161, 191, 215
Van Natten, Steve, 165
Vatican II, 176, 180

Virgin birth. *See* Jesus Christ, virgin
  birth of
Voltaire, 172
Voodoo, 168

Walker, James, 107
Walston, Rick, 201–2, 221
Walt Disney Corporation, 88
Warfield, Benjamin B., 64
Warnke, Mike, 217
Watchman Fellowship (WF), 17, 95, 97;
  and Freedom of Religion, 106–10
Watchtower Bible and Tract Society. *See*
  Jehovah's Witnesses, as Watchtower
  Bible and Tract Society
Watters, Randall, 125
Weldon, John, 37, 45, 47, 49–50, 76, 200,
  206; countercult colleagues on, 198;
  educational credentials of, 113, 200,
  202–4; and First Amendment,
  100–101; on the Latter-day Saints,
  136; Mosser and Owen on, 140–41
Wessinger, Catherine, 120
White, James R., 140, 206; anti-
  Catholicism of, 178–81, 183, 188, 189;
  countercult colleagues on, 198;

  educational credentials of, 113,
  200–202, 221
Wicca, 77, 117, 123–24, 126–28, 163–64;
  Wiccans, 127
Wilber, Ken, 31–32
Wilson, Jennie, 159
Wimber, John, 194, 198
Wise, Robert, 194, 198, 199
Witchcraft, 41, 47, 90–91, 123–24, 168
Word Faith movement, 51, 171–72
World Parliament of Religions (1893),
  65–66
World Trade Center: 1991 attack on,
  152–53; 2001 attacks on, 91, 150,
  152–53. *See also* September 11 attacks
Worldview, Christian, 6; hygienics,
  48–51; integration, 52–53;
  maintenance, 28, 36, 39, 41, 105–6,
  125, 133–34, 178–86, 205–6;
  nihilation, 35, 51–52, 53–54, 66, 70,
  105, 134, 145, 162; pathology and
  diagnostics, 48, 51–52; therapy, 48,
  52–54. *See also* Reality
Wozniak, Steven, 88
Wright, George Frederick, 64

Yousef, Ramzi, 152

About the Author

DOUGLAS E. COWAN is Assistant Professor of Religious Studies and Sociology at the University of Missouri, Kansas City. He is the co-editor of *Religion
on the Internet: Research Prospects and Promises.*